The Material Basis
of the Postbellum
Tenant Plantation

The Material Basis of the Postbellum Tenant Plantation

Historical Archaeology
in the South Carolina Piedmont

CHARLES E. ORSER, JR.

THE UNIVERSITY OF GEORGIA PRESS

Athens and London

© 1988 by the University of Georgia Press
Athens, Georgia 30602
All rights reserved

Designed by Madelaine Cooke
Set in Linotron 202 ten on thirteen Baskerville
The paper in this book meets the guidelines for
permanence and durability of the Committee on
Production Guidelines for Book Longevity of the
Council on Library Resources.

Printed in the United States of America
92 91 90 89 88   5 4 3 2 1

Library of Congress Cataloging in Publication Data

Orser, Charles E.
    The material basis of the Postbellum tenant plantation:
historical archaeology in the South Carolina Piedmont / Charles E.
Orser, Jr.
        p.   cm.
    Bibliography: p.
    Includes index.
    ISBN 0-8203-0986-9 (alk. paper)
    1. Plantations—South Carolina—History.   2. South Carolina—
Antiquities.   3. Plantation life—South Carolina—History.
4. Landlord and tenant—South Carolina—History.   5. Archaeology and
history—South Carolina.   I. Title.
F270.O77 1988
975.7'04—dc19   87-12535
                                                            CIP

British Library Cataloging in Publication Data available

To Janice, Erin, Emily, and Christine,
and in the memory of
Earl J. Krebel, a southern Illinois share renter

Contents

Tables

Illustrations

Preface

THE ARCHAEOLOGICAL STUDY of plantation tenancy has just begun. The research reported in this book is the result of one of only two large-scale investigations of a postbellum tenant plantation. It is the only such study to concentrate on South Carolina and the Piedmont.

As I prepared this book, I kept in mind that archaeologists, particularly historical archaeologists, must learn to present their research findings to nonarchaeologists. One group with which historical archaeologists must learn to communicate is historians. Toward this end, I have explained many terms and concepts already well known to archaeologists.

I also seek to demonstrate a future direction for historical archaeology. I have tried to present information in a manner that will appeal to scholars in other fields, perhaps most particularly to historians. Still, I have tried to do so in a way that will not compromise historical archaeology. I have not tried to present a formal history or to make historical archaeology a subsection of the academic discipline of history. Although I have been trained in anthropology, my inclination is toward the sort of anthropology sometimes called "historical anthropology." Notable historical anthropologists whose work I most admire are Sidney W. Mintz, Eric R. Wolf, and Jerome S. Handler. My viewpoint is that historical archaeology, like many formal academic disciplines, should transcend narrow, artificial boundaries. Historical archaeology, as one way of examining the past, is neither just anthropology *nor* just history. Rather, historical archaeology is both anthropology *and* history—and many other formal disciplines as well.

All the archaeological and some of the historical data used in this book were collected as part of a contract research project supervised by Archaeological Services Division, National Park Service, Atlanta, and generously funded by the U.S. Army Corps of Engineers, Savannah District. The original report of investigations, completed in 1982 and published by the National Park Service in 1987, is more than 1,000 pages long, which precludes its easy reproduction and wide dissemination. Regardless of length, however, this report is of consequence only to a few professional archaeologists; its exhaustive description of all the data collected is usually not of interest to nonarchaeologists. Because this is so, I believe that archaeologists who conduct contract research have a responsibility to provide readable archaeological information to interested nonarchaeologists. The data collected by archaeologists are simply too important to be confined to technical contract reports having limited distribution. This book, about an aspect of American history seldom studied by archaeologists, was written with this in mind; however, this book goes beyond the original contract report and is an original research effort. It is not merely a summary of the contract report; new information is presented, and fresh interpretations are offered.

In my exploration of the idea that many historians are interested in historical archaeology, provided that it is presented without the jargon and the almost endless artifact measurements so common to archaeology, I have benefited from discussions with several talented historians. James L. Roark of Emory University has been most influential among them. Without his encouragement and kind words, this book would not have been written in its present form. His interest in historical archaeology showed me that historical archaeologists must reach beyond the boundaries some have set for the field. Other historians who have reinforced this idea are Amy Friedlander, George McDaniel, and Peter Wood. These historians support historical archaeology and encourage its practitioners to discover the significant contribution they can make to the study of the past.

I am also grateful to the following individuals: John D. Pitzer of Erskine College in Due West, South Carolina, for kindly sending me a second copy of Dundas's *The Calhoun Settlement;* Professor Ernest McPherson Lander, Jr., of Clemson University, for sharing his knowledge about, and love for, South Carolina; Ronald L. Michael, editor of *Historical Archaeology*, for allowing me to reprint the photographs appearing here as figures 23 and 25; and Mary Lee Eggart of the Cartographic Section of the Department of Geography and Anthropology, Louisiana State University, for skillfully and patiently drafting the figures for this book.

I also wish to thank Malcolm L. Call, director of the University of Georgia Press, for his interest in historical archaeology and for his faith in this book. The assistance of Debbie Winter, managing editor, and Madelaine Cooke, copy editor and designer, has immeasurably improved the presentation of this book. Their attention and care is sincerely appreciated.

My parents, Charles and Mildred Orser, deserve my deepest thanks for their understanding and encouragement. They believed in the importance of past events, and it was they who took me, then nine years old, to visit the first excavation project at Fort Michilimackinac, Michigan. That experience made a lasting impression on me.

Finally, archaeological fieldwork, contrary to the image portrayed in today's popular media, includes a great deal of hard, dirty, and exhausting physical labor. I especially owe a deep debt of gratitude, in fact more than I can ever express, to my wife, Janice Krebel Orser, the daughter of a tenant farmer, who accepts my fieldwork with very good humor. Without her support, I could not do it. In addition, she serves as my typist, word processor, devil's advocate, editor, and proofreader. None of this book could have been written without her never-ending thoughtful assistance. Also, although they do not fully understand what this book is about, my three girls, Erin, Emily, and Christine, know that it is mine. They gave much to it without even realizing it.

Chapter One

The Archaeology
of Southern Plantations

IN 1930 A GROUP OF SCHOLARS published a collection of essays entitled *I'll Take My Stand: The South and the Agrarian Tradition.* This book extolled the virtues of the agricultural South and condemned those who increasingly called for southern industrialization. Although all the attacks on the growth of southern industry were quite explicit, the comments made by Herman Clarence Nixon summarize the content of most of the essays: "It is deplorable that the South's agricultural philosophy is imperiled by a nonphilosophical pattern of society in which the highest aim of life is success in industry."[1] Echoing Nixon's statements, other authors in the book commented upon the agrarian tradition of the South and the familiarity of her people with the soil.

The views expressed by these scholars, men who were intimately acquainted with the South and its problems, were obviously romantic ones. In their minds, the South was rural, agricultural, and good; the North was urban, industrial, and bad. Although their call for conservatism in industrial growth was more wishful thinking than future reality, these men had a point: before 1930 the South was largely rural and agricultural, and, unlike the North, the South did have one important characteristic that bound many people to the land—a well-developed plantation tradition. This tradition was immensely important to southern identity, economy, and society.

Even though most southerners in 1860 had no connection with slavery and were not plantation owners, the plantation continues to fascinate scholars and nonscholars alike.[2] In some ways, the plantation is synonymous with the American South because of its occurrence there.

That a portion of the South was a place of large plantations, small

1

tenant farms, and fields of thriving cotton is a historical fact. This trinity—plantation, tenancy, and cotton—set the South apart as a distinctive American region. In the South, the tradition of slavery was hard to forget, and plantation tenancy, the postwar legacy of slavery, was often seen as a major social and economic problem.

Developed initially as a means of providing economic security for rich planters, the plantation soon became a way of life that incorporated its own labor organization, social rules, and physical form. Still, the plantation was a highly adaptable organization that could be altered to meet the conditions and challenges of changing times.

The greatest forces that affected southern cotton plantations were brought by the Civil War and the emancipation of some four million slaves. When the war ended in the spring of 1865, much of the agricultural base of the South was in confusion: many of the large plantations were burned or in ruins, great stretches of once arable land were trampled or left unattended, and many of the former slaves, most of whom had grown up working in the fields, had left the estates or were unwilling to work for former slave owners.[3] Wanting their own land, former slaves desired to make the plantation South resemble the surrounding nonplantation South with its many small farms. Freed slaves interested in agriculture wanted their own farms, free from white supervision.

The farm tenancy that eventually developed from the needs and hopes of these former slaves, along with the entrepreneurial ambitions of plantation owners, worked in concert with other complex issues to shape the modern South. The cotton tenancy from 1865 to 1925 was not a simple reorganization of the antebellum cotton plantation, for tenancy transformed the South. The cotton South that developed after the Civil War was not the cotton South that had existed earlier, even though similarities did remain, the greatest of which was the continued existence of plantations. Still, the social, economic, and political changes that were wrought by a nation at war with itself forever changed the way southern cotton would be grown. Arranged to occupy as little space as possible so as not to limit cotton production, the homes of tenants sprang up across the cotton South on antebellum plantation lands; rigid Jim Crow laws were enacted by fearful whites in the attempt to control the social roles of their newly emancipated black neighbors; and a rural poverty settled over cotton country as large landowners sought to recapture their former power, prestige, and wealth.

The complicated events of the postbellum period perhaps have been more significant in shaping the contemporary South than have those of the antebellum period. Even so, the antebellum period, and particularly the antebellum plantation, has generally attracted more attention than its postwar counterpart.

This interest in the antebellum plantation has not been confined to the general public, and many historians, anthropologists, sociologists, economists, and geographers have focused their attention on antebellum plantations. Some scholars, however, who did understand the importance of the postbellum plantation, presented excellent studies of it. Some studies, like those of Howard W. Odum and Rupert B. Vance, concentrated on the geographic and social issues of the postbellum plantation, while others, like those of Robert E. Park, Edgar T. Thompson, and W. Lloyd Warner, focused upon race relations and social structure.[4] The research of these scholars and their students, many of whom became prominent in their fields, provides a starting point for understanding the postbellum plantation South. The practitioners of other disciplines, notably history and anthropological archaeology, have been slower to examine the postbellum plantation. In history, however, a number of contemporary scholars have successfully built upon the research of the scholars who preceded them to expand our understanding of the postbellum plantation in historical and cultural terms.[5]

Cultural anthropologists have studied the agrarian systems of the world for many years. In the Western Hemisphere, this tradition goes back at least as far as the early 1930s, with the research of Robert Redfield and Paul Taylor in Mexican peasant communities.[6] Anthropologists have continued to conduct these kinds of studies and in some cases have examined the cross-cultural nature of sharecropping and plantation tenancy.[7] Today, anthropologists are examining the many aspects of agricultural life and agrarian development around the world.[8] Even though great effort has been expended to understand the farming systems of other cultures, anthropologists have not spent an equal amount of time studying the farmers of the American South. Whereas a few students have concentrated on the nature of status in southern farming communities, little real effort has been made to study agricultural life itself.[9]

A notable exception to this is a study by Morton Rubin.[10] This study provides a brilliant analysis of one plantation area (called "plantation county") by employing an anthropological approach to examine plantation organization, the change in this organization through time, the differences between black and white social standing, the place of small farmers in society, the role of the church in rural society, and the life cycle of the farm family.

Rubin's study uses the multifaceted approach that characterizes American anthropology. American anthropology, composed of four subfields—cultural anthropology, physical anthropology, anthropological linguistics, and archaeology—includes the study of every aspect of human life, and so finds value in all the areas specifically studied by the formal disciplines of history, sociology, economics, and political science. Nonetheless, while scholars in each of these disciplines have presented detailed studies of the plantation South, this great tradition has no counterpart in American archaeology, and archaeologists have been slow to turn their interpretive powers to the southern plantation. This lack of interest is not surprising, because only recently has American archaeology become interested in the most recent, literate past.

Of the two kinds of archaeology practiced in the United States—prehistorical and historical—the study of plantations falls within the domain of historical archaeology. Prehistorical archaeology involves the study of the nonliterate Native Americans who lived in North America before European colonization. Its focus extends from about thirty-five thousand years ago, when the first people came to this continent by way of the Bering Straits land bridge, up to about the sixteenth century, when Europeans began arriving on the shores of the New World. In some regions, the historic period began later. Prehistorians study mounds, villages, and burial sites related to these ancient first Americans.[11]

Historical archaeology, on the other hand, begins where prehistory ends, with the presence of European contact and colonization, written documents, and literacy. A comprehensive definition of historical archaeology is difficult to present because of its multidisciplinary nature, but the best definitions stress its emphasis on the study of the material expressions of the expansion of European culture into the non-European world beginning in the sixteenth century and continuing to the present.[12] Whereas prehistorical archaeology has been of interest to people almost since the first days of the European settlement of North America, historical archaeology has been recognized as a respectable kind of archaeology only since the 1950s.[13] After all, the early colonists, some of whom speculated about human antiquity in North America, are the subject of today's historical archaeology. Even though historical archaeology does not have a long history, its purview is wide, and historical archaeologists study colonial, Native American, and frontier history, urban development, ethnic history, cultural processes, and physical restoration and reconstruction.[14] So, rather than being just the study of a particular period, historical archaeology studies a particular topic, the spread and manifestation of European culture throughout the world.

At first glance, one might suppose that historical archaeology is really just a special kind of history, perhaps closely akin to local history because of its inherent interest in individual sites and small regions. This view of the field has been expressed by prominent historical archaeologists during the field's early development. Of those who held this view, perhaps most notable among them are Ivor Noël Hume, the foundation archaeologist of Colonial Williamsburg, Virginia, who has called historical archaeology the "handmaiden to history," and J. C. Harrington, an early pioneer in historical archaeology, who referred to the field as "an auxiliary science to American history."[15] Such comments imply that historical archaeology is nothing more than history with dirt on it. In other words, historical archaeology exists to supplement historical knowledge. This perspective is misleading because even though most of today's historical archaeologists have been trained in anthropology, historical archaeology has the ability to transcend the narrow boundaries of formal academic disciplines.

Still, historical archaeology is currently conducted both as history and as anthropology, whether or not its practitioners claim to be anthropologists. Ultimately, some historical archaeologists view their research as historical; others, as anthropological. The groups formed by these scholars are not exactly mutually exclusive, and neither group works without knowledge of the other's research. In fact, a survey of contemporary historical archaeologists might reveal that these groups exist only on a theoretical level. Nevertheless, an appreciable difference can appear in the ways those trained in history and those trained in anthropology approach, analyze, and interpret what they excavate.[16] This difference provides a healthy diversity to historical archaeology and helps it ma-

ture. Historical archaeologists will learn one day that they should be neither historians nor anthropologists, but rather merely historical archaeologists. Importantly, those scholars who have examined the epistemo-
logical bases of history and anthropology have generally concluded that
little theoretical difference exists between them.[17]

If historical archaeology is similar to any kind of history, that history
would probably be social history even though its methodological links
with local history are strong. Although social history has its antecedents
in the writings of Herodotus, no readily agreed-upon definition of the
field exists. The best definitions of social history are perhaps those that
emphasize the historical study of culture and society, social structures,
the development of social classes, and the relations between them.
Among its other characteristics, social history seeks to illuminate the social organizations of past peoples and to understand the relationships
among the various historical classes of people.[18]

Historical archaeology, like social history, is interested in people who
are not necessarily members of the ruling classes. Historical archaeologists excavate slave cabins, miners' homes, workers' quarters, and so
forth. However, because historical archaeologists also excavate sites inhabited by the kind of people termed "elite policy actors,"[19] historical
archaeologists have an excellent opportunity to view historical social
classes and the relations among them. This aspect of historical archaeology holds great promise for the future of the discipline.

Although often expensive and always time-consuming, historical archaeology is perfectly suited to the study of the southern plantation.
Largely as a result of their close association with history, historical archaeologists have learned that although usually invaluable, written documents can present an incomplete, inaccurate, and even contradictory
view of the past. Information of vital interest to historical archaeologists
is often not mentioned by past observers, or when mentioned, it is often
mistakenly or intentionally misrepresented. In many cases, the information most sought by archaeologists was too commonplace to have been
recorded. As a result, written records taken alone are inadequate for
archaeological research.

Because historical archaeology is an expansive field that transcends
normal academic description, members of many disciplines should see
much that is familiar here. Local historians, rural sociologists, folklorists,
and others will find aspects of their own disciplines in this book. A com-

mon thread that runs through both historical archaeology and these formal disciplines is an interest in material culture.

Defined in its broadest sense, *material culture* is "that segment of man's physical environment which is purposely shaped by him according to culturally dictated plans."[20] Defined in another way, material culture incorporates the symbols of power, one's place in the world, and the relationship of a person to his neighbors.[21] Because the study of material culture does not neatly fit into any one academic discipline, scholars trained in many disciplines are involved in material culture research.[22] As a multifaceted discipline that draws on many different kinds of sources—letters, account books, photographs, excavated artifacts, keepsakes, standing buildings, building ruins, excavated building remains, and the remembrances of informants—historical archaeology is truly "the study of American material culture in historical perspective."[23] Historical archaeology has a prominent place within the study of material culture, and as a discipline that should not be the handmaiden to history, or to any other discipline, it has much to offer.[24]

This book, whose emphasis is on the study of material culture, follows a theoretical orientation generally referred to as *historical materialism* and composed of a complex body of theoretical thought. Although historical materialism cannot be fully explained here, a brief outline is presented to provide a framework for understanding the foundation of this study.

Although historical materialism is not a recent development, its modern form was devised by Karl Marx and Frederick Engels.[25] As explained by Marx and Engels, the historical materialist model of society incorporates three basic elements—in order of importance: the economic base, the political superstructure, and the social ideologies.[26] Historical materialists assume that society is constantly changing and that change occurs as a result of conflict rather than of consensus.

For historical materialists, the economic base constitutes the footing for all else in society. Still, historical materialism is not mere economic determinism, because the other elements of society work together to structure the human world. Starting with the understanding that the natural bases—climate, land contour, and water resources—limit and affect human subsistence efforts, historical materialists consider human production of primary importance in history. One way humans distinguish themselves from the rest of the animal kingdom is through this production. As Engels wrote in 1877, humans "must first of all eat, drink, have shelter and clothing, therefore must *work*, before they can fight for domination, pursue politics, religion, philosophy, etc."[27] This production, however, is complex and includes the way people grow food, make clothing, and build homes (called the *mode of production* by historical materialists); the relations of ownership and the division of labor (the *relations of production*); the raw materials, tools, and techniques used in production (the *means of production*); the ways in which consumers obtain goods from producers (the *mode of exchange*); and the ways in which people divide what is produced (the *mode of distribution*). In short, production includes most of the tangible actions and products of people who are working toward ensuring their own survival. As society grows, certain distinctions develop between those people who are the society's producers and those people who are the society's owners. The logic of materialism for archaeology is obvious because of the kind of information archaeologists collect. In fact, materialism in archaeology is as old as the discipline itself, and a reliance on material culture is central to archaeological research;[28] however, an interest in material culture does not make one a materialist.[29]

Following the lead of the renowned British archaeologist V. Gordon Childe, a number of archaeologists have recently realized their commitment to materialism, specifically, historical materialism.[30] Prehistorians have generally had difficulty using historical materialism in their research, because of an imperfect understanding of the preliterate world in materialist thought.[31] Historical archaeologists should have a somewhat easier time because they concentrate on the kinds of societies most studied by historical materialists, modern, literate, capitalistic ones. If one accepts the proposition put forth that "historical archaeology has always been about capitalism,"[32] then the union between historical archaeology and historical materialism is a natural one.

A word of caution is in order here. Upon reading the words "Karl Marx" and "historical materialism," many people immediately relate them, perhaps unconsciously, to political issues. The concern over associating archaeology with politics via historical materialism has been voiced by archaeologist Mark Leone, who has demonstrated that historical materialism is an important intellectual tool that can be used to understand America's historical past.[33] History has shown us, for example, that most people who came to the North American continent from Europe did so as part of a global search for wealth. This search eventually led to full-scale capitalism.[34] These immigrants came to reap profits from a huge land inhabited only by people perceived as ignorant savages largely unconcerned with profits. Historical materialism, being interested in the development and manifestations of capitalism, is perfect for understanding this worldwide expansion and search for wealth. Although Leone has been criticized for his stance on historical materialism in archaeology, his position is consistent with that of Childe.[35] While it may be true, as Engels said at Marx's grave, that "Marx was before all else a revolutionary," and that "divorced from its revolutionary practice the materialistic theory of history would be lifeless,"[36] historical archaeologists who adopt historical materialism are only part of a revolution within archaeology, not within society as a whole. Although all archaeology exists within a political framework of some kind,[37] American historical archaeologists who adopt historical materialism as a framework for understanding the past do not necessarily attach themselves to contemporary Marxist political beliefs. Thus, the distinction between *Marxian* studies—using the philosophical and socioeconomic concepts explained in Karl Marx's view of history—and *Marxist* studies—incorporating a belief in the political agenda of today's Marxist regimes—must be made explicit.[38] This study should be considered Marxian.

This book examines the first element in the historical materialist view of society: the material basis of society. The society studied is the postbellum tenant plantation. Plantation landlords were interested in profits, and plantation tenants were generally interested in getting away from the plantations. All the activities conducted by these plantation inhabitants—sleeping, eating, dreaming, celebrating, and dying—occurred within a capitalist world. The material aspects of the lives of plantation inhabitants—landlords, managers, and tenants—must be studied first in order that other analyses focused on different aspects of plantation life might eventually follow. The emphasis here is on the basic physical aspects of tenant plantation existence: settlement, housing, and material possessions.

This study in historical archaeology might be conceptualized as a subtype of historic-sites archaeology called plantation archaeology. As explained by historical archaeologist Robert L. Schuyler, *historic-sites archaeology* is composed of the many specialties within the wider field of historical archaeology.[39] These specialties are defined on the basis of their spatial, temporal, cultural, and ethnic characteristics. When viewed in this framework, *plantation archaeology* is a kind of historic-sites archaeology that focuses upon the diverse ethnic, occupational, social, spatial, and economic aspects of plantation organization throughout the world.

Of the many different kinds of historic-sites archaeology conducted in the United States, plantation archaeology is perhaps the most recent.[40] One early example of archaeology at a southern plantation was the exploration of the Elizafield ruins on the Georgia coast by James A. Ford.[41] As an example of historical archaeology, Ford's study was pathbreaking and unusual. Unfortunately, this research was insignificant to the development of plantation archaeology because Ford's major concern was the location and study of early Spanish mission sites. He made no attempt to study the discovered sites within a plantation context.

Even though his work was not plantation oriented, Ford's investigation at least demonstrated that plantation remains did exist and that they were available for archaeological investigation if anyone cared to excavate them. Nonetheless, another thirty years would pass before plantation archaeology in the southern United States would begin in earnest.

In the 1960s, the civil rights movement, the war in Vietnam, and other factors combined to cause archaeologists, and most social scientists, to reevaluate the social relevance of their fields. An interest in plantations, as the homes of slaves, grew out of this general concern. Much of the early research was conducted by Charles H. Fairbanks, professor of anthropology at the University of Florida. Fairbanks's archaeological study of plantations began with his limited excavation, in the late 1960s, of the Von Bulow Plantation near Daytona Beach, Florida. This promising research revealed the existence of slave cabins, but because of a shortage of funds, these remains were never fully excavated.[42] Fortunately, Fairbanks maintained his interest in plantation archaeology, particularly as it pertained to slavery, and later conducted excavations at Kingsley Plantation on Fort George Island, Florida, and at Rayfield Plantation on Cumberland Island, Georgia.[43]

This research by Fairbanks dramatically documented the material culture used by slaves and illustrated the inadequacies of using only written records for studying southern slave life. In addition, Fairbanks was the first plantation archaeologist to demonstrate one of the main tenets of historical archaeology—that the thoughtful combination of written documents and archaeological information, in addition to many other kinds of information, is the best possible means for providing detailed knowledge about the historical past. In fact, the innovative approach used in presenting the Rayfield slave cabin research, that of interlacing the comments of former slaves with the archaeological findings, provides a substance to slavery that has been seldom duplicated.[44]

The research conducted by Fairbanks and his students illustrates the promise and potential of plantation archaeology.[45] Although many aspects of plantation life and organization have been examined by historical archaeologists, the anthropological studies have generally focused upon plantation slavery and antebellum plantation social structure.

Encouraged by the work at slave sites in the South and the Caribbean and at free blacks sites in the Northeast, many historical archaeologists have examined plantation slavery in some detail.[46] Along this line, some studies have provided inventories of the kinds of artifacts used by American slaves; others have expanded our understanding of plantation slavery in specific, material ways. Examples of this last kind of research are Theresa Singleton's examination of slave households in coastal Georgia, Suzanne McFarlane's study of the Couper Plantation slave community, and the reconstructions of slave life presented by Charles Fairbanks and Sue Mullins Moore and John Solomon Otto.[47] Some of the most promising studies are those that provide information about slave diet and nutrition based upon the tangible remains left at plantation homesites.[48] The kind of information presented in these studies is not often available in records written at the time.

One important area of study for the archaeologist interested in the antebellum plantation is slave acculturation and resistance. *Acculturation,* a complex process that has been variously defined, is perhaps best viewed as the changes in culture that occur when two different groups come into prolonged contact.[49] Acculturation occurred on the plantations of the American South as African and Caribbean laborers came into daily contact with their white masters and overseers. This acculturation was a two-way process as masters and slaves learned from one another. At the same time, plantation slaves resisted white dominance in several ways, including the stubborn retention of certain African cultural traits. The exact results of past acculturation and resistance are difficult to observe because beliefs, morals, ideals, language skills, and work habits were also transmitted between slave and master.[50] As a result, the best evidence for acculturation and resistance often resides in the tangible aspects of plantation life. The collection and study of these tangible items falls well within the domain of historical archaeology.

The problems inherent in studying Afro-American acculturation and the survival of African traits in the United States were indirectly addressed by historian John W. Blassingame when he stated that primary documents must be closely scrutinized to arrive at even "tentative conclusions" about African survivals.[51] This comment unintentionally demonstrates how archaeological research can be used. Although a few historical archaeologists have provided detailed comments about Afro-American acculturation and the survival of Africanisms,[52] a brief examination of two classes of material culture studied by archaeologists—ceramics and housing—can illustrate the nature of this research.

One of the most intriguing expressions of antebellum Afro-American culture in the southern United States appears in the pottery that is found on some colonial and early antebellum plantations. Although slave food and food allotments were always of interest to plantation owners,[53] little has been written about the kinds of ceramics used for the preparation and serving of slave meals. As a result, information about the use of ceramics by slaves and the changing use of ceramics must come almost entirely from archaeological research. In fact, most historical archaeologists now believe that some changes in ceramic usage indicate slave acculturation and, perhaps, slave resistance.[54]

First identified as pottery made by Native Americans who lived near plantations, the thick-bodied ware of simple construction originally called Colono-Indian pottery, is now thought to have been produced by slaves and is called Colono ware.[55] Even though this pottery does bear similarities to a Native American pottery style found in the South, its surface decorations and vessel shapes are strongly reminiscent of West African wares.

The presence of this pottery in the American South is an interesting example of the retention of African traits by American slaves. The production of African ceramics obviously continued as part of an earlier ceramic tradition that appeared on Caribbean islands such as Barbados.[56] That knowledge of pottery manufacture was carried from West Africa to the Lesser Antilles and then to the plantations of the American South is not surprising. Still, the discovery of this pottery in the South provides concrete evidence for the persistence of Africanisms there. This find, however, leads to the question of how this African-like ceramic was incorporated into the plantation system, a system controlled by non-Africans.

Research suggests that Colono ware was used by both slaves and masters. For example, at Middleton Place, a rice plantation in South Carolina dating from 1727, Colono ware was found in the remains of the slave dwellings and in the kitchen of the main house. The discovery of this ware in the kitchen implies that Colono ware was used by slave cooks to prepare their masters' meals, or even that planter families used these ceramics.[57] That planters and their families may actually have used these wares in the same ways that they would have used European ceramics is not only intriguing but perhaps indicative of the acculturation of non-Africans to certain African traits. Further evidence, found at Limerick Plantation, another eighteenth- and nineteenth-century rice plantation in South Carolina, suggests that Colono ware may have been used when European ceramics were difficult to obtain.[58] Excavation has shown that Colono wares decreased in popularity at the plantation between 1725 and 1824. Whereas Colono ware comprised 82 percent of the ceramics dating from 1725 to 1749, it accounted for only 21 percent of the entire ceramic collection by 1824. Concurrently, European ceramics increased in the ceramic sample from 18 percent to 79 percent for the same period.[59] Economic factors, such as the growth of the English ceramic industry, probably played some part in the disuse of Colono ware during the nineteenth century, but it remains possible that second- and third-generation slaves were never taught how to make the traditional Colono ware and that they simply used the more common European ceramics. Another possibility is that plantation owners made their slaves stop producing Colono ware after a few years.

The amount of Colono ware found has been used to establish the degree of acculturation suffered by the plantation slaves at two low country plantations in South Carolina. At these plantations, Yaughan and Curriboo, the smaller the percentage of Colono ware, the greater the amount of acculturation.[60] Interestingly, a decrease in Colono ware at the slave sites was accompanied by an increase in European items, a trend similarly observed at Limerick Plantation. This steady decline of Colono ware may suggest that American slaves were increasingly removed from their African ceramic traditions, perhaps because the hold of the planters over them was becoming stronger.

The changing use of European ceramics by slaves has also been studied. At Cannon's Point Plantation, a long-staple cotton plantation on St. Simon's Island, Georgia, built in 1794, evidence has been found that slaves replaced commercial ceramics for traditional ones at a fairly rapid rate.[61] The excavation of one slave cabin yielded a diverse collection of European, American, and Oriental plates, bowls, and cups. This five-hundred-piece collection, although seemingly large for a slave dwelling, was only about half as large as that from the master's kitchen refuse; however, although larger, the master's ceramic collection was more homogeneous and included many specimens from single-ceramic sets.

A combination of many economic, social, and aesthetic factors might explain the differences between the ceramics used by masters and those used by slaves. Perhaps the owner purchased fine, matched sets for his family and cheap, mismatched sets for his slaves; perhaps slaves purchased individual pieces with the little money they were allowed to earn on their own; or perhaps owners consciously bought cheap ceramics for their slaves to impress upon them the "enforced personal feeling of inferiority."[62] The possibility also exists that the slaves were not interested in nicely matched sets of dishes because they were more concerned about the daily business of survival.[63] Many other reasons can be presented to explain this difference in ceramic usage, and plantation archaeologists are deeply interested in this topic.

Regardless of which explanation best fits one's personal interpretation, the use of ceramics was not only different between slaves and masters, it changed through time. Historical information about this usage is rare, and comments like that made by former slave Cicely Cawthon are even rarer. When speaking about the ceramics used at her former plantation, Cawthon replied: "All the dishes [at Master's house] was flowered. I don't know as I ever saw a plain plate, except in the [slave] quarters. They [Master's family] had blue and yellow flowered plates, cups and saucers flowered, too, and great big, long, covered dishes to match."[64]

Plantation archaeology provides the best means for providing tangible information about the material culture used at southern plantations and provides bountiful evidence for the historical and cultural life on the plantations of the American South. Fortunately, the same kind of evidence that can be provided for ceramic usage also exists for plantation housing.

Planters were well aware of the need to provide adequate housing for their slaves. Ideally, slave housing was expected to be sufficiently commodious, well heated, and well ventilated, but in reality, slave cabins were often shamefully inadequate. The size of nineteenth-century slave cabins, those for which the best historical evidence remains, varied considerably from plantation to plantation, but the recommended size ranged from between 16 by 18 feet (288 square feet) to 16 by 20 feet (320 square feet). The smaller cabin was considered adequate for a family of five or six. The most important aspects of slave housing were size and ventilation.[65]

Although plantation owners generally viewed their slave quarters as the resting places of their human property when not at work, slaves remembered their cabins for what they were: primitive shelters for use at the end of a long work day. When asked about their slave homes, ex-slaves responded in amazingly similar ways. For example, in discussing her former slave home in Marshall County, Mississippi, Belle Caruthers offered a fairly typical description: The "houses were log cabins, with stick chimneys, daubed with mud. We cooked, ate and slept in one room, no matter how big the family."[66] Similar descriptions provided by other former slaves imply that most slave housing was simple, inadequate, and far from the ideal.

Descriptions of the interiors of these slave homes are also quite uniform. The comments of Gabe Butler of Amite County, Mississippi, are representative: "The house we lived in was just one big room with a big fireplace at one end and mammy done cookin' on that fireplace. We had one window and had no glass in it, but one big shutter. I remember the room we lived in; it had three beds in the corners of the room, and them beds had just one leg and the other side was nailed to the wall."[67]

These memories of former slaves, although invaluable, do not provide the kind of physical detail that archaeological research does. Plantation archaeology is particularly well suited to provide concrete information about slave cabin size. Research at Rayfield Plantation on Cumberland Island, Georgia, for example, has shown that slave cabins there measured 18 feet on a side (324 square feet); at Stafford Plantation along the Georgia coast, the cabins measured 16 by 20 feet (336 square feet); at Kingsley Plantation in northeastern Florida, one room of an excavated duplex cabin measured about 12.5 by 16 feet (200 square feet); and at Cannon's Point Plantation on St. Simon's Island, Georgia, the cabins were 17 by 20 feet (340 square feet).[68]

Unlike the oral information, these archaeological data cannot be questioned on the grounds of faulty memory. Instead, they provide tangible evidence for the crowded living conditions of at least some of the South's slave people. If the generally accepted estimates that either between 4 and 9 persons or 5.2 persons inhabited each slave dwelling in the South is used, then at the dwellings mentioned above, the slave families would have had between 22 and 85 square feet of living space per person with the first estimate (4 to 9 persons), and between 38 and 65 square feet with the second (5.2 persons).[69] If cubic-feet estimates are used, as proposed by Richard Sutch,[70] these cabins would have contained between 1,600 and 2,720 cubic feet of space, assuming an 8-foot ceiling. Using Sutch's estimate that a child would use half the airspace of an adult, the space per person would have ranged from 291 cubic feet (using Blassingame's figure of 9 persons per dwelling: 2 adults and 7 children, or 5.5 space-using people) to 907 cubic feet (using Blassingame's figure of 4 persons per dwelling: 2 adults and 2 children, or 3 space-using people). Neither figure falls within Sutch's estimate that an average adult needs between 400 and 600 cubic feet.

These estimates are enlightening, but an even better picture of slave space can be gathered by examining further archaeological evidence from Rayfield Plantation.[71] At this site, examination of an excavated slave cabin's standing chimney revealed that the roof peak was 11.5 feet above the base of the fireplace hearth. Because the walls of the cabin were calculated to have been about 6 feet high, this slave cabin had about 2,532 cubic feet of space, including the airspace between the eaves and the roof peak. Blassingame's slave family would have had between 400 and 844 cubic feet of space in this cabin; Sutch's slave family would have had 675 cubic feet of living space. Historical information from Rayfield Plantation is incomplete and cannot provide a good indication of how many slaves actually lived there; however, the records consulted during the research showed that fifty-three slaves had lived there at one time. Because two rows of nine cabins each existed at Rayfield, an average of three slaves would have lived in each cabin. This estimate suggests that the typical Rayfield slave had an average of 844 cubic feet of available living space. The possibility remains, nonetheless, that slaves not mentioned in the documents were also housed in the quarters and that the available-space figures should be much lower.[72]

Unique evidence about slave cabin construction is collected every time a historical archaeologist excavates a cabin. This research supports historical documents in their claim that slave cabins were simple structures made from locally available materials. At one cabin excavated at Cannon's Point Plantation, a number of locally made hinges and other building hardware were located. All of these items were hand-wrought and probably made by slave blacksmiths. The lack of window glass fragments at this structure implies that the building did not have glass windows, a finding consistent with the observations of many former slaves. Research at the Jones Creek Settlement on Butler Island, Georgia, shows that the slave cabins there were frame duplexes with foundations made of wooden posts set in trenches. These cabins had earthen floors and red brick fireplaces.[73] Further unique construction details can be cited from every slave cabin excavation in the South.

One of the best sequences of housing change was documented at Yaughan and Curriboo plantations in South Carolina. In the earliest years of these plantations, before 1740, the slave cabins were constructed with closely spaced wooden posts set in trenches and were reminiscent of West African and Caribbean house forms; later, the cabins were built with more widely spaced posts set both in trenches and individually; and finally, the cabins were built on brick piers and contained brick fireplaces. In addition to these design changes, the archaeological evidence also indicates that these buildings changed from rectangular to square, from mud-walled to frame, and from irregular to regular.[74] These changes provide evidence of slave acculturation or greater control and management by owners, or perhaps both, and also demonstrate that African housing forms were incorporated into some American plantations during the earliest period of their existence.[75]

In addition to producing these studies that shed light on the physical aspects of the antebellum plantation, a few archaeologists have studied plantation social order. These studies have been anthropological studies that have used archaeological materials in conjunction with detailed historical records.

John Solomon Otto was the first archaeologist to make an effort to understand antebellum plantation social position as revealed in archaeological remains.[76] Using housing, ceramics, glass, other artifacts, and food remains, Otto argues that planters, overseers, and slaves at Cannon's Point Plantation left distinctly different refuse deposits. Even though Otto's early conclusion that "archaeological remains from the plantation sites generally reflect social status differences" was somewhat tempered in his later work, his general finding that plantation social groups can be identified from their physical remains has important implications for plantation archaeology.[77]

In another study, Sue Mullins Moore takes Otto's ideas further by proposing that economic position rather than strict social position may be what is really identifiable in the physical evidence. Using three sites on St. Simon's Island, Georgia, Moore argues that plantation size may be the most important element in influencing the kinds of artifacts used there.[78] Her conclusion, that the material possessions of the small planter are similar to those of an overseer on a large plantation, correlates well with historical information.[79] Although the studies by Moore and Otto are not without problem,[80] they deserve the serious attention of plantation archaeologists.

These archaeological studies of antebellum plantations significantly further our understanding of the American plantation system by providing physical evidence of the kinds of conditions faced every day by plantation inhabitants. These studies have even stronger interpretive value when they incorporate historical research. The only unfortunate aspect of this research is that it has been largely confined to antebellum plantations; regrettably, only a few archaeologists have turned their attention to postbellum plantations.

The failure of archaeologists to study postbellum plantations can be rectified by the requirements of the federal government's cultural resource management legislation enacted during the 1960s and 1970s. This legislation requires construction projects using federal funds to allocate a portion of these monies for archaeological research. This research begins with simple ground surveys and literature reviews and terminates with full-scale excavation. The last step is reserved only for those sites deemed highly significant during the earlier research steps. The goal of such legislation is to protect and to study as many sites as possible before they are destroyed or irreparably altered by construction.[81]

While some people may choose to view this use of federal money as frivolous, most see this legislation for what it is: an attempt to save irreplaceable archaeological and historical resources from complete destruction. This federal legislation has been a boon for plantation archaeology because a vast number of sites, sites that otherwise would never have been studied, have been examined within this program. Fortunately, postbellum plantations have been included, for without this federal effort, the few postbellum plantations that have been excavated would have been destroyed before any study.

The main focus of this book, Millwood Plantation in Abbeville County, South Carolina, and Elbert County, Georgia, was studied as part of this federal program. Because the only other postbellum tenant plantation ever studied archaeologically was located in Mississippi,[82] Millwood Plantation is the only tenant plantation in the southern Piedmont that has been studied in any detail.

After the American Civil War, Millwood Plantation, like a great many others, was reorganized as a tenant plantation. As defined by the United States Census Bureau in 1910, the first postwar year in which plantations were explicitly enumerated, a tenant plantation was "a continuous tract of land of considerable area under the general supervision or control of a single individual or firm, all or a part of such tract being divided into at least five small tracts, which are leased to tenants."[83] Up until this time, plantation tenant farms had been counted as individual farms, and the continued presence of plantations in the South was largely overlooked.[84] The census of 1910 demonstrated that the plantation was still very much a part of the South, occurring in an area that stretched from North Carolina to Texas and including almost three hundred counties. Millwood Plantation was one of 39,073 tenant plantations that existed in 1910.

In an important study of the tenant plantation, historical economist Jay R. Mandle makes the case that the postbellum plantation provided a significant means by which white planters could keep their black labor force under control.[85] Although a more "indirect" institution than the slave plantation, the tenant plantation was nonetheless part of a plantation framework that ultimately required a large, subservient work force. The tenant plantation, an extension of its antebellum progenitor, provided the roots of black poverty. As such, the study of the postbellum tenant plantation helps provide information about the modern South.

The issues raised by Mandle are important ones that require further examination. As shown above, plantation archaeology is uniquely qualified to provide an examination that focuses on the tangible aspects of plantation life and culture. The goal of this book, then, is to examine the material culture of a postbellum tenant plantation. Before starting this task, however, the historical antecedents of Millwood Plantation must be presented, and the general aspects of all postbellum plantations must be addressed.

Chapter Two

The Colonial Antecedents
and Antebellum Beginnings
of Millwood Plantation

MILLWOOD PLANTATION WAS THIRTY-THREE YEARS OLD when slavery ended in 1865. By this time, Millwood had been built into a fairly consistent producer of short-staple, or green-seed, cotton. However, just ninety years earlier, when naturalist William Bartram rode past the future site of Millwood Plantation on May 10, 1775, the area consisted of an "uninhabited wilderness" composed of "a body of excellent fertile land, well watered by innumerable rivers, creeks, and brooks."[1]

Long after Bartram's visit to the area, cotton cultivation was synonymous with the South. During Bartram's time, however, cotton was not king in the region and would not be for some time. The experimental cultivation of cotton had occurred in "Carolina" by 1666, but its potential as a major cash crop was not immediately recognized. Even if the eventual value of cotton had been perceived, the technology to gin the short-staple, or upland, cotton would not exist until the 1790s.[2] As such, an interest in cotton cultivation did not contribute to the earliest white settlement of the South Carolina Piedmont.

The white settlement of the South Carolina Piedmont, defined here as the fifteen present counties in the northwestern corner of the state (figure 1), took place slowly as settlers moved northwest from the coast and south over the Appalachian Mountains. The Piedmont, or more accurately the Piedmont Physiographic Province, extends from New York State to Alabama and encompasses all of the northwestern part of South Carolina except a mountainous thin strip of Oconee and Pickens coun-

Figure 1. Counties of the South Carolina Piedmont.

ties.[3] The southern Piedmont, consisting of rolling hills and rich forests, is situated between the Blue Ridge Province, formed by the Appalachian mountain chain, and the flat Atlantic Coastal Plain. The topographic difference between these three regions is readily apparent in South Carolina, and persons traveling northwestward from Charleston would reach at Columbia what Bartram described as an "uneven" country "undulated by ridges or chains of hills, sometimes rough with rocks."[4] In geological terms, the relief in the Piedmont is caused by the presence of igneous and metamorphic rocks that form the many shoals along the Savannah River.[5]

Prehistorical archaeologists, in their frequent study of pre-European environments, generally divide large physiographic regions into smaller, more easily analyzed, environmental zones; they have defined four such zones along the Savannah River in Abbeville County: the Savannah River channel, the floodplain, the valley slopes, and the uplands.[6] Although these zones are not important to the present study, archaeological surveys have determined that all four were inhabited during prehistoric and historic times, with most of the sites located on ridgetops overlooking the Savannah River floodplain.[7] The region's many plantations used all four environmental zones in some fashion, for the location of dams and ferries, homes, or industrial sites.

In the early eighteenth century, the Piedmont was still inhabited by the Cherokee and Creek, who had lived in the area for centuries. After a series of battles and treaties, these Native Americans, like all eastern native groups, were pushed farther and farther west in front of a steady advance of whites.[8] The settlement of whites in the South Carolina Piedmont was slow, and by 1756, only about twenty-five families lived there. Included in this group was the Ezekiel Calhoun family, who had settled with four other Calhoun families near the present-day site of Abbeville.[9] In time this family figured prominently in local, state, and national politics, and was intimately familiar with Millwood Plantation.

In the mid-eighteenth century, the Piedmont was a beautiful but dangerous place for whites who intended to move onto Native American land. In the 1770s, the area that according to Bartram presented "a body of excellent fertile land" was still the scene of often intense Indian-white conflict. Although the town of Abbeville, first named New Bordeaux, had been founded in 1764 by a group of French Protestants seeking religious freedom, many white inhabitants in the area still found it necessary to defend themselves against Indian retaliation.[10] During this period, most whites followed the Native American example and settled along the area's largest rivers, the main source of transportation and communication in a region considered by whites to be undeveloped.

Archaeological evidence for the white settlement of the South Carolina Piedmont, and specifically Abbeville County, is extremely sparse, and a field survey of the region conducted in the mid-1970s failed to discover indisputable physical evidence with which to document it. Still, some archaeologists have made important discoveries in the Piedmont. For example, the excavations at Fort Independence, an eighteenth-century outpost, have provided important new data to document the early white settlement of the area.[11] The lack of physical evidence for these white settlements stems from their often temporary nature, the amount of time since they were built, and the degree of disturbance they may have experienced as new buildings were constructed to replace them. This paucity of evidence is clearly not caused by a lack of settlement, for whites had cast their eyes on the South Carolina Piedmont fairly early in the state's history.

Following a series of treaties and further conflicts with the Native Americans in the area, the white population of Abbeville County grew steadily. In 1793 the *State Gazette of South Carolina* reported that Pendleton and Greenville districts—that area that would become Anderson, Greenville, Oconee, and Pickens counties—contained at least 20,000 people. Seven years earlier, only forty families were reported living there. In 1794 a Charleston paper reported that Abbeville and Edgefield counties—encompassing the present counties of Abbeville, Edgefield, Greenwood, McCormick, and Saluda—contained 17,280 people.[12] This rapid population increase demonstrates either that the region's Native Americans had been removed by this time or that they were no longer a serious hostile threat, and that extensive white settlement was possible without major opposition.

In 1790 the Piedmont, with 81,533 inhabitants, comprised 32.7 percent of the entire population of South Carolina. Within the Piedmont, Abbeville County contained 9,197 inhabitants, or 11.3 percent of the region's population. By 1800 the population of the Piedmont was reported at 120,805, an increase of 48.2 percent over the previous decade. In Abbeville County alone, the population increased to 13,553, or by 47.4 percent, during this period. During this same decade, the population of the entire state increased by only 38.8 percent, or 8.6 percent less than the Piedmont.[13] The population of South Carolina continued to grow, and the spread of whites throughout the state was an accomplished fact by 1800.[14]

One obvious reason for the white population increase in the Piedmont was the promise of good, arable land. Although the first waves of settlers on the southern frontier were mostly herders, tobacco cultivation was a major preoccupation in the South Carolina Piedmont by 1800.[15] However, when the price of tobacco fell a few years later in conjunction with the development of a cotton gin capable of separating the short fiber of upland cotton from its tenacious seeds, many farmers in the upcountry shifted to the cultivation of upland cotton.[16] As French traveler François André Michaux wrote at the time, this shift was a "great advantage" to the inhabitants "many of whom have since made their fortunes by it."[17]

In the decades following 1800, the cultivation of cotton and the importation of slaves to produce it steadily grew in Abbeville County. From 1790 to 1800, the slave population in the county increased from 18.1 to 21.9 percent, or from 1,665 to 2,964 persons. The white population grew by 40.5 percent, but the black population grew by 77.8 percent. In the next decade, the white population grew by 36.5 percent, while the black population expanded by an incredible 125.1 percent. At that time, 6,672 slaves and 14,396 free whites lived in Abbeville County. This population trend continued, and in 1820, slaves accounted for 41.5 percent of Abbeville County's entire population. In 1820 the entire Piedmont contributed 35.0 percent of the state's slave population. Abbeville County in turn contributed 18.2 percent of the Piedmont's slaves.[18]

When William Robertson made his survey of Abbeville County for Robert Mills's *Atlas of South Carolina* in 1820, the county contained 23,167 persons, 9,615 of whom were slaves.[19] The map drawn by Robertson and later refined by Mills shows the county seat, Abbeville, located in the center of the county with a series of roads radiating outward from it. On the extreme western edge of the county, on the Savannah River, an area called Trotter's Shoals occurs between the Rocky River and the small town of Vienna. In 1820 this area contained Bickley's Mill, Bickley's Store, Allen's Mill, and Midway Plantation (figure 2). This is the area that would soon contain Millwood Plantation.

Millwood Plantation, the subject of this book, was not created until 1832 and so does not appear on the map; however, the earliest germ of thought about Millwood developed while James Edward Calhoun, its owner, lived at Midway Plantation. Calhoun, the owner of both plantations, was a member of one of the pioneer, and eventually most prominent, white families in the South Carolina Piedmont.

In 1820 the operation of a cotton plantation was new to Calhoun.[20] Although born into the Abbeville County planting aristocracy in 1798, James Edward Calhoun—the grandson of colonist Ezekiel Calhoun and the son of John Ewing Calhoun, a prominent planter and United States senator, and Floride Bonneau Calhoun—sought his career, not from the land, but from the sea. Local tradition holds that Calhoun joined the United States Navy while still in his teens, traveled the world, and

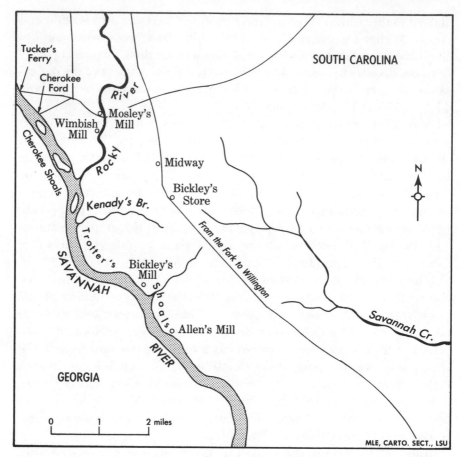

Figure 2. Area of James Edward Calhoun's activities as it appeared in Mills' Atlas *in 1820.*

learned seventeen languages, of which his favorite was Portuguese.[21] By all accounts, Calhoun was a brilliant man whose interests ranged from ethnography to machinery to astronomy. When he was twenty-seven years old, Calhoun was selected—through the intervention of Secretary of War John C. Calhoun, who was also his cousin and brother-in-law (having married James Edward's sister, Floride Bonneau Calhoun, in 1811)—to join the Stephen H. Long Expedition as its astronomer.[22]

The Long Expedition of 1823 was a massive undertaking that began in Philadelphia, traveled across the Midwest, up the Mississippi River into Minnesota, along the old fur trade routes in Manitoba and Ontario, through the Great Lakes to the Erie Canal, and then back to Philadelphia. The expedition had many purposes, including the collection of cartographic details on the Upper Midwest and information about the northern Native Americans. Another purpose—to collect intelligence on British activities south of the forty-ninth parallel—gave the expedition a national significance.[23] Calhoun's participation in this undertaking was undoubtedly an important personal event.

The diary Calhoun kept during this expedition aptly demonstrates both the breadth of his knowledge and his innate intelligence. His comments on the Native Americans he encountered are detailed, and his astronomical measurements indicate his interest in scientific accuracy. Calhoun refers to a number of books throughout the diary, and footnotes them with Greek letters. Little doubt exists that Calhoun was an asset to the expedition both as a scientist and as an affable companion.[24] Although in later life Calhoun would be known largely for his eccentricities, having been described by one acquaintance in 1837 as "the eccentric, & wicked, but highly-gifted James Edward Calhoun,"[25] no hint of these character traits was apparently manifested during the Long Expedition. A strong likelihood exists, however, that even while he was a participant of the Long Expedition, young James Edward had his mind on his planting operations in far-off Abbeville County.

Years before he joined the Long Expedition, James Edward Calhoun had become the owner of several large tracts of land in the South Carolina districts of Abbeville and Pendleton. At the age of four he had inherited this land from his father.[26] However, by choosing a career in the navy, James Edward showed that he was not interested in living the planter's life. Nonetheless, he was the absentee owner of Midway Plantation, and he probably at least thought about his planting concerns throughout his naval career.

Little is known about Midway Plantation. Early in its history, the operation of the plantation was managed by Andrew Norris, Calhoun's uncle, and later by James Edward's brother, John Ewing Calhoun, a planter in Pendleton District. Both men conveyed the wishes of James Edward to the overseers and sometimes directed the operations outright. For example, in September 1822, Norris notified James Edward that his cotton crop at Midway was quite good but that the crop from last year was still sitting unsold in Augusta.[27] Norris continued to direct the work of Calhoun's overseers at Midway until he became ill in 1824. At this point, John Ewing assumed this responsibility.[28]

Throughout the period of James Edward's absentee ownership, the slaves of Midway Plantation produced a consistent cotton crop, with 65 bales produced in 1823, 50 in 1826, and 60 in 1827.[29] Nonetheless, economic factors outside Calhoun's control placed him always on the edge of financial ruin. His uncle told him in 1822, for instance, that "money as well as purchasers [are] very scarce," and five years later his brother informed him that his cotton sale would not do more "than meet the current expense of the plantation."[30] One year later, in 1828, John C. Calhoun told James Edward that the return from staple crops hardly compensated the expense of cultivation, because the prices of land and slaves were at "depressed rates."[31]

Still, Midway Plantation offered great promise, and in 1823, Norris reported that the overseer believed that the place was large enough to employ as many as ten more hands.[32] To buy more slaves, Calhoun required capital, and this was in short supply in the Piedmont during the early 1820s. One way to acquire more usable capital was through the sale of land, but whereas Norris was approached many times about selling Calhoun's Pendleton District property in 1818, by 1822 no one was asking. In 1823 Norris reported that he was unsuccessfully trying to sell land to pay the carpenters who had built Calhoun's cotton gin house.[33] Four years later, in December of 1827, Calhoun's brother was still trying to sell the Pendleton lands. In May of that year, John Ewing had told James Edward that "the times are so dreadful that there is no possibility of selling any kind of property" and that "there must be a change of staple, or we shall be most of us ruined."[34] Times continued to be bad, and in 1828 John Ewing wrote to James Edward: "There is no prospect of collecting what is due to you, . . . your place has not much more than cleared expenses since you left here."[35]

The economic problems faced by James Edward Calhoun were compounded by problems presented by his managers. From at least 1818 to 1825 Calhoun retained an overseer named Speed.[36] Although nothing is known of this Speed, his length of employment and his efforts to produce cotton steadily suggest that he was an adequate plantation overseer. Even though the term of employment for many southern plantation overseers was notoriously short, a term of seven years for a manager of an absentee estate was not unusual.[37] However, trouble had obviously arisen with Speed, because on January 27, 1825, a new manager named William Clark was mentioned by John Ewing Calhoun in a letter stating that he was sending him seven more slaves.[38] John Ewing reported that Clark was an expensive manager at $365 a year but that he was well worth the money. On the other hand, Speed, the former overseer, was causing some sort of presently indeterminable trouble within the area.[39]

Although mentioned by John Ewing Calhoun, almost nothing concrete is known about the Midway slave force; however, in his letter to Clark in January 1825, he does refer to a slave rebellion that had occurred either at Midway or at an adjoining plantation. In light of this activity, John Ewing warned Clark that "the only method is to be decisive and punish on the spot all attempts at insubordination."[40] Clearly, within an environment of a poor economy and possible slave insurrections, Midway Plantation was facing difficult times.

These difficult times may have caused James Edward to think more seriously about the life of a resident planter. Throughout his service in the navy, Calhoun made frequent visits to his plantation, and he was aware of both its potential and its problems. For example, in 1822 Andrew Norris made reference in a letter to Calhoun's having visited Midway. By 1828, when James Edward was on furlough from the navy, John C. Calhoun told him in a fatherly tone that "we are much pleased, that you directed the erection of a building for your residence at Midway, and hope, that we may have much of your company the next two, or three years." Nonetheless, only four months later, when James Edward was ready to go back to sea, John C. Calhoun told him, "It is not my wish to disuade you from a tour, which you have so much at heart, and on which you have made up your determination."[41]

By early 1831 James Edward was once again thinking about giving up the sea for the plantation. In January he wrote, "I have not determined definitely on my future arrangement," and two months later, while staying at Fort Hill, John C. Calhoun's home north of Midway, he informed a friend that he was undecided about remaining "in the country."[42] Obviously, Calhoun was weighing the possibility of moving permanently to his Abbeville plantation and had thought about it for some time. A statement made in the same letter is significant because Calhoun mentions that if he did settle permanently in the Piedmont he would not want to live at Midway, but would rather prefer building on one of his other tracts. Although in this letter he was referring to lands he owned on

Twenty-six Mile Creek in south-central Pendleton District, this brief comment serves as the first mention of his plan to organize and settle at Millwood Plantation. By this time, Calhoun had probably had a good taste of the resident planter's life because navy records indicate that he had received a year-long furlough on April 1, 1830. His indecision in March 1831 must have been resolved, because on April 1, 1831, he apparently received another twelve-month leave. He finally resigned his commission in late 1833 or early 1834.[43]

With Calhoun's resignation, he began to concentrate fully on planting. His diary, written during these early days of resident planting, reads like any planter's notes, being filled with comments on slaves, plows, and the weather. His interests in science began to show as he started to experiment with many crops that, in the South Carolina upcountry were exotic, but with which he had obviously become acquainted during his worldwide travels—various strains of wheat, including Mexican and Malayan, wild orange trees, Brazilian tea, and different varieties of rye, clover, corn, and oats.[44]

By January 1832 James Edward was fully involved in planting and was well on the way to implementing what he referred to as his "new plan." Calhoun wrote in his diary, "Being able, at last, to bestow individual attention to my affairs, I have commenced the improvement of my lands, which have been shamefully abused by overseers." He began by directing his slaves to clean the plantation, to fill the gullies with brush and trash, and not to cultivate those tracts of land that had always been planted. James Edward's active and experimental mind caused him to invent his own system of contour farming called loxotising. Although this kind of horizontal farming was "troublesome, tedious & uncertain," Calhoun believed that it would "keep up the land."[45] Calhoun's plan of contour farming was resisted by his neighbors, who were not as well-read or perhaps merely not as adventurous as he. In fact, one even told him that he would ruin his land because "fresh ground cannot bear the sun!" The scientist in Calhoun caused him to relegate such ideas to the realm of "notions" lacking "rational reason."[46]

Calhoun's vision for his planting operations included other tracts that were uncleared in January 1832. In an effort to expand his enterprise in the spring of that year, Calhoun began what would become his major operation, Millwood Plantation, by sending "2 men, 1 woman & 1 girl" there to form a settlement. He also hired a man named Absalom Roberts at $100 a year to oversee and to labor alongside his slaves there. At this time, sixty acres were cleared and planted in corn and peas. On July 30, James Edward "began a crib Dam at the upper part of Trotter's Shoals, Savannah River, intending to erect Mills at [his] Millwood place, the site where Trotter had his built before the Revolutionary War."[47] With these activities, Millwood Plantation was born.

Whether the Millwood lands were purchased by Calhoun after he began to live at Midway, or whether these formed part of the "other tracts" he frequently mentioned, cannot be determined. However, in the early 1830s, Calhoun started to acquire at a rapid pace the five miles of land between Midway and Millwood. In November 1832 he bought a 422.5-acre piece of land adjoining Millwood, called the Hamilton Tract, for $4 an acre, or $1,690, payable in three annual installments. The following month he bought another 200 acres for $400 from Richard Covington, payable on January 1, 1835. Almost one year later, he purchased 310 acres on the Rocky River adjacent to the Hamilton Tract for $4 an acre, or $1,240. In addition, Calhoun purchased two islands in the Savannah River, containing 4.5 acres, from a William Fleming for $27.12; in December 1833 he paid $500 for 100 acres next to Midway; and in March of the following year, Calhoun traded a piece of land with a Colonel Harleston for "mutual benefits."[48]

These real estate acquisitions demonstrate Calhoun's serious intent to build a large planting empire and to pursue the planter's life in earnest. He was clearly intent on becoming one of the larger planters in the South Carolina Piedmont. In 1832 and 1833, he acquired 1,037 acres, he traded for another piece of land, and he owed creditors more than $3,000 for land alone. Even after 1834, Calhoun's thirst for land was not easily quenched. Between 1834 and 1838 he acquired 10,853 more acres in Pickens District, and between 1848 and 1860 he purchased another 1,423 acres in Elbert County, Georgia. For all this land Calhoun paid more than $5,000.[49]

The energy Calhoun displayed in land acquisition was no greater than his dream of a planting empire, and in the 1830s, Calhoun had an estate that included three different plantations: the Hamilton Tract, which he called Stockdale, Millwood, and Midway, which was his home. He had an overseer and a slave work force at each place. At Stockdale, he had John B. Gapping and four slaves, at Millwood was Delancy Chisenhall and at least the four slaves he had sent there when it was first cleared, and at Midway were William McCrary and the remaining forty-seven slaves enumerated in the 1830 census.[50]

Although 61.8 percent of the 55 slaves owned by Calhoun in 1830 were between the ages of 10 and 55, Calhoun was nonetheless rich in land and poor in labor. When he began remodeling the settlement at Midway in August 1833, he obviously intended to make the plantation his career. Without labor, however, his plans would quickly evaporate. In the antebellum South, there were at least two ways in which Calhoun could acquire the labor he needed to build his large tracts of land into a lasting financial empire: by purchase and through childbirth. Census records reveal that Calhoun's slave labor force increased through both means. For example, in 1840 his slave force increased to 155 slaves, or 181.8 percent above the 1830 figure of 47. Much of this increase was undoubtedly due to purchase. In later years, Calhoun's purchase of slaves apparently became less frequent, because in 1850 and 1860, the increase in the slave population was less dramatic than the increase from 1830 to 1840. In 1850 Calhoun owned 183 slaves, an increase of 18.1 percent since 1840; and in 1860 he owned 195 slaves, an increase of 6.6 percent in a decade[51] (table 1). After 1840 Calhoun's work force was beginning to reach the level where they could transform his large land-holdings into capital.

Almost nothing is known about Calhoun's slaves as individuals, and little is known about how they lived or how they were treated. Historical archaeology has added considerable information about slave life, but because the postbellum occupation of Millwood Plantation obliterated almost all the evidence for the antebellum period, little has been learned about this period.[52] This lack of information is particularly unfortunate because these slaves became the tenant farmers and their ancestors who lived at Millwood after 1865. Thus, much of the antebellum documentation concerns Calhoun and his activities.

Some evidence about Calhoun's early slave force, however, is provided in a unique source, an unsigned slave ledger. Although unidentified, the ledger is written in Calhoun's characteristic handwriting. This ledger, although not without problem, provides information available in no other historical source and permits some small understanding of Calhoun's antebellum slave force.

The ledger consists of three parts. The first section contains a list of names and numbers that probably represent the ages of the slaves Cal-

Table 1

James Edward Calhoun's Slave Force, 1830–60

Age	1830 Male	1830 Female	1834 Male	1834 Female	1840 Male	1840 Female	1850 Male	1850 Female	1860 Male	1860 Female
<10, not sexed							61			
<10	7	12	14	15	35	29			26	40
10–24	6	10	8	11	21	25	13	16	33	27
25–36	8	3	4	3	6	17	14	10	21	17
37–55	4	3	3	2	9	6	7	9	11	13
>55	1	1	0	3	2	5	3	2	4	3
10–75, not sexed			3	6			48			
Subtotal	26	29	32	40	73	82	37 (not sexed 109)	37	95	100
Total	55		72		155		183		195	

Sources: Unidentified slave ledger; 1830, 1840, 1850, 1860 Slave Schedules, James Edward Calhoun, Abbeville District, Magnolia Township, South Carolina.

houn held in 1834. Some of the names are preceded by an *x* or have a line drawn through them, suggesting that they were either sold or dead. A second section of the ledger presents a list of names and dates from February 1835 to June 1847. These are probably slave births. The third section of the ledger provides a list of slaves who, in 1839, comprised an as yet unidentified agricultural work force called the Edgefield Gang.[53]

One hundred and twenty-six slaves are listed in the first section of the ledger. Of this number, only 72, or 57.1 percent, are not crossed out or identified with an *x*. The remaining 54 slaves were apparently deceased by 1834. The cause of their deaths cannot be determined, except in the case of Old Polydore, who had drowned. Among males, the highest mortality rate was among those slaves who were younger than 10 years old. Of these 25 males, only 14 (56.0 percent) survived. Among females, the highest mortality rate occurred in the 10- to 24-year-old class, where 7 out of 11 (63.6 percent) died. Most of the slaves enumerated were younger than 10 years old. This distribution seems to support the suggestion that natural increase played some role in structuring James Edward Calhoun's slave force. Mortality rates were high and 30 out of 62 males (48.4 percent) and 24 out of 64 females (37.5 percent) died by 1834.

The information presented in the second part of the ledger also provides limited evidence that Calhoun was an active slave buyer. Although 72 slaves were enumerated in 1834, and 155 in 1840 (an increase of 115.3 percent), the ledger lists the birth of only 59 children, of which 43, or 72.9 percent, survived. When 43 is added to the number shown in 1834, 40 slaves are unaccounted for in 1840. Although this evidence is extremely incomplete, it does support the contention that Calhoun made many slave purchases, even though some slave births may not have been recorded in the ledger.

Regardless of slave fertility and mortality rates, the available evidence indicates that a sizable percentage of Calhoun's slaves were within the optimal working ages. In 1830 61.8 percent of his slaves were between 10 and 55; in 1840, 54.2 percent were; and in 1850, 63.4 percent of his slaves were within this age group. Ten years later, 66.2 percent of his slaves were between the ages of 10 and 55.

In 1840, eighty-nine of Calhoun's slaves were employed in agriculture, and at least three were involved in manufacturing and trades. Because eighty-four slaves were between the ages of 10 and 55, it can be assumed that some agricultural workers were either younger than 10 or older than 55. At least one of those engaged in nonagricultural pursuits probably worked under the direction of the white male listed in the census.[54] This white male may have been Delancy Chisenhall, the millwright hired by Calhoun in 1832. In addition to this nonagricultural slave worker, Calhoun also had slave artisans. Written evidence of these craftsmen is not abundant, but it does exist. For example, in October 1842 a man in Abbeville wrote to Calhoun to inquire about hiring Andy and Alak at $2.50 per day or for one-half of whatever they produced. Although these men may have been agricultural laborers, known skilled artisans did live at Millwood. In April 1843, John C. Calhoun wrote to James Edward Calhoun: "I regret to hear of Polydore's attack. He is a very valuable Negro and his death would be a great loss to you."[55] Polydore's skill is not known, but he might have been the Big Polydore listed in the slave ledger in 1834. In 1843 he would have been thirty-one years old. A slave artisan in the prime of his working life would have been viewed as a great financial asset and upon his death a great loss for an antebellum planter who relied on the labor of his slaves for his economic security. Of course, no mention was made of the effect of the loss of Polydore on his family or the slave community. James Edward Calhoun also owned a slave mason named Andrew, who, in 1845, was hired by John C. Calhoun for two months' work on the family memorial plot. In 1839 a bricklayer named Andrew who worked in the Edgefield Gang was listed in the slave ledger. Calhoun obviously continued to hire his skilled laborers out, for in 1856 his masons were hired out to build a brick chimney.[56]

Almost nothing can be inferred from the documents about the society and life of Calhoun's slave force. Sketchy evidence suggests, however, that at least some slave families were kept together either by slave inventiveness or by Calhoun's design.[57] For example, the Edgefield Gang was composed of at least three slave families. The first family was composed of Andrew, the bricklayer, estimated age 23, Harriet, aged 21, Little Andrew, aged 4, Frances, aged 2, and an infant named Martha. A second family was composed of Maria, aged 29 (who was apparently married to Damon, who was not in the gang but who appeared in the 1834 list), Paul, aged 14, Emmeline, aged 8, Susan, aged 7 (who may not have been in the gang), William, aged 6, George, aged 4, and Edward, aged 6 months. A third family was composed of Charlotte, aged 24, who was possibly married to Favor (who was not in the gang but who appeared in the 1834 list), Moses, aged 8, Comfort, aged 6, Wilson, aged 4, and Richmond, an infant. Assuming that the ages of those in the Edgefield Gang were only estimates, two of these families can be identified in the 1850 census, eleven years later.[58] In fact, the 1850 census is presented in a manner that suggests family groupings, in that an adult male or female is presented first, followed by a list of minor children (all of whom are unnamed). After the minors, other adults appear, followed by more minors. The 183 slaves are thus separated into thirty-three groups. Of these, twenty-one, or 63.6 percent, were male-female households, seven (21.2 percent) were headed by females, and the remainder were aggregates of grouped males, grouped females, or combinations. These were possibly unmarried slaves or slaves married to slaves on other plantations. The size of these groups ranged from two to ten persons, an average of five per group.

Little more is known about the slaves, and even less is known about Calhoun's treatment of them. The scant evidence, however, implies that Calhoun was a harsh master. On March 18, 1835, for example, he wrote to Andrew Calhoun that one of his slaves had "lodged a complaint against Abbeville William," who promptly fled into the woods. Calhoun told Andrew to "have a good lookout kept for the rascal, and if you can catch him give him, in the first place, as soon as he can be tied, 100 lashes and then have him put in jail." In a postscript, Calhoun told his nephew that he would send a slave catcher after the runaway, but that he reserved the right "to punish him as an example." Calhoun also demonstrated that he was aware that his slaves formed a tightly knit social community when he told Andrew not to tell his slaves about William, because "they would be sure to caution him."[59]

Some knowledge of Calhoun's treatment of his slaves remains fixed in the oral tradition of the Millwood area. When questioned about the antebellum years of the plantation, some of Calhoun's former tenants commented upon the way their slave ancestors were treated. At least three people remembered that Calhoun never whipped his slaves, preferring instead to have a slave driver whip them. As one informant said, "I guess this slave might have done something bad and he'd give him so many licks." After using the whip a few times, the slave overseer would say " 'Master, you don't want to kill him, that'd be enough.' "[60] If this statement is true, then Calhoun's slaves played an active role in both punishment and reward on the plantation.

The increase in the slave population was good for Calhoun's economic development, if not good for the slaves themselves. In view of the subject of this study, however, another way Calhoun tried to acquire a larger work force is perhaps more intriguing. Early in the 1830s, when Calhoun was just beginning to expand his operations, and before his slave force was large enough to work all of his land, he rented selected tracts to tenant farmers. On January 23, 1833, he rented an unspecified amount of land on the Hamilton Place—or Stockdale as he called it—to Absalom Roberts, the man who had served him earlier as the overseer at Millwood. Calhoun set the rent at one-quarter of the corn, one-third of the cotton, and one-half of the oats grown by Roberts and agreed to supply him with oat seed. In addition to renting to this sharecropper, Calhoun rented land to Elihu Beard for $35, and the next year he rented to John E. Lyon. Lyon had obviously been a renter of Calhoun's before, because Calhoun noted that Lyon "again rents the cleared land on the Bickley & part of Hamilton tracts, say together 50 or 60 acres & comfortable houses for $50."[61]

Plantation tenancy—the hiring of farm laborers for a portion of the crop, a fixed amount of money, or a combination of each—was first used well before the postbellum period. In fact, tenancy in the United States was an outgrowth of the agricultural practices adopted in Europe during the Middle Ages. These practices were many and varied. One system used in England, the *service-tenancy system,* usually required the tenant either to spend a certain number of days working for the landlord or to perform a specified number of tasks for him. This system was flexible, however, and the tenant was sometimes able to use produce or money instead of actual labor, and sometimes the rent was paid with a combination of money, crops, and labor. In medieval England, service-tenancies were established when slaves became less available and more costly or when a landlord had recently cleared new lands and simply needed more laborers.[62]

When European colonists came to North America they brought the idea of tenancy with them. In colonial Louisiana, for example, Governor Jean Baptiste Le Moyne, Sieur de Bienville, had sharecropping tenants on his land as early as 1723. This tenancy occurred within the seigneurial regime that characterized one system of land tenure in early New France. Although not a true system of tenancy as it would later be practiced, the colonial French system did incorporate many of the same elements of the tenant-landlord relationship that would later seem universal of tenancy.[63]

In the English-speaking colonies, renting and sharecropping appeared as early as the seventeenth century in South Carolina and Virginia, as settlers sought both security from Indian attack and cleared land.[64] Throughout the seventeenth and eighteenth centuries, a variety of sharecropping and renting arrangements were practiced in the South. As early as 1689, a planter in Westmoreland County, Virginia, named William Fitzhugh, noted that only three of his tenants were able "to pay their Rent in money" because they were such "poor needy men."[65] The collection of rents from tenants was obviously a serious problem, because in 1695 the government of South Carolina enacted "An Act to Ascertain the Prices of Land, the Forms of Conveyances, and the Manner of Recovering Rents for Lands, and the Prices of the Several Commodities the Same May Be Paid In." This act was repealed in favor of the Quit Rent Act of August 20, 1731, by other acts of 1738, 1808, and 1817, and by later antebellum rulings.[66]

Further evidence for the antebellum presence of tenant farming in the South appears elsewhere. For example, in 1800, in *An Historical and Practical Essay on the Culture and Commerce of Tobacco,* William Tatham wrote that "independent cultivators," or "croppers," were common in tobacco country. These croppers worked on shares and received a portion of the crop based upon how much the landholder, called the crop master, had contributed toward cultivation. Accordingly, if the crop master supplied the land and everything needed for cultivation, he would receive two-thirds of the crop. If the crop master supplied only the land, then his share would be one-third of the crop. Tatham's comment that the share-croppers received their portion of the crop according to the "custom of the country" suggests that the tenancy laws either were not enforced or perhaps were not widely heeded by 1800.[67] Tenant farming, particularly sharecropping, was widely practiced in the South Carolina Piedmont by the 1840s, and by the 1850s these South Carolina upcountry tenant farmers were spoken of as a distinct social class.[68] As such, Calhoun's decision to hire tenant farmers in the 1830s was not revolutionary.

Coupled with Calhoun's urge to mold his three plantations into one major planting concern was his desire to develop a strong mechanical component within his empire. Millwood, located at Trotter's Shoals in an area already known for its mills, was well suited to such activity, and

Calhoun consciously selected this plantation to be the site of these new developments. Calhoun was obviously quite familiar with Bickley's Mill, a mill so well known that it appeared on the Abbeville County map in *Mills' Atlas* on land that would become part of Millwood Plantation.[69]

Calhoun turned his attention to mechanization early in his planting career. In 1832 a man named Edmund Roberts, possibly a relative of Calhoun overseer and later tenant farmer Absalom Roberts, had spent eight days at 50 cents a day working on the Millwood Plantation crib dam. The quality of Roberts's work was apparently less than Calhoun expected, because when high water carried the dam away only twelve days after Roberts was discharged, Calhoun said that the dam "proves badly built." On January 1 of the next year, James Edward rehired Delancy Chisenhall, "a good Millwright" to superintend at Millwood. Seven months later, Calhoun began to blast through the granite outcroppings that line the Savannah River at Trotter's Shoals to construct a new millrace. By August, the pier head was in place, and in September the crib dam was ready to be set. The following April the millrace was leveled, and a dam was being constructed.[70] This activity demonstrates that Calhoun was deeply interested in mechanical pursuits. Calhoun's interest in mills, in fact, has been immortalized in the folklore of the Millwood Plantation area. A historical plaque, once located on the side of the highway near the location of Millwood, proclaimed that Calhoun "was among the first to encourage the use of southern water power."[71]

At about the same time Calhoun began using his slaves seriously to make Millwood a well-integrated agricultural and mechanical enterprise, he was beginning to think about moving his residence there. In February 1834, while living at Midway Plantation, he notified a relative that he was "preparing materials for building at Millwood & hope[d] to move there long before the termination of the . . . year."[72] James Edward's plans were realized less than a month later, when he wrote in his diary, "At Millwood getting out stuff for an overseer's house, but which I shall occupy until I have leisure to build there a better house." This "Dwelling House" was raised on April 25, and in August its chimney was built.[73] At this point, James Edward Calhoun became, at age 36, the resident planter of Millwood Plantation.

Once Calhoun started to enjoy what he called "cottage life" at Millwood,[74] his activity there became even more accelerated. In the 1830s he sought to expand his interests even further by asking his brother-in-law,

John C. Calhoun, to inquire into certain operations for him. In March 1837 John C. Calhoun wrote, "I attended to your business at Washington, and have collected a good deal of information in relation to the manufacture of cotton seed oil, of the success of which I have very flattering accounts."[75] James Edward was perhaps contemplating expanding the manufacturing side of Millwood, because almost one year later to the day, John C. Calhoun wrote to James Edward to introduce a John Hastings of Philadelphia who was traveling throughout the Piedmont. Hastings was a "skilful [sic] & faithful superintendent of cotton manufactures." While in the South Carolina upcountry, Hastings had an itinerary that included meetings with many prominent southern planters, but John C. Calhoun wanted him to meet James Edward because he considered that James Edward had "the best situation for a cotton manufacturing establishment that [he knew] of." A month later John C. Calhoun advised him that if he were in James Edward's place he "would not hesitate. You could commence almost for nothing, and make your women & children your most valuable hands."[76] Clearly, the elder statesman was advising his younger kinsman that he should put all of his heretofore "unprofitable" slaves to work.

Regardless of whether James Edward actually had built any large manufacturing buildings at Millwood, and he almost certainly had not, his plans to build his empire did not diminish during his earliest days as a planter. In April 1840, for example, James Edward wrote, "I have never been more constantly busy." During this period, in addition to all his other plans, he had become intrigued by the gold deposits often found in the South Carolina Piedmont and frequently corresponded with John C. Calhoun about exploring his lands.[77] In 1843 the elder Calhoun told him that the Piedmont was becoming a gold region and that he should look to his property for gold, for "a good gold mine would be of service at a period of such low prices." Obviously, James Edward heeded this advice, because shortly thereafter, John C. Calhoun had the sorry task of saying to Calhoun, "I doubt whether the specimen you sent contains metal of any discreption [sic]."[78] James Edward Calhoun, however, obviously maintained his enthusiasm for his gold ventures, because in 1845 he received a letter from a geologist in Columbia telling him that he was "Truly glad that you have taken up mineralogy and geology for your amusement."[79] Unfortunately for Calhoun, the gold mine was more of an "amusement" than a paying enterprise; it never became profitable.

Nonetheless, its existence is well remembered in the area's local tradition.[80]

During this same period, it seems that Calhoun was contemplating the construction of a cotton-bag factory at Millwood. In 1843 he sent to New York for a "loom for weaving cotton Bagging, osnaburgs [coarse cotton fabric], and Negro clothing."[81] Two years later he corresponded with a factory superintendent in Tallahassee, Florida. This machinist assured Calhoun that he could have his $2,000 worth of machinery in operation before too long. Although employed at that moment, he told Calhoun that he could possibly "get away sooner than August, but that would depend entirely on circumstances."[82]

Probably, little, if anything, was produced at this factory, and all was not well for Calhoun at Millwood.[83] In the early 1840s, Calhoun received inquiries about the sale of six hundred acres of land that he had advertised.[84] Calhoun had obviously discussed his planned sale with John C. Calhoun, because in February 1843 the elder statesman had informed him that "the present state of things" would make it impossible for him to sell any land "to Northern Capitalists." However, by November of that year, John C. Calhoun wrote, "I am much gratified to learn that you have made a conditional sale of your Millwood property on such favorable terms. I think you have done well to sell. It took more capital than you could command to Develope [sic] its resources."[85] But the sale of Millwood Plantation was not concluded, and James Edward Calhoun remained at the plantation for the rest of his life.

Another factor that played on James Edward's mind in the early 1840s was the insolvency of his brother, John Ewing Calhoun. In early 1843 John Ewing's life as a planter was over when his estate was sold at auction by the sheriff.[86] James Edward was deeply affected by the failure of his brother, and he was probably all too well aware of his own possible failure and how he had tried to stretch his finances to the limit. Calhoun undoubtedly hoped that he could be successful using what John C. Calhoun described as his "naval habits & zeal."[87]

Although these circumstances were important to Calhoun during the critical period of the late 1830s and early 1840s, probably more important to him was his marriage, at age forty-one, to Maria Edgeworth Simkins, aged twenty-three, on February 4, 1839.[88]

Unfortunately, little is known about Maria Simkins, and even less is known about her life as Mrs. James Edward Calhoun. Born in 1816,

Maria Simkins was the daughter of Eldred Simkins of Edgefield District. Simkins, a former state representative and South Carolina lieutenant governor, was a respected member of the upcountry planter aristocracy, and when John C. Calhoun's daughter Anna Maria attended a female academy in Edgefield in the 1820s, she had stayed with the Simkins family.[89] Letters written by John C. Calhoun to Anna Maria suggest that she and Maria Simkins were close friends, and in a letter written on September 12, 1838, Gregory A. Perdicaris, the United States consul at Athens, Greece, referred to Maria Simkins as the "interesting companion" of Anna Maria.[90] Clearly, Maria Simkins was well known to the Calhouns prior to her marriage and, in fact, seems to have been regarded as a member of the family.

After her marriage, Maria Edgeworth Simkins Calhoun probably did not move to Millwood Plantation. At this time, Millwood was a rustic place that had been inhabited for only seven years. Just five years earlier, the overseer had killed two rattlesnakes under the houses there.[91] Although poisonous snakes are certainly not unknown to the South Carolina Piedmont even today, their presence under the Millwood dwellings suggests something of its character in the early 1830s. Soon after his marriage, however, James Edward did begin to purchase new furnishings for the Millwood dwelling, probably in an effort to make the plantation a more appealing place to his new wife. He undoubtedly planned that she would live there one day as the plantation mistress.[92]

In early 1840, James Edward and Maria communicated largely by mail because he lived at Millwood and she lived at her parents' home in Edgefield District, about fifty miles to the south. In April 1840, after receiving a letter from his young wife, James Edward wrote to her, "I hanker for your presence and you must not be surprised, if I run down, soon after my return from Pendleton, to pay you a visit."[93] In early 1844, Maria still did not live at Millwood, but the letters that passed between her and James Edward imply that he frequently visited her in Edgefield District. Nonetheless, it seems that Maria did direct some of the operations of the plantation from afar. For example, on March 16, 1844, James Edward wrote to her, presumably after paying her a visit: "Your instructions have been attended to, all the Shirts are cut out and some Pantaloons. Sam's and Caroline's clothes are put in order for traveling."[94] Although her wishes were obeyed, the historical evidence implies that she never did more than visit the plantation.

In 1844 Maria Simkins Calhoun became seriously ill when dangerous epidemics ravaged the South Carolina Piedmont. On March 16, in the same letter mentioning the clothing, James Edward told her that she should keep her spirits high and call for the doctor often. Maria, however, did not recover, and she died sometime before June 29, as evidenced by John C. Calhoun's advice to James Edward: "You must not think of remaining alone at Millwood. The scenes around you will but serve to remind you of your loss."[95] Even though this letter implies that Maria had once lived at Millwood, it probably refers to the improvements James Edward had made for her there rather than her actual residence on the plantation.

Maria's death is remembered in the legends of the Millwood Plantation area. The most prevalent is that James Edward was still in the navy and away at sea when Maria died in childbirth. Francis de Sales Dundas, a knowledgeable person about Millwood because his parents had been quite friendly with Calhoun, stated in his book *The Calhoun Settlement* that Maria died shortly before she gave birth, "before Lt. Calhoun could return home from sea duty." However, on the same page, Dundas writes that Calhoun resigned his commission on November 11, 1833.[96] Since they were married on February 4, 1839, this scenario is not realistic. This story was later repeated in local newspapers and has been ingrained in the folklore that surrounds James Edward Calhoun and Millwood Plantation.[97]

Another legend was precipitated by a 1933 newspaper article stating that Calhoun married Maria Simkins after he returned home from the navy and had begun Millwood. According to the story, shortly after their marriage, James Edward received a letter from John C. Calhoun, stating that "there was a mission to be performed which only a most trustworthy person could be allowed to take." John C. Calhoun reportedly asked James Edward to undertake this mission to England because he held "the most absolute trust" in him. According to the story, James Edward reached England after many weeks on board a war vessel that had sailed from New York. Upon his return to New York, he learned that his newborn son had died and that his wife lay "desperately ill." Because Calhoun had to take a train home, his return to Millwood was further delayed. When he finally reached the plantation, he learned that Maria had died and that "her body had been carried back to her old home at Edgefield."[98] Evidence for the "secret mission" has not been found and, in fact, seems most unlikely, given the dates of the existing correspondence. Maria most certainly died in Edgefield, not at Millwood. Although short and without embellishment, perhaps the most accurate account of Maria's death appeared in Calhoun's locally published obituary shortly after his death. This account simply stated that after resigning his commission he "came home, and married Miss Simpkins [*sic*] of Edgefield, who died soon after their marriage, and left no children."[99]

Regardless of the exact circumstances of Maria Simkins Calhoun's death—and it seems certain that she fell ill during the period of sickness in the South Carolina upcountry in 1844 while Calhoun was a resident planter at Millwood—the historical evidence clearly documents that she was never a full-time resident of the plantation. In this light, her overall role in affecting the life of the plantation seems to have been minor.

Throughout this period, Calhoun continued to use his slaves to build his plantation, even though he again tried to sell Millwood in 1848 for $300,000. In the same year, he planned to persuade German immigrants to work on his land as tenants.[100] Calhoun, however, was never able to entice large numbers of Germans to come to his plantation, so he continued to expand both his agricultural and mechanical enterprises with the labor of his growing slave force. The census for 1850 shows that Calhoun used two hands at his water-powered mills to process corn, wheat, and logs. In addition, the Millwood slaves produced seventy bales of cotton, a variety of other crops, and used livestock worth $1,869.[101] In June 1854 Calhoun hired D. U. Sloan for $15 a month to oversee those hands who were sent to construct a millrace at the "Allen Mill Place (now called Calhoun's Landing)."[102] Allen's Mill appeared on Mills's map of Abbeville County, south of Bickley's Mill (figure 2). The 1860 census indicates that Calhoun's plantation continued to prosper and that his slaves produced sixty-three bales of cotton, a thousand pounds of tobacco, and many other crops, including $1,000 worth of orchard products. The value of the livestock on the plantation rose to $9,608. Also, in partnership with a man named Rogers, Calhoun owned gristmills, a sawmill, a tannery, and a smith shop. These industries annually produced products worth $8,400, and put eight hands to work.[103]

When the first shots of the Civil War were fired in Charleston Harbor in the spring of 1861, James Edward Calhoun was sixty-three years old. As a well-entrenched member of the planter aristocracy and a stalwart son of one of South Carolina's most prominent families, little doubt existed concerning his loyalties. Calhoun expressed his feelings early in the war by sending a "keg of choice whiskey" to the "suffering soldiers" of the Confederacy in September 1861.[104] Calhoun's concern for the men who fought against the Union was consistent, and in May 1864, he wrote to Andrew Calhoun to notify him of the process used to make pemmican and "Confederate Cracker," a mixture of pepper tea, syrup, and flour.[105] Pemmican was a traditional food made by Native Americans in the Plains and Great Lakes regions by mixing slices of sun-dried, pounded meat with melted fat, bone marrow, and the dry paste made by crushing wild cherries and other berries.[106] One of the advantages of pemmican was that an individual could easily carry an abundance of it a great distance. Calhoun had probably learned about pemmican during his trip through Minnesota with the Long Expedition. Impressed with its qualities, Calhoun had fed pemmican to his slaves at Millwood Plantation "for several years." Calhoun believed that both pemmican and Confederate Cracker were inexpensive ways to feed the Confederate troops.

Calhoun also assisted in the war effort by sending slaves to Charleston to work. In February 1864 he received notice that he would be sent $371.80 from the Engineer Department for the work of thirteen slaves. However, even though the government was willing to pay for their labor, they "refused to pay anything for the Axes, Shovels, & Hoes which were stolen" from them.[107] The likelihood exists, given the late date of their work, that these slaves may have been pressed into service by the Confederate government, but this cannot be determined from the documents.[108]

Calhoun also seems to have tried to do his part to assist his fellow planters during the crisis caused by the war. In February 1863 he received a letter from his cousin Mary Calhoun Garvin asking for financial assistance because her "husband and sons are all in the army." Her youngest son was at home, but he was "to [sic] small to make a crop."[109] Later that year, Calhoun received a letter from John W. Lewis thanking him for his help in assisting Lewis enough "to plant a sufficiency of land and of getting food for [his] negroes." No record remains to indicate what Calhoun actually did for Lewis, but Lewis remembered it as "kind and just treatment of me (a refugee), so different from my experience in the Upper portion of the State."[110] Calhoun also attempted to help other planters who were displaced by the war. When James Gregorie, a former "school fellow" of James Edward's, wrote to him in August 1863 to inform Calhoun that he had been forced to abandon his coastal plantation because of the war and to ask whether Calhoun knew of any plantations in Abbeville District he could "hire for the war," Calhoun offered him his land in Pickens District. Gregorie was grateful for the offer but said that it would be more than he could handle at age sixty-five.[111]

Although Calhoun was clearly an ardent Confederate, he apparently did not agree with everything the Confederate government did. Even though he could boast, in 1864, that he was "free from debt," he did not agree with what he called the government's "monstrous tax scheme." Writing to Andrew Calhoun, James Edward stated that these taxes would prove "sorely grievous of every Planter, ruinous to many." He believed that the Congress was composed almost entirely of "refugees, stript [*sic*] of property, lawyers, speculators, blockade runners, non-producers, consumers, impatient at the enhanced cost of living." Calhoun further explained that "no agricultural people can stand a tax of more than 1 pr. ct. on real estate." Later in the letter, Calhoun told Andrew that many years ago, he had told Andrew's father, John C. Calhoun, "that we should never have changed from the Articles of Confederation, & that the Constitution of '89 was a failure."[112] Calhoun's mind was not quickly changed, for in 1877 a brief note appeared in the Abbeville newspaper stating that Calhoun made his tenants pay real estate taxes so "that they may feel some of the oppression of a robbing government."[113]

Calhoun also did not agree with other actions of the Confederate government. For example, in 1864 when he was sixty-six years old and could look back on a long and successful military career, he expressed his disapproval of the act that allowed slave owners with more than fifteen slaves to stay home "to make provisions." James Edward referred to this act as "a humbug," and a pretext for thousands of "skulkers." To him, they should all serve in the army, because "the hands are in the country, and the old men & the women will make them work."[114] Calhoun obviously believed that the government had gone too far to protect the planter class by permitting them to avoid military service in what was obviously becoming an increasingly lost cause.

In spite of his opinions about the political situation that faced South Carolina planters, James Edward Calhoun continued to have Millwood Plantation developed at this time. Although evidence on this subject is slim, Calhoun's comments to Andrew Calhoun that he looked for "an extraordinary crop" and that he "never before was so well prepared" suggest, at the very least, that he thought he was prepared for the future that would come after the war.[115] That Calhoun was not totally ready for the changes that would occur in the agricultural organization of the post-war South does not suggest that he was out of touch with what was happening around him. Rather, his lack of preparation was a sign of the times.

On plantations, of course, the greatest changes that would occur concerned the emancipation of the slave work force and the full scale development of plantation tenancy. These subjects are explored in the next chapter.

Chapter Three

The Postbellum Tenant Plantation
and the South Carolina
Piedmont, 1865–1925

THE EVENTS THAT OCCURRED in the South's plantation belt after 1865 were far-ranging and significant. The many changes caused by the American Civil War are too complex and multifaceted to be fully explored here. Rather, these changes are only summarized so that the major emphasis can be placed on the physical changes that occurred on the plantations of the South after 1865—those changes related to settlement pattern, housing design, and material possessions. This chapter provides a historical context for the rest of this book, just as chapter 4 provides a context for understanding the physical changes experienced on the cotton plantations of the southern United States after 1865.

Immediately after the Civil War, the reestablishment of agricultural operations on the many cotton plantations of the South was prompted by exceptionally high cotton prices. Southern cotton planters who had retained their land and tools were interested in these potential profits, especially given the hardships of the recent war. This desire on the part of most southern planters was something of a mania. One planter expressed the opinion that an "epidemic cotton fever" had swept the South and that every kind of land had been planted, the "rich and poor, wet and dry, well and badly prepared." Another cotton planter said that planters had an "insanity" called "cotton on the brain." According to him, southern planters had this malady in its more acute form and would produce cotton at all costs.[1] The only element missing from the plantations of these planters was the most important one, labor. Although some four million slaves had been freed by the events of the war, many were unwilling to work for their former owners or had left the immediate area of their former slavery in search of an illusive freedom. As an Englishman who was traveling through the South immediately after the war said, "Thirty-seven thousand negroes, according to newspaper estimates, have left South Carolina already, travelling west."[2]

Faced with freedom and the problem of nowhere to go, many slaves decided to stay with their former masters; others left as soon as the opportunity arose. The decision to leave or to stay was based, of course, on each freed man's and woman's feelings and circumstances. Former slaves who stayed in their plantation homes reported that they did so often out of loyalty to their master, or because they simply had no place else to go. For example, Charlie Davenport, who lived in Adams County, Mississippi, and stayed until his "white folks died off," said, "when I looked at my masse and knew he needed me, I [was] pleased to stay." Another reported that he "couldn't get nothing to do" so he "just stayed and made a crop." Other slaves reported that they moved away from the plantations of their bondage quickly and without equivocation. For example, John Gilstrap of Marshall County, Mississippi, remarked that "all the others stayed on" with the master except his father, who "moved right away." Times were hard for all freedmen, but they may have been even harsher for those freedmen who immediately moved away from their former plantation homes, because, as one former slave said, "Didn't nobody tell us how to go about nothing"; or, if they had been told, they "didn't pay no attention to them because we sure did have a hard go."[3] In any case, perhaps one historian summarized the situation best when he wrote that movement for freedmen "came to be regarded as the test of freedom."[4]

During this period, southern planters, who were confused and frightened about the future, began to search for a profitable and workable substitute for slavery. Planters could not predict their futures by any means, but they were certain of at least one thing: they were "resolved never to give up their farms" to their former slaves.[5] One solution to the sticky problem of plantation labor reorganization was presented by the Union army, which directed the development of a full-scale wage-labor system.[6] In this system, former slaves were hired and paid wages as were all freed laborers. Imposed on the South by a conquering army, this system was controversial and not readily accepted by all planters. For example, one writer remembered being told by one planter, who had recently returned home from a prisoner of war camp in July 1865, that good feelings existed between the whites and their former slaves and that "everything was going on as before the war except that negroes were free and receiving wages." This supposedly happy arrangement worked well until a Freedman's Bureau agent appeared and "declared all contracts null and void and that no negro should work for a white except under contract written and approved by him."[7] The intervention of this federal agent upset the workings of a system that was obviously established by former slave-owning planters and that functioned, at least according to this one white planter, quite well. The contract-holding ex-slaves were apparently not asked what they thought of the system; if they were asked, their responses were not recorded.

In September 1865, in response to the development of the Freedman's Bureau, which had been established in March 1865, the legislature of South Carolina passed the Black Code, which was designed to regulate the status of freedmen.[8] This Black Code contained a number of provisions for restricting the labor and movement of plantation freedmen and their families. For example, freed slaves were not permitted to sell farm produce without the written permission of their landlords, they could not keep any weapons except fowling pieces, and if they were under eighteen years old, they could be "moderately" whipped. Stiff vagrancy provisions kept freedmen on their plantations, and if a freedman was judged to be a vagrant, he could be hired out to a landlord for minimal wages.[9] Although certain token legal protections were legislated for freedmen—legitimacy of children, passage of the Thirteenth Amendment, and the right to acquire property and to bring suit in court—freed slaves were only nominally freed. The Black Code merely extended the restrictions on southern blacks. Even though its harsher clauses were repealed in September 1866, the Black Code had established what whites wanted for blacks: a nominal freedom that would lead them to a new kind of slavery. At the very least, the Black Code showed that whites still thought they could control the labor of their former slaves.[10]

Many planters did not like the Black Code either, believing that its provisions "greatly hampered the economic recovery of the South." This code had, they thought, forced them into a period of confusion.[11] In other words, the Black Code was not harsh enough, even though it placed severe restraints on their labor force.

One of the elements of the wage-labor system that helped complicate the lives of both black plantation farmers and their landlords was a legal contract between them. This wage contract was an expedient method for planters to make their plantations productive units once again. These contracts placed restrictions on the freedmen who supplied the labor so that planters could increase their wealth. In 1867, for example, thirty-six wage laborers on the Peter B. Bacot plantation in Darlington District, South Carolina, agreed to work ten hours per day, to perform a wide variety of tasks, and, in short, to be good and faithful laborers for Bacot.[12] The rules governing freedmen contractors working on the William J. Minor plantations in the sugar region of south Louisiana show just how restrictive some contracts could be. On these plantations, the morning bell rang first at 5:00 A.M., again at 6:30 A.M., and finally at 7:00 A.M., and all those hands who were not in the fields when the bell rang for the last time were docked a quarter of the day's pay. Wage hands also lost a quarter of their daily pay by working less than ten hours, for any sort of insubordination, and for arriving to the fields late after lunch. The hands were charged for all tools and implements that were lost, they were not allowed to use any of the plantations' mules or horses unless they were regular teamsters, and they could not leave the plantation without their employer's, or his agent's, permission. Other restrictions made the wage system even more oppressive.[13]

Many different forms of contracts appeared immediately after the war. In fact, so many forms of contracting existed during this period of experimentation and adjustment that one Arkansas planter is reported to have said, "On twenty plantations around me, there are ten different styles of contracts."[14] According to historical economist Ralph Shlomowitz, seven major variations of the wage system were practiced during this period.[15] Each variation had a specific name and engendered a particular kind of landlord-laborer relationship. In the *standing-wage* arrangement, the planter paid the freedman a fixed wage in addition to a weekly ration of meat and meal; in the *crop-sharing* arrangement, the freedman provided his labor and received only a portion of the crop he made, and the planter supplied the land, seed, tools, animals, and feed; and in the *time-sharing* plan, the freedman received rent-free land in return for working for the landlord a set number of days per week. This last arrangement was later known as *private cropping,* or *the four-day plan.*[16] The other wage arrangements noted by Shlomowitz are the *standing-rent* arrangement, where the laborer paid the landlord a specified amount of farm produce as rent; *wages in kind,* where the freedman received a certain amount of farm produce in the place of cash wages; and *incentive schemes,* where freedmen received pay for extra work completed. On the South Carolina coast, a work task system was instituted where laborers received wages for each task they finished. The most practical forms of wage labor were, at least according to one planter, crop-sharing and straight-wage labor.[17]

The amount of wages received by freedmen varied widely and ranged from as little as two dollars per month to as high as twenty-five dollars, depending upon the region and the kind of work performed.[18] However, the organization of the wage-labor plantation did not differ greatly from that of the antebellum plantation. In 1866, Whitelaw Reid, a twenty-nine-year-old Ohio newspaper reporter, provided an excellent description of the organization of a wage-labor plantation in Mississippi. The plantation was divided into two gangs, a plow gang and a trash gang, each headed by a black driver. The gangs worked from 4:00 A.M. to noon and from 1:30 P.M. to sunset. According to Reid, wages were paid daily with tickets, with the laborer receiving a white ticket for a full day's work and a red one for a half day's work. The laborers kept these tickets until the end of the month, when they redeemed them for cash. Reid learned from the overseer that few laborers reported sick under this arrangement and that the owner of the plantation was pleased with the labor of the freedmen and expected to make one hundred thousand dollars in profit that year.[19] A similar plan of dividing the workers into two gangs under the direction of a foreman, or manager, was used in northeastern Georgia, where the two gangs were made to compete against each other to produce the best crop.[20]

With all the restrictions placed on black plantation farmers after the war, coupled with the clear fact that the plantations were not going to be broken up and the land distributed to them, the wage-labor system caused tension between whites and blacks living on the South's plantations.[21] Although legally quite powerless, plantation blacks had some means of protest available to them.

The clearest form of protest available to freedmen plantation farmers was to break their wage contracts, leave their plantation homes, move to new estates, and begin new contracts. With high cotton prices and a scarcity of labor, this mechanism worked well for freedmen and created consternation among planters. As one planter in central Mississippi complained, freedmen were unreliable as contract laborers because they were a "wonder-seeking, credulous, improvident people," who would sometimes leave their neighbors "en masse, deserting comfortable homes for something better."[22] Many freedmen believed, correctly in most cases, that in signing a contract they were signing away their freedom. As a result, most freedmen began to dream even more earnestly for their own land.[23]

Planters were aware of the freedmen's desire to own land. One planter probably spoke for many when he said that freedmen would "starve and go naked before they will work for a white man if they can get a patch of ground to live on, and get from under his control!" Another planter said that "the tendency of heads of families was to own their own stock and operate independently of the landlord," and still another said that hired labor was "sorry . . . unreliable . . . [and] scarce."[24] All in all, an observation made in the late 1890s may have expressed a commonly held belief of twenty years earlier: "the dream of the wage-earner is to become at least a renter."[25]

One reason freedmen disliked the wage-labor system was the rigid regimen of work imposed by most owners. A twentieth-century tenant farmer, Ed Brown, said that the wage hand had no time to himself because his "time belong to the boss man." After the crop was planted or harvested, the owner would order the wage hand to spend his time cutting logs, repairing roads, digging ditches, hauling manure, or cleaning fence corners.[26] This kind of labor system left wage earners with little spare time and was too reminiscent of slavery for most freedmen.

Most planters did not like the wage-labor system because of the latitude it gave their laborers. For example, one planter stated a commonly held complaint of many planters when he noted that freedmen who failed to complete the terms of their wage contracts could not be sued for damages because they did not own property. In his opinion, these freedmen would become like white sailors and soldiers, "above all law, and worthless as laborers." Another planter reported how he and his "club" blacklisted freedmen who broke their contracts or failed to conform to the club's behavioral ideals. He said that they took these restrictive steps not to "oppress the freedmen, but as the quickest and surest means of enabling them to appreciate the obligation of contracts." Another planter said that the rules imposed on freed slaves caused them to "work harmoniously" and served to "preserve discipline, encourage industry, and promote contentment and happiness."[27] As historians have noted, however, if most planters had had their wish, black wage laborers would have been only slightly better off than they had been as slaves.[28]

This period of wage-labor agriculture has been described as one of "experimentation" during which a variety of "alternative arrangements" were tested on the South's plantations as blacks and whites tried to re-organize themselves in relation to one another.[29] One of these experi-mental arrangements has been termed the *squad system*. This system, al-though it bore similarities to the work-gang system characteristic of the antebellum and wage-labor periods, was a distinctly different form of land tenure. Nonetheless, in spite of its unique nature, the squad system is difficult to identify in historical records because many contemporary observers confused it with the more common gang system.

In his careful examination of the available written evidence, historical economist Shlomowitz found that the words *gang* and *squad* had dis-tinctly different meanings in the immediate postwar period. To over-come the confusion between the gang and the squad, Shlomowitz identi-fies four main characteristics of the squad.[30] The first characteristic of the squad system is that its members usually received a share of the crop by prior arrangement. Although wage laborers also often received pro-duce instead of wages, they did so because of the scarcity of ready cash, not because this share was given by prior agreement.[31] The distinguish-ing factor, then, concerns the time at which the wage tenant knew he would receive a share of the crop. A second characteristic is that kin-ship was central to squad membership. Most people in a squad were members of the same nuclear family or were united through some other bond of kinship. The importance of kinship to the squad was noted by British newspaper editor Robert Somers in the early 1870s when he wrote that "a strong family group, who can bring odd hands to work at proper seasons, makes a choice, if not always attainable, nucleus of a 'squad.' "[32] Embedded within the family organization of the squad is the third characteristic, its small size. Each squad usually contained between two and ten laboring hands, with an average size of around seven hands. The gangs of the antebellum and immediate postbellum periods were usually much larger and were created, not around family lines, but around the needs and whims of the plantation owner. In sum, as a "nonbureaucratic, self-regulating, and self-selecting worker peer group," the squad is a significant departure from the gang.[33] Although these characteristics help define the squad system, the fourth aspect of the squad, its unique settlement form, is perhaps most immediately important to the historical archaeologist. This aspect of the squad is considered in detail in the next chapter.

The squad system was one of many experimental systems tried during the immediate postwar period, and its exact distribution throughout the South has not yet been determined. One thing, however, is clear: on those plantations where experimentation did not occur, the problems inherent in the wage-labor system became quickly obvious. Even where experimentation did occur, the problems faced by freedmen plantation farmers were significant. With time, black plantation farmers became unwilling to work for wages and began to demand their own land. According to at least one historian, this struggle for land in many ways structured the black experience in the South during the nineteenth century.[34]

With the realization that they had a certain amount of power within the labor market because of their numbers, skills, and desires to live and to work as agriculturalists, some freedmen probably sought to climb what white agricultural economists called the *agricultural ladder*. In American agriculture during the period from 1865 to 1935, the agricultural ladder began with the wage earner and extended to the independent farm owner-operator.[35] Freedmen realized that to accomplish this ascent, they would require land, capital, and housing; however, lacking all three, freedmen found the climb difficult if not utterly impossible when faced with southern plantation tenancy.[36]

Southern tenancy represents a complex system of agricultural land tenure.[37] For present purposes, the basic structure of tenancy need only be summarized.

In simple terms, two kinds of tenancy—sharecropping and renting—existed in the postbellum plantation South. Each was defined on the basis of the arrangement the tenant was able to make with the landlord. On the most basic level, *sharecropping* required the tenant to pay his landlord part of the crop he produced; *renting* required the tenant to pay a fixed rent in either crops or money. The sharecropper was merely a wage laborer who received his portion of the crop *from* the landlord even though he had produced it. The renter, on the other hand, paid his rent *to* the landlord.[38] State courts in the South generally upheld this distinction, and the direction of payment determined a tenant's status. The North Carolina Supreme Court justices made this distinction in 1874 when they stated that if the tenant "pays a share of the crop for rent it is he that divides off to the landlord his share, and until such division the right of property and of possession in the whole is his." This right of division distinguished the renter. The sharecropper, on the other hand, had no legal claim to the land, and "although he has, in some sense, the possession of the crop, it is only the possession of a servant, and it is in law that of the landlord." Because the landlord divided the crop, the cropper was only a "laborer receiving pay in a share of the crop." The justices of the Georgia Supreme Court held the same opinion two years earlier when they ruled that "the case of the cropper is rather a mode of paying wages than a tenancy."[39]

The South Carolina Supreme Court made the same distinction as early as 1833, and although this decision was often challenged, it remained in force throughout the period under consideration here.[40] By 1921, the South Carolina Court could rule that "it is well settled in this State that the laborer or 'share cropper' has no title to the crop until after the division is made."[41]

The difference between who divided the crop and how a plantation farmer received his pay provides a significant distinction between the sharecropper and the renter; however, other differences in the arrangements also distinguish them. In general, three different arrangements—sharecropping, share renting, and cash renting—were common in the South from about 1880 to the 1930s.[42]

In the *sharecropping* arrangement, the tenant supplied his labor and one-half of the fertilizer he needed; the landlord furnished everything else—land, house, tools, work animals, animal feed, seed, wood for fuel, and the other half of the fertilizer. In some cases, the landlord agreed to pay for all the fertilizer in exchange for keeping all the cotton seed.[43] At harvest time, the landlord was supposed to divide the crop equally between himself and the tenant. Tenants referred to this arrangement as "working on halves," and they were variously known as *croppers, half hands,* or *half tenants.*[44]

Many of the problems faced by black sharecroppers involved the landlord's ownership of the crop. This problem was insightfully addressed by Georgia sharecropper Ed Brown. According to him, in January, when he

was breaking and turning the land with the landlord's mule, the landlord
would come by and ask him, "'How is your crop, and how is you gettin'
along turnin' your land?'" He would also remind Brown to take care of
the mule. In April, the landlord would again inquire about Brown's
crop, but by June, the landlord would ask, "'Is our cotton doin' pretty
good?'" By September, when cotton picking started, the landlord referred to "'My cotton, my corn, my crop.'"[45]

Not coincidentally, just about the time when the landlord would start
to think of the crop in more personal terms, the tenant's "furnishing
time" would end. *Furnishings* were the advances against the crop sharecroppers and the other kinds of tenants received when they did not have
enough money to purchase the basic necessities of life. In Ellis County,
Texas, in the rich Black Waxy region of the east-central part of the state,
tenants were carried on credit until October in two principal ways. In the
first method, tenants gave their personal notes for the amount of goods
they estimated they would need for that year to the merchant or landlord, who would then supply them with the goods. This note carried an
interest rate of 10 percent; however, because tenants paid interest on the
total sum for nine months, they actually paid an interest of about 20
percent. In the second arrangement, 10 percent was added at the time of
purchase to every purchase the tenant made.[46]

In some areas, a major source of income for landlords derived from
furnishing their tenants. In bad years, tenants were given small advances
and told to exist as best they could, but in good years, plantation tenants
could develop large debts because they were given large advances.[47] Regardless of how their furnishing was arranged, tenants usually saw a
drastic cut in their incomes after accounts were settled. The cash received by tenants after settlement, the "cash after settling," was the
money they received from the crop after the advances for food, cost of
farming supplies, and interest were subtracted.[48] Landlords on some
plantations encouraged their tenants to spend their cash after settling on
unnecessary items in order to increase the tenants' dependence on them.
The assumption made by these landlords was that a tenant deep in debt
would make a more obedient and, therefore, better worker.[49] Also, as a
debtor the tenant would have the force of law against him; the courts
were firmly on the side of the landlord.

Sharecroppers were not able to divide their own crops. As Ed Brown
explained, because the landlord made the division, the tenant was usu-

ally ignorant of its exact proportions. Because his landlord would not show him the papers from the gin and warehouse, he did not know how much his crop had made, or what his rightful share was. In this case, Brown said, his landlord "took his share and all of mine and claim I owe him twenty-four dollars in addition."[50] Under this kind of arrangement and during a time that blacks were routinely beaten, lynched, and murdered, the sharecropper had little recourse but to agree with the landlord or to leave the estate in utter poverty. To compensate for his financial shortfall, Brown worked for his landlord for wages when the crop was laid by.[51]

In the *share-renting* arrangement, the landlord supplied the land, housing, and either one-quarter or one-third of the fertilizer costs; the tenant supplied the labor, animals, animal feed, tools, seed, and the remainder of the fertilizer. The crop was divided so that each party received a portion equal to the amount of fertilizer he had supplied. If the landlord paid for one-third of the fertilizer costs, then he received one-third of the crop.

Many different share-renting variations occurred in the postbellum plantation South.[52] The most common form, *third and fourth*, was an arrangement whereby the landlord received one-quarter of the cotton and one-third of all other crops. In the early 1920s, this popular arrangement was practiced almost everywhere except North Carolina and South Carolina. Another common form of share renting was called *straight-third*. In this arrangement, used most predominantly in the Red River Valley of northwestern Louisiana and in the Mississippi Delta, the landlord received one-third of all the crops. In the *straight-fourth* arrangement, the landlord received a fourth of all cotton and corn grown. During the 1920s, this arrangement was found in the less-fertile parts of Louisiana and Mississippi, where the tenant was known as a *fourth tenant*.[53] In a final kind of share renting the landlord received one-half of all crops grown by the tenant, who was known as a *half-share tenant*. This arrangement was similar to sharecropping only as far as crop division was concerned because the half-share tenant had to provide his own animals, feed, tools, seed, and fertilizer. This arrangement was extremely rare in the plantation South in the early 1920s, but it did appear in Autauga County, Alabama.

The similarities between sharecroppers and share renters were great enough to cause a confusion in terminology. For example, the terms *cropper, sharecropper,* and *half cropper,* were all used to refer to sharecroppers. In South Carolina and Georgia, however, these terms were also used to refer to share renters. In the western part of the postbellum plantation South, the terms *half tenant* and *half hand* were also used to refer to sharecroppers.[54] The use of these regional terms makes an absolute understanding of plantation tenancy difficult.

In the *cash-renting* arrangement, the landlord supplied the land and the housing, and the tenant supplied everything else needed to produce the crop. The landlord received a fixed rent per acre in cash. The amount of rent paid depended upon many factors, including the availability of tenants, the soil quality, and, from 1892 to 1921, the amount of damage caused by the cotton boll weevil. Between 1922 and 1932, many lands were rent-free in some areas because of the recent attack of the weevil.[55]

Another plantation tenure arrangement was called *standing renting*. This arrangement was similar to cash renting, but as a standing renter, the tenant paid the landlord a fixed amount of the staple crop rather than cash. Although found in all sections of the plantation South, standing renting was most popular, at least in the early 1920s, in Georgia.[56]

In summary, the kinds of plantation tenure that were used after 1880 can be divided into two main categories. The first is defined on the basis of who divided the crop at harvest time. In those arrangements considered to be highest on the agricultural ladder—standing renting and cash renting—the tenant held estate rights over his crop and either sold it to obtain the cash he needed for rent or divided it and gave a certain portion of it to the landlord in lieu of a cash payment. In those arrangements considered to be on the lower end of the agricultural ladder—sharecropping and share renting—the landlord held estate rights over the crop and was in charge of dividing it. A second way to distinguish between these systems of tenure is based on the success of the crop itself. On the higher end of the agricultural ladder, the rent to be given to the landlord was fixed, or established, prior to the planting of the crop. Regardless of the size of the harvest, the rent would ideally remain the same. On the lower end of the ladder, the rent was not fixed and so was free to vary, depending upon the success or failure of the harvest. This variation made the share forms of tenancy risky for both the direct producers and the landlords.

Postbellum plantation tenure was further complicated because all the different kinds of tenure could occur on a single plantation. For example, a landlord who preferred sharecropping might accept a standing or cash renter if he had vacant land.[57] In other cases, landlords might have made one agreement with one group of tenants, only to accept different terms from other tenants later.

The distributions of various kinds of arrangements were studied by many scholars during the first few decades of the twentieth century. These studies demonstrate the extent of the tenures in both time and location and illustrate the fluid nature of tenancy from decade to decade.[58]

A similar analysis can be conducted for the South Carolina Piedmont for the years from 1880 to 1925 using information presented in the published census books (table 2).[59] Although these published census records must be used carefully, this analysis shows the changing nature of tenancy in the Piedmont.

In general, the number of owners, cash renters, and sharecroppers rose steadily in the South Carolina Piedmont from 1880 to 1925. During this period, the number of owner-operated farms increased by 35.3 percent, but in 1925 the number of owners declined. The increase in cash renters and sharecroppers was even more remarkable: cash renters increased by 375.4 percent, and sharecroppers increased by 155.8 percent. In 1925 the number of sharecroppers decreased. Given the short time span and in spite of the minor declines, these increases are remarkable.

In 1880, 35,222 farmers lived in the South Carolina Piedmont. An examination of the data for owners and nonowning tenants reveals that 1880 was the only year between 1880 and 1925 during which the majority of Piedmont farmers were owners. An obvious majority of owners (more than 50 percent) appeared in only three counties: Laurens (58.6 percent), Oconee (69.1 percent), and York (54.5 percent). In the next decade, owners held a majority (54.7 percent) only in the mountainous, and marginally Piedmont, county of Oconee. In the following decades, the percentage of owners operating farms throughout the Piedmont declined steadily, reaching a low of 21.2 percent, in Chester County, in 1900. The population of owner-operators in the Piedmont remained at around 30 percent after 1900 (figure 3).

The pattern of ownership in the entire Piedmont was mirrored in Abbeville County. In 1880, 40.0 percent of the farmers were owners, in 1910 a low of 22.5 percent was reached, and by 1925 owners accounted for 25.4 percent of the county's farmers (figure 3). Of the 16,171 owners

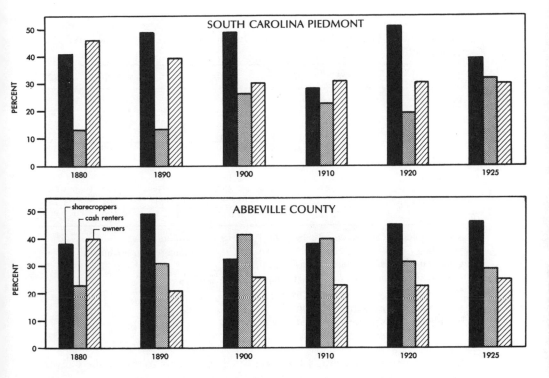

Figure 3. Major tenure groups, South Carolina Piedmont and Abbeville County, 1880– 1925, by percentage.

in the South Carolina Piedmont in 1880, 1,639 (10.1 percent) were in Abbeville County. In 1890 this number climbed to 1,710, or 1.4 percent of the Piedmont total. This number declined to a low of 966 owners in 1925, but rather than reflecting a true decline in the number of owner-operated farms in Abbeville County, this decrease more accurately reflects a decline in county size after Greenwood and McCormick counties were created from part of Abbeville County in 1897 and 1916, respectively (table 2).

Cash renting was not prevalent in the Piedmont between 1880 and 1925. Its lowest occurrence was in the northernmost tier of counties— Anderson, Cherokee, Oconee, Pickens, and Spartanburg—with a low of 1.6 percent in Pickens County in 1880. The highest concentration of cash renters appeared in Abbeville County, and in the two counties later

Table 2

Major Tenure Groups, South Carolina Piedmont and Abbeville County,
1880–1925

	1880	1890	1900	1910	1920	1925
Piedmont						
Owners	16,171	16,383	17,605*	20,393	21,872	19,967†
Cash renters	4,487	5,491	14,986	14,898	13,779‡	21,330§
Sharecroppers	14,564	20,549	26,058	30,667	37,248‖	26,035
Total	35,222	42,423	58,649	65,958	72,899	67,332
Abbeville County						
Owners	1,639	1,710	1,185	1,233	1,015	966
Cash renters	948	1,145	1,865	2,210	1,417	1,096
Sharecroppers	1,508	2,690	1,524	2,028	1,994	1,741
Total	4,095	5,545	4,574	5,471	4,426	3,803

Sources: Census of Agriculture, 1880, 1890, 1900, 1910, 1920, and 1925.

*Combines owners, part owners, owner-tenants, and managers according to the suggestion in the *1900 Census of Agriculture,* p. xliii.

†Combines owners, part owners, and managers.

‡Combines cash and standing renters.

§Combines cash renters and "others."

‖Combines sharecroppers and share tenants.

created from it. In 1900, 40.8 percent of the farms in Abbeville County were worked by cash renters. In 1880 Abbeville County contained 948 cash renters, and in 1910 a high of 2,210 cash renters was reached, even after Greenwood County was created; by 1925 the county contained 1,096 cash renters (table 2). The entire South Carolina Piedmont experienced a tremendous increase in cash renting between 1890 and 1900 as the total number of cash renters climbed from 5,491 to 14,986, an increase of 172.9 percent. This number declined slightly in the next two decades but climbed again in 1925. The highest percentage between 1880 and 1925 was 31.7 percent, in 1925.[60]

The sharecropper population was quite high in the South Carolina Piedmont from 1880 to 1925. In 1880 more than half the farms in three counties—Anderson (50.6 percent), Pickens (50.7 percent), and Union (52.1 percent)—were operated by sharecroppers. By 1920 the number of counties wherein more than one-half the farms were worked by sharecroppers rose to 8 and included Anderson (60.5 percent), Cherokee (60.0 percent), Laurens (51.0 percent), Oconee (51.3 percent), Pickens (50.4 percent), Spartanburg (61.1 percent), Union (52.4 percent), and York (53.9 percent). This meant that in 1920 slightly more than one-half (51.1 percent) the 72,899 farms in the South Carolina Piedmont were worked on shares. In terms of sharecropping, Abbeville County usually ranked in the middle of the extremes, containing 36.8 percent sharecroppers in 1880 and a high of 48.5 percent in 1890. By 1925 Abbeville County contained only 6.7 percent of the 26,035 sharecropped farms in the South Carolina Piedmont (table 2).

Another perspective on farming in the South Carolina Piedmont can be gained by examining farm size. Unfortunately, these statistics are difficult to use authoritatively because of the manner in which they were originally collected. Between 1880 and 1910, census enumerators counted every farm as one unit whether or not it existed as part of a larger plantation. In doing this, the Census Bureau counted the farms of the South as they had counted the farms of the North—as individual agricultural units. Accordingly, if a plantation owner had thirty-five tenant farmers on his land, then thirty-five separate farms would have been counted by the census takers.[61] The use of this recording method makes it difficult to rely strongly on these data. Still, they can be used to present at least a rough image of farm size in the Piedmont between 1880 and 1925.

In the decades between 1880 and 1925, the size of the average farm in the South Carolina Piedmont decreased. This decrease is to be expected, given the manner of reporting and the changing nature of southern agriculture during these years. In 1880, 34.4 percent of the farms were between 100 and 499 acres, but 32.6 percent were between 20 and 49 acres. Only 17.2 percent were between 50 and 99 acres. Ten years later, the percentage of farms between 20 and 49 acres increased to 38.3 percent, and that of those between 100 and 499 acres fell to 30.3 percent even though the actual number of farms this size increased (table 3). By 1910 more than one-third (42.4 percent) the farms in the Piedmont were between 20 and 49 acres, and in the next decade almost half (45.8 percent) were of this size. In 1925 this figure had fallen to 40.6 percent, but the 20- to 49-acre farm was still the most common in the region. During this period, the number of large farms (more than 500 acres) severely declined. In fact, farms of between 500 and 999 acres decreased 72.9 percent, while farms of over 1,000 acres decreased by 78.9 percent (figure 4).

64

The Material Basis of the Postbellum Tenant Plantation

This trend was repeated in Abbeville County. In 1880, 36.6 percent of the farms were between 20 and 49 acres, and only 32.0 percent were between 100 and 499 acres. One decade later, almost half (46.1 percent) the farms in the county were in the 20- to 49-acre class. This trend continued until 1925, when 42.5 percent of the farms in the county were in this class. Farms of between 500 and 999 acres decreased by 90.7 percent, and farms of more than 1,000 acres decreased by 96.0 percent (table 3). Overall, the percentage of farms of less than 20 acres increased in Abbeville County between 1880 and 1925 (figure 5).

Even though the published censuses are not completely reliable, the 1880 and 1890 statistics provide a partial glimpse of the relationship between tenure type and farm size in the South Carolina Piedmont and in Abbeville County (table 4). As would be expected, owners worked the largest farms. In 1880 more than one-half the owner-operated farms both in the region and in the county were between 100 and 499 acres (58.1 percent in the Piedmont, 59.4 percent in Abbeville County). The same was true in 1890, when 54.6 percent of the owner-operated farms were of this size in the Piedmont, and 55.4 percent in Abbeville County.

Table 3

Farm Size Distribution, South Carolina Piedmont and Abbeville County, 1880–1925

| | | | | *Acres* | | | |
	<10	*10–19*	*20–49*	*50–99*	*100–499*	*500–999*	*>1,000*	*Total*
Piedmont								
1880	710	3,261	11,502	6,086	12,166	1,262	331	35,318
1890	803	3,247	16,318	7,915	12,895	979	454	42,611
1900	1,463	4,546	22,772	14,445	14,764	572	120	58,682
1910	2,394	7,771	29,041	15,476	13,173	488	121	68,464
1920	2,094	9,323	32,450	16,018	10,501	340	82	70,808
1925	3,468	12,464	26,521	13,289	9,175	342	70	65,329
Abbeville County								
1880	108	352	1,496	598	1,309	182	50	4,095
1890	165	502	2,556	791	1,378	126	27	5,545
1900	146	261	2,006	1,055	1,064	35	7	4,574
1910	208	476	2,180	1,581	1,131	24	6	5,606
1920	122	649	1,897	1,059	723	15	4	4,469
1925	386	756	1,296	736	610	17	2	3,803

Sources: Census of Agriculture, 1880, 1890, 1900, 1910, 1920, and 1925.

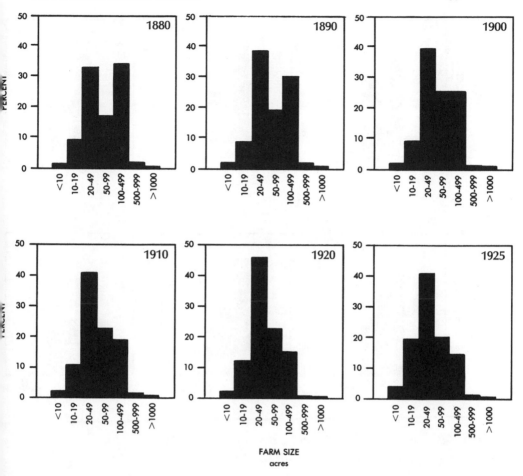

Figure 4. Major tenure groups, Abbeville County, 1880–1925, by percentage.

During this same period, the farms worked by cash renters were generally smaller. In the Piedmont, 50.3 percent of the farms were between 20
and 49 acres, and in Abbeville County, 49.1 percent were this size in
1880. Little change had occurred ten years later, as 49.2 percent of the
farms worked by cash renters in the Piedmont were between 20 and 49
acres, whereas 54.4 percent of the cash renter farms in Abbeville County
were this size.

This same pattern occurred among the sharecroppers both in the

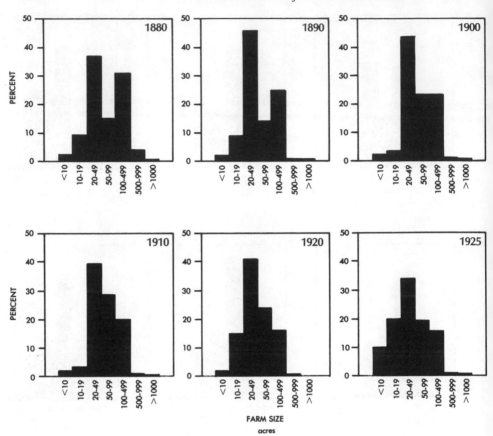

Figure 5. Trends in farm size, South Carolina Piedmont, 1880–1925.

Piedmont and in Abbeville County. In 1880, 52.8 percent of the farms in the South Carolina Piedmont worked by sharecroppers were between 20 and 49 acres; in Abbeville County, 58.0 percent of the sharecropper farms were this size. In the next decade, 5.0 percent of the farms were between 20 and 49 acres, and 64.0 percent of the farms in Abbeville County were this size.

Another way to examine the relationship between farm size and tenure type is by computing the percentage of each tenure class within each farm size class. This permits a somewhat better view of the association of tenure groups with specific farm sizes (figures 6 and 7).

In both the Piedmont and in Abbeville County, owners were over-

Table 4

Farm Size Distribution, South Carolina Piedmont and Abbeville County, 1880 and 1890, by Tenure Class

	Acres							
	<10	10–19	20–49	50–99	100–499	500–999	>1,000	Total
Piedmont								
1880								
Owners	181	348	1,505	3,357	9,393	1,065	322	16,171
Cash renters	98	453	2,304	800	849	75	4	4,583
Sharecroppers	431	2,460	7,693	1,929	1,924	122	5	14,564
Total	710	3,261	11,502	6,086	12,166	1,262	331	35,318
1890								
Owners	269	388	1,911	3,838	8,944	805	228	16,383
Cash renters	89	438	2,702	1,040	1,146	56	20	5,491
Sharecroppers	445	2,421	11,705	3,037	2,805	118	18	20,549
Total	803	3,247	16,318	7,915	12,895	979	266	42,423
Abbeville County								
1880								
Owners	18	44	156	254	973	153	41	1,639
Cash renters	37	115	465	144	165	18	4	948
Sharecroppers	53	193	875	200	171	11	5	1,508
Total	108	352	1,496	598	1,309	182	50	4,095
1890								
Owners	51	51	211	321	947	104	25	1,710
Cash renters	25	129	623	176	180	12	0	1,145
Sharecroppers	89	322	1,722	294	251	10	2	2,690
Total	165	502	2,556	791	1,378	126	27	5,545

Sources: Census of Agriculture, 1880 and 1890.

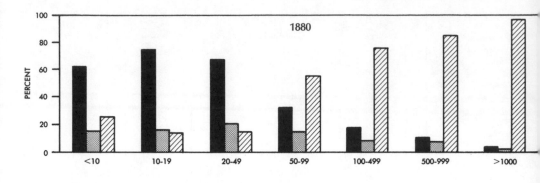

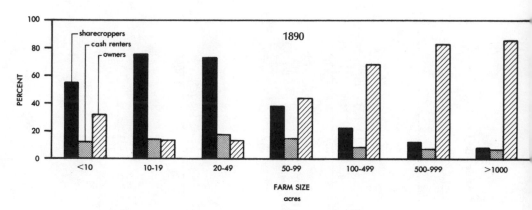

Figure 6. Relationship between farm size and tenure, South Carolina Piedmont, 1880 and 1890.

whelmingly associated with farms of more than 50 acres in both 1880 and 1890. Sharecroppers were associated with farms of less than 50 acres. In the Piedmont as a whole, cash renters were fairly equally associated with all farm sizes (figure 6), but in Abbeville County, cash renters were associated more with farms of less than 50 acres in 1880 and between 10 and 99 acres in 1890 (figure 7).

When the South Carolina Piedmont is examined for the forty years between 1880 and 1920, a consistent pattern of agricultural expansion appears. The total number of farms increased, and more acreage was committed to cultivation. This trend continued until 1920; however, between 1920 and 1925, a dramatic downward trend occurred in all areas of agriculture. Whereas in 1920 the Piedmont contained 73,489 farms, five years later it contained only 67,332, a decline of 8.4 percent, or a loss of 6,157 farms. In Abbeville County, the number of farms fell from 4,456 to 3,803, or 14.7 percent, almost double the statewide rate. Between 1910 and 1920, the number of farms in the Piedmont increased 7.8 percent; in the preceding decade, an increase of 16.2 percent had occurred. Against this steady increase, the decline between 1920 and 1925 seems even more significant.

Accompanying the decline in the number of farms was a decline in cotton production. Again, between 1910 and 1920, the production in the Piedmont increased, only to fall between 1920 and 1925. In 1910 the South Carolina Piedmont produced 418,422 bales of cotton on 1,040,212 acres. A decade later, 566,204 bales were produced on 1,092,738 acres, an increase of 35.3 percent in bales and 5.0 percent in acreage. Just five years later, the output of cotton bales fell to 416,071 bales on 864,439 acres, a decline of 26.5 percent in cotton production. The 1925 production was even slightly lower (0.6 percent) than that of fifteen years earlier. In cotton acreage, the percentage fell by 20.9 percent from 1920 to 1925. The 1925 figure was 16.9 percent lower than that of 1910. Cotton production declined in Abbeville County from 30,096 bales in 1920 to 20,182 bales in 1925, or by 32.9 percent. The acreage allocated to cotton production fell by 33.6 percent, or 23,359 acres in those same five years.

The reasons for this dramatic drop in cotton production in the South Carolina Piedmont between 1920 and 1925 are complex, and a full examination of them is outside the scope of this study. Two prominent reasons for this decline, however, must be mentioned because of their immediate effect on the tenants who lived in Abbeville County and in the South Carolina Piedmont: the cumulative effects of severe erosion and the advance of the cotton boll weevil into the Piedmont.

One of the problems faced by southern agriculture early in its history was soil erosion. Whereas the Native American farmers who had lived by cultivation did so strictly on a scale small enough to feed their immediate families and close relatives, the Euro-American settlers who moved into the South began large-scale agriculture for both home consumption and sale.[62] Shortly after the white settlement of the South and the commencement of full-scale land clearing operations necessary for Euro-American, profit-oriented agriculture, soil erosion, and its counterpart,

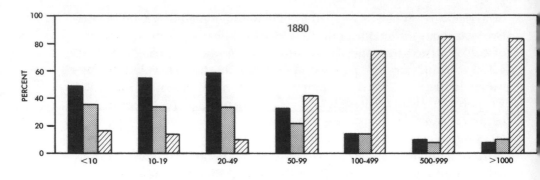

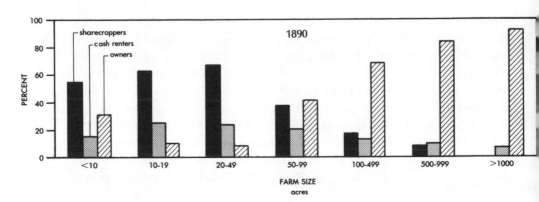

Figure 7. Relationship between farm size and tenure, Abbeville County, 1880 and 1890.

soil exhaustion, were considered inseparable partners of the one-crop plantation system. At a time when the resources of the United States were new and thought to be everlasting, the loss of a few inches of top-soil seemed a small problem. But as hillsides were plowed, and as crops such as cotton were replanted in the same fields year after year, the land began to wear out. With new (that is, Native American) land abundant and apparently available for clearing and planting, many planters believed that the labor of their expensive slave forces would be better spent working on the cultivation of cash crops rather than on the problem of soil conservation.[63] When unwise and shortsighted farming practices such as deep plowing, large-scale land clearing, and slope plowing were used on newly cleared lands, the high annual rainfalls of the South (as much as sixty inches in portions of the Deep South) helped wash soil away. With the lack of deep ground freezing in the South, the conditions for soil loss were disastrously present, and soil exhaustion and soil erosion were significant factors in southern agriculture during the antebellum period.[64]

Soil erosion was particularly severe in the South Carolina Piedmont because of the area's physiography. The soils of the region were always geologically young because they were washed away before they could naturally disintegrate and mature. Both sheet erosion—the uniform removal of large sections of fields—and gully erosion—the removal of deep channels of soil—regularly occurred in the South Carolina Piedmont.[65] By 1860 a belt of severe erosion stretched from Lee County, Alabama, to Lancaster County, South Carolina. In South Carolina soil erosion caused by humans was most severe in the northeastern part of the state in the area of Chester, Fairfield, Newberry, and Union counties. Less severe erosion stretched into the rest of the South Carolina Piedmont, and almost all of the area was affected by it to some degree.[66]

The period of severest erosion in the South came after 1865 with the rise of plantation tenancy. Tenant farmers, who had no long-term commitment to the land they farmed, had no interest in spending their time conserving soil from which they would most likely not benefit. One good solution to the problem of erosion—paying tenants for adopting soil conservation measures—was apparently unattractive to plantation owners.[67] When put in this light, soil erosion was obviously as much a social problem as a natural one. It was said at the time that "the plantation system causes gullies more by what it does to man than by what it does to land."[68] Although this statement is somewhat of an oversimplification, it does contain a bit of truth.

In the sixty years between 1860 and 1920, erosion in the Piedmont was extreme. The belt of severe erosion in South Carolina moved northwest from its location before 1860 to form a wide strip that extended from Chester, Fairfield, and York counties on the east to Abbeville, Greenwood, and McCormick counties on the west.[69] An early twentieth-century survey conducted in Fairfield County, on the southeastern edge of the South Carolina Piedmont, revealed that 90,560 acres had become rough and gullied and unfit for cultivation. Another 46,656 acres were classified as meadow because of past erosion. These 137,216 acres of once arable soil could not be restored and so were judged "permanently destroyed."[70] This unusable land was almost as extensive as the total amount of cropland in all of Fairfield County in 1910, which was then 180,949 acres.[71] A 1936 survey of Spartanburg County revealed that soil erosion had "seriously affected most of the agricultural land" in the county, with between 25 and 75 percent of the topsoil removed from at least three-fourths of the county.[72]

A number of preventative measures for soil erosion and exhaustion had been proposed as early as 1869, and a number of plantation owners (including James Edward Calhoun) had experimented with field terracing, crop rotation, the use of clover as ground cover, and the application of new fertilizers such as bone phosphates.[73] By 1936, however, the South Carolina Piedmont still experienced severe erosion even though experimentation had shown that higher yields could be produced through a process of careful, resourceful agriculture.[74]

Although erosion was a major problem in the South Carolina Piedmont since relatively early in its plantation history, the problems presented by the cotton boll weevil were more immediate and more quickly ruinous to the plantation farmer. Unlike soil erosion, which slowly worked against the farmer as the result of his own actions, the boll weevil appeared quickly and spread its destructive force rapidly.

The cotton boll weevil, *Anthonomus grandis,* was known in Cuba as early as 1871, but it did not appear in the United States until 1892, when it entered southern Texas.[75] The weevil is a small insect whose female lays eggs in the cotton buds and fruit during the spring. Newly hatched grubs feed upon the cotton, thereby destroying it. Perhaps a more pertinent description is one offered by someone whose life was directly affected by it, tenant farmer Nate Shaw. Once Shaw discovered that this small insect could destroy his entire crop, he said, "All God's dangers ain't a white man." The weevil would "go to depositin his eggs in them squares, that's when he'll kill you." Once the eggs hatched, the young weevils would stay in the cotton pod until they were developed. Once the weevil had matured, it would "cut a hole and come out of there, little sneakin devil." According to Shaw, a boll weevil could "ruin a stalk of cotton in a night's time"; when it finished with one plant, it would simply move to another. Shaw saw as many as six weevils on one cotton plant at a time.[76]

The boll weevil gradually worked its way east across the cotton South, reaching the Texas-Louisiana border in 1903; it moved into Alabama in

1910 and into Georgia in 1915. Two years later, the boll weevil reached the southern tip of South Carolina, and by 1919 it had reached Oconee County. By 1922 the boll weevil had made a full sweep over the entire cotton South and had reached Virginia.[77] Years with an unusually high amount of rainfall or with a mild winter were particularly well suited to the growth and spread of weevils. Although the actual damage caused by weevils varied considerably from year to year, an estimate of crop damage of over two hundred thousand dollars per year is not unreasonable.[78]

Many studies of the effects of boll weevil infestation were completed during the first two decades of the twentieth century, but none are more indicative of the weevil's destructive power than one that appeared in 1914, the year that the weevil reached the southern Alabama-Georgia border. In this study, a number of statistics were presented to show the average cotton bale yield before the attack of the weevil, the yield during the worst year of infestation, and the percentage of crop decline for fifteen areas in Texas, Louisiana, and Mississippi.[79] In the twenty-eight counties selected for this study in eastern Texas, cotton production fell from 383,354 bales to 116,288 bales, a decline of 69.7 percent; in the fourteen parishes in southern Louisiana, production decreased from 274,734 bales to 33,326 bales, a decline of 87.9 percent. Along the fertile Mississippi River in the Louisiana Delta, cotton production fell from 129,537 bales to 40,589 bales, a decline of 68.7 percent, and in the rest of Louisiana, cotton production was down by 72.5 percent, from 432,673 bales to 118,781 bales. In the three counties surveyed in the Mississippi Delta, production was down from 83,359 bales to 40,975 bales, or 50.8 percent, and in the other nineteen Mississippi counties, production fell from 371,405 bales to 76,974 bales, a decrease of 79.3 percent. In total, the cotton production of the counties surveyed fell from 1,675,062 bales to 426,933 bales, a decline of 74.5 percent.

Although dramatic, the destruction caused by the boll weevil was not immediately catastrophic for all farmers. The weevil did not move into an area, destroy its entire cotton crop, and then move to a new area, leaving waste and destruction behind. The destruction that would be caused was difficult for farmers to predict.

A study conducted by Arthur F. Raper in Greene County, Georgia, a county in the northeastern part of the state bordering the Georgia Piedmont, shows the actual mechanism of the boll weevil's attack.[80] At first glance, it appears that the devastation caused by the weevil in Greene County was extensive. When the weevil reached the county in 1916, cotton production fell from 14,581 bales to 11,964 bales, or by 17.9 percent. The following year, however, cotton production rose 20.3 percent to 14,396 bales. In 1918 and 1919, with almost no weevils in the county and with more money spent on fertilizers and insecticides, the farmers in Greene County began to believe that the weevils did not like their county. With land prices high and yields good after World War I, many farmers—owners and tenants alike—had money and wanted more land. As a result, more cotton was produced in the "weevilproof" county, and in 1919, cotton production had risen to a high of 20,030 bales. This production was the highest since 1911, when 23,015 bales were made. Then the weevils returned. The cotton production of 1921 was only 1,487 bales, down 88.9 percent from the 1920 production of 13,414 bales. Only 333 bales were made the following year. While production was up to 5,969 bales in 1926, it never again reached pre-weevil levels. Many factors may have been responsible for this decline, but the farmers of Greene County would have fared better if they had not become optimistic after the weevil left their county after its first appearance.

The actual impacts of the boll weevil and soil erosion on the Piedmont remains poorly understood, and the destructive force of these two agricultural impediments may be overstated in some cases. Two geographers, Merle C. Prunty and Charles S. Aiken, have suggested that the evolution of mechanized harvesters, an increase in farm size, and the increasing distance between cotton gins may have had more impact on the demise of Piedmont cotton production than did the plantation tradition, sharecropping, the boll weevil, or changes in the landscape.[81]

This provocative study by Prunty and Aiken can be partially tested by using published census data. On the basis of available evidence, it would seem that the greatest threat to cotton production occurred in the Piedmont between 1918 and 1920 from the boll weevil and from 1880 to 1925 from soil erosion. If the boll weevil and soil erosion had a significant impact on cotton production, it would have been most evident during these years by a sharp decline in production.

Although the complex problem of decreased cotton production cannot be exhaustively pursued in this book, at least some impression of the decrease in Piedmont cotton production can be presented.[82] A simple analysis can be conducted by comparing the cotton production of the

South Carolina Piedmont with a group of non-Piedmont counties in the state and with the entire state of South Carolina. The counties chosen for the comparison are those in the Red Hills subdivision of the Coastal Plain physiographic province. These counties—Allendale, Bamberg, Barnwell, Calhoun, Clarendon, Darlington, Dillon, Florence, Lee, Marion, Orangeburg, and Sumter—were cotton-producing counties that were within the postbellum plantation tradition but which never faced the severe erosion of the Piedmont.[83] If these counties were affected by the boll weevil, they should have suffered a decrease in cotton production between 1917 and 1919, or slightly before the Piedmont experienced the weevil. These counties should show no decrease at all from soil erosion. Overall, any decrease in cotton production in these counties should be less severe than that experienced in the Piedmont. If a decline did occur because of the advance of the cotton boll weevil, it should have occurred earlier than that experienced in the Piedmont.

A comparison of cotton-bale production, the number of bales produced per acre, and the total farm acreage in the three areas—the Piedmont, the non-Piedmont, and the state—shows the same pattern (table 5). Cotton production increased in the state and in both areas until 1910. From 1880 to 1910 production increased in the non-Piedmont counties by 229.1 percent, in the Piedmont it increased by 77.6 percent, and in the entire state, production increased by 144.9 percent. By the next decade, however, cotton bale production decreased in the non-Piedmont counties by 26.3 percent. Cotton production was up both in the Piedmont and in the state, having increased by 35.3 percent in the Piedmont and in the state by 15.4 percent; however, between 1920 and 1925, cotton production fell in the Piedmont by 26.5 percent, in the non-Piedmont counties by 35.9 percent, and throughout the state by 42.8 percent. When viewed in this manner, the decrease in cotton production in the Piedmont is, in fact, much less severe than in the entire state.

A slightly different pattern emerges when the number of cotton bales produced per acre is examined. From 1880 to 1910 the production of cotton per acre increased in the non-Piedmont counties and the entire state. The overall increase in the non-Piedmont counties was more extreme than that experienced statewide. A decrease, however, appeared in the Piedmont from 1890 to 1900. After 1910 the non-Piedmont counties suffered a severe decline in production per acre, and production both in the Piedmont and in the state continued to rise until 1920. Be-

Table 5

Cotton Production and Farms, Piedmont Counties, Non-Piedmont Counties, and South Carolina, 1880–1925

	1880	1890	1900	1910	1920	1925
Piedmont						
Number of farms	35,222	42,423	58,649	68,156	73,478	67,332
Improved farm acreage	1,870,459	2,152,040	2,159,078	2,342,196	2,345,795	1,909,554
Bales	235,650	332,614	349,484	418,422	566,204	416,071
Bales/acre	.37	.38	.36	.40	.52	.48
Non-Piedmont						
Number of farms	21,634	25,788	27,056	41,898	49,075	42,889
Improved farm acreage	957,638	1,343,841	1,484,863	1,620,175	1,679,261	1,388,158
Bales	129,968	211,877	269,357	427,713	315,341	202,064
Bales/acre	.39	.38	.51	.59	.46	.35
South Carolina						
Number of farms	93,864	115,008	155,355	175,571	191,955	172,767
Improved farm acreage	4,132,050	5,255,237	5,775,741	6,097,999	6,184,159	5,035,956
Bales	522,548	747,190	872,213	1,279,866	1,476,645	844,224
Bales/acre	.38	.38	.43	.50	.56	.42

Sources: *Census of Agriculture*, 1880, 1890, 1900, 1910, 1920, and 1925.

tween 1920 and 1925, the production decreased in all areas, with the smallest decline occurring in the Piedmont. In the entire state a decrease of 25.0 percent was recorded; in the non-Piedmont counties a decrease of 23.9 percent occurred, but in the Piedmont the decline was only 7.7 percent.

A similar pattern appears when improved farm acreage is examined. In the Piedmont, the non-Piedmont, and the state, the amount of acreage cultivated grew steadily from 1880 to 1920. This increase grew 49.7 percent in the state, 75.4 percent in the non-Piedmont counties, and 25.4 percent in the Piedmont. The greatest increases in the Piedmont occurred in those counties along the northern edge of the state in the more mountainous part of the region bordering the Blue Ridge physiographic province. For example, in 1880 only 21.0 percent of the farm land in Oconee County was improved; by 1920, 44.9 percent was improved. Similarly, only 30.9 percent of the farm land in Spartanburg County was improved in 1880; in 1920, 60.7 percent was improved.

As with the other measures used, improved farm acreage declined in all areas between 1920 and 1925. In the Piedmont, whereas 53.2 percent of the farm land was improved in 1920, five years later less than half (48.9 percent) the land was improved. The decline was much less severe in the entire state, where the incidence of improved land dropped from 49.8 to 47.3 percent. The decline was negligible in the non-Piedmont counties (from 59.5 to 59.4 percent).

When these three measures are examined, it does seem that a decline in cotton production occurred in the cotton Piedmont between 1910 and 1925, when the farmers there would have experienced great pressures from soil erosion and boll weevil infestation. The decrease, however, was not unique within the state, and the conclusion that soil erosion and boll weevil infestation were the only direct causes of this decrease cannot be defended. The decrease was felt throughout South Carolina, even in those areas, such as the non-Piedmont, that did not experience severe erosion.

Erosion and the boll weevil did have an effect on the cotton-producing South Carolina Piedmont, but a complete understanding of the decline of cotton production between 1920 and 1925 is difficult to obtain. The decline in the number of farms in the Piedmont, the non-Piedmont counties, and the entire state of South Carolina is an obvious contributing factor in the drop in cotton production. In each area, the number of farms steadily increased from 1880 to 1920, but then fell from 1920 to 1925. In the Piedmont, the increase from 1880 to 1920 amounted to 108.6 percent; in the non-Piedmont, to 126.8 percent; and in the entire state, to 104.5 percent (table 5). In each area, however, the number of farms decreased between 1920 and 1925. In the Piedmont a decrease of 8.4 percent was recorded; in the non-Piedmont counties the decline was 12.6 percent; and in the entire state the decline was 10.0 percent.

That cotton production fell as the number of farms decreased is not startling. This conclusion, though, permits the asking of the next logical question: did the number of farms fall because of erosion and the boll weevil, or did other factors contribute to it? While both soil erosion and the attack of the boll weevil undoubtedly played a part in the decline of cotton, they were related to a much larger circumstance that affected cotton production: the migration of large numbers of black farmers out of the cotton South between 1910 and 1925.

Between 1916 and 1930, more than 400,000 southern blacks moved north in the Great Migration.[84] Although many early scholars have argued that this migration reflected a black tendency for movement,[85] scholars now agree that social and economic factors comprised the major reasons for the black migration out of the cotton South. Specifically, the migration was caused by the treatment blacks received from many southern whites; lynching was a major, justifiable fear of many rural blacks. Poor schools and Jim Crow practices also figured prominently in many decisions to move. In addition, the economic depression of 1914–15, the poor cotton crop of 1916, the appearance of the boll weevil, floods, the sharecropping system, low wages, and the growing need for laborers in the North all made emigration from the South or to southern cities attractive to many southern rural blacks.[86]

The social conditions faced by blacks in the rural South from 1880 to 1925 have been studied by many scholars and cannot be recounted here.[87] A brief glimpse of the fears of at least one black tenant farmer were expressed by Ed Brown when he said that when the sheriff got a posse together "you didn't know who they was goin to kill and more than likely they didn't either." Because these men "would walk right into your house," many people would run from "house to house," and many even left home to hide in the woods "to keep from havin anythin to do with it."[88] Besides this kind of terrorism, some rural blacks faced added pressures when they were blamed for the presence of the boll weevil in their counties. As Nate Shaw reported, some landlords threatened to cease furnishing their tenants if they did not work harder to destroy the weevils.[89] Perhaps Ed Brown summed up his feelings best when he said, "Your two worstest enemies if you was a sharecropper was the boll weevil and the landlord."[90]

The black migration from South Carolina was not of the magnitude of that from southern Georgia, central Alabama, the Mississippi and Louisiana deltas, and east-central Texas, but rural blacks did move to the developing cities of South Carolina and to other states.[91] Although blacks migrated from South Carolina in the 1880s and 1890s, these movements did not affect the overall population of the Piedmont, the non-Piedmont, or the state (table 6). In all areas, the overall population rose between 1880 and 1930.[92] A decline appeared only in the black population between 1920 and 1930. The total population of the state rose 74.6 percent between 1880 and 1930, with the white population increasing 141.4 percent. While the black population increased 43.1 percent between 1880 and 1920, it decreased 8.2 percent in 1930, showing that 71,038 blacks had left the state within that decade. A similar pattern appeared in the Piedmont. The white population increased 185.8 percent between 1880 and 1930; the black population increased 44.5 percent between 1880 and 1920 but decreased 11.1 percent between 1920 and 1930. In the non-Piedmont counties examined, the white population increased 116.7 percent between 1880 and 1930; the black population experienced an increase of 82.3 percent between 1880 and 1920, but a decrease of 4.5 percent between 1920 and 1930. In Abbeville County both the white and the black populations declined between 1890 and 1900 (25.2 percent for whites, 30.4 percent for blacks) and increased between 1900 and 1910 (8.4 percent for whites, 2.1 percent for blacks); however, between 1910 and 1930, the black population of the county decreased by 50.9 percent. The white population suffered a decline of 4.7 percent between 1910 and 1920, but increased 4.8 percent in 1930, meaning that from 1910 to 1930, the total white population declined only 0.2 percent.

Clearly, many factors were responsible for the decrease in cotton production in the South Carolina Piedmont from 1920 to 1925—among these, the advance of the boll weevil, the cumulative and deleterious effects of soil erosion coupled with poor conservation measures, and black migration. That no single element can be identified as *the* cause of the

Table 6

Population, Piedmont Counties, Non-Piedmont Counties, and South Carolina, 1880–1925

	1880	1890	1900	1910	1920	1930
Piedmont						
White	162,963	197,688	250,022	316,610	380,187	465,828
Black	182,582	205,055	243,579	265,274	263,767	234,609
Total	345,545	402,743	493,601	581,884	643,954	700,437
Non-Piedmont						
White	71,866	84,387	96,774	115,786	141,901	155,726
Black	134,204	159,566	191,118	220,171	244,624	233,694
Total	206,070	243,953	287,892	335,957	386,525	389,420
South Carolina						
White	391,105	462,008	557,807	679,161	818,538	944,040
Black	604,332	688,934	782,321	835,843	864,719	793,681
Total	995,437	1,150,942	1,340,128	1,515,004	1,683,257	1,737,721

Sources: Census of Population, 1880, 1890, 1900, 1910, 1920, and 1930.

decline demonstrates the complexity of southern agriculture during the postbellum period. As is shown in chapter 5, the decline in cotton production in the South Carolina Piedmont was mirrored at James Edward Calhoun's Millwood Plantation. Before this particular plantation can be discussed again, however, further contextual information on southern cotton tenancy is required. Therefore, the next chapter presents information on the physical aspects of tenancy: the settlement forms, the housing, and the material possessions of southern plantation tenant farmers.

The Material Basis of Plantation Tenancy: Settlement, Houses, and Personal Possessions

THE STUDY OF THE MATERIAL BASIS of past cultures is a major aspect of all archaeological research. The material basis of the postbellum plantation—its settlement, its housing, and the material possessions of its inhabitants—is no less a topic for serious archaeological investigation.

An interest in settlement has been important in anthropological and archaeological research for many years. A major tenet of the archaeological study of abandoned settlements is that the spatial arrangement of people's homes, graves, work places, and so on, provides information about past culture and society that is available in no other source. In fact, the study of the distribution of past settlements, known as *settlement archaeology* or by a more encompassing term, *spatial archaeology*, is in many ways the study of past social relationships expressed in physical terms.[1]

Although developed independently, this kind of archaeological inquiry is linked to the anthropological study of *proxemics*. As defined by its creator, anthropologist Edward T. Hall, proxemics is comprised of "the interrelated observations and theories of man's use of space as a specialized elaboration of culture." The subject matter of proxemics is the human use of space, "the distance between men in the conduct of daily transactions, the organization of space in his houses and buildings, and ultimately the layout of his towns."[2] Hall demonstrates that many kinds of space exist—visual, auditory, olfactory, and tactile—and that the use of space is culturally determined. Even though every culture uses space differently, three general kinds of space are found in all cultures: fixed feature space, semifixed-feature space, and informal, or dynamic, space. In a general sense, *fixed-feature space* refers to those spatial items of a culture that are not movable. This category includes buildings, wells, icehouses, and the layouts of villages. *Semifixed-feature space* generally refers to movable items such as chairs, screens, and tables. *Dynamic space,* or *informal space,* refers to the use of space in human communication. This kind of space refers to the intangible, or nonmaterial, uses of space, such as the distance people maintain during a business meeting or when speaking to a friend.[3]

Hall's examination of proxemics includes a strong commitment to *ethology,* the study of animal behavior. Thus, the differential use of space can be observed in many, if not all, animal species. The use of space by humans, however, must not be tied too closely to general animal behavior.

Noted scholar Henri Lefebvre refined Hall's ideas about proxemics when he argued that space is a social product that cannot be explained by reference to the environment, human nature, or even culture. Rather, space has its own reality within the existing mode of production. The use of space is therefore not only culture-specific but intrinsic in the way the material world is produced. For Lefebvre, space has at least four functions: it is a means of production, an object of consumption, an aspect of class struggle, and a political instrument.[4] Within this view, space can be allocated, controlled, and policed within a culture-specific hierarchy of social classes. Thus, to distinguish this more social view of the use of space from the more directly ethological brand devised by Hall, the term *social proxemics* is used.

Social proxemics, the study of social space in cultural contexts, is a perfect subject for archaeological inquiry. Archaeologists, however, face severe difficulties conducting proxemic analysis, because they study only the remaining evidence of human behavior and interaction, not the behavior itself. As a result, archaeologists find it almost impossible to study dynamic space and extremely difficult to study semifixed-feature space. Prehistorians who attempt to conduct proxemic analyses must necessarily rely only on the physical remains they uncover to understand the fixed-feature space usage of the people who lived at a particular locality. To go beyond this kind of spatial analysis, prehistorians must interpret and induce. Historical archaeologists, on the other hand, often have at least partial access to the past use of semifixed-feature space and dynamic space through written records. Without these documents, historical archaeologists are on the same relative footing as prehistorians where spatial analysis is concerned, even though historical archaeologists still have a greater body of comparative information from which to draw.

Although settlement pattern studies are now common in archaeology, explicit proxemic studies are rare. Of the few studies in existence, Bruce Wright's examination of the sixteenth- and seventeenth-century Iroquois of northern New York State and southern Ontario illustrates the problems archaeologists face when conducting true proxemic analysis.[5] As a result of these problems, archaeologists have concentrated more on the fixed-feature space revealed in regional and community settlement patterns.

This archaeological research on settlement has shown that at least three levels can be examined: individual buildings, communities (groups of buildings), and zones or regions (groups of communities). These levels of settlement concomitantly incorporate special kinds of interaction between the people who inhabited them, and each requires a specific approach in order to understand it. Social models can be used to explain the factors that shape the design, construction, and layout of individual buildings; social and architectural models help provide an understanding of communities; and geographic and economic models are useful for examining regional settlement patterns.[6]

These models help archaeologists understand the house, community, and regional settlement patterns at a particular time; archaeologists can also use these methods of analysis to study the changes in settlement over time. This interest in settlement change is embedded within a wider anthropological interest in general cultural change.[7]

In this study of the postbellum tenant plantation, both the house and community levels of settlement are examined, with particular emphasis on their changes over time. This examination is crucial to an understanding of the settlement forms and changes at Millwood Plantation.

When the Civil War was over and the postwar period of plantation organization had begun, southern plantations still had the spatial form of antebellum estates. In general, most antebellum cotton plantations were characterized by clusters of buildings. The planter's house was usually at the center of the estate in a cluster of buildings that contained the service buildings used by the planter and his family. These buildings were typically carriage houses, servants' quarters, smokehouses, and sheds. A second cluster was formed by the slave quarters, the overseer's house, and the buildings used by the slaves for the storage of agricultural tools. This sort of nucleated settlement has been termed the "ante bellum plantation occupance form" by geographer Merle Prunty.[8] As plantation scholar Edgar Thompson wrote: "The spatial pattern of the settlement reflected its political and social structure. The special position of the planter found expression not only in a larger and better equipped house, but in its detachment from the quarters of the laborers."[9]

The nucleated antebellum plantation layout was described by novelist J. T. Trowbridge when he spent the summer and winter of 1865 in the South. Trowbridge wrote that "the buildings of a first-class plantation form a little village by themselves." The planter's home was surrounded by a number of smaller buildings, including a pantry, a dairy, a kitchen, and a smokehouse. According to Trowbridge: "Next in importance to the planter's house [was] the overseer's house. Then [came] the negro quarters." Trowbridge said that barns were rarely found on plantations but that other structures—corn cribs, grain bins, mule pens, gin houses, and sorghum mills—were often present.[10]

One of the best descriptions of the planter's portion of an antebellum plantation is that presented by James Battle Avirett in his recollections of his plantation home in North Carolina.[11] Avirett's narrative is presented as a walking tour of the plantation from the planter's home to the surrounding woods. The plantation big house was approached by a "broad avenue of lovely elms" that was about 400 yards long and 40 feet wide. The plantation orchards and a number of service buildings were placed along this avenue. Avirett describes the kitchen as a "plazza" that may have been detached. Behind the kitchen was a quadrangle of about one hundred feet on a side that contained a well, three smokehouses, a flour house, a coffee house, a grocery storehouse, and a few other buildings. Behind these structures were others used for potato and oyster storage. A poultry yard, containing peacock, turkey, guinea fowl, duck, and chicken houses, was placed near these storage buildings. Next to this barnyard were a one-acre vegetable garden and a weaving room. The servants' quarters, consisting of six separate structures, were located beyond this area.

The immense plantation described by Avirett may not be typical of all southern plantations. The clarity of his remembrances, written in 1901, might be clouded or unintentionally embellished to make the plantation seem ideal. Nonetheless, his description of the grounds surrounding the planter's home is useful.

Perhaps even more interesting is the planter's compound recollected by Charles Ball, a fugitive slave from South Carolina.[12] Remembering the planter's home, Ball says that a five-acre garden, containing both vegetables and flowers, was located behind the planter's large, brick mansion. Farther behind the mansion were the kitchen, a pigeon house, and a large wooden building called the "kitchen quarters." This last building was where the house servants slept, ate, and did "all the rough or unpleasant work of the kitchen department," such as cleaning fish and preparing meat. Although the plantation did not contain a barn, it did have a combination carriage house and stable presumably located behind the kitchen quarters.

In the planter's portion of the antebellum plantation, the planter's home was surrounded by small, detached outbuildings reserved for specific functions. This plan, although seemingly typical, was judged "unnecessary and inconvenient" by at least one nineteenth-century architect who devised a ranch-style home for southern planters. The planter's home of his design was attached to the kitchen by a narrow corridor. The servants' quarters, rather than being detached, were adjacent to the kitchen. Accordingly, this plan would "bring the family of the planter, himself, and their servants, although under different roofs, into convenient proximity with each other."[13]

Most contemporary observers were impressed by the planter's portion of the plantation, but the slave quarters also attracted much attention. On larger plantations, antebellum field slaves usually lived in a group of buildings called *quarters*. Although the quarters could be arranged in any way to suit the planter, they were usually arranged in rows of identical dwellings placed along short roads. Many ex-slaves reported living in this kind of quarters complex. Charlie Hudson of Elbert County, Georgia, commented that "slave quarters was laid out like streets."[14] Charles Ball described the slave quarters with which he was familiar as "standing in rows, much like the Indian villages which I have seen in the country of the Cherokees."[15] A more detailed description, if accurate, has been offered by Avirett, who said that the quarters on his plantation contained two cross-streets, called Broadway and Chestnut, that were lined by long rows of elms and maples. The slave cabins along Broadway were spaced about fifty feet apart. A hen house, a pig house, and a garden were located in the rear of each house. The industrial and agricultural service buildings—the cotton gin, pork house, and carpenters' workshop—were located on Chestnut Street.[16] A similar description was offered by Whitelaw Reid, who, in speaking of a Mississippi plantation immediately after the war, said that the quarters consisted of a double row of frame houses that fronted each other across a street. Two or three brick cisterns were placed in the middle of the street, and a church was located at the end of the street. A fenced garden stood behind each cabin. Behind the garden was a large expanse of level land that terminated in a cypress swamp.[17]

The typical distance between the slave quarters and the planter's home is difficult to determine. In the eighteenth century, while speaking of Louisiana plantations, Antoine Simon Le Page du Pratz wrote, "Prudence requires that your negroes be lodged at a proper distance, to prevent them from being troublesome or offensive; but at the same time near enough for your conveniently observing what passes among them."[18] A former nineteenth-century slave said that the slave cabins were located "in calling distance" of the big house, another said that the cabins were "some distance behind the master's house," and still another said that the quarters were clustered "approximately one block from the planter's home." Of all the available comments on this subject, that by Charles Ball is the most explicit. He said that the quarters on his former plantation were placed "about a quarter of a mile from the dwelling house."[19] A less explicit, but perhaps more interesting comment, was offered by an ex-slave from Tennessee, who said that the house servants' houses were whitewashed and closer to the big house than were the quarters, "so the white folks could get to them easy if they wanted them" but far enough away so that they would "keep from spoiling the looks of the big house."[20]

Archaeologists have successfully provided exact distance measurements between masters' houses and slave quarters. These measurements indicate that the distance between the two kinds of dwellings was variable and probably depended upon a number of factors. For example, at Limerick Plantation in the South Carolina low country, the slave quarters were from 250 to 625 feet from the main house, and at Hampton Plantation on the Georgia coast, the quarters were 328 feet from the planter's complex; however, at Stafford Plantation, another plantation in coastal Georgia, the slave quarters were just over one-half mile from the main house, and at Shirley Plantation in Virginia, the quarters were about a mile from the planter's home.[21] Archaeological research thereby supports the historical information that shows that great variety existed in the distances between slave quarters and planters' homes.

Not all slaves were housed in quarters. Many freed slaves reported that their homes were scattered at various locations behind the master's house.[22] Even though this arrangement might usually be associated with small plantations, at least one former slave, George Fleming of Laurens County, South Carolina, said that this pattern occurred on his plantation, which housed two hundred slaves.[23] Other seemingly aberrant forms of slave quarter settlement have also been reported. For example, Minerva Grubbs, a former slave from a plantation in Simpson County, Mississippi, that housed seventy-five slaves, said that the slave cabins on this plantation were "in rows under tall shady oak trees in the front of Mar's house." She found this odd because "most all the slave owners had [their slaves] living at the back," and that she "never did know how come he didn't have his like that."[24] Another ex-slave, Callie Elder of Floyd County, Georgia, reported that on her plantation, where "there was too many slaves" for her to count, "the cabins was built in a circle."[25] Obviously, not all antebellum slave quarters were the regularly designed complexes that have often been reported.

Regardless of how far the slave quarters were located from the planter's complex, the exact placement of slave quarters was partly affected by the time necessary to transport slaves to their workplaces. For example, Marcus Robinson, a former slave in North Carolina, reported that his master kept his slaves housed at places "convenient to the different parts" of the estate. As he said, "some of [the cabins] was close to the barn and stables, then there was two or three close to the big house for the servants and maids to live, others was near the fields and pastures." Another former slave made a similar comment, perhaps speaking of the same plantation.[26] Such reports imply that plantation labor organization helped structure the antebellum settlement pattern.

Not all slaves were housed in the quarters or even in the detached dependencies within the planter's area. On small plantations, of course, planters commonly lived and labored alongside their slaves,[27] but even on larger plantations, the separation of whites and blacks was not absolute. Many slaves lived inside their master's home to render special services such as tending fires or emptying the chamber pots at night.[28] For example, Bob Mobley, a former slave in Pulaski County, Georgia, claimed that he had slept on a trundle bed in his master's room just in case he needed anything. Another former slave, whose mother was the master's cook, said that he "was raised right in the house with the white folks," even though his sister and four brothers stayed in the quarters. His mother, who also served as a wet nurse, lived in the big house until her usefulness for this task was over, at which time she went back to live in the quarters. He remained in the house, however, sleeping on a trundle bed. When he grew up, he too was sent to the quarters. Another slave reported that as "mistress' pet" he "slept under the stairway in the closet."[29] Thus, the physical separation of blacks and whites on antebellum plantations rested on more than just skin color. Simple division of labor also figured prominently in the settlement location of plantation inhabitants.

Great variations also occurred in the other fixed-feature spaces in the slave quarters, spaces such as gardens, overseers' cabins, and other structures. Some slaves had personal gardens. Frederick Law Olmsted reported in 1856, for example, that on a South Carolina rice plantation each slave family was given a garden of one-half acre. Fugitive slave, Charles Ball, noted that slaves on every plantation with which he was acquainted were allowed to make "patches," or gardens. These patches, however, were not located near the slave cabins but "in some remote and unprofitable part of the estate, generally in the woods."[30] Many other slaves, however, report that they were not allowed to have gardens. One ex-slave, in fact, said, "How could slaves have gardens?" as if the question that had been put to her was ridiculous. Other slaves without gardens reported obtaining fresh vegetables from their masters' gardens.[31]

Overseers on large plantations generally lived somewhere near the quarters, symbolically between them and the planter's home. Ball reported that the overseer's cabin on one cotton plantation in South Carolina was located about 100 yards from the rows of cabins that comprised the quarters. Another former slave remarked that the overseer's house on her plantation was "up the road a piece from the Big House." Avirett reported that the two homes of the black foremen on his plantation were located at the end of Broadway Street. Another ex-slave, from Louisiana, reported that the black drivers' cabins were 150 yards from the master's house.[32]

Many slave quarters on larger plantations contained special buildings used as hospitals or nurseries. Regarding the last kind of building, one ex-slave said that the quarters usually contained a larger house with two or three rooms, called the "chilun house." Young children were kept in this house during the day while their parents worked in the fields.[33]

With the Civil War and emancipation, the nucleated settlement of the plantation generally broke up as freed slaves began living as independent farmers. The immediate postwar period of experimentation on plantations mentioned in the last chapter was accompanied by a modification of settlement form. The clustered pattern of the antebellum plantation was modified on some estates immediately after the war as former slaves became members of squads.

The squad system, an experimental form of plantation agriculture found on some South Carolina plantations, had a settlement pattern that was between antebellum nucleation and postbellum dispersion. Individual squads were located in a cluster of buildings across the plantation lands some distance from the administrative center. This unique settlement was observed in the 1870s by Edward King, a writer for *Scribner's Monthly.* King reported that under slavery, the slaves were "all quartered at night in a kind of central group of huts, known as the 'quarters.'" With emancipation, however, planters found it "an excellent idea to divide up the hundred or five hundred laborers among a number of these little villages, each located on the section of the plantation which they have leased." King referred to this settlement form as the "segregation of quarters."[34] A similar settlement pattern was noted by David Crenshaw Barrow, Jr., at his father's plantation in Oglethorpe County, Georgia. Barrow observed that the two original postbellum squads split into "smaller and still smaller squads" until full dispersion had occurred.[35]

Experimental forms of land tenure changed the nature of the postbellum tenant plantation; however, on those estates where true experimentation did not occur, but where wages were paid immediately after 1865, the settlement pattern of the plantation did not radically change. In fact, one great advantage planters found in the wage system was that the physical form of the plantation did not require expensive modification. Freed men and women wage laborers lived, for the most part, in small, cramped, and inadequate antebellum slave quarters.

The continued habitation of slave cabins by freed blacks is one outstanding feature of the postbellum plantation wage system. James Lucas, an ex-slave from Adams County, Mississippi, said that when he lived in the quarters after he was granted freedom his life "wasn't much different from slavery." According to him: "We lived in quarters, used the white folks horses and ploughs and helped raise our own food. We just changed a master for a boss."[36] Another former slave, from Elbert County, Georgia, said that "telling the slaves they was free didn't make much difference on our place, for most of them stayed on there and worked with old Marster just like [they] always done." Still another freed slave said, "The only difference we knowed [between slavery and freedom] was we got money for our work."[37]

Considering the poor financial situation of most planters after the war, the lack of settlement change, or more accurately, the failure of planters to build new houses for their freed, but even poorer, laborers, is not surprising. Freed slaves often remarked that their former masters had nothing but land and simply could not afford to build houses in the postwar era. When one ex-slave remarked that his former master said "there is a house for you, and wood to keep you warm, and a mule to work,"[38] he was undoubtedly referring to a slave cabin.

Many newly freed slaves apparently accepted their old slave homes, while others clearly did not. Many freed families sought almost desperate measures to escape the quarters. Joe Hawkins's family, for instance, lived "under the oak trees [for] two years" before getting a house. In his words, they camped "with a shelter of limbs and leaves." He said that houses simply did not exist and that landlords were too poor to build them. He does not mention what had happened to the plantation quarters buildings or whether anyone lived in them. Another freed slave reported that her father built a "shack" with a mud and rock chimney on land he rented.[39] This cabin was probably similar to the one they had just left on the plantation.

The relationships between plantation buildings radically changed when tenancy was established on southern plantations. To be practical, tenancy required that each farmer live near his fields. Most freed slaves were happy to accept this arrangement because it provided some escape from white supervision and because it presented some minor means of control over land and animals. A house near the fields took the tenant out of the quarters forever. David Crenshaw Barrow observed the shift from settlement nucleation to dispersion when he wrote that some of the tenants on his father's plantation had to walk a mile to reach their fields when they still lived in the old slave quarters. When tenant farmers began to "want more elbow-room," they moved directly on their own farms.[40] According to one scholar, this early settlement was by "trial and error," and tenants occupied "whatever land could be acquired."[41]

The decision to move out of the quarters resulted from at least two factors: planters wanted to diminish their tenants' transportation time, and tenants wanted some freedom from supervision and a sense of separation that could come only from living in individual homes, even if they were not their own. Robert Somers, an Englishman traveling in the South, observed in 1871 that the black sharecropper "loves to have a mule of his own to ride on Sundays and in idle times of the year." Somers noted that the planters' convenience was found in putting tenant farmers and their animals "near his work, where, if so inclined, he may protect both his own and his employer's property." In 1879 a member of the British Parliament, Sir George Campbell, noted, "The large farms have for the most part been broken up or let to small farmers."[42] This disbursed settlement pattern, characteristic of the postbellum tenant plantation, has been termed the "post bellum 'fragmented' occupance form."[43] This settlement design was merely a modification of the antebellum settlement form. That is, plantation settlement did not disappear after the war; it had only been modified.

Two settlement subtypes are generally identified within the "'fragmented' occupance form": the cropper subtype and the tenant-renter subtype. With the exception of the dispersed location of the tenants' houses, the cropper subtype was similar to the antebellum plantation in that the barns, sheds, and other outbuildings were part of the landlord's settlement complex. As a result, sharecroppers who wanted to use a mule or a plow were required to go to the landlord's part of the plantation to obtain it. This spatial organization symbolized the tenant's position vis-à-vis the landlord and reflected his relative lack of personal choice in labor matters. A major difference existed in the tenant-renter settlement form in that barns, sheds, and outbuildings were placed near the renter's home. When a tenant became a full renter, owning his own work animals and tools, his part of the plantation theoretically began to appear as a distinct little farm. Because the tenant's home and the surrounding buildings looked like an independent farm, census takers undoubtedly failed to recognize the continuation of the plantation in the South after 1865. These houses were generally located on unpaved roads, a practice that could be observed until well into the 1920s.[44]

Descriptions of the homes inhabited by tenant farmers vary after 1865. Although the information from 1865 to 1925 is scant, with the identification of tenancy as a social problem by sociologists after 1925, abundant information on tenant housing exists for the years 1925 to 1941.

The interest in tenant housing reflects both the visibility of the houses and the common perception of tenancy as a social problem during the 1920s, 1930s, and early 1940s. Tenants' homes were a reminder and physical symbol of the "problem." American sociologists who conducted fieldwork in the rural South were affected by the inadequacies of tenant housing, and most wrote about it with impassioned precision. The publication of sociologist Rupert B. Vance's *How the Other Half Is Housed,* a picture book of tenant housing, is a further indication that at least some social scientists attached great importance to tenant housing as a physical representation of tenancy.[45]

The homes of plantation wage laborers were essentially slave cabins. As a result, many descriptions of these cabins exist in the extant narratives of ex-slaves. Even though some of the characteristics of slave cabins are addressed in chapter 1, a more complete examination is now in order.

Although wide variations in slave cabin construction undoubtedly occurred across the plantation South, the remembrances of ex-slaves concerning their homes are remarkably similar. The statement of Vinnie Rusby, of Rankin County, Mississippi, is fairly typical: "The cabins we lived in was built of logs split open and pegged together. The fire places was big that held long logs. . . . These chimneys was made of sticks, dirt, and straw. The cabins didn't have but about one window and two doors. One door at the front and one at the back."[46] These cabins usually consisted of a single room and had windows that were covered only by a large wooden shutter. Some had dirt floors; others had wooden floors.[47] On plantations where slaves were not fed at a central kitchen, the most commonly remembered interior feature was the fireplace, a focal point of the cabin where the cooking was done.

Stick-and-mud chimneys were common in slave cabins, but other kinds of chimneys were also used. According to James J. Butler in his 1851 article entitled "Management of Negroes," the recommended chimney was one made of brick, if only for economic reasons: "in soils where the clay will make brick, the saving of fuel, and the greater security against fire, render it a matter of economy to build brick chimneys."[48] In the same decade, Olmsted had seen brick chimneys on slave cabins, but he had remarked that they were "more commonly of lath or split sticks, laid up like log-work and plastered with mud." George Fleming, a former slave in Laurens County, South Carolina, remembered that many different kinds of chimneys had appeared on the cabins of his plantation, "some brick, some rock and some of [the] old stick and mud kind."[49]

The cabin with a stick-and-mud chimney was the simplest and most inexpensive kind to build. Most freed slaves, if they were able to build a house, built houses with stick-and-mud chimneys. Although the comments of former slave John Hunter of North Carolina are ambiguous and may refer to antebellum days, his statement that some blacks "just built up a log house and dobbed it with dirt to keep the air from coming through" implies that some of the homes built after the war were modeled on slave cabins.[50] At any rate, the stick-and-mud chimney did not disappear from the rural South. An excellent example of this sort of construction was photographed by Farm Security Administration photographer Marion Post Wolcott in December 1938, near Beaufort, South Carolina (figure 8).

The homes of tenant farmers, of whatever tenure class, were simple structures. Although Vance's picture book of tenant housing aptly demonstrates the great variety of tenant housing, George Brown Tindall's assessment is generally accurate: "home [for the tenant] was a dilapidated, unpainted, weatherbeaten frame cabin leaning out of plumb on rock or brick pilings—unceiled, unscreened, covered with a leaky roof."[51] This description has been repeated by many different writers. Of all the descriptions presented, one of the best is provided by W. O. Atwater and Charles D. Woods in their innovative study of black dietary patterns in Alabama in 1895 and 1896. This study helps fill a gap in the knowledge of tenant housing through time, because the best and most detailed descriptions of tenant housing were written during the 1930s and early 1940s.

In describing the tenant dwellings in the region around Tuskegee, Alabama, Atwater and Woods note that both small, one-room houses, and larger two-room, dog-trot houses existed. Both kinds of houses were log dwellings with simple shingle or board roofs. Many of these houses were built so that spaces appeared between the logs; others were chinked

Figure 8. "Negroes' Home Near Beaufort, South Carolina," 1938, an illustration of the persistence of stick-and-mud chimneys in the rural South. (Library of Congress)

with earth or boards. These houses, built on posts, were entered by stepping up on a box or rough steps. Many of the floorboards were an inch or more apart, and in at least one instance, water moccasins were able to enter the house through the floor. The windows in these houses were covered with wooden boards rather than with glass.

The one-room cabins were built with a single door, a fireplace on one side, and one or two windows. Sometimes a small storeroom was annexed to the building.

The two-room cabin was a typical dog-trot house: one room was used as a combination kitchen and living room, and the other was used as a bedroom. The open, central passage was used as a porch.[52]

Tenant housing did not change much by the twentieth century. For example, Ed Brown described his tenant home as "just a shell of a house, not sealed in any way—no plaster, no ceilin—had a chimney goin up from a fireplace openin on to two rooms, so some called it a stacked chimney double pen house." He said that in place of glass windows, the house had "shutters of upright boards that swung out on hinges like a gate." Flour sacks were used as curtains.[53] In the late 1930s, sociologist Margaret Jarmon Hagood described tenant houses in terms of a few "modal traits": unpainted, one-story, weatherbeaten, and without electricity. Still, she did note that "in spite of the existence of these modal traits, variation from them was so frequent and great that there was little suggestion of uniformity."[54]

The great variation in housing makes it difficult to generalize about tenant housing across the entire plantation South; nonetheless, the housing of the plantation South has been studied in two major ways: by region and by occupants' race.[55]

Two detailed regional studies of farmhouses, including those of tenants, were conducted in 1934 by the Bureau of Home Economics of the United States Department of Agriculture.[56] In the first of these studies, the Bureau of Home Economics recommended the kinds of housing that would, in its view, be adequate for farm families in the United States. To the bureau, the farmhouse was not merely a rural example of an urban house. The farmhouse, which had closer ties to the land than did the house in the city, was the administrative, food preparation, and food preservative center of the farm. Thus, the farmhouse was a special place. To make recommendations on the form of these special places, the Bureau of Home Economics divided the forty-eight states into fourteen regions. One of these regions, stretching from North Carolina to Texas, was called the Cotton Belt.

The report's author said that "southern comfort is of the greatest importance in planning both the design and the orientation of the house[57] and that every effort should be made to protect the house from the severe heat of the South. Doors and windows should be located in order to create drafts and should have transoms, windowsills should be low, and floors should be doubled.

This ideal design was more wishful thinking than reality, however, and the second study presented by the Bureau of Home Economics, a survey including data on 595,855 farmhouses in 308 counties in forty-six states, demonstrated how far the reality deviated from the ideal. Statistics for two southern cotton states—South Carolina and Georgia—and for two northern corn and winter wheat states—Illinois and Indiana—can be used to demonstrate regional differences (table 7).[58]

Significant distinctions appear in the quality of farmhouses in the two areas. Farmhouses in Illinois and Indiana were generally older than those in South Carolina and Georgia. Whereas more than 30 percent of the houses in the northern states were more than fifty years old, less than half that amount were of this age in the two southern states. Age, however, had little relation to house quality. Most of the houses in Illinois and Indiana were painted, but in South Carolina and Georgia, most were unpainted. In addition, the farmhouses of the southern states were overwhelmingly single-storied; those of the northern states were normally more than one story. The southern farmhouses averaged fewer than five rooms; those in the North averaged more than six rooms. These figures indicate not only the kind of housing that existed in the South but also how the homes of southern farmers differed from those

Table 7

Farmhouses, South Carolina, Georgia, Illinois, and Indiana, 1934, by Percentage

	South Carolina (n = 15,505)	*Georgia* (n = 33,139)	*Illinois* (n = 21,318)	*Indiana* (n = 15,755)
<10 years old	12.7	9.7	6.0	7.1
10–24 years old	36.6	31.2	16.8	16.5
25–49 years old	38.0	44.6	43.3	41.3
>50 years old	12.7	14.5	33.9	35.1
Frame				
Unpainted	79.4	73.6	8.0	9.1
Painted	18.0	23.0	85.6	82.1
Stucco	–	0.1	1.5	2.0
Log	2.3	3.2	1.5	1.9
Brick	0.2	0.1	2.9	4.4
Stone	0.1	–	0.2	0.2
Concrete	–	–	0.3	0.3
One story	91.1	93.4	28.2	22.4
More than one story	8.9	6.6	71.8	77.6

Source: U.S. Department of Agriculture, Bureau of Home Economics, *Farm-Housing Survey*, pp. 3, 4, 7, 8, 9.

of northern farmers. The homes in the South were not as old as those in the North, but they were painted less often, were more likely to be made of logs, and were single-storied more often than their northern counterparts.

In addition to presenting quantitative figures on farm housing, the 1934 farm housing survey also provides qualitative statistics (table 8). Ten housing elements—foundations, exterior walls, roofs, chimneys, doors and windows, screens, exterior paint, interior walls and ceilings, floors, and stairs—are evaluated as "good," "fair," "poor," and "not reported" (meaning not present). As is true of the quantitative measures, significant differences occur between the farmhouses in South Carolina and Georgia and those in Illinois and Indiana.

In general, the quality of the farmhouses in the two northern states was appreciatively better than those in the two southern states. When the "good," "fair," and "poor" categories are averaged, fairly even figures result for all three categories in South Carolina and Georgia, meaning that equal proportions of houses were good, fair, or poor. A different pattern appears for the houses in Illinois and Indiana, where "good" appears most often. In nearly every category, the majority of the homes surveyed in Illinois and Indiana fell within the "good" category; the only exception was "exterior paint." The farmhouses surveyed in the two southern states were most often judged to be "fair" or "poor." The only predominantly "good" element of the southern homes was the chimneys.

Four counties in South Carolina were surveyed as part of the 1934 study. One of these counties (York) was in the Piedmont and one (Orangeburg) was in the non-Piedmont area examined in the preceding chapter (table 9).

The houses in York County were slightly older than those in Orangeburg County. Whereas 24.3 percent of the houses in York County were more than fifty years old, only 8.9 percent of the farmhouses in Orangeburg County were this old. Even though York County contained more painted houses than did Orangeburg County, it contained many more log dwellings. Orangeburg County contained more one-story houses, but houses in both counties were partitioned into about the same average number of rooms.

An examination of farmhouse quality, however, indicates that the houses in York County were of higher quality than those in Orangeburg

Table 8

Farmhouse Quality, South Carolina, Georgia, Illinois, and Indiana, 1934, by Percentage

	Southern States								Northern States							
	South Carolina				Georgia				Illinois				Indiana			
	G	F	P	N*	G	F	P	N	G	F	P	N	G	F	P	N
Foundations	28.2	34.3	37.5	—	27.9	31.9	40.2	—	51.2	32.3	16.5	—	55.4	29.1	15.5	—
Exterior walls	30.9	38.2	30.9	—	32.3	42.3	25.4	—	56.8	32.6	10.6	—	63.3	28.2	8.5	—
Roofs	27.0	26.0	47.0	—	31.3	29.5	39.2	—	57.7	27.0	15.3	—	59.0	26.3	14.7	—
Chimneys	40.2	33.3	26.0	0.5	48.9	32.2	17.9	1.0	77.4	17.5	4.5	0.6	79.8	15.8	4.1	0.3
Door and windows	22.3	29.7	48.0	—	22.2	36.5	41.3	—	49.5	38.0	12.5	—	53.1	36.4	10.5	—
Screens	9.8	9.2	11.2	69.8	10.0	9.6	11.5	68.9	44.7	30.8	18.0	6.5	43.2	30.3	20.3	6.2
Exterior paint	4.0	4.7	9.5	81.8	4.3	6.4	12.4	76.9	27.0	35.3	27.1	10.6	25.5	28.9	32.8	12.8
Interior walls and ceilings	21.9	35.2	42.9	—	20.5	34.4	45.1	—	42.7	42.0	15.3	—	50.8	36.2	13.0	—
Floors	29.1	38.3	32.6	—	31.5	41.8	26.7	—	51.0	37.0	12.0	—	61.3	29.7	9.0	—
Stairs	5.0	2.8	1.1	91.1	3.4	2.1	1.1	93.4	47.8	19.3	4.7	28.2	62.5	12.3	2.8	22.4
Mean:	21.8	25.2	28.7		23.2	26.7	26.1		50.6	31.2	13.7		55.4	27.3	13.1	

Source: U.S. Department of Agriculture, Bureau of Home Economics, Farm-Housing Survey, pp. 20–23.

*G = good; F = fair; P = poor; N = none.

Table 9

Farm Housing, York and Orangeburg Counties, South Carolina, 1934, by Percentage

Characteristics	York County (n = 3,923)	Orangeburg County (n = 5,310)
<10 years old	8.1	10.7
10–24 years old	22.6	39.8
25–49 years old	45.0	40.6
>50 years old	24.3	8.9
Frame		
Unpainted	69.1	83.1
Painted	26.0	16.5
Stucco	–	–
Log	3.8	0.2
Brick	0.4	0.2
Stone	0.1	–
Concrete	–	–
One story	81.5	94.7
More than one story	18.5	5.3

Source: U.S. Department of Agriculture, Bureau of Home Economics, *Farm-Housing Survey*, pp. 4, 8.

County (table 10). When the percentages of the qualitative features are averaged, roughly equal percentages of "good," "fair," and "poor" houses exist in York County. A different pattern, however, appears for Orangeburg County, where most of the homes were judged to be "poor." This simple measure suggests that the farmhouses in York County were generally of slightly better quality than those in Orangeburg County.

A sample from only two counties is not sufficient to make reasonable qualitative assessments about the farm housing of South Carolina. Nonetheless, the obvious differences between the farmhouses in South Carolina and Georgia and those in Illinois and Indiana, and the quality of housing in two South Carolina counties generally supports the contention that southern tenant housing was substandard and inadequate.

While reasons for the poor quality of southern farm housing are complex, many scholars have reduced the complexity to a simple matter of skin color. Generally, black farmers inhabited homes of poorer quality than those of white farmers. Whereas black farmers composed 46.2 percent and 29.3 percent of the farm population of South Carolina and Georgia, respectively, the black farmers in Illinois and Indiana comprised only 0.2 percent and 0.5 percent of the total farm population in 1935.[59] This disparity in housing between blacks and whites in the North and the South was explained by some sociologists in terms of a "color line" that served to separate blacks and whites in the American South. Accordingly, the South was divided into two endogamous, or non-intermarrying, castes.

Sociologist W. Lloyd Warner and his students were the first American scholars to examine the castelike nature of southern society in any detail.[60] Warner used a rectangle divided by a diagonal line to represent the southern social order. The diagonal line, which Warner called the "caste line," separated the white "caste," placed symbolically on the top half of the rectangle, from the black "caste," located in the bottom half of the rectangle. Horizontal lines within each caste represented upper, middle, and lower classes. The opposing right triangles created by Warner's caste line illustrated that the small black upper class was on a horizontal social level with the white middle class. The white upper class was above all other classes.[61]

Some scholars accepted Warner's idea and adapted this caste/class concept to southern plantations. For example, in 1939 Edgar Thompson

Table 10

Farmhouse Quality, York and Orangeburg Counties, South Carolina, 1934, by Percentage

Characteristics	York County				Orangeburg County			
	G	F	P	N*	G	F	P	N
Foundations	32.0	40.3	27.7	–	22.4	28.3	49.3	–
Exterior walls	29.0	43.0	28.0	–	23.7	36.0	40.3	–
Roofs	33.8	28.3	37.9	–	19.5	21.9	58.6	–
Chimneys	45.5	32.3	21.1	1.1	32.0	34.6	32.9	0.5
Door and windows	24.5	35.5	40.0	–	16.4	19.0	64.6	–
Screens	12.1	10.6	11.3	66.0	9.7	6.4	10.5	73.4
Exterior paint	5.6	7.3	13.6	73.5	4.2	3.0	9.4	83.4
Interior walls and ceilings	29.2	40.3	30.5	–	15.9	25.9	58.2	–
Floors	31.4	42.7	25.9	–	23.7	34.0	42.3	–
Stairs	9.9	5.9	2.7	81.5	3.0	1.8	0.5	94.7
Mean:	25.3	28.6	23.9		17.1	21.1	36.7	

Source: U.S. Department of Agriculture, Bureau of Home Economics, *Farm-Housing Survey,* pp. 22–23.

*G = good; F = fair; P = poor; N = none.

wrote about the way in which plantation organization worked both to maintain the color line and to bring blacks and whites together occupationally.[62] In another study, published in 1942, Wilbert F. Moore and Robin M. Williams presented a model of the antebellum plantation that relied heavily on Warner's ideas.[63] Moore and Williams diagrammed plantation society as a triangle containing white and black castes separated by a diagonal caste line. The white caste contained four classes: large planters, small planters and merchants, yeomen farmers and artisans, and laborers and servants. The black caste contained three classes: free blacks, house slaves, and field slaves.

The idea that the American South contained color castes or quasi-castes has been rejected by most sociologists and anthropologists, though some still continue to use this term to describe southern society.[64] One by-product of this interest in the color caste system and its color line was that many sociologists turned their attention to southern tenancy as a complex labor system. Many of these scholars used combined notions about skin color and labor in fairly equal measure. The awareness that skin color and tenure status were related is perhaps demonstrated by the United States Census Bureau's first publication of tenure figures by color in 1925.[65]

An excellent analysis demonstrating the approach of uniting tenure with skin color is Arthur F. Raper's study of Greene and Macon counties, Georgia.[66] Raper used these counties to show that the homes of black farmers were generally smaller, less finished, and cruder than those of white farmers.

In the course of his study, however, Raper discovered an important fact of tenant housing: the homes of whites and blacks were more similar within tenure classes than across tenure classes according to skin color. That is, the homes of white sharecroppers were more like the homes of black sharecroppers than those of white owners. Just because a sharecropper was white did not ensure that he would live in a fine home. As Raper and a co-author would write in 1941, "Plantation owners do not have tenant houses for whites and tenant houses for Negroes—they have tenant houses, little cabins of two or three rooms usually built of a single thickness of rough boards."[67] Interestingly, this same conclusion had been reached in the early 1920s in a survey of 2,886 white farm families in New Hampshire, Vermont, Massachusetts, Connecticut, Kansas, Missouri, Iowa, Ohio, Kentucky, Alabama, and South Carolina (including two Piedmont counties, Greenwood and Newberry), where the finding was that owners lived in better housing than did tenants or hired men.[68]

Of the many good descriptions of tenant houses, few allow the exact tenure status of the inhabitants to be ascertained. An exception to this appears in James Agee and Walker Evans's wonderful book *Let Us Now Praise Famous Men*.[69] Agee and Evans described the typical white tenant farmer's home as a one-room unpainted shack. None of the houses inhabited by the three families interviewed by Agee could be described as adequate; nevertheless, subtle differences between them do appear in his comments. Careful reading reveals that one of the farmers interviewed was a sharecropper who worked on halves; the other two were share renters who worked a variation of the third-and-fourth system, with the landlord receiving one-third of their cotton and one-fourth of their corn. None of these tenant families owned their house or land, but one share-renting family owned one mule, and the other owned two mules. Both families owned their own tools. Even though the homes of all three families were similar, the share renter who owned two mules lived in the only house that had double walls and a fireplace large enough to provide adequate heat. This house could "as easily as not be the home of an owner at the bottom of the owning class." The other two houses, that of the sharecropper and that of the share renter who owned one mule, would never belong to the small owner, "no matter how small."[70]

That owners would have had better houses than sharecroppers is not surprising, because wealth and tenure status were obviously highly interrelated. Under ideal circumstances, the higher one's position on the agricultural ladder, the higher the opportunity to acquire wealth. This simple fact of economics seemingly has been demonstrated many times. For example, in a 1913 study of the Yazoo-Mississippi Delta, researchers found that the average income after expenditures was $333 for sharecroppers, $398 for share renters, and $478 for cash renters. These figures show how wealth and the agricultural ladder were related, but unfortunately, they are somewhat oversimplified and misleading. A further examination of the figures reveals that members of each non-owning tenure group—sharecroppers, share renters, and cash tenants—earned from less than $10 to more than $1,000 annually. Some sharecroppers earned more than some cash renters. The highest number of sharecroppers (32.1 percent) and share renters (18.4 percent) were in the $300 to $399 annual income range; the highest number of cash renters (16.9 percent) were in the $200 to $299 income range.

Even though it seems odd that the median income of sharecroppers and share renters would be more than for cash renters, the real difference between the tenure groups is more apparent in the upper incomes. For example, 10.9 percent of the sharecroppers, 26.6 percent of the share renters, and 37.0 percent of the cash renters made more than $500. This distribution is predictable, but what is truly surprising is that two sharecroppers (0.5 percent) and four share renters (3.0 percent) made more than $1,000 each and that thirteen (4.4 percent) of the cash renters made less than $100.[71] In short, these statistics, some predictable, others not, demonstrate the complex relationship between tenure and wealth and illustrate the pitfalls in making gross generalizations about this relationship.

A survey conducted in 1934 upheld these earlier findings. In this study of the entire cotton South, the average net income was reported as $2,313 for owners, $180 for wage laborers, $312 for sharecroppers, $417 for share tenants, and $354 for cash renters. In the Upper Piedmont Region—including the South Carolina Piedmont and parts of North Carolina, Georgia, and Alabama—the net income was $1,424 for owners, $104 for sharecroppers, and $170 for share renters.[72] The average value of owners' homes in all seven cotton states surveyed was $1,188 for owners ($815 for whites; $373 for blacks) and $625 for tenants ($380 for whites; $245 for blacks). In South Carolina, the average owner's home was valued at $1,431 ($1,083 for whites; $348 for blacks), and the average value of the tenant's home was $692 ($454 for whites; $238 for blacks).[73] These figures show not only a relationship between housing and tenure status but also an appreciable difference between the homes of blacks and whites.

More exact estimates of the value of farm buildings can be gathered from the published agricultural censuses. The three censuses completed between 1900 and 1920 contain figures for the accumulated value of farm buildings in all counties in the United States.[74] The values for the South Carolina Piedmont are presented in table 11.

In 1900 the average value of farm buildings in the South Carolina Piedmont ranged from about $145.00 to $245.48. A ranking of counties according to these values from lowest value to highest shows that

Table 11

Farm Building Values, South Carolina Piedmont, 1900–1920,
Ranked by County

1900		1910		1920	
County	*Dollars*	*County*	*Dollars*	*County*	*Dollars*
Oconee	144.99	Union	284.31	McCormick	659.62
Union	162.50	Fairfield	296.43	Fairfield	670.33
Pickens	164.40	Abbeville	311.20	Union	752.11
Cherokee	164.69	Oconee	325.51	McCormick/Abbeville	756.98
Abbeville	165.27	Cherokee	336.19	Cherokee	786.71
Fairfield	168.77	York	373.72	York	789.77
Spartanburg	178.75	Chester	385.67	Newberry	792.76
Greenwood	179.39	Laurens	391.99	Chester	797.33
Laurens	197.81	Pickens	394.53	Abbeville	820.40
Chester	200.78	Spartanburg	407.26	Laurens	830.71
Anderson	201.51	Newberry	424.61	Oconee	855.93
Greenville	203.39	Greenville	427.27	Spartanburg	967.44
York	210.61	Greenwood	435.28	Greenville	983.91
Newberry	245.48	Anderson	525.04	Pickens	1,034.92
				Anderson	1,198.96
				Greenwood	1,247.07
Mean:	184.88		379.93		879.20

Sources: Census of Agriculture, 1900, 1910, and 1920.

Note: To obtain an average value of farm buildings per farm within each county, the values listed in the censuses for each county were divided by the total number of farms.

Abbeville County appears fifth from the bottom (table 11 and figure 9). In 1910 the values ranged from $284.31 to $525.04. Abbeville County ranks third from the bottom. In the next decade, the farm building values range from more than $659 to $1,247. Abbeville County appears in the middle of this ranking. The 1920 figures imply that the farm building values in Abbeville County rose substantially relative to the other counties. This change, however, is an illusion. The relative rank of Abbeville County rises only because the housing in McCormick County, created in 1916, was computed separately for the first time in 1920. When the values for McCormick County, a county that obviously contained poor farm housing, and Abbeville County are combined, this combined county ranks third from the bottom just as in 1910. It would seem, then, judging by reported farm building values, that the farm housing in Abbeville County was slightly below average within the South Carolina Piedmont.

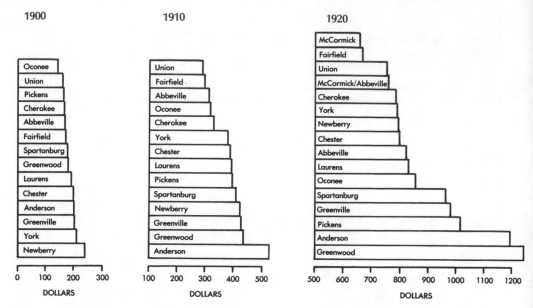

Figure 9. Farm building values, South Carolina Piedmont, 1900–1920, ranked by county.

It is interesting to note the growing differentiation between the value of the houses on both ends of the scale. Whereas the difference between the least valuable houses (in Oconee County) and the most valuable houses (in Newberry) in 1900 is small, this difference is great in 1920, when the houses in Greenwood County are valued at almost double those of McCormick County (figure 9).

The censuses unfortunately do not provide details about the relationship between tenure, skin color, and farm housing in the South Carolina Piedmont. The 1925 and 1930 censuses, however, do provide descriptive farm value statistics by tenure and by skin color.[75] Although these figures are presented with the building and the land values combined, they are nonetheless instructive (table 12).

In 1925 the value of land and buildings for Piedmont white owners ranged from almost $3,397 to just over $6,722. The land and building values for black owners was considerably less, ranging from $1,577 to $3,511. As would be expected, land and building values were lower for tenant farmers. The property of white cash renters ranged from more than $1,029 to more than $4,442. As was true of black owners, black cash

Table 12

Average Land and Building Values for Individual Farmers, South Carolina Piedmont Counties, 1925, by Race

	Owner		Cash		Share	
	White	Black	White	Black	White	Black
Abbeville	$5,371.19	$2,118.87	$2,145.22	$ 768.89	$1,072.45	$1,681.54
Anderson	6,722.19	3,511.14	3,211.00	1,091.67	1,725.69	1,994.53
Cherokee	4,687.79	2,416.13	3,271.43	2,473.33	2,322.74	2,197.14
Chester	5,464.29	2,147.14	2,244.55	619.17	1,428.43	987.68
Fairfield	6,134.37	1,977.02	2,220.00	1,099.52	939.99	752.47
Greenville	5,179.20	3,043.67	4,442.76	2,858.33	2,025.30	2,313.12
Greenwood	5,521.17	2,116.38	3,571.45	1,695.48	1,536.67	1,434.94
Laurens	4,569.20	2,302.07	2,077.57	643.64	1,510.98	1,235.81
McCormick	3,686.07	1,666.54	1,029.55	637.50	815.34	661.52
Newberry	4,721.45	1,577.13	2,341.25	1,509.04	1,918.64	959.24
Oconee	3,704.36	2,307.37	1,692.10	1,625.00	1,585.39	1,701.65
Pickens	3,396.96	2,387.65	2,456.55	1,275.00	1,890.49	2,113.38
Spartanburg	5,508.88	3,186.94	3,617.92	2,750.00	2,589.90	2,140.59
Union	5,103.06	2,295.73	3,160.00	530.00	2,092.03	1,166.25
York	5,471.92	1,997.33	3,514.85	2,441.36	2,465.11	1,551.10
Range:	3,396.96	1,577.13	1,029.55	530.00	815.34	661.52
	6,722.19	3,511.14	4,442.76	2,858.33	2,589.90	2,313.12
Mean:	5,016.14	2,336.74	2,733.08	1,467.86	1,727.94	1,526.06
Combined Mean:	3,676.44		2,100.47		1,627.00	

Source: 1930 Census of Agriculture.

renters had property valued at about half that of white cash renters. Their property values ranged from $530 to just over $2,858. The property of white sharecroppers ranged from more than $815 to almost $2,590; for black sharecroppers, the values ranged from more than $661 to $2,313.

The values for 1930 can be similarly arranged (table 13). The land and building values for white owners ranged from $3,282 to more than $5,428; for black owners, the land and building values ranged from more than $1,358 to more than $2,821. White cash renters' land and building values ranged from more than $2,104 to almost $4,250; for black cash renters, the values ranged from more than $709 to $2,626. The land and building values for sharecroppers ranged from almost $825 to just over $2,262, and from more than $735 to almost $2,108.

These figures seem to suggest that the poorest farmhouses inhabited by whites were located in Pickens County for owners, and McCormick County for cash renters and sharecroppers. The best houses for these tenure classes were generally found in Anderson County for owners, and Greenville County for cash renters and sharecroppers. The best homes for black owners were located in Anderson County and for cash renters and sharecroppers in Greenville County; the worst homes were in Newberry, Union, and McCormick counties for owners, cash renters, and sharecroppers, respectively. The best housing for owners of both colors was found in Anderson County, and the best housing for cash renters was in Greenville County. The worst housing for sharecroppers was found in McCormick County.

In 1930 the worst homes for both white and black owners and for white and black sharecroppers were found in Abbeville County. Greenville County seems to have been, at least in an abstract statistical sense, a good place for black farmers to live. The most valuable homes for blacks of all tenure groups were located there. Fairfield County was seemingly a good place for white owners, but not equally good for white cash renters.

A further examination of these values proves enlightening in a purely economic sense. When the 1925 mean values for each tenure group are compared by color, the difference between white and black owners was $2,679.40, between white and black cash renters, $1,265.22, and between white and black sharecroppers, $201.88. This pattern of decreased value was repeated five years later when the difference between

Table 13

Average Land and Building Values for Individual Farmers, South Carolina Piedmont Counties, 1930, by Race

	Owner		Cash		Share	
	White	Black	White	Black	White	Black
Abbeville	$3,282.00	$1,358.46	$2,201.50	$ 913.93	$ 824.93	$ 735.28
Anderson	4,383.90	1,997.35	3,376.37	1,078.75	1,482.36	1,375.27
Cherokee	3,609.14	1,949.98	2,314.73	1,050.00	1,836.03	1,662.03
Chester	4,526.17	1,669.49	2,198.70	709.50	1,474.96	851.34
Fairfield	5,428.51	1,484.41	2,104.45	826.49	2,222.92	820.80
Greenville	4,432.59	2,821.56	3,723.08	2,626.00	2,171.57	2,107.80
Greenwood	4,464.12	1,894.61	2,670.51	1,384.89	1,834.44	1,130.78
Laurens	3,940.54	2,012.48	3,062.40	1,361.54	1,531.50	1,234.93
McCormick	4,048.89	1,459.63	2,281.39	1,884.56	1,417.80	814.94
Newberry	4,238.41	1,674.71	2,323.05	1,290.54	1,755.16	1,045.48
Oconee	3,311.62	2,134.33	2,425.40	1,075.00	1,428.26	1,407.14
Pickens	3,433.22	2,032.07	2,309.40	2,355.00	1,520.88	1,508.25
Spartanburg	4,356.98	2,666.38	4,249.62	1,910.00	2,262.34	1,993.04
Union	4,066.70	1,710.35	4,190.37	1,822.19	1,880.10	1,334.14
York	4,112.48	1,775.98	2,124.92	765.48	2,080.79	1,371.50
Range:	3,282.00	1,358.46	2,104.45	709.50	824.93	735.28
	5,428.51	2,821.56	4,249.62	2,626.00	2,262.34	2,107.80
Mean:	4,109.02	1,909.45	2,770.39	1,403.59	1,714.94	1,292.85
Combined Mean:	3,009.24		2,086.99		1,503.90	

Source: 1930 Census of Agriculture.

white and black owners was $2,199.57, between white and black cash renters, $1,366.80, and between white and black sharecroppers, $422.09. These figures show not only that blacks were associated with land and houses of lower value than were whites but that the differences between the tenure groups lessened as one descended the agricultural ladder. Whereas in both 1925 and 1930 cash renters were associated with land and buildings having a value of approximately one-half that of owners, the values associated with sharecroppers were much less than half those associated with cash renters (figure 10). In both years white owners, cash renters, and sharecroppers are arranged in a steplike fashion according to land and building values, but black owners, cash renters, and sharecroppers are relatively level. Thus, the houses occupied by black owners might not have been too dissimilar from those occupied by black sharecroppers and cash renters, while clear distinctions existed between the homes of white owners and those of white sharecroppers.

The apparent housing differences between black and white agriculturalists in the South Carolina Piedmont make it possible to suggest that the agricultural ladder (that is, wealth accumulation through farming) was more accessible to white farmers than to black farmers. The differences in land and building values between white owners and white sharecroppers perhaps provided tangible evidence of the agricultural ladder. The relative similarity between black tenure groups may represent their exclusion from the ladder. In other words, black sharecroppers may not have had many purely economic incentives for climbing the agricultural ladder.

To summarize, plantation blacks generally lived in houses of lower quality, smaller size, and less secure construction than plantation whites. In addition, the quality of houses generally decreased as one moved down the agricultural ladder, regardless of skin color, although the differences among white farmers were more distinct than those among black farmers. These distinctions were seen first hand by sociologists who worked among the South's plantation tenants in the 1920s, 1930s, and early 1940s.

These differences between tenure groups should be readily recognizable in archaeological deposits. One archaeologist has made the claim that the archaeological deposits left by white tenants can be distinguished from those of black tenants.[76] Unfortunately, such is not the

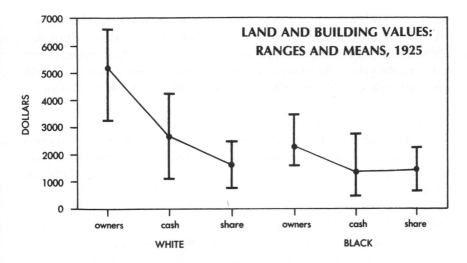

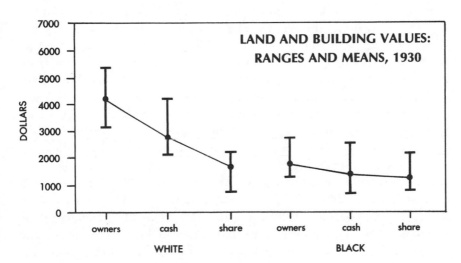

Figure 10. Land and building values, South Carolina Piedmont counties, 1925 and 1930, by race. The dots represent means.

case, and as with most aspects of plantation tenancy, the situation is not so straightforward. Rather, a practice called shifting has serious implications for the archaeological recognition of ethnicity on southern tenant farms.

The term *shifting* refers to the relocation of farmers from one farm to another. Shifting can occur between regions, between individual farms, or between farms located on the same plantation. Shifting is not synonymous with migration. *Migration* refers to a change in residence from one area to another or from a rural environment to an urban one. Shifting, like migration, was common immediately after the Civil War, as black freedmen started the search for freedom and as displaced whites began to look for a place to settle.

The presence of shifting in a state, region, or plantation means that any particular farmhouse could have been occupied by many different tenant families in only a few years. As a result, knowledge of shifting patterns is crucial to understanding plantation housing during the postbellum period, particularly for archaeologists.

Statements about shifting among freed black farmers are not abundant, but they do occur. For example, when speaking specifically about shifting, Mose Evans of Arkansas said that he became a sharecropper after having been a share renter for some time. During all his experience in tenancy, the longest he had worked for anyone was twelve years. Before this lengthy stay he rented from different landlords for six years, four years, two years, and then for three years. Another tenant from Arkansas, a share renter, said that her family moved only three times and that they stayed at one location for fifteen years.[77]

Although many freed slaves mentioned the length of time they stayed with their former masters after emancipation, few talked specifically about shifting. As such, the best information derives from studies that explicitly mention shifting.

In an early study of shifting conducted in the first years of the twentieth century in Dane County, Wisconsin, Richard T. Ely and Charles J. Galpin discovered that between 1909 and 1918, 429 tenants had changed their residences. The agricultural census compiled in 1910 shows that Dane County had 1,572 tenants in 1910; this means that 27.3 percent moved at least once. Of these shifting tenants, 253 (59.0 percent) shifted within their community. The remaining 176 tenants (41.0 percent) shifted to and from other communities.[78] Thus, even in the North, shifting was a fact of rural life.

A more pertinent study of tenant shifting was conducted in the South in 1920.[79] This study of ninety-three selected plantation counties revealed that 48.3 percent of all "share tenants" (share renters, share-cash renters, and share croppers) had lived on their then-current farm for less than two years, 33.5 percent had lived there for from two to four years, and only 18.2 percent had lived there for more than five years. Among "cash tenants" (cash and standing renters), 30.0 percent had lived on their present farm less than two years, 33.8 percent from two to four years, and 36.2 percent for longer than five years. A comparison of blacks and whites revealed that 53.2 percent of the whites had lived in their homes for less than two years, whereas 39.6 percent of the black tenants had lived in their homes for this period. Most white tenants (30.5 percent) had lived in their current homes for one year; most black tenants (35.1 percent), from two to four years. Eleven percent of the blacks surveyed had lived in their current homes for more than ten years, whereas only 6.9 percent of the white tenants had lived in their houses for that long.

A similar study of shifting was presented by Raper in his study of 1,468 rural families in Greene and Macon counties, Georgia, during the early 1930s. Raper also found that plantation blacks tended to live longer in one place than did plantation whites. Of the white families, 23.1 percent had lived in their homes for one year; 31.9 percent of the black families had lived in their homes for this length of time. And, whereas 21.4 percent of the whites had lived in their homes for more than fifteen years, only 10.0 percent of the blacks had lived in their homes for this long. Sharecroppers and cash renters of both colors had lived in their houses for much shorter lengths than did owners. Nonetheless, the median length of stay for whites was 2.4 years for sharecroppers, 2.9 years for cash renters, and 11.6 years for owners. The median lengths of residence for blacks was 2.8 years for sharecroppers, 3.7 years for cash renters, and 11.9 years for owners. These statistics, however, are puzzling because they contradict Raper's earlier statement that blacks were more mobile than whites. In fact, his statement that "length of residence . . . varies with tenure class and farm conditions rather than with race" seems more accurate than his earlier assessment that skin color was one determining factor for length of residence.[80] This conclusion that tenure was more important than skin color in affecting length of farm residence was later upheld by E. A. Schuler's study in the 1930s. In this study, Schuler found that the shortest period of farm occupancy occurred within the lowest tenure classes, regardless of skin color.[81] No appreciable difference between white and black tenants was noted.

A further investigation of shifting was presented by Woofter and others in their study of cotton plantation farms occupied in 1934. Their findings revealed that the average time spent on a farm was 8.2 years. The average among black farmers was 8.6 years, but was only 5.9 years among whites. When examined by tenure classes, the length of residence increased from wage hands to cash renters. In each class, blacks lived in their houses longer than whites. The average length of residence for wage hands was 6.5 years (4.3 years for whites, 6.7 years for blacks); for sharecroppers, 6.9 years (4.7 years for whites, 7.3 years for blacks); for share renters, 11.2 years (7.2 years for whites, 12.6 years for blacks); and for cash renters, 12.8 years (9.2 years for whites, 13.7 years for blacks). This study added weight to the idea that white tenants were more mobile than were black tenants.[82]

Included in the larger study by Woofter and others was an analysis of shifting among 1,830 farmers in South Carolina in 1933. This examination revealed that most of these farmers had moved an average of 4.3 times since 1904. No major difference was obvious among whites and blacks; whites moved an average of 4.2 times in 28.6 years, whereas blacks moved an average of 4.3 times in 28.1 years. The only apparent difference was between tenure groups: white tenants moved an average of 5.6 times in 24.4 years; white owners moved an average of 2.9 times in 32.9 years. Black tenants moved an average of 4.6 times in 27.5 years; black owners moved an average of 3.0 times in 34.6 years.

Further analysis by Woofter and others revealed that white owners who had become owners by climbing the agricultural ladder had made 38.5 percent of their total moves as tenants, even though they had spent only 18.0 percent of their working lives as tenants. Black owners, who had spent an average of 25.3 years of their working lives as tenants, made 42.5 percent of their moves then. On the other hand, white tenants, who had spent 74.7 percent of their working years as tenants, made 77.4 percent of their moves then. Similarly, black tenants, who had spent 84.8 percent of their working years as tenants, made 81.4 percent of their moves then.[83] These statistics suggest that owners, whether white or black, tended to move less frequently than they had as tenants. Conversely, tenants of both colors moved frequently.

Patterns of shifting in South Carolina, and, more specifically, in the South Carolina Piedmont, can be seen by using figures appearing in the agricultural census of 1935 (table 14).[84] During this census, enumerators apparently asked farmers how long they had lived on their present farm.

Table 14

Years on Farm, South Carolina Piedmont, 1935, Owners and Tenants, by County

	Owners								
	<1	1	2	3	4	5–9	10–14	>14	Total
Abbeville	47 (6.6)*	30 (4.2)	28 (3.9)	27 (3.8)	36 (5.0)	104 (14.5)	101 (14.1)	344 (48.0)	717
Anderson	150 (7.9)	69 (3.6)	75 (3.9)	57 (3.0)	94 (4.9)	303 (15.9)	270 (14.2)	888 (46.6)	1,906
Cherokee	92 (10.3)	31 (3.5)	35 (3.9)	47 (5.3)	39 (4.4)	144 (16.2)	125 (14.0)	378 (42.4)	891
Chester	54 (6.5)	24 (2.9)	28 (3.4)	22 (2.6)	38 (4.6)	117 (14.0)	131 (15.7)	421 (50.4)	835
Fairfield	46 (6.9)	29 (4.3)	25 (3.7)	20 (3.0)	24 (3.6)	95 (14.2)	83 (12.4)	348 (51.9)	670
Greenville	226 (8.6)	95 (3.6)	100 (3.8)	93 (3.5)	149 (5.7)	427 (16.2)	449 (17.0)	1,095 (41.6)	2,634
Greenwood	49 (6.4)	31 (4.0)	40 (5.2)	43 (5.6)	56 (7.3)	108 (14.0)	110 (14.3)	333 (43.2)	770
Laurens	100 (8.8)	40 (3.5)	45 (3.9)	43 (3.8)	91 (8.0)	178 (15.6)	149 (13.0)	496 (43.4)	1,142
McCormick	18 (5.5)	15 (4.6)	15 (4.6)	17 (5.2)	18 (5.5)	48 (14.6)	45 (13.7)	152 (46.3)	328
Newberry	68 (6.5)	28 (2.7)	41 (3.9)	32 (3.1)	68 (6.5)	150 (14.4)	138 (13.2)	517 (49.6)	1,042
Oconee	79 (6.5)	70 (5.8)	38 (3.1)	42 (3.5)	53 (4.4)	167 (13.8)	182 (15.1)	576 (47.7)	1,207

(continued)

Table 14 (Continued)

Owners

	<1	1	2	3	4	5–9	10–14	>14	Total
Pickens	93 (7.1)	45 (3.5)	57 (4.4)	46 (3.5)	79 (6.1)	215 (16.5)	203 (15.6)	564 (43.3)	1,302
Spartanburg	183 (8.2)	62 (2.8)	91 (4.1)	91 (4.1)	135 (6.0)	380 (17.0)	340 (15.2)	958 (42.8)	2,240
Union	54 (8.7)	31 (5.0)	27 (4.4)	24 (3.9)	35 (5.7)	96 (15.5)	85 (13.8)	266 (43.0)	618
York	74 (6.1)	39 (3.2)	57 (4.7)	50 (4.1)	68 (5.6)	201 (16.6)	184 (15.2)	539 (44.5)	1,212
	1,333 (7.6)	639 (3.6)	702 (4.0)	654 (3.7)	983 (5.6)	2,733 (15.6)	2,595 (14.8)	7,875 (45.0)	17,514

Tenants

	<1	1	2	3	4	5+	Total
Abbeville	827 (37.3)	239 (10.8)	185 (8.4)	155 (7.0)	161 (7.3)	648 (29.3)	2,215
Anderson	2,225 (41.2)	713 (13.2)	407 (7.5)	344 (6.4)	395 (7.3)	1,323 (24.5)	5,407
Cherokee	1,001 (45.4)	288 (13.0)	219 (9.9)	135 (6.1)	133 (6.0)	431 (19.5)	2,207
Chester	536 (28.4)	182 (9.6)	189 (10.0)	143 (7.6)	145 (7.7)	693 (36.7)	1,880
Fairfield	328 (22.4)	148 (10.1)	111 (7.6)	111 (7.6)	119 (8.1)	649 (44.3)	1,466
Greenville	1,787 (40.7)	494 (11.2)	456 (10.4)	301 (6.9)	338 (7.7)	1,017 (23.2)	4,393

Greenwood	553 (30.4)	190 (10.4)	178 (9.8)	149 (8.2)	213 (11.7)	539 (29.6)	1,822
Laurens	1,177 (37.9)	351 (11.3)	251 (8.1)	216 (7.0)	263 (8.5)	848 (27.3)	3,106
McCormick	371 (28.1)	110 (8.3)	126 (9.5)	97 (7.3)	140 (10.6)	478 (36.2)	1,322
Newberry	611 (29.2)	194 (9.3)	225 (10.8)	170 (8.1)	174 (8.3)	715 (34.2)	2,089
Oconee	1,670 (54.9)	269 (8.8)	260 (8.5)	169 (5.6)	183 (6.0)	492 (16.2)	3,043
Pickens	1,055 (49.3)	253 (11.8)	203 (9.5)	120 (5.6)	126 (5.9)	385 (18.0)	2,142
Spartanburg	2,302 (40.1)	666 (11.6)	515 (9.0)	381 (6.6)	450 (7.8)	1,422 (24.8)	5,736
Union	602 (32.0)	234 (12.4)	163 (8.7)	120 (6.4)	156 (8.3)	607 (32.3)	1,882
York	1,239 (34.6)	354 (9.9)	375 (10.5)	268 (7.5)	345 (9.6)	997 (27.9)	3,578
	15,748 (39.0)	4,503 (11.1)	3,674 (9.1)	2,736 (6.8)	3,196 (7.9)	10,551 (26.1)	40,408

Source: 1935 Census of Agriculture.
*Numbers in parentheses are percentages.

These census figures are presented for owners and for tenants, but not for the more exact tenure classes or skin color groups. The figures for owners range from less than one year to more than fifteen years; the figures for tenants range from less than one year to more than five years.

An examination of the statistics presented reveals that 75.4 percent of the 17,514 owners in the South Carolina Piedmont included in the census had lived in their then-current homes for at least five years. Only 15.2 percent had resided in their homes for two years or less (figure 11). None of the counties in the Piedmont deviated greatly from this pattern. In Abbeville County, 76.6 percent of the owners had lived in their homes for at least fifteen years; only 14.7 percent had lived in their houses for two years or less.

The figures presented for the 40,408 tenants living in the South Carolina Piedmont show that 39.0 percent had lived in their then-current homes for less than one year; 26.1 percent had occupied their homes for at least five years (figure 11). The residence pattern for Abbeville County is fairly consistent with this pattern in that 37.3 percent of the tenants had lived in their homes for less than one year, and 29.3 percent had lived there for at least five years. This bimodal pattern with large percentages of tenants on both ends of the scale, however, did not appear in all of the Piedmont counties. For example, in four of the five counties located in the northwestern part of the region—Cherokee, Greenville, Oconee, and Pickens—the percentage of tenants who had lived in their homes for less than one year was greater than that of all others. These tenants accounted for 45.4 percent, 40.7 percent, 54.9 percent, and 49.3 percent of all of the tenants in those counties, respectively. Conversely, in four counties—Chester, Fairfield, McCormick, and Newberry—the percentage of tenants who had lived in their homes for less than one year was relatively small (28.4 percent in Chester, 22.4 percent in Fairfield, 28.1 percent in McCormick, and 29.2 percent in Newberry).

One reason for the high percentage of short-term, or frequently shifting, tenants might be the high percentage of white farmers in Cherokee, Greenville, Oconee, and Pickens counties, where whites comprised 69.1 percent, 71.9 percent, 84.2 percent, and 87.8 percent of the farm population, respectively. By the same token, Chester, Fairfield, and McCormick counties contained black farm populations of 68.2 percent, 75.7 percent, and 70.3 percent, respectively. Blacks in Newberry County only slightly outnumbered whites, comprising 53.5 percent of the population.

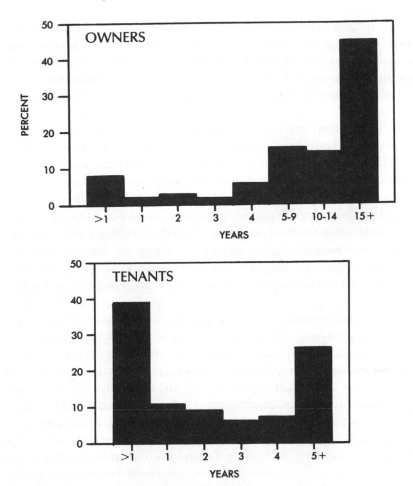

Figure 11. Years on farm, South Carolina Piedmont, 1935, owners and tenants, by percentage.

Ethnicity is only a partial explanation of shifting, because other counties in the Piedmont share the black-to-white population proportions found in the high-shifting counties. These counties do not contain an unusually large percentage of tenants who either move frequently or stayed on the same farm for a long time. For example, in Spartanburg County, where whites comprised 69.3 percent of the total farm population, only 40.1 percent of the tenants had lived in their homes for less than one year. Nonetheless, even though such deviations do occur, the correlation between the racial composition of the population and the frequency of tenant shifting does seem to have been fairly consistent.

At any rate, it seems logical that the homes of owners would be better maintained than would those of tenants. This distinction, however, is not due to some character flaw in tenants, but results from the simple fact that tenants did not own their homes. Tenants had to purchase the necessities of life with what little cash they received after settling with the owners. After buying those essentials, some tenants undoubtedly made a few somewhat frivolous purchases rather than spend all of their cash on window screens or roofing material for homes they did not own and were likely to leave anyway.

The assumption that all tenants lived in small homes while all owners lived in big houses, however, is not necessarily correct. Raper's report of a plantation "big house" inhabited by a black tenant family belies the idea that a consistent correlation exists between house size and tenure status. The particular house mentioned in the report was a large, white two-story house with two large brick fireplaces and a two-story front porch supported by five square pillars. Although this home did not have the outward appearance of a tenant's home, a black tenant family lived in a few of the rooms on the first floor. Similarly, Raper's reference to a small, unpainted house, with a T-shaped floor plan and two brick and stone chimneys, illustrates the fallacy of relating housing with tenure class because of shifting. This home was originally owned by a white owner who had lost it to creditors. After the owner lost the house, three black tenant families and two white tenant families lived there.[85] This house was occupied on the basis of availability and not tenure status or racial affiliation.

The presence of shifting in the postbellum plantation South presents a significant problem for historical archaeologists. To make accurate interpretations about the tenure status of the people who once inhabited a house site that is today a pile of broken artifacts or a few scattered building fragments, archaeologists generally rely on "focus" and "visibility"; both can be affected by tenant shifting. *Focus* refers to the degree to which the remains of a past building—postholes, walls, fireplace hearths, and so on—represent the building that once stood there. *Visibility* refers to the actual physical remains at a building site.[86] Building remains can have any combination of focus and visibility. A house with a brick fireplace hearth and a stone foundation has both high focus and high visibility. A corncrib made of posts might have high focus if the postholes are distinct and neatly arranged when discovered during excavation, but it would have low visibility because the postholes would not be apparent until they were completely uncovered and their pattern understood.

The kinds of houses inhabited by postbellum tenants have various levels of focus and visibility. A wage laborer's house with a stick-and-mud chimney and log walls might have both low focus and low visibility; a well-constructed home belonging to an owner, on the other hand, would most likely have both high focus and visibility.[87]

Shifting affects focus and visibility because a house that has been altered or remodeled with each new occupant can have low focus even if it has high visibility. In addition, the frequent habitation of a single house by families with different tenure arrangements will reduce the focus of each preceding family's occupation. If a particular house is first occupied by sharecroppers and then by cash renters, the cash renters can seriously alter and sometimes even erase the archaeological evidence of the sharecroppers. When this sequence of occupation is lengthened, the focus of the archaeological deposits is even further reduced. For example, the house shown by Raper to have been occupied by six families in ten years—one white owner family, three black tenant families, and two white tenant families—would have low focus. If disturbed after abandonment, its stone chimney and pilings might also give it low visibility.[88] The historical archaeologist excavating this site would probably have a difficult task separating the deposits of the individual families. Because each tenant family lived in this house for only a short time, the archaeological deposits would be thin and difficult to differentiate.

The problems with focus and visibility apply equally to material possessions, which when broken, lost, or consciously thrown away, become the archaeologist's artifacts. Of the many kinds of material possessions available during the period from 1865 to 1925, two kinds are considered here: home furnishings and personal items.

Comments made about the antebellum period—both by freed slaves and by nonslaves—can be used to provide information about the kinds of home furnishings wage earners and other newly freed plantation tenants had available directly after the war. Freed slaves' memories of the house furnishings they had as slaves were remarkably similar. This uniformity is not surprising, for a quick perusal of the extant narratives reveals that slave homes did not contain many furnishings. One owner from Mississippi, expressing his opinion in the New York *Tribune* in 1854, said that this was because "Negroes have no need of furniture."[89]

Most freed slaves who discussed the furnishings in their homes first mentioned their beds and mattresses. Their comments reveal that most slave beds were constructed with one side nailed to the wall and supported by either one or two legs. In Mississippi the beds with one leg were referred to as "one legged aggies," and those with two legs were called "two legged aggies." Others referred to their beds as "jinnies." A mattress was usually a sack stuffed with hay or corn shucks, and supported on the bed by ropes.[90] On at least one plantation, a mat of white oak splits was placed over the ropes to protect the mattress and to make it smooth.[91]

The frequent mention of mattresses by freed slaves implies that this item was an important one; in some ways, a focal point of the semifixed-feature space within the small and sparsely furnished cabin. Mattresses seemed to be an important aspect of plantation housing even into the twentieth century. Tenant farmer Ed Brown said, "every time you come up in the world you got a better mattress." Thus, a hierarchy of mattresses occurred within the agricultural ladder. According to Brown, wage hands usually had mattresses stuffed with straw or crabgrass. Sharecroppers, who could hold back a little cotton from their landlords, usually had mattresses made of unginned cotton and had to tolerate the feel of the cotton boll shells through the ticking. Standing renters and cash renters, who theoretically controlled the disposition of their cotton, most likely had mattresses of ginned cotton. This kind of mattress was the best, and was the kind for which Brown's wife strived.[92]

Some slaves apparently had pillows made of dirty cotton and hay; others had none. As former slave Georgia Baker, from Taliaferro County, Georgia, said in 1938, "Us never knowed what pillows was." For coverings, slaves commonly used quilts and coverlets made from scraps of old clothing by females who were too old to work in the fields.[93]

The only other furniture in the slave house, and presumably within the home of the early free wage earner as well, were simple stools or chairs. Fugitive slave Charles Ball said that the only furniture in one slave cabin consisted of "a few blocks of wood for seats" and "a short bench, made of a pine board, which served as a table." Another former slave remarked that his family used homemade chairs with bottoms made of rye splits, oak splits, or cane and that the preferred ones were those made out of rye splits. Some also used chairs with cowhide seats.[94]

As is true of the houses of the period, a gap exists in our knowledge about tenant house furnishings between 1865 and the 1920s and 1930s.

This gap is partly filled by Atwater and Woods's description of the interior of a tenant's cabin in the mid-1890s. Their description suggests that the legal transition from slavery to tenancy was not manifest in home furnishings. In each cabin they examined, Atwater and Woods found a bedstead, a corn shuck mattress, and a patchwork quilt; a wooden cupboard containing a few dishes; a wooden chest or trunk containing food and clothing; a simple pine table; and a few homemade chairs.[95]

Similar descriptions were provided in the 1920s and 1930s when rural sociologists entered the homes of the South's tenants. For example, a study of 2,886 white farm families in the 1920s revealed that the average amount spent on furnishings was $40.20 per family.[96] The expenditures are not presented in a manner that is conducive to further analysis, but they do suggest the amount of money spent by some farmers for home furnishings during the early part of the twentieth century.

Home furnishings were mentioned by Raper in his study of Greene and Macon counties, Georgia. He notes that in some tenant homes "some of the beds [were] made by nailing rough planks to the wall" in a manner reminiscent of former slave beds. According to Raper, even though black tenants generally had fewer household furnishings than did white tenants, they still had more furnishings than landless whites. And, while owners of both colors tended to invest their surplus money in land, Raper suggests that black tenants tended to spend their cash on household goods, fine clothing, and automobiles. Of the black families studied, Raper reports that 82 percent of them owned dressers and bureaus, 55 percent owned sewing machines, 23 percent owned pianos or organs, 19 percent owned phonographs, and 15 percent owned ranges.[97]

When Margaret Jarman Hagood conducted her study of white tenant farm women during the 1930s, she found that the furniture inside the 254 homes she visited could be easily listed. The kitchens she visited usually contained a wood stove or range, a table covered with oilcloth, a food safe, a worktable, and an occasional closet or cabinet for the dishes. In the combination sitting room–bedroom, Hagood usually found one or two double beds, a sewing machine, a dresser, several chairs, and sometimes a table, radio, record player, or organ. In the home of a family with children, a cradle could be found in any of the rooms. In general, she reported, the interiors of the tenant homes were characterized by a lack of color and a general drabness.[98]

The farm-housing survey of 1934 provides important information on farmhouse interiors.[99] These statistics reinforce others' comments about

Table 15

Farmhouse Furnishings, South Carolina, Georgia, Illinois, and Indiana, 1934, by Percentage

	South Carolina (n = 15,505)	Georgia (n = 33,139)	Illinois (n = 21,318)	Indiana (n = 15,755)
Water supply				
Pump in house	10.0	2.5	33.4	33.8
Piped, cold	3.5	3.8	16.8	18.1
hot and cold	1.5	1.0	10.4	8.2
Indoor toilet				
Chemical	–	0.1	0.6	0.5
Flush	1.7	1.4	11.2	9.5
Tub	2.6	1.8	15.9	13.7
Lavatory	1.7	1.5	12.7	10.3
Kitchen sink with drain	3.2	2.6	51.0	48.9
Lighting				
Gas	0.8	0.8	3.6	5.7
Electricity	3.6	3.5	20.4	24.4
Central heating				
Pipeless	–	–	5.7	3.9
Air, steam, water	0.1	0.1	19.9	13.7
Refrigeration				
Ice	14.5	18.7	27.4	20.6
Mechanical	0.7	0.7	2.3	1.8
Cooking stove				
Kerosene, gasoline	2.6	3.1	45.1	52.0
Gas	0.1	0.1	2.8	4.8
Electric	0.2	0.3	1.7	1.5
Power washing machine	0.1	0.1	44.2	36.5

Source: U.S. Department of Agriculture, Bureau of Home Economics, *Farm-Housing Survey*, pp. 11, 13, 15, 17.

the general lack of home furnishings in southern farmhouses. When the housing statistics for South Carolina and Georgia are compared with those for Illinois and Indiana (table 15), the southern farmhouses appear much more poorly furnished. Similarly, the farmhouses in South Carolina and Georgia were poorer than those in the two northern states in every category. One of the most glaring differences appears in the water supply, where a much greater percentage of farmhouses in Illinois and Indiana had indoor water.

Using the same statistics, a similar examination of the South Carolina Piedmont is possible (table 16). The differences between York County, a Piedmont county, and Orangeburg County, a non-Piedmont county are only minor. The most significant differences occur in the greater pres-

Table 16

Farmhouse Furnishings, York and Orangeburg Counties, South Carolina, 1934, by Percentage

	York County (n = 3,923)	Orangeburg County (n = 5,310)
Water supply		
Pump in house	1.3	16.3
Piped, cold	4.0	4.8
hot and cold	1.2	2.9
Indoor toilet		
Chemical	–	–
Flush	1.7	2.9
Tub	2.8	4.2
Lavatory	2.1	2.6
Kitchen sink with drain	3.8	3.9
Lighting		
Gas	1.4	0.5
Electricity	4.2	4.9
Central heating		
Pipeless	0.1	–
Air, steam, water	0.1	0.1
Refrigeration		
Ice	19.0	17.0
Mechanical	0.5	1.0
Cooking stove		
Kerosene, gasoline	3.1	3.7
Gas	0.1	–
Electric	0.4	0.2
Power washing machine	0.1	0.2

Source: U.S. Department of Agriculture, Bureau of Home Economics, *Farm-Housing Survey*, pp. 13, 17.

ence of indoor pumps, bathtubs, and indoor flush toilets in Orangeburg County. Houses in York County with gaslights and ice refrigeration slightly outnumbered those in Orangeburg County. Nonetheless, the overall differences between the two counties are not striking.

As was noted previously, these statistics do not provide any specific information about plantation housing. While it must be assumed that some plantation homes were included in the sample, this cannot be substantiated. An interesting view of tenant home facilities, however, has been provided by Schuler in his study of farm families during the 1930s.[100] As one part of his study, Schuler asked housewives who were owners, tenants (renters and sharecroppers), and laborers about the home facilities they had and about those they wished they had.

In his examination of the cotton belt,[101] Schuler found that 14 percent of the white owners questioned had running water, whereas 65 percent of those who did not have it wanted it. Only 6 percent of the white tenants had running water, and 58 percent wanted it; only 25 percent of the white laborers had running water, and 62 percent wanted it. Only one of the 114 black tenant farm women questioned had running water in her home; 32 percent wanted it. None of the black owners or black laborers had running water in their houses, even though 53 percent of the black owners and 21 percent of the laborers wanted it. Most people questioned did not own, and did not care to own, indoor toilets. Only 10 percent of the white owners and 12 percent of the white tenants said they would prefer indoor toilets. None of the white laborers expressed this preference. (Only 9 percent of the owners, 1 percent of the tenants, and none of the white laborers had indoor toilets.) Among the blacks interviewed, only 12 percent of the owners, 24 percent of the tenants, and 26 percent of the laborers said they would prefer to have indoor toilets. None of them had inside toilets.

Most of the farm women questioned showed a greater interest in owning sewing machines, washing machines, and iceboxes or refrigerators than in owning other household conveniences. The greatest interest was shown in sewing machines: more than half of all women questioned wanted to own one (59 percent of white owners, 53 percent of white tenants, 62 percent of white laborers, 62 percent of black owners, 63 percent of black tenants, and 68 percent of black laborers). The majority of owners (72 percent for whites, 73 percent for blacks) and white tenants (78 percent) and almost half the remaining blacks (44 percent for tenants, 42 percent for laborers) already had sewing machines. Only one of the eight white laborers questioned had a sewing machine. Fewer of the women questioned either had or wanted a washing machine or refrigerator. Of the whites, only 14 percent of the owners, 15 percent of the tenants, and 25 percent of the laborers wanted washing machines. Of the blacks, only 9 percent of the owners, 16 percent of the tenants, and 16 percent of the laborers wanted washing machines. Of the 138 whites questioned, only 25 (18.1 percent) had these machines, and only one of the 167 (0.6 percent) blacks had them. More of the people questioned wanted an icebox or refrigerator more than a washing machine, but the numbers did not constitute a majority. Only 28 percent of the white owners, 32 percent of the white tenants, 12 percent of the white laborers, 26 percent of the black owners, 20 percent of the black tenants, and 16 percent of the black laborers wanted refrigeration devices. A greater percentage of whites than blacks had them, but these percentages are still fairly small (29 percent for white owners, 18 percent for black owners, 29 percent for white tenants, 8 percent for black tenants, 12 percent of white laborers, and 5 percent of black laborers).

These figures reveal that the ownership of large amounts of interior home furnishings or conveniences was not a fact of life for southern farm families, at least not during the Depression years of the 1930s. The comparative statistics presented for 138 farms in the North[102] show that 98 percent of the owners, 93 percent of the tenants, and 64 percent of the laborers there had sewing machines; 75 percent of the owners, 77 percent of the tenants, and 64 percent of the laborers had washing machines. Again, these statistics illustrate the disparity between at least some of the farms in the southern Cotton Belt and some in the northern Corn Belt.

An excellent view of tenant home furnishings is presented by Agee and Evans in *Let Us Now Praise Famous Men.*[103] This work has little statistical or regional utility because information is provided for only three white tenant families. Nonetheless, these comments are useful because of their depth.

The sharecropper family of six interviewed by Agee lived in a four-room dog-trot house. Each room contained a small amount of easily inventoried furniture. The front bedroom included a simple cast-iron bed, a cane settee with a broken seat, a small table, a bureau, a trunk, and a treadle sewing machine. The rear bedroom contained three iron beds, a trunk similar to that in the front bedroom, and nails on the walls for closets. The beds were so insecure that every motion in them had to be carefully made and "to some extent thought out beforehand"; the pillows and bedding were the "cheapest available" and "not very pleasant."[104] The third room was a lean-to kitchen addition that contained a rusting iron stove, a cupboard or cabinet, a simple table, a wood box, and six ladderback chairs with cane seats. The fourth room in the house was called a storeroom and did not contain any furniture.

One of the two share tenant families interviewed contained six members and lived in a three-room house. The bedroom contained a small tin trunk, a broken hickory-bottom chair, an iron bed, and an old mirror. The second room, a combination bedroom and sitting room, had a weak iron bed that was nailed to the wall, a chair with a pine seat, and a table. The last room, the kitchen, contained a small wood stove and a small, bare table. The home of the other share tenant family, containing nine members, was not described in detail but was presented instead as being quite similar to the other two houses in terms of furnishings.[105]

All the evidence examined strongly suggests that the furnishings of southern tenants' homes, and possibly even those of owners, were neither extensive nor expensive. Most postbellum plantation homes were simply and sparsely furnished. Given the poor quality of the houses themselves, the quality of the furnishings is not surprising. Furniture was an expensive luxury that most plantation inhabitants could not afford and perhaps did not particularly want. On the other hand, the price of small, mundane objects used in the daily process of living—ceramics, tools, clothing, and so forth—were not as expensive as the larger articles of furniture. Because they were used frequently, these items had a higher probability of being broken and discarded than did the larger items.

These smaller, more common objects, mentioned in detail only by Agee and Evans, constitute a major source of information for historical archaeologists. Many of these items, once discarded, were never meant to be seen again. A tenant with a severe but well concealed drinking problem, for example, could feel secure in tossing his empty whiskey bottles down the backyard privy, safe in the knowledge that no one would ever find them, not even the prying eyes of Agee and Evans. This tenant could not foresee the development of historical archaeology and probably in his wildest imagination could not conceive that anyone would be interested in the contents of his privy. Such deposits, however, are of great value to historical archaeology simply because they were never meant to be examined. Herein, then, lies one great value of historical archaeology: the ability to examine the common objects of daily life that, once discarded, were never meant to be seen by anyone.

Although historical documents do not provide abundant references to the personal items owned by plantation inhabitants, scattered references do appear. As with much of the other evidence that has bearing on the postbellum period, such references were first made by freed slaves.

Freed slaves frequently made comments about their former cabins but seldom mentioned any of their personal belongings. The items they did mention were usually associated with the immovable focal point of the cabin, the fireplace. One ex-slave in Georgia, for instance, in speaking of the fireplace equipment said that it "consisted of an iron pot suspended by a hanger and a skillet with long legs that enabled the cook to place fire beneath it." Another ex-slave, from Laurens County, South Carolina, said that he remembered "big iron pots" hanging on hooks extending from the fireplace. In addition to the pots, his slave family had pans and lids "and things to bake in." Other freed slaves mentioned their iron pot for cooking, and one writer even went so far as to state that "the household utensils consisted of one pot" even though an occasional frying pan was also seen.[106]

Almost every ex-slave who mentioned his old fireplace commented upon its use for cooking, but few mentioned what vessels were used to prepare these foods. Though slaves obviously had access to other kinds of vessels, the one large iron pot is all that is usually remembered. For example, in speaking of the vessels used in the large plantation kitchen, one former slave said that the cooking utensils consisted of "pots and big ovens and little ovens and big, thick iron frying pans with long handles and hefty iron lids." This kitchen held enough utensils to cook for one hundred people at once.[107] Other comments about slave utensils have been made, but they are rare. For example, one former Mississippi slave reported that they ate and drank from gourds, and Olmsted reported having seen a "shelf of crockery" in a slave cabin near Natchitoches, Louisiana.[108]

These comments, along with those presented in chapter 1 on slave ceramics, illustrate some of the everyday materials used by southern slaves during the nineteenth century and provide a rough guide to the kinds of items available to freed families in 1865. Unfortunately, it is not likely that planters permitted many freedmen to take from their former plantations the implements they used as slaves. It could be surmised that under usual circumstances, freed slaves were allowed to leave their plantations with only their clothing and the few small personal items they had acquired themselves. These items would most likely have been the beads, shoe buckles, buttons, smoking pipes, and other miscellaneous personal items found by archaeologists at slave cabin sites.[109] Thus, it can be assumed that the material possessions of the earliest postbellum wage laborers mirrored those of slaves.

More difficulty is encountered in the attempt to identify the material possessions of nonwage-laboring tenant farm families. Although scholars in the 1920s, 1930s, and 1940s described tenant housing and house furnishings, almost none spoke in detail about a tenant family's personal possessions. Again, Agee and Evans's study of the three white tenant families provides the notable exception.[110]

Unfortunately, because of the small number of tenant families interviewed and because many of his more detailed comments were made from memory, Agee's comments cannot be considered definitive. Although there is no reason to think all plantation tenants throughout the South used similar items, Agee's comments serve as a useful guide to the personal items of the tenant family.

Agee provides an incredibly thorough inventory of the material possessions of the sharecropper family he interviewed. (At the same time, Evans made equally invaluable photographs.) The inventory is presented as if the tenants left Agee and Evans alone in their house with instructions that they were free to examine anything and everything. Agee and Evans did not miss much. Inside the trunk that was inside the front bedroom, Agee and Evans found an old cotton slip, a little boy's gray cap, a baby's dress, a baby's knit shoe, a pair of blue socks, and a pair of blue doll's eyes. On the bureau in this same room they found an almost toothless rubber comb; a white clamshell holding a small white button; a small pincushion; a small, broken ceramic rabbit; a small ceramic bovine and three calves; and a Bible. Many things found in the drawers were not listed, but the items that were listed are schoolbooks; a number of pieces of neatly folded, but previously used, wrapping paper; and a few pieces of string, some wound around spools, matches, and nails. On the table in this bedroom, Agee and Evans observed a white ceramic swan sitting in a

small, green fluted-glass bowl, and on the mantle, they found two irides-
cent glass vases and a milk glass saucer. A number of photographs, cal-
endars, pictures, and other pieces of memorabilia were tacked to the
walls. In examining the contents of the table drawer, Agee and Evans
found six baby dresses, a handmade blue cloth cat, a hat, an empty box
of talcum powder, a child's glove, a hexagonal piece of newspaper, both
parts of a broken button, a small, black hook and eye, a black hook, and a
small needle.

Agee and Evans continued their thorough search in the rear bedroom. On the mantle in this room they found a small, round cardboard
box of face powder, an almost empty jar of menthol salve, a half-empty
spool of white thread, a ceramic shaving mug decorated with roses (containing a worn varnish brush, eleven rusty nails, one blue button, one
pin with an imitation pearl head, three kitchen matches, and a lump of
soap), a pink comb missing three teeth, sixteen rhinestones, a nailfile,
and a small mirror on a wire stand. A fireplace poker made from an old
automobile part, a square pincushion (containing several pins, two large
safety pins, three or four pins with glass heads, a small brooch, and a
needle), and a calendar were hung by nails on the walls. A number of
dresses, overalls, quilts, and shoes were observed inside a shallow closet.

In the kitchen, Agee and Evans found an assortment of utensils, including dishpans, a coffeepot, a kettle, a set of canisters, a large iron
skillet, a broom, and a butter churn. Their inventory of the kitchen table
and its dinnerware is the most complete account available.

On this table, they found "two stainless steel knives and forks" with
black handles, a number of cheaper forks, knives, and spoons, and an
assortment of ceramic dishes. The tines of the forks were all bent, and
few of the plates, glasses, or saucers matched. One of the cups was a
cheap imitation of an expensive blue and white willow pattern cup, but
the others were the plain, thick, white cups "of the sort used in lunch
wagons." This last type, usually referred to as ironstone, or hotelware, by
historical archaeologists, was a common and inexpensive ceramic first
made in the 1880s and used extensively during the first half of the twentieth century.[111] Two of the plates were of this "lunch wagon" variety,
one was translucent white (perhaps glass), and one was cream-colored
and decorated with yellow corn and green leaves. The food was placed
on the table in pans, two shallow soup plates, and a small thick platter.
The children ate from saucers and bowls, and the adults used plates. In

the middle of the table was a canning jar containing sorghum, a box of black pepper, a saltshaker with a green top, and an unlit lamp.

Three dozen canning jars and fifteen or twenty jelly glasses were found in the storeroom. These jars, about half of which were empty, held jams, jellies, peaches, tomatoes, and string beans.

Agee and Evans did not describe the material possessions of the two share renting families, and no comparison can be made with those of the sharecropper family. Nonetheless, the importance of Agee's observations and Evans's photographs must not be diminished. In describing the sharecropper's home and material possessions, Agee and Evans approached the subject as ethnographers studying another culture. Although their observations have no statistical validity, they provide an unparalleled view of at least one tenant family's material possessions.

Archaeologists studying tenant farmer homesites are not able to provide the same kind of personal detail as that provided by Agee and Evans. The information provided by archaeologists may be more precise, from the standpoint that each excavated object can be measured, remeasured, and described in minute detail, but it lacks the rich, personal context offered by direct observation. Importantly, archaeological research provides another kind of detail, that gained from studying the actual objects used by past plantation inhabitants.

Recent historical archaeological research at tenant farm sites has increased our knowledge of the material items used by postbellum tenant farmers. This information is obviously fragmentary because the artifacts excavated represent only a small portion of the activities that actually occurred at a site. Also, given the potential problems caused by tenant shifting, archaeologists can seldom provide exact dates of tenant house occupation using the excavated artifacts alone. Even so, the examination of a few of the tenant farm studies conducted to date can provide further evidence about the material possessions of tenant farmers.

While conducting an archaeological survey in Clarendon County, South Carolina, archaeologists found surface evidence for four separate tenant farm homesites occupied sometime between 1920 and 1950.[112] These sites all had low focus and low visibility because they consisted of only a surface scatter of artifacts.

The artifact collections retrieved from each site were not large. In fact, the largest collection contained only 186 artifacts. The smallest collection contained only 33 artifacts. Many different kinds of artifacts were found, including ceramics. Historical archaeologists frequently use ceramics to learn about past sites. Ceramics are useful because they are durable when buried for long periods of time, they can be dated fairly well, and their decorations can be identified and compared with ceramic collections from other archaeological sites. Also, ceramics are thought to be useful in learning about the social positions of people who inhabited past houses and settlements. An examination of the ceramics suggests that the tenants who lived at these four sites used a variety of decorated wares, various kinds of stoneware crockery, and even some porcelain. A brief outline of the ceramics collected from one of the homesites shows the variety used at the site.[113] Fifty-three pieces of ceramics were located. The sherds were plain white, plain white with a raised-dot design, brown transfer-printed, greenish yellow transfer-printed, blue transfer-printed floral, and blue hand-painted. In addition, plain porcelain, molded porcelain, and two different kinds of stoneware crockery were found. In this one small collection, then, were at least twelve different kinds of ceramics. Other artifacts found at this site include pieces of colored glass (dark blue, amethyst, aquamarine, clear, and white), one piece of iron from a stove or plow, and one piece of rubber.

Other archaeological research at tenant farm sites in South Carolina adds weight to the notion that tenant families used a wide array of material goods in their daily life. The predominance of ceramics at tenant farm sites, however, has led one archaeologist to posit the existence of a "tenant artifact pattern" that relies on the relative abundance of ceramics.[114]

The idea that artifact collections should exhibit a certain patterned regularity underlies much archaeological research, but in historical archaeology, the idea was first explored in detail by South Carolina historical archaeologist Stanley South.[115] In simple terms, South postulates that members of past cultures, because of their attitudes, beliefs, and perceived needs, lived their lives, as we do today, in culturally patterned ways. He maintains that this basic anthropological precept should be observable in archaeological deposits. As such, if the members of a past culture held a belief that blindness would result from eating from flat plates, then the archaeological remains from a site inhabited by these people should contain few plate fragments.

Since South first formalized this concept, historical archaeologists have described patterns in almost every conceivable kind of archaeological deposit. This pattern concept, although seemingly logical, is difficult to accept for many reasons. Perhaps the most pertinent reason involves the concept's failure to incorporate a sometimes irrational individual element. For example, when South states that a similarity should exist between sites in British colonial Charleston, Savannah, and Philadelphia because its inhabitants shared the world view, attitudes, and behaviors of Englishmen, he ignores the individual vagaries of humans. On a more important level, South's "laws" are not the more realistic "laws of tendency," but rather the "iron laws of society."[116] In studies of tenant farmers, the need to incorporate the specifics of tenure and plantation organization reduce the effectiveness of South's pattern concept.[117]

One implication of the past studies of tenant farming is that much of what archaeologists can learn will derive from ceramics. On the other hand, this implication suggests that the perception an archaeologist develops about tenancy from using only artifacts can be one-sided and inaccurate. The disparity between the artifacts Agee observed and the artifacts collected from the South Carolina tenant sites mentioned above ably demonstrates this. Nonetheless, the predominance of ceramic sherds in the archaeological deposits allows historical archaeologists to make two important observations about the material possessions of southern tenant farm families. First, the variation in the sherds present in ceramic collections reveals, as historical archaeologist William H. Adams has noted, that ceramics seem "to have been purchased as replacement items rather than in sets."[118] At Waverly Plantation, examined in more detail below, Adams substantiated this contention by illustrating the wide diversity of decorated ceramic sherds found during excavation and by an examination of plantation store ledgers showing that plantation inhabitants seldom bought whole sets of dishes. Second, the predominance of ceramics in archaeological deposits made by postbellum tenant farmers may be a strong indication of a rather obvious fact: when tenants moved they took everything they could with them; all that remained behind were small, useless, broken pieces of ceramics and glass. This conclusion leads to a more important piece of information about the material possessions of postbellum plantation tenant farmers: summarized by Agee and Evans, "nothing is thrown away," a conclusion also reached by historical archaeologists.[119] This finding, although not startling, is significant for archaeologists because it means that the archaeological data on tenancy might be sparse indeed. Past research in South Carolina seems to substantiate this idea.

Figure 12. A tenant house, Coffee County, Alabama, 1939. The photo illustrates the effects of yard sweeping on archaeological deposits. (Library of Congress)

The paucity of artifacts found at tenant sites also can be affected by cultural practices such as yard sweeping. The effects on the archaeological deposits of cleaning the ground around a tenant house appears in many of the photographs made by the Farm Security Administration, particularly one made by Marion Post Walcott in Coffee County, Alabama, in August 1939 (figure 12). Yard sweeping, however, did not necessarily obliterate the remains at the entire site; it only changed them. Research at a number of tenant farm sites in Texas indicates that the presence of artifacts increases as the distance from the house increases.[120] Thus, yard sweeping serves merely to push the artifacts from immediately around the building to the periphery of the site.

Not all tenant farms excavated by archaeologists have yielded few artifacts. For example, at Waverly Plantation in northeastern Mississippi,

54,495 artifacts were collected from six tenant homesites. Interestingly, glass items accounted for 45.7 percent of the entire collection, and ceramics comprised only 8.5 percent of the collection. Metal items comprised 44.0 percent of the collection.[121] The material collected at this postbellum tenant plantation obviously presents a different picture of tenant material possessions than do the items excavated at other sites, where ceramics outweigh all other kinds of artifacts.

For an overview of the kinds of artifacts collected at Waverly Plantation, a brief discussion of one site, called the Aaron Mathews House, is instructive. Extensive archival research and thorough interviewing of former plantation inhabitants revealed that this house may have been built and occupied as early as 1880, but most of the building's use occurred between 1910 and 1970, when the house was torn down.[122] Aaron Mathews was a tenant farmer who resided in the house with his family from the early 1920s until 1941. The possibility is strong that the twenty-nine years between 1941 and 1970 saw a great many changes at the property, and many of the artifacts recovered were probably from this later period.

A brief inventory of some of the nonceramic and nonglass items recovered through excavation demonstrates the range of materials found at this one tenant site. Many of the metal objects were tools: files, chisels, chain links, an ax head, hacksaw blades, a drill bit, a screwdriver, hammer heads, pully wheels, and a C-clamp. Pieces of barbed wire, a hoe blade, a plowshare, a harrow tooth, harness equipment, horseshoes, and muleshoes were among the agricultural artifacts found. Included in the collection were items that could be considered personal in nature: pocket watch parts, wristwatch fragments, pendants, a locket, a necklace, twenty-four different kinds of buttons, a pants snap, zipper pieces, suspender clips and buckles, a thimble, scissors, pins, double- and single-edged razor blades, lipstick containers, a toy sadiron, a toy Junior G-Man badge, a hair curler, a hairpin, and pen caps. Stove parts; a collection of forks, spoons, and knives; and a number of cans from commercially sold foods all provide information about dietary and food preparation habits of the past inhabitants of the house that once stood at the Aaron Mathews Site.[123]

Using these artifacts and the others collected at this site, archaeologists were able to present a well-balanced and detailed picture of life at the plantation. One practical problem with this site, however, is its occupation between 1941 and 1970, which undoubtedly severely altered the focus and visibility of the site. Because the depth of the archaeological deposits was only eight inches, the degree of disturbance by later inhabitants is assumed to have been extensive.

The unsolvable problem of long post-tenancy occupation was not a significant issue at Millwood Plantation because full-scale occupation of the property largely ended by 1925. The visibility of the antebellum occupation, however, was severely compromised by the postbellum occupation. Coupled with the severe erosion of the Piedmont, the postbellum activities at Millwood obliterated most of the physical evidence for the existence of the plantation from 1834 to 1865. As a result, archaeological research provided little information about the antebellum history and society of the plantation. This problem did not occur for the postbellum occupation, and the evidence from Millwood is the best yet encountered in the United States.

Before considering this evidence, the postbellum history of Millwood Plantation as presented in the documentary record must be considered. This record, although not extensive, provides vital information about Millwood Plantation as a postbellum tenant plantation.

Chapter Five

Millwood Plantation
Transformed, 1865–1985

IMMEDIATELY AFTER THE AMERICAN CIVIL WAR, the Freedmen's Bureau began the difficult task of overseeing the change of the plantation South to the free-labor system. Although the individuals themselves had not changed, slaves had become free farmers, and masters had become landlords. Specifically, the bureau's job consisted of aiding in the definition of new labor arrangements between white landholders and newly freed black farmers. The immediate postwar period was generally one of confusion and violence, as southern whites and blacks sought to define their places in the new social order, and the job of the Freedmen's Bureau was not easy.

Stationed in Abbeville County at this difficult time of transition, Captain C. R. Becker, like most of the bureau agents stationed throughout the South, found that the adjustments would be difficult to make.[1] Writing to his superior, Lieutenant Colonel John Devereau, Becker conveyed the confusion and general lawlessness that was widespread in Abbeville County. Becker found outlaws and horse thieves in the area who preyed, almost without retaliation, on both blacks and whites.

Concerning labor, Becker reported that the planters in the area were in great need of laborers and that every day he had applications "from planters who [were] in want of hands and unable to obtain them." The problems in obtaining laborers undoubtedly stemmed from the intractableness of both planters and freedmen. Becker reported that planters were still whipping their laborers in Abbeville County, and freedmen wanted to avoid working for someone who would inflict physical punishment. Freedmen, on the other hand, were being accused by planters of stealing from surrounding plantations because "it seem[ed] to be part of their nature to steal."[2] Becker was forced to conclude, after working with both planters and freedmen, that his problems in resolving labor disputes were compounded because "both will lie." Becker's difficulty in learning the truth was further aggravated by the distances between Abbeville, his home base, and the outlying plantations. He decided that "where the parties live 18 or 20 miles away it is very hard to arrive at the truth in every case."[3]

By the summer of 1866 many of the planters in Abbeville County employed emancipated blacks as wage hands. Becker reported that the planters who employed wage hands had been "turning them off" during the lay-by season—that time between cotton cultivation and picking—with the intent of hiring a few back during harvest. Although two months later Becker reported that this forced unemployment continued in Abbeville County, he did concede that "the free labor system has worked well" and that he was told by the "intelligent portion of the citizens" (obviously white planters) that the freedmen had "worked better under the circumstances than could have been expected."[4]

Only one year later changes were being made in the organization of plantation agriculture in Abbeville County. As was typical of that period, several different forms of labor were tried. A contract between W. V. Clinkscales and a number of freedmen demonstrates that a modified wage system continued to be used in Abbeville County. Instead of paying the hands a monthly wage, and thereby retaining the luxury of turning them out during slack times, Clinkscales paid yearly wages to the male heads of freed households. Clinkscales agreed to pay $50 a year to the males and between $125 and $148 for family labor. In addition, he provided two pounds of meat and a peck of meal each week for the children and one-half acre to each family for the cultivation of potatoes. The hands were to provide all the labor needed for the upkeep of the plantation, they were to work at all reasonable times and meet all fair demands, and they were required to be polite at all times. Clinkscales had the right to deduct fifty cents from the yearly wage of any laborer who missed a day's work.[5] The contract does not state this, but the possibility is strong that other deductions and penalties would be levied for insubordination or any other "impolite" actions on the part of any freed laborer.

On another plantation in the area, John A. Calhoun signed a different kind of agreement with the freedmen on his estate. This plan was a cropsharing arrangement where the tenant farmer gave up two-thirds of his farm produce in return for housing, mules and horses, wagons, and tools. All provisions were supplied by the landlord, but their price was deducted from the tenant's one-third share of the crop. While at work, all the freedmen agreed to be "directed," and any refusal of duty could be punished by the tenant's dismissal, his expulsion from the plantation, and the loss of his share, regardless of the time of year or the progress of the crop. Calhoun agreed to treat the freedmen kindly only insofar as they agreed to be "industrious and attentive to their duties," prompt to obey "all proper orders," and "respectful in their conduct" to their employers.[6]

At Millwood Plantation James Edward Calhoun made yet another kind of arrangement with seven freedmen—Butler Irving, Jasper Calhoun, Charles Calhoun, Andrew Calhoun, Winter Bryan, George Bryan, and Cuff Walker—who wanted to work on his estate. Three of these freedmen, whose last name was Calhoun, were probably former Calhoun slaves, and Andrew Calhoun was undoubtedly the stonemason whose skills were so valued by James Edward Calhoun before 1865. Signed on January 1, 1867, and approved by Captain Becker at the Abbeville County Courthouse on February 5, 1867, this agreement suggests that the squad system mentioned in chapter 3 was experimented with at Millwood Plantation.[7]

Each of the seven named in the contract was to hire others to cultivate at the plantation, provided that they not hire anyone "objectionable" to Calhoun. The seven freedmen were "to cultivate carefully and industriously" with the intent of paying Calhoun a "Rentage of one half of all they raise" with the understanding that the other workers would toil for them. These seven were also charged with maintaining their portion of the estate by making improvements and by keeping the fences, farm buildings, and roads in good repair. They, or their hands, were permitted the freedom to seek outside employment if they so desired, but Calhoun was entitled to receive one-third of what they earned. In addition, they were neither allowed to leave the plantation nor to receive visitors without Calhoun's permission. Above all else, the seven men and their employees were required "to be obedient & respectful to the said Calhoun & to his agent, not to quarrel or to fight, [and] not to abuse the work animals in their charge." If any animal was stolen or neglected, the man judged responsible was answerable for its full value.

Calhoun carefully spelled out a number of other restrictions on the seven freedmen and their hands that further narrowed the limits of their newfound "freedom." For each offense committed by one of the freedmen—either one of the seven or their hands—Calhoun would levy a fine of twenty-five cents. Calhoun reserved the right to dismiss them, for any other offense, whereby they would forfeit all their claims against him, and he would "place their effects in the public road." The freedmen were not permitted to sell or to transport any portion of their crops off the plantation until Calhoun had received his rent and had all his orders obeyed. Furthermore, the tenants were "to watch & defend the Premises night & day" and to assist Calhoun in the collection of rents. In addition, Calhoun ordered them "to pay all Stamp & Internal Revenue Taxes and all other Taxes incident to & consequent upon this agreement." This question of taxation was obviously important to Calhoun, and his insistence that his tenants pay their own taxes was a personal quirk rather than a general attitude of postbellum planters near Abbeville. Taxation was a constant issue for James Edward Calhoun throughout his life. For example, a short notice appearing in an Abbeville newspaper on March 7, 1877, states that the sixty-five tenants on Calhoun's estate were required to pay a tax of ten cents an acre "in order that they may feel some of the oppression of a robbing government."[8]

The 1867 contract also stipulated that all Millwood Plantation tenants were required to obtain all necessary supplies exclusively from Calhoun's storerooms. In addition, Calhoun was to receive "one third part of all the fresh eggs" from the chickens he supplied the tenants, and every month he was to receive a "roasting pig" out of the hogs he had given them. Accordingly, in November and December, each of the seven contract signers was to supply Calhoun with a "well fatted Hog, weighing at least 150 lbs."

All these restrictions obviously worked for Calhoun's benefit and against the independence of the freedmen involved. This contract enumerated both economic and social stipulations that were undoubtedly designed to keep Calhoun in the exalted position of planter and the freedmen in the unenviable positions of dependent farmers. Calhoun's tenants were required to be constantly on their guard, both socially and in terms of productivity, lest their belongings become placed in the middle of the road. While this eviction may have had some potentially long-term advantages to freedmen, whose labor was in great demand on southern plantations, it would have caused most to leave the area they had known for many years, perhaps all their lives. Also, with the stiff vagrancy laws of the immediate postwar period in full force, turned-out blacks had very real fears of landing in jail or becoming part of a forced work detail.

The arrangement Calhoun made with the freedmen farmers was not the only plan he had for operating his plantation after the war. His plans for Millwood involved both agricultural and mechanical development.

One scheme Calhoun revived during this immediate postwar period was his plan, first formulated during the 1840s, to settle Germans on his plantation as tenants. Writing to Calhoun in July 1865, a Mr. Goldsmith in Columbia, South Carolina, informed him that he was sending letters "to the German people" that would appear in "the Cologne Gazette in translation."[9] As was the case twenty years earlier, however, large numbers of Germans did not settle at Millwood Plantation as tenants; Calhoun's advertisements seemed to have gone largely unnoticed.

Perhaps even more important to Calhoun than agriculture was his life-long interest in the mechanization of the plantation. He had a number of plans for the mechanical operation of Millwood. In June 1866 he informed Thomas Green Clemson, the Yankee husband of his niece Anna Maria Calhoun, that he had recently leased two hundred yards of land on the Georgia side of his ferry "to be improved immediately" and "leased the Allen Mill Place, on this side," just below his home at Millwood[10] (see figure 2). One year later Calhoun made an agreement with a man who was to build "a Superior Cotton Boat," presumably to be launched from his ferry landing.[11]

In addition to these enterprises, Calhoun's interest in gold mining continued during this period. Along these lines, Calhoun made an agreement with a Dr. John L. Vertrees that was amazingly similar to the agricultural agreement he had made with the seven freedmen shortly before.[12] This agreement created a mineralogical sharecropping arrangement between Vertrees and Calhoun. Signed on August 21, 1867, this agreement permitted Vertrees "to mine, bore, and explore for Gold and other minerals" at Calhoun's gold mine near "The Bickley field" for two years and nine months, in return for two-ninths of "the gross proceeds of all Gold, Minerals, and other substances yielded by the Mining operations." As was the case with the seven agricultural squad leaders, Vertrees was not allowed to employ anyone objectionable to Calhoun or to enter into any associations or partnerships without Calhoun's permission. Similarly, Vertrees was not to interfere with the work of any of Calhoun's tenants or to obstruct any of the roads or waterways on the estate. To ensure that Vertrees was doing a good job, Calhoun required him to keep accurate and detailed books and accounts that were "subject at any time to inspection by the said Calhoun" or his agent. Calhoun's agent in this matter was to be the son of Anna Maria and Thomas Green Clemson, John Calhoun Clemson, called Calhoun Clemson because of the many Johns in the family. Calhoun Clemson, who was to die in a train accident only four years later,[13] was to receive one-sixth the proceeds from the gold and minerals after Calhoun's two-ninths had been subtracted. As one might expect, Vertrees was also required to pay all the taxes that would result from the agreement, including stamp and internal revenue taxes.

Although this lease demonstrates the continued breadth of Calhoun's approach to building and maintaining his empire, the agreement was short-lived. When Vertrees ceased operations at the gold mine on August 4, 1868, Calhoun pronounced the lease to be forfeited.[14] This part of Calhoun's enterprise was, at least for the moment, dead.

Even though Calhoun was apparently making an effort, through the labor of freedmen farmers and white entrepreneurs, to rebuild his empire after the war, he faced problems encountered by many planters, not the least of which was the acquisition of the capital necessary to transform his plans into realities. For example, in his June 14, 1866, letter to Thomas Green Clemson he said that "the Pickens estate," his land in Pickens County, had "been such a pickpocket" that he had "resolved to bestow no further expenditure on it."[15] Three years later, on June 3, 1869, Calhoun told Anna Maria Calhoun Clemson, that his losses were "immense" and that they were not yet over. He told her that his house was "rotting over [his] head, past repairs." He could not afford to build another and wrote, "I can do no more than try to gather enough to enable me to modify one of my outbuildings that I may have some convenience & more security." In the same letter, however, Calhoun informed her that he could lend her five hundred dollars to help with the wedding of her daughter Floride on August 1, 1869.[16] Interestingly enough, although Calhoun did not attend the wedding, he sent a gift to Floride of "a gold chain and a lump of pure gold, from [his] Mine, for the wedding ring, &c." He also sent "some wines & liquors of [his] own importing, respectively, 24 & 12 years old & 1 bottle Madeira, 43 yrs.

old," presumably for the wedding itself.[17] While times might have been somewhat more difficult for Calhoun after the war, it seems that he was still solvent enough to lend large sums of money to relatives and to keep a stock of imported liquor, even if it had been purchased before the war. Also, it would seem from Calhoun's wedding gift that Vertrees had had some success at the gold mine before his lease was terminated.

Still, all was apparently not well in the area of agriculture, and it appears that Calhoun was having difficulty with some of his tenants. Calhoun leased land not only to the seven squads and their unknown number of employees but also to an undetermined number of white tenants. On December 17, 1869, he notified a W. F. Anderson: As "the only one of the white tenants on this portion of the Estate who has not come to a satisfactory arrangement, you owe me a considerable amount." Calhoun was concerned because he had learned on that very day that Anderson, who had told him he was planning to go to the Abbeville County Courthouse to arrange fire insurance for the gin house, had instead planned to take his cotton to "Augusta & Thence [go] to Arkansas." In light of this attempted subterfuge, Calhoun gave Anderson eight days to liquidate his notes and accounts, as he would "no longer rent land to you or to your brothers."[18] On the same day, Calhoun also wrote to a Mr. Boyd to instruct him to "hasten to deliver" his letter to Anderson "before he leaves." In the event that Anderson was already gone, Boyd was to "shew [sic] it to both of his Brothers & give it to the one who goes in the Boat, to deliver it in Augusta."[19]

These letters to Anderson indicate that Millwood Plantation, in addition to being farmed by a number of black squads, was also being worked by an undetermined number of white tenants. These whites may have been cash or standing renters, because in his letter Calhoun spoke of "your cotton" to Anderson. If Anderson was not a cash or a standing renter, he would not have been able to remove the cotton to Augusta, and Calhoun, instead of sending a letter, probably would have sent the sheriff.

Except for these brief references appearing in the Calhoun correspondence, little is known about Millwood during the immediate postwar period. For an unknown reason, Calhoun does not appear in the 1870 agricultural or mechanical censuses, and the history of the plantation during the critical transition period is largely unknown. That Calhoun still lived at Millwood is without question, because bills of sale remain for this period.[20]

Some of Calhoun's tenants, however, can be identified in the censuses. At least five of these tenants can be named: Aaron Blue, Joe Burton, Washington Hill, Amos Johnson, and Cuff Walker. These farmers worked between 20 and 60 improved acres and held up to 60 unimproved acres. The mean cash value of these five farms was $460, and the mean cash value of the farm tools and machinery was $45. Each man held at least some livestock whose mean value was $117. Four of the tenants—Burton, Hill, Johnson, and Walker—each produced one bale of cotton; Aaron Blue produced three. Aaron Blue was the only one of the five who produced anything else, having made 80 bushels of Indian corn. As a result, Aaron Blue's farm, consisting of 28 improved acres, was valued at $320; each of the others was valued at $80.[21] Although scant, this census information about the reorganization of the plantation labor system is important.

Much more significant in documenting the changes at the plantation is a contract, signed in 1875, between Calhoun and thirty-six of his tenant farmers.[22] This document is significant because, when added to the information in the 1870 census, it demonstrates that the squad system, as headed by the seven freedmen named in 1867, had been changed to a standing-rent arrangement shortly thereafter. Of the farmers listed in the 1867 document, five—Butler Irving, Andrew Calhoun, Winter Bryan [or Bryant], George Bryan, and Cuff Walker—appear along with the rest of the tenants, with no special mention of foremen or leaders.

In this agreement each tenant was required to pay Calhoun between 300 and 3,500 pounds of unginned cotton, between 4 and 35 bushels of unshucked corn, between 50 and 300 bundles of fodder, and either one-quarter or one-half of their oats. When the figures are totaled, it can be seen that Calhoun expected to receive 57,400 pounds of cotton, 648 bushels of corn, and 6,280 bundles of fodder from the tenants. The share of oats he would receive cannot be calculated.

As with all of the agreements Calhoun made with his agricultural producers, this document placed stringent requirements on them. The tenants were required to put the prime portion of their crops into Calhoun's storehouses as directed by him or his agent and were directed not to remove or dispose of the crop until the final settlement was made. They agreed to cultivate the soil "so as to improve its fertility," to keep the roads and fences in repair, to employ no one objectionable to Calhoun, neither to sublet nor to clear land without his permission, and to use the "Mill, Gin, and Smith shop of said Calhoun, if required to do so." In addition, the tenants agreed to sow one-quarter of their allotted land—land that had been "laid off and agreed upon" before the contract was signed—in wheat, even though they could not claim "to remain on the premises the ensuing year, or to come to watch or to harvest it." Calhoun would, however, on the removal of a tenant, pay him "for the seed sown as exhibited by the stand towards the end of the year." As a further concession, the tenants agreed that they could not charge Calhoun for any "clearing, ditching, fencing, repairing, building and other improvements" they might undertake. Any tenant who wanted to clean up his plot would have to bear all the costs. As a final stipulation, each tenant was required to pay all the taxes levied.

In addition to specific information, this document provides two important clues about the agricultural relationships at Millwood Plantation in the mid-1870s. At first glance, it appears that Calhoun was fairly lenient with his tenants in not forcing them to accept wage labor or sharecropping, systems wherein they would realize little opportunity for the accumulation of wealth. The contract implies that his black tenants were standing or share renters, who would have occupied fairly high positions on the agricultural ladder. While they did not hold clear title to their land, they do seem to have been autonomous to some small degree. Given all the constraints imposed by the 1867 contract, Calhoun made, or was forced to make, fewer demands on his tenants by 1875. At least, fewer demands are mentioned in the document, and the available correspondence implies that Calhoun would have been careful to spell out his demands if he had made them.

Looked at another way, however, Calhoun's having black tenants as standing or share renters indicates that he did not want to bear any of the risk in their farming ventures. A tenant farmer with a poor yield one year could be worse off as a standing renter than as a sharecropper if his entire crop consisted of a bale of cotton. As a sharecropper, he would lose only half of the bale, but as a standing renter, he would probably lose the whole bale as rent.

The second piece of information that is revealed in this document is circumstantial. The letter Calhoun sent to W. F. Anderson in 1869 suggests that white cash renters also lived at Millwood. Because the afore-mentioned 1877 newspaper notice stated that Calhoun had sixty-five tenants, who were required to pay their own taxes, it can be suggested that Calhoun had thirty-six black tenants (those mentioned in the 1875 contract) and twenty-nine white tenants (the number remaining when the black tenants are subtracted from the 1877 number). This conclusion is conjectural.

The late 1870s again saw further entrepreneurial activity at the plantation. In 1875 the estate was visited by a Georgian named W. S. Logan who inquired about the possibility of leasing the Calhoun gold mine.[23] No record exists to determine whether Calhoun granted the lease, and Logan's name does not appear again in the correspondence. Still, the gold mine was an interesting diversion for the scientifically oriented Calhoun but never a truly prominent part of the Millwood enterprise.

More important during this period was Calhoun's renewed attempt to sell Millwood Plantation. In June 1877 Calhoun wrote a letter to Chicago industrialist Cyrus M. McCormick. This letter was so important to Calhoun that he asked one of the sons of his "eldest nephew," probably one of the five sons of Andrew Pickens Calhoun, to transmit it to Thomas C. Reynolds in Saint Louis for publication in a newspaper there, thereby giving it a "wide circulation." To aid in the publicity he would receive, Calhoun enclosed two maps of Millwood.[24] Reynolds, a former Confederate governor of Missouri who fled to Mexico in 1865 and returned only after general amnesty was granted in December 1868, replied that he unfortunately had no relations with the newspapers that he could use to persuade them to publish Calhoun's letter. Reynolds was sorry that he could not assist Calhoun in this endeavor.[25]

The letter, dated June 5, 1877, and one of the maps was eventually published in an undetermined location, probably during that same year.[26] In essence, the letter is an attempt by Calhoun to convince McCormick that "the region embraced by Aiken and Anderson Court House," or, in other words, the area of Millwood Plantation, "enjoys one of the happiest climates on earth." According to Calhoun's information, McCormick had the intention of relocating some of his enterprises in the South "to escape the horrible winter of the North." After a glowing account of the glories of the region—with its "sunshine and showers," few insects, "constant set of the air from a higher elevation," and cool nights—Calhoun proceeded to mention the long life span of everyone who lived in the area. For example, one planter was "one hundred and fourteen years old" when Calhoun "last saw him," a woman named Mrs. Fleming "numbered her ninety-eight years on this estate," "Aunt Peggy" died from "the effects of a fall" at age 106, and "her mother went to 115." Speaking of his tenants, Calhoun said that many of them who were older than he— "including an octogenarian with the fresh vitality of twenty-five"—"still use the hoe." In short, Calhoun said that "this is the country in which to grow old comfortably."

In addition to the quality of life in the region, Calhoun noted the many business advantages it offered. Accordingly, "southern spinners" would easily "put themselves beyond the competition," and the estate was large enough to accommodate both industry and agriculture. To Calhoun's mind, the "operatives" could go home at night "to their parents," who in turn could be rented land that would "in great part balance wages." Furthermore, labor strikes "would be obviated" because provisions for the workers would be cheap along the Savannah River, "this great water transit." The final benefit would be new achievements in manufacturing techniques that would "go far toward meeting expenses."

Calhoun claimed that his land was the perfect place for McCormick, or any other industrialist, to build a southern manufacturing empire. The area offered the best of everything: a great climate, human longevity, a ready work force of children, enough land to rent to their parents for agriculture, and great economic advantages to the entrepreneur.

The map that Calhoun included with this letter is particularly intriguing because it shows all the existing or potential features of the property that Calhoun thought were most appealing to the industrialist or potential buyer (figure 13). The main settlement, where his house was situated, appears on the map as "Millwood House." On the South Carolina side are four mill races, two on the Savannah River and two on the Rocky River, and on the Georgia side is one long race. The Calhoun gold mine appears on a small tributary of Collins Creek, and four other locales containing gold are indicated throughout the estate. The Calhoun Ferry is positioned between Davis and Cedar islands near the gold mill. Calhoun suggested the best location for an industrial works, by indicating "grand site for manufacturing city" that could be reached from a "dock for steamers."

A number of additions appear in Calhoun's characteristic handwriting on an extant copy of the map. He added the proposed location of the

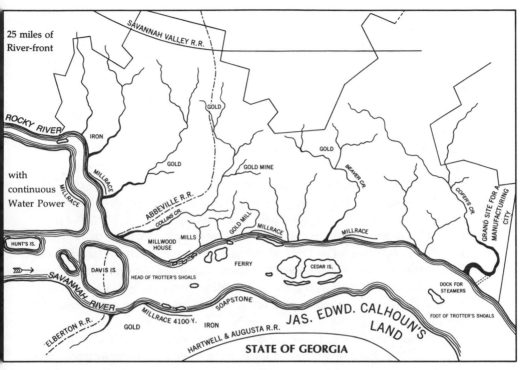

Figure 13. Promotional map, Millwood Plantation, 1877. Calhoun used this map to demonstrate the advantages his plantation offered in terms of industrial development.

railroad from Abbeville, South Carolina, to Elberton, Georgia (now called the Seaboard Air Line), and the notation "25 miles of River-front with continuous Water-Power" on the side of the map. Along the top of this version of the map was a typeset notice that "for further Particulars than those herein stated" the interested party should contact "Jas. Ewd. Calhoun."

Even though Cyrus McCormick, or any other Northern industrialist for that matter, never purchased Millwood Plantation, Calhoun's claims were apparently more than just boast. In 1885, for example, George F. Swain wrote in *Reports on the Water-Power of the United States* that the most important shoal on the Savannah River was Trotter's Shoals, at Calhoun's Millwood Plantation. Swain mentioned the advantages of the area, including its wonderful climate, the abundance of building materials, and its suitability to the construction of canals. On the basis of these characteristics, Swain concluded that Trotter's Shoals "offers the finest power on the river above Augusta." Nonetheless, Trotter's Shoals was "almost entirely unutilized, being only used for a couple of small grist-mills."[27]

The similarity between Swain's comments and those made by Calhoun in his letter to Cyrus McCormick were not mere coincidence. Interestingly, Swain had never visited Trotter's Shoals but had relied exclusively on information provided by Calhoun. As a check on Calhoun's information, however, Swain did question others, and they all agreed that Trotter's Shoals "afforded one of the finest powers they had ever seen." He concluded that Trotter's Shoals was "certainly worthy of attention."

One disadvantage of Trotter's Shoals was that it was "rather inaccessible." This inaccessibility could be solved by the construction of railroads and by the opening of steamboat navigation above Augusta. In 1879 the U.S. Army Corps of Engineers reported that for $124,000 a steamboat channel could be dug in the Savannah River from Augusta to Trotter's Shoals, a distance of sixty-four river miles. A pole boat channel could be completed for only $45,000.[28]

Calhoun's grandiose plans for Millwood Plantation, whether he continued to live there or whether McCormick built a major manufacturing city there, were further expressed in August 1877 when he signed a contract with a black tenant named Washington Hill for a gin house to be constructed according to plans and directions given to him by Calhoun.[29] Hill was to start the job on August 4 and finish by August 30. For "the faithful performance" of the construction, Hill would be paid $25 for the framing, $20 for the roof, $10 for the weatherboarding, $9 "for the three floors," and $1 for each door and window "with all fastenings, fittings, &c." If for any reason Hill could not finish the work, including sickness and accident, he was to "forfeit all compensation for the work he may have done on it." The circumstances surrounding this construction are not known, but the suggestion is that Calhoun either needed the gin house for his tenants or he wanted it built to make his property more attractive to future investors. At any rate, by 1880 Millwood Plantation was a fully developed tenant plantation.

The 1880 agricultural census shows that Calhoun had only 5 acres of improved land, 6,664 acres of permanent meadows and pastures, and 2,500 unimproved acres. The value of his land, buildings, and fences is reported as $27,507, and the value of his farm implements and machinery is $766. His livestock, consisting of three horses, two mules, four working oxen, eight milch cows, eight other cattle, and six sheep, is valued at $658. Calhoun produced one bale of cotton on two acres, and twenty bushels of cowpeas, his only other crop.[30]

These figures imply that Calhoun was not deeply involved in agriculture in 1879 when the statistics were collected. This does not seem unreasonable, because at this time Calhoun was eighty-one years old. At any rate, as the 1875 contract shows, he did not need to labor for his wealth; his tenants did it for him.

Thirty-three of Calhoun's tenants can be identified in the 1880 agricultural schedule. Of this number, twenty-two were fixed cash renters, and the other eleven rented for a share of the crop.[31] An examination of the amount of improved acreage, the farm values, and the agricultural production of each tenure group provides important information (table 17).

Different amounts of land were farmed by the fixed renters. While one fixed tenant farmed only 8 acres, another farmed 83 acres. Four (18.2 percent) farmed more than 40 acres, but nine (40.9 percent) farmed 20 acres or less. The wide range in acreage farmed was mirrored in the land and building values—where one tenant had property valued as low as $32, and another had property valued as high as $400—and in the values of tools and machinery—where one had only one dollar's worth and another had $62 worth. The greatest gap between individual fixed renters appeared in production. In the value of all farm products sold in 1879, four tenants (18.2 percent) reported no products sold and no production of Indian corn or cotton. Thirteen (59.1 percent) did not grow oats, and fourteen (63.6 percent) did not grow wheat.

Similar differences existed among the Millwood Plantation share renters. The differences in improved acreage was not as great as among fixed renters, because only one (9.1 percent) farmed more than 40 acres, and only four (36.4 percent) farmed 20 acres or less. The values of land and buildings and of tools and machinery varied within the tenure group, however. Whereas, one share renter reported land and buildings worth $50, another reported their value at $300; whereas one reported using tools and machinery worth only $2, another reported the value of his at $73. Gaps also existed in agricultural production. Whereas a single tenant in each case reported growing 180 bushels of Indian corn, 50

Table 17

Tenant Farms, Millwood Plantation, 1880

	Fixed (n = 22)			Share (n = 11)		
	Range	Mean	Median	Range	Mean	Median
All Tenants						
Improved acreage	8–83	27.9	22.5	15–50	27.0	30.0
Values ($)						
Land, buildings	32–400	133.5	100.0	50–300	121.8	80.0
Tools, machinery	1–62	16.3	5.6	2–73	20.2	7.0
Livestock	0–234	64.6	51.0	5–285	95.0	70.0
Fence cost	0–40	12.1	7.5	0–12	11.4	10.0
All products	0–622	207.1	17.0	0–514	201.8	198.0
Indian corn (bu)	0–150	46.5	35.0	0–180	64.0	65.0
Oats (bu)	0–50	6.8	0.0	0–50	9.1	0.0
Wheat (bu)	0–49	9.0	0.0	0–51	5.0	0.0
Cotton (bales)	0–12	3.4	2.0	0–13	4.5	4.0
Those Reporting Products						
Value ($)						
All products	58–622	253.1	224.0	52–514	222.0	199.5
Indian corn (bu)	3–150	56.8	67.5	4–180	70.4	70.0
Oats (bu)	3–50	16.7	12.0	5–50	25.0	22.5
Wheat (bu)	15–49	24.8	20.5	4–51	27.5	27.5
Cotton (bales)	1–12	4.1	3.0	2–13	4.9	4.0

Source: 1880 Agricultural Schedule, Abbeville County, Magnolia Township, South Carolina.

bushels of oats, 51 bushels of wheat, and 13 bales of cotton, one (9.1 percent) reported growing no corn or cotton, seven (63.6 percent) reported raising no oats, and nine (81.8 percent) reported growing no wheat.

The differences between the two tenure groups can be illustrated by examining both the means and the medians of the figures (table 17). An examination of the means indicates that both fixed renters and share renters farmed approximately the same amount of land (27.9 acres for fixed renters, 27.0 acres for share renters). A study of the medians, however, shows that share renters actually farmed slightly larger farms overall (30.0 acres for share renters, 22.5 acres for fixed renters). Fixed tenants had a higher estimated value of land and buildings than share renters ($100 for fixed tenants, $80 for share renters), but share renters owned more livestock and produced more crops, as a group, than did fixed renters. This difference shows most clearly in corn and cotton production, where share renters produced twice as much cotton (4.0 bales to 2.0 bales) and almost twice as much corn as fixed renters (65.0 bushels to 35.0 bushels). The actual differences between the two tenure groups are better illustrated by removing those tenants who did not report production (table 17). The differences between the two tenure groups are lessened, but share renters still produced more than did fixed renters.

The differences between the Millwood Plantation fixed and share tenants who can be identified in the 1880 census carry over into livestock ownership to a lesser degree (table 18). Fairly equal proportions of fixed renters and share renters owned each kind of livestock enumerated,

Table 18

Millwood Plantation Tenants Having Livestock, 1880, by Percentage

Animal	Fixed (n = 22)	Share (n = 11)
Horses	22.7	9.1
Mules and asses	40.9	81.8
Working oxen	50.0	45.5
Milch cows	81.8	81.8
Other cattle	77.3	72.7
Sheep	4.5	9.1
Swine	68.2	63.6
Poultry	95.5	90.9

Source: 1880 Agricultural Schedule, Abbeville County, Magnolia Township, South Carolina.

with the greatest differences appearing in the ownership of horses, mules and asses, and sheep. Most informative of these differences is probably mule and ass ownership, because twice as many share renters as fixed renters owned them. Even though an equal number of share tenants and fixed tenants (nine) owned mules and asses (eight fixed tenants owned one, one fixed tenant owned two; six share tenants owned one, three share tenants owned two), the greater percentage of mules and asses on share renter farms suggests that this group had more access to these animals.

These figures suggest that the share renters were slightly better off than were the fixed rent tenants. Depending upon the exact terms of the share arrangements, which cannot be determined, the better position of share tenants, even though they were slightly below fixed renters on the agricultural ladder, can be expected. Calhoun's production of one bale of cotton and twenty bushels of cowpeas, probably actually produced by wage laborers, was considerably below the production of the average share renter. As illustrated in the last chapter, this disparity is to be expected because the tenants were, after all, working for the landlord. Calhoun received income not only from his own farm but also from the many other farms on his property. The wealth he accrued from the labor of his tenant farmers was considerable. A statement from his Augusta cotton factors, George R. Sibley and Company, showed that on September 19, 1884, Calhoun had $9,694.31 on account there.[32] This money undoubtedly came largely from the sale of tenant farm cotton.

The 1880 Industrial Schedule shows that Millwood Plantation contained a gristmill and a sawmill, each employing two hands. The gristmill hands were paid fifty cents for a ten-hour day and worked two months at full time, three months at three-quarter time, and three months at half time. This mill, a center discharge variety consisting of one milling stone, was idle for four months of each year, but processed 48,000 bushels of corn and other products worth $1,250 in 1879. The sawmill hands were paid seventy-five cents a day and worked full time for half the year and one-half time for the rest of the year. Consisting of one saw and a flutter-wheel turbine, this mill processed logs procured from the plantation. In 1879 this eight-horsepower mill produced 20,000 board feet of wood.[33]

The wealth Calhoun received from his tenants and workers was what allowed him to expand the operations of his estate. Calhoun's interest in new enterprises and his eccentricity almost took a unique turn in 1880 when he expressed a desire to make Millwood into a tea plantation. On January 2 of that year, Calhoun wrote to William G. Le Duc, commissioner of the Department of Agriculture, to inquire about the department's plan to establish a one-hundred-acre tea plantation somewhere in the South. Le Duc replied that if the bill to do so passed through Congress, he would make a tour of the South to determine the site of the farm. Le Duc said that he would do himself "the long wished for & long promised pleasure" of visiting Calhoun's "hospitable abode."[34] The Department of Agriculture had received numerous inquiries from farmers interested in cultivating tea, and in 1879 alone they distributed sixty-nine thousand tea plants.[35] Calhoun, however, had been growing tea at Millwood since 1859, when he received six tea plants from China. This experiment in tea cultivation convinced Calhoun that the South Carolina Piedmont, particularly his part of it, presented "the perfect climate for the tea-plant."[36] Millwood did not become a tea plantation, but tea was grown there for many years.[37]

The activities at Millwood during the 1880s continued much as they had in earlier decades. In November 1886 Calhoun ordered a pair of mill gears from a foundry in Augusta, and a few months later he received a request from a man in Georgia who wanted to prospect for gold on his property.[38] Nonetheless, in the mid-1880s, Calhoun was nearing ninety years of age and was beginning to narrow the range of his activities. In April 1885, he wrote that his seclusion was "so great." Two years later he refused the invitation of Mrs. George Robinson and the "Ladies Associated with the Calhoun Monument" to attend an "interesting occasion." Calhoun wrote that "after so many years of quiet routine, in a delightful location," which procured for him "perfect health & contentment" he believed that at his "extreme age any changes [would] be a hazardous episode."[39] This comment suggests the accuracy of those who called James Edward Calhoun the Hermit of Millwood in his later years.[40]

While Calhoun may not have ventured far from his estate in the mid-1880s, many people knew that he was still there and wrote to him to test his philanthropy. In February 1886, for example, Maggie McNinch of Williamston, South Carolina, wrote to thank Calhoun for his "great kindness"; one month later an orphan from Newberry, South Carolina, wrote for assistance with her education; in July of the same year, a partially blind man from Ninety-Six, South Carolina, wrote to ask for one hundred dollars so that he might visit "the celebrated oculist, Dr. Calhoun" in Atlanta.[41] These letters imply that Calhoun was widely known, at least in the northwestern corner of the South Carolina Piedmont, as a kind and generous benefactor.

In 1887 he donated a number of boxes of books to an academy operated by Professor George C. Hodges in Greenwood, South Carolina. Also, to a scholar researching the early history of the Huguenots in South Carolina, he said that he would examine his papers and forward "anything that may be useful to you."[42]

Further evidence for Calhoun's continued activity appears in a letter the proprietors of the Elberton (Georgia) Machine Works sent to him on June 17, 1887. In this letter, Phillips and Garbutt wrote that they had heard from one of their friends that Calhoun was "intending to purchase a gin and Cotton Press and other Machinery."[43] The available evidence does not indicate whether Calhoun was actually seeking to buy a gin and a cotton press, or whether this letter was an unsolicited piece of salesmanship, but the possibility exists that what Phillips and Garbutt had been told was the truth: perhaps Calhoun was seeking to purchase new industrial machinery for his Millwood Plantation. If so, then Millwood was still capable, at least in Calhoun's mind, of being expanded even further.

An intriguing letter from Calhoun's nephew, Edward B. Calhoun, sheds a different light on Calhoun during the 1880s, however. On December 5, 1888, "Teddy" Calhoun, as he was known in the area,[44] wrote to his uncle to express a number of things that he had found difficult to communicate face to face. This letter provides interesting insights into the situation at Millwood during the latter part of Calhoun's life.

Edward's letter concerned the fact that Calhoun had told him the year before that he could stay at the "Enright Place" as long as he wished. In the meantime, however, Calhoun had sold the property, and Edward found himself "all at sea again." Apparently, when he mentioned the earlier promise of his uncle, Edward was told that he would get "five per cent commission on the purchase money." Calhoun had obviously not lived up to his end of the bargain, and Edward felt compelled to bring it to his uncle's attention. Because Calhoun was obviously "so short of funds," Edward proposed to sell some of Calhoun's cotton seed for his 5 percent of the Enright selling price. Edward added, with obvious irritation, that "for a long time you have allowed nearly all of your money to go to the benefit of totally unworthy parties, so I think that it is about time to give those who are friendly towards you some chance." Without the money, Edward said, his wife, Sallie, would be forced to take a position as housekeeper to support their children. A few years earlier Calhoun had recommended against Sallie's working, but now, Edward said, "we have got to do something for a support."[45]

Whether Edward received Calhoun's support cannot be determined. Nonetheless, interesting facts are revealed in this letter. First, it provides the first reference to the Enright Place in the Calhoun correspondence. The events surrounding this property provide further insights into Calhoun's character. John J. Enright was an Irishman who settled in Abbeville in the early 1800s. In his will, Enright left two acres of land in Abbeville to the Diocese of Charleston for the construction of a Catholic church. Enright's two sons, John and Thomas, inherited the elder Enright's home, general store, and plantation, all located near Millwood's northern boundary. When the brothers died, the property was conveyed to the Diocese of Charleston by Thomas's daughter, Mary H. Enright (better known as Madame Patricia of the Ursuline Nuns of Valle Crucis, near Columbia, South Carolina), who was charged to sell it to raise the money for the construction of the church. Calhoun bought the property in May 1883, and the money was used to build the Church of the Sacred Heart in Abbeville. Local legend says that Calhoun donated the wood for the altar and confessional.[46] Second, Edward adds support to the idea that Calhoun was indeed known for his philanthropy. The likelihood is strong that Edward was merely being sarcastic when he said that his uncle was "short of funds." Calhoun obviously received income from his tenants, but apparently he was generous only to those who he felt were deserving.

Less than one year after he received Edward's letter, Calhoun died, on October 31, 1889, at the age of ninety-one, at Millwood Plantation. The obituary that appeared in the Abbeville newspaper on November 6 paints a sentimental picture of Calhoun's last days.[47] According to this account, about two weeks before his death Calhoun began to refuse "to take his usual stimulants and refreshments," including solid food. Then, surrounded by Edward Kieser (a German fixed rent tenant), Miss Margaret Calhoun (Calhoun's greatniece, the daughter of Andrew Pickens Calhoun), Mrs. Edward B. Calhoun and her two daughters, Sadie and Coodie, or "Cuddy," and an unnamed "servant woman" (probably Caroline Walker "Calhoun"), Calhoun decided that he had lived "beyond the allotted time" and was ready to die. He passed away at 5:10 A.M.

The sentimentality of the obituary was further evidenced by the stereotypical comments about the wake held the next morning. This article reports that "perhaps a hundred of his faithful old tenants and former slaves" came to view his body. Accordingly, they "all seemed deeply affected and many felt that they had lost their best friend." While some of the tenants viewed his body, others sang a hymn in the yard and then joined each other in solemn prayer. Some of the tenants were pallbearers, and seventy-five of them followed his coffin to the train station even though "rain was falling at the time." Calhoun's body was carried to Pendleton for burial next to his sister, Floride Bonneau Calhoun, wife of John C. Calhoun.

At the time of Calhoun's death, considerable local speculation centered on the terms of his will. The author of the obituary said that Calhoun had intended to leave the entire estate to Patrick Calhoun, the son of one of James Edward's nephews, Andrew Pickens Calhoun, but that Patrick Calhoun "preferred only a part," wishing instead "that his cousins . . . receive a share." At any rate, the obituary correctly reported that Calhoun was "no doubt a rich man" because he owned a great deal of land but incorrectly added that "he never contracted any debts, nor loaned any money." Finally, the obituary stated that if Calhoun had not left a will Edward B. Calhoun, of Abbeville, would inherit the entire estate because he was a nephew and everyone else "who are supposed to be named in the will" were only grandnephews and grandnieces. The obituary writer ended by commenting that the will could be contested on the grounds that Calhoun "was not of a sound and disposing mind at the time he made the will—only a few days before he died." Author Lewis Perrin incorrectly stated that Edward never contested the will because a clause in the will required the claimant to forfeit his portion upon making the claim.[48]

In truth, Calhoun wrote his will on October 19, 1889, twelve days before his death.[49] This document spelled out the disposition of Calhoun's estate in careful detail and did not contain a clause about forfeiture. The language contained in the will did not imply that Calhoun was of unsound mind at the time of its writing. Rather, the will suggested that Calhoun had a clear plan for the final division of his property among his relatives.

In the first clause, Calhoun directed his executor to pay all his debts, including that of the funeral, out of the portion of his money that was most accessible. In the second clause, he directed his executor to designate and deed 150 acres of his land in Elbert County, Georgia, to his "faithful servant Caroline Calhoun" for her to hold for life.

Caroline "Calhoun," being the first-named person in the will, was obviously someone of great importance to Calhoun. Information about her can be gleaned from the censuses. In 1870 Caroline Walker, called Caroline Calhoun by James Edward, appears in dwelling 75. Calhoun appears in dwelling 74. Caroline is listed as a 50-year-old, black domestic servant born in South Carolina. She reported three mulatto children: John, aged 17, Letty, aged 15, and Kitty, aged 13. In 1880 she appears as an illiterate, married domestic servant who is the head of her household. She stated that her father was born in Georgia, and her mother in Virginia. In this census she is listed in dwelling 469, and Calhoun is in 472. In 1900 she is reported as an 82-year-old widow who was married for thirty-seven years. She is a farmer and head of her household. After her name, the census lists six persons, referred to as sons and daughters: Emma, aged 50, Carrie, aged 35, Henry, aged 13, Margie, aged 11, Edward, aged 9, and Leo, aged 7. Carrie was probably really Letty, who appears in the 1870 census, but the identity of Emma is a mystery. The younger children are undoubtedly Caroline's grandchildren, probably Carrie's children. All members of Caroline's household are listed as "black," not "mulatto," in the 1900 census.[50]

When interviewed in 1981, two of Caroline Walker's great-great-grandsons felt that Caroline was Calhoun's "mistress, because she stayed in the house all the time." They felt that Calhoun had purchased Caroline from Edgefield, South Carolina.[51] Although it cannot conclusively be proven, the evidence does provide support for the idea that Caroline Walker was Calhoun's companion at Millwood Plantation during the last few decades of his life.

The third clause of Calhoun's will was similar to the second in that Calhoun requested that his executor deed 150 acres in either Abbeville County or Elbert County, Georgia, to Edward Kieser to be held in fee simple. Kieser is more difficult to identify than is Caroline Walker, but some of his life can be reconstructed. In 1880 Kieser was a twenty-three-year-old fixed rent tenant of James Edward Calhoun, originally from Wittenburg, Germany. He was single and farmed 45 acres, on which he raised 75 bushels of Indian corn, 50 bushels of oats, 20 bushels of wheat, 15 bushels of cowpeas, 40 bushels of sweet potatoes, and four bales of cotton. In 1900 Kieser, who reported that he had arrived in the United States in 1874, was still single; his occupation was listed as "merchant."[52] Kieser's rise from tenant farmer to merchant may have been occasioned by Calhoun's land grant. Calhoun may have had a certain fondness for Kieser because he may have come to America as a result of one of Calhoun's advertisements abroad.

In the fourth clause in the will, Calhoun directed that the remainder of his land in Abbeville County and in Elbert County, Georgia, be divided equally "in such manner and at such time" as his executor would "deem best." Those who would receive property were his nephew Edward B. Calhoun, and his living grandnieces and grandnephews, John C. Calhoun, Patrick Calhoun, and Margaret Maria Calhoun (children of nephew Andrew Pickens Calhoun who had died in 1865), and Benjamin Putnam Calhoun and John C. Calhoun (sons of nephew John Caldwell Calhoun, Jr., who had died in 1855). Also included was great-grand-nephew Andrew P. Calhoun, the son of Calhoun's deceased grand-nephew Duff Green Calhoun.[53] Calhoun left it to the executor to decide how and when to make the actual land divisions.

In the fifth clause, Calhoun expressed the same wishes as in the fourth clause for his land in Oconee and Pickens counties. All of those named in the preceding clause appeared in this clause with the exception of Benjamin P. Calhoun, who was replaced by Isabella Lee (daughter of Calhoun's grandniece, Floride Elizabeth Clemson Lee) and Maria Pickens Butler (niece of Calhoun's "lamented wife," Maria Simkins). Calhoun again left to the executor the decision about how and when to divide this property. The executor was also directed, in the sixth clause, to divide any "residue" of the estate equally among those mentioned in the fourth clause. In the seventh clause, Calhoun directed that the executor hold all the interest bequeathed to Andrew Pickens Calhoun until his twenty-first birthday, and in the eighth clause, Calhoun finally named grandnephew Patrick Calhoun, of Atlanta, Georgia, the sole executor of his estate.

In the final clause of the will, Calhoun requested that the executor hold the land bequeathed to Edward B. Calhoun, Patrick Calhoun's uncle, in trust for "the sole, separate use, benefit and behoof of my said nephew Edward B., his wife and children." This land could not be used against any of Edward's debts or obligations, past or future. Patrick was further empowered to pay Edward the annual interest from his inheritance for the remainder of Edward's life. Upon Edward's death, his portion of the estate would be divided equally among his heirs. This clause suggests that, for some reason, Calhoun simply did not trust Edward Calhoun with money. Calhoun was trying either to protect him or to punish him. At any rate, this clause is interesting in light of Edward's harsh letter of the year before.

Shortly after Calhoun's death, the probate court of Abbeville County called for the inventory and appraisal of Calhoun's estate. Sometime between November 1, 1889, and March 10, 1890, Calhoun's estate was inventoried.[54]

This inventory revealed the scope and breadth of Calhoun's material possessions during his last years. His personal property totaled $24,180.48. Of this amount, $20,367.23, or 84.2 percent, consisted of personal loan notes, made mostly to Calhoun's tenants. Some of these loans, however, dated to 1864. The notes, ranging in size from $5 to $3,000, attest to Calhoun's generosity. Other interesting items include one Chinese clothes basket, two porcelain-lined coffeepots, eight champagne glasses, one theodolite and two surveying compasses, and $100 worth of Confederate 6 percent bonds. The remainder of the items are those that would be expected to be found in the home of a rural planter and landlord: agricultural implements, hardware and tools, an assortment of dishes and flatware, personal items (watches, buttons, and so forth), hunting rifles, and foodstuffs.

With the inventory completed, an estate sale was held on March 10 and 11, 1890, by order of the probate court of Abbeville County. The list of sales provides information about who purchased what and how much was paid for it.[55] Local planters, Millwood tenants, and Edward Kieser purchased most of the agricultural implements and tools. Patrick Calhoun bought many items that might have had sentimental value for the family, such as a pair of dueling pistols for $20.00; a rifle for $5.50; a brass watch for $1.30; three gold watches for $22.00, $40.00, and $41.00; a telescope for $2.00; a pocket compass for $4.00; a silver dog whistle for $5.00; and a silver watch key for $3.00. Edward B. Calhoun bought one clock for $1.80 (Edward Kieser bought one for $11.00); the Chinese clothes basket for $1.55; a stove for $10.00; a table for $5.00; a pump for $2.00; and a number of silver items: a sugar dish for $40.00, a tea pot for $50.00, a cream pitcher for $30.00, and a coffeepot for

$50.00. Edward Calhoun's wife bought a writing desk for $7.00. In all, the estate sale netted $1,644.27.

Calhoun's death and the settlement of his estate attracted considerable attention in Abbeville County. In 1885 the Abbeville newspaper stated that James Edward Calhoun was the largest taxpayer in the county.[56] Even though this was partly an illusion, because his tenants actually paid their own taxes, Calhoun was still probably the largest landowner, and the local white inhabitants of the county were interested in his affairs. The depth of this interest was expressed in an 1891 newspaper article entitled "Will There Be a Sensation?"[57] This article was founded on a rumor, then "current on the streets," that a number of heretofore unknown heirs of James Edward Calhoun had come forward to contest the will and to gain their just portion of the estate. While the estate attorneys, Grayson and Grayson, would not discuss the situation with the reporter, they did admit that they had received a letter making this claim. The reporter was able to learn that these claimants stated that their deceased mother had been married to James Edward Calhoun. When she and Calhoun developed an "unhappy domestic life," they had separated, and she had moved "West" about forty years before, or around 1851. The children said that nobody in Abbeville County remembered them because they had lived there so long ago. The reporter astutely observed that the claim was "nothing more than a nine day's wonder" and that "those of our fellow citizens who may be looking for the excitement incident to a big law-suit, may be disappointed." The extant records provide no further information about this possible legal challenge or Calhoun's "first" wife, and the whole incident constitutes a footnote in the history of Millwood Plantation.

While the speculation about Calhoun's will and the rumor of "new" heirs circulated through the county, Calhoun's tenants were still faced with the mundane task of making a living as tenant farmers. The plantation did not die with Calhoun, and the tenants discovered that, economically, one landlord was simply replaced by another. The plantation was not subdivided by executor Patrick Calhoun, and its operation continued much as it had while Calhoun was alive.

Remarkable information about the organization and operation of Millwood Plantation during the period after Calhoun's death is presented in the annual estate returns filed by agents William P. Calhoun from 1890 to 1893 and by Granville Beal from 1894 to 1910 for Patrick Calhoun. These returns provide a superb account of the continued operation of the plantation.[58]

A review of these returns, composed of the receipts collected and the expenditures made by the agents of the estate, reveals that the estate made money in all years except 1893 (table 19). The returns provide details about how this money was acquired and disbursed. For example, in 1890, the estate paid $625.75 in taxes in Abbeville County, $130.00 in taxes in Oconee County, and $73.80 in taxes in Elbert County, Georgia. These tax figures show not only that the majority of Calhoun's lands were in Abbeville County but also that his land in Pickens County had been sold by this date. Expenditures for foodstuffs, hauling cottonseed to the railroad, ginning cotton, and paying wages demonstrate that Millwood Plantation was an active and fully operational tenant plantation during the late nineteenth and early twentieth centuries. On June 23, 1891, a millwright named Johnson was paid $1.25; on September 18,

Table 19

Annual Receipts, Expenditures, and Balance for James Edward Calhoun Estate, 1890–1910

Year	Receipts	Expenditures	Balance
1890	$ 4,595.25	$4,449.41	$ 145.84
1891	5,142.59	2,723.10	2,419.49
1892	4,957.46	2,413.00	2,544.46
1893	5,734.88	6,560.15	−825.27
1894	3,266.64	2,088.87	1,177.77
1895	5,521.70	1,478.20	4,043.50
1896	4,700.81	1,773.63	2,927.18
1897	3,810.38	2,033.35	1,777.03
1898	3,987.57	1,763.02	2,224.55
1899	5,277.18	2,441.56	2,835.62
1900	6,590.08	2,304.34	4,285.74
1901	5,848.20	4,142.83	1,705.37
1902	5,624.71	2,710.60	2,914.11
1903	8,780.39	5,603.26	3,177.13
1904	7,484.70	3,843.14	3,641.56
1905	8,561.21	5,760.19	2,801.02
1906	10,147.59	1,723.91	8,423.68
1907	8,727.78	3,146.54	5,581.24
1908	6,872.19	3,100.40	3,771.79
1909	9,345.46	3,013.33	6,332.13
1910	10,377.19	3,308.20	7,068.99

Source: Annual returns of the James Edward Calhoun estate, 1890–1910, probate court of Abbeville County, Abbeville, South Carolina.

1891, a man named Burton was paid for work on the millrace; the well was cleaned in 1893; fences were built in 1896; and three cabins were constructed in 1904. Millwood Plantation was obviously still active.

More important than the everyday operation of the plantation by the estate agents were the activities of the tenants. The annual returns indicate that a significant change in the landlord-tenant relationship occurred at Millwood Plantation in 1891, when tenants began paying their rent in cotton. This change was not as significant as the change that had occurred in 1865, but it demonstrates the fluidity of the tenure relationships on postbellum tenant plantations.

The estate returns show that the vast majority of the income collected on the Calhoun estate was from the tenants. The tenants provided from 76.8 (in 1893) to 99.7 percent of the income (in 1909) (table 20). In 1890 this tenant-derived income came from cash paid to the estate for rent. The annual return for this year lists the name of each tenant and how much rent he paid. Ninety-five tenants are listed, and the rents they paid range from $2.50 to $108.00.

The receipt of these cash rents correlates well with the earlier census information that indicates that most of the Millwood Plantation tenants were cash renters. In 1891, however, the tenants began paying their rent in cotton. In the returns filed after 1891, the receipts show that the estate received "rent cotton." Whether this cotton represents a fixed rent in cotton, such as that paid by standing renters, or a share of the cotton produced, such as that paid by share renters, cannot be determined; however, because none of the returns show any expenditures for fertilizer by the estate, it appears that the tenants were standing renters. This means that in the twenty-six years since 1865, Millwood Plantation had been farmed by squad members, sharecroppers, fixed rent tenants, and finally by standing renters. Through all these changes, the bulk of the wealth from the plantation was supplied by tenant farmers.

While the sale of cotton provided most of the money for the Calhoun estate, other receipts came annually from the sale of the estate's wood and from rent for the Calhoun Ferry. An occasional sale of corn also brought money to the estate.

The tenants continued to live their lives on Millwood Plantation as farmers, but a legal battle over the final disposition of the plantation was brewing. At some point between 1890 and 1903, the assembled heirs of James Edward Calhoun grew tired of having Patrick Calhoun serve them

Table 20

Total Annual Receipts from All Sources, Receipts from Cotton Sales, and Receipts from Rents, Millwood Plantation, 1890–1910

Year	Total receipts	Cotton sales	Rents from tenants
1890	$ 4,595.25	$ 424.55 (9.2)*	$4,117.02 (89.6)*
1891	5,142.59	4,225.48 (82.2)	0
1892	4,957.46	4,065.00 (82.0)	54.00 (1.1)
1893	5,734.88	4,315.40 (75.2)	89.37 (1.6)
1894	3,266.64	3,096.12 (94.8)	41.00 (1.3)
1895	5,521.70	4,891.20 (88.6)	41.00 (0.7)
1896	4,700.81	4,634.76 (98.6)	15.00 (0.3)
1897	3,810.38	3,745.83 (98.3)	15.00 (0.4)
1898	3,987.57	3,853.70 (96.6)	15.00 (0.4)
1899	5,277.18	5,251.78 (99.5)	8.00 (0.2)
1900	6,590.08	6,544.88 (99.3)	8.00 (0.1)
1901	5,848.20	5,728.20 (97.9)	8.00 (0.1)
1902	5,624.71	5,581.31 (99.2)	0
1903	8,780.39	8,587.86 (97.8)	0
1904	7,484.70	6,953.10 (92.9)	0
1905	8,561.21	8,388.13 (98.0)	0
1906	10,147.59	8,475.50 (83.5)	0
1907	8,727.78	7,863.28 (90.1)	0
1908	6,872.19	6,760.87 (97.6)	0
1909	9,345.46	9,320.66 (99.7)	0
1910	10,377.19	10,304.18 (99.3)	0

Source: Annual returns of the James Edward Calhoun estate, 1890–1910, probate court of Abbeville County, Abbeville, South Carolina.

*Percentage of total receipts.

as executor. Patrick Calhoun was apparently content to have the estate perpetuated as a tenant plantation and was in no hurry to subdivide it among the heirs. With Andrew P. Calhoun, of San Antonio, Texas, leading them, Edward B. Calhoun, Sarah N. Calhoun, and the other heirs filed suit to have the estate sold. On January 29, 1903, Patrick Calhoun filed a bill of complaint against Andrew Calhoun and the others to halt the sale of the estate, but he lost when the court of common pleas of Abbeville County found against him on May 24, 1906. The court ordered him to offer the sale of the estate at the door of the Abbeville County Courthouse in the town square on Monday, October 1, 1906.[59] In all, 11,773.5 acres in Abbeville County (consisting of two tracts: one of 11,664 acres; the other, 109.5 acres), 2,384 acres in Elbert County, and 65,000 acres in Oconee County were to be offered for sale. The land in

Abbeville and Elbert counties comprised Millwood Plantation (figure 14). Not included in the sale were the 150 acres Calhoun willed to Caroline Walker and the 150 acres left to Edward Kieser. Both parcels were located in Elbert County, Georgia. Also exempt were four tracts that Patrick Calhoun had sold: two acres to a man named Edward Simpson, six-tenths of an acre to the Georgia, Carolina, & Northern Railroad for a right-of-way, one acre to a Mr. J. S. Norwood, and two acres to Millwood Plantation manager Granville Beal. For the lands in Abbeville and Elbert counties, to be sold as a single plantation unit, Patrick Calhoun would accept no less than $165,000, with $5,000 in cash or certified check; for the Oconee County lands, he would not accept less than $10,000, with $1,000 in cash or certified check. The terms of the sale were simple enough. The down payment was to be paid within thirty days after the sale, one-third of it in cash. The balance was to be paid in one or two years at 7 percent interest.[60]

By noon on the day of the sale, a large crowd had gathered outside the Abbeville County Courthouse, but because of rain, the sale was moved inside. In the crowd were a number of men representing large corporations, including W. S. Montgomery from Spartanburg, South Carolina, William S. Lee from the Southern Power Company of Charlotte, North Carolina, and E. H. Jennings from Pittsburgh, Pennsylvania. Interest in the Calhoun estate obviously was not confined to the local area.

Granville Beal, the Millwood manager, served as auctioneer, and the bidding lasted only thirty minutes. When the bidding was over, Andrew P. Calhoun, one of the original complainants against Patrick Calhoun in 1903, was the successful bidder, having purchased all property for $260,500, $86,634 of which was cash. This price was considerably above the $175,000 minimum asking price, so it can be assumed that the bidding was brisk. Andrew Calhoun agreed to pay the balance in two annual installments.[61]

In actuality, the real purchaser of the Calhoun estate was its executor, Patrick Calhoun. As executor, hence the holder of the sale, Patrick Calhoun was unable to bid on the property. The purchaser of record, however, was Andrew P. Calhoun, and it was he who would be in default if the balance was not paid.[62]

Almost three months after Andrew P. Calhoun bought the property and only one month after he had received the final deed, the Calhoun Falls Company was formed. The Calhoun Falls Company was a South

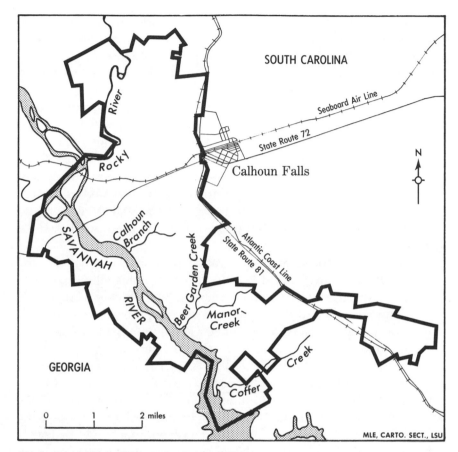

Figure 14. Millwood Plantation lands, 1903.

Carolina corporation established by Mathew C. Butler, Augustine T. Smythe, and Henry J. Bowdoin. Butler was an Army general who had served as one of three witnesses to the signing of James Edward Calhoun's will in 1889. He had been present at the estate sale, and although he lived in Washington, D.C., he was still deeply interested in Calhoun's Millwood Plantation. Smythe was an attorney in Charleston, South Carolina, whose firm represented Patrick Calhoun.[63]

The purpose of the Calhoun Falls Company was simple. It would seek to do what would eventually cause Millwood Plantation to receive the attention of modern scholars: to build one or more dams across the Savannah River for the express purpose of generating water power. Another aspect of the company's grandiose scheme was the construction of a grand manufacturing city at Millwood—the realization of James Edward Calhoun's original dream. The Calhoun Falls Company sought to erect factories "for the purpose of manufacturing, spinning, dyeing, printing, finishing, and selling goods of every kind made of cotton, wool, or wood" and to build "such dams, mills, buildings, machine shops, stores, dwellings, and other houses as may be necessary or required to carry on any or all of such branches of manufacture and business." The company also planned to condemn as much land as necessary to accomplish this plan. A total of twenty-eight hundred shares at $100 each were to be sold as capital stock in the company.[64] The $280,000 raised would cover the cost of the Calhoun property, which had been purchased for $260,500.

The corporate articles of incorporation were drawn up under the names of Butler, Smythe, and Bowdoin, but Patrick Calhoun actually held the controlling interest in the company, 60.5 percent of the stock. Butler, Smythe, and Bowdoin held 14.3 percent, 3.6 percent, and 9.1 percent of the stock, respectively. Andrew P. Calhoun held 11.8 percent, and two minor investors each held less than 0.5 percent.[65]

On January 2, 1907, Andrew P. Calhoun, who stated that he had originally acted not only for himself but as agent for the Calhoun Falls Company, sold the company to the Calhoun estate for the token price of one dollar. Andrew Calhoun did this because he said that he had originally intended to hold the property only until a corporation could be legally established.[66] Patrick Calhoun, who obviously enjoyed his position as estate executor and who undoubtedly held the same vision for Millwood as had its original owner, never lost his control over the property during this period.

Some years later, the vision of the Calhoun Falls Company had not materialized or even begun. Millwood Plantation was not a grand center of manufacturing and water power, but a tenant farming plantation. Granville Beal continued to collect rent cotton until 1912; after him the collections were made briefly by a Mr. Parker, and then by John G. Carlisle.[67] The business of the company was in complete disarray by this time, and Augustine T. Smythe, the estate lawyer who held a 3.6 percent interest in the company, was appointed by the court to be the receiver of the corporation on January 30, 1914. The taxes on the land had not been paid and a real danger existed that both Millwood Plantation and Calhoun's lands in Oconee County would be once again sold at auction. No provisions for planting on the plantation had been made, and the tenants were reportedly "at a standstill." To keep the estate functioning, Smythe proposed to borrow somewhere less than twelve thousand dollars against receiver's certificates at 7 percent interest.[68]

Smythe again petitioned the court the following month to appoint a surveyor and a hydraulic engineer to make a thorough survey of Millwood Plantation so that he might be better able to judge which land was suited to agriculture and which to water power. A few of the heirs had inquired about paying the eighty-thousand-dollar mortgage debt owed by the Calhoun Falls Company. Smythe wanted the property surveyed so that the land suitable for agriculture could be divided "into farms of ordinary size, suitable for ready sale for small planters." The land found useful for the development of water power, obviously that along the Savannah River, would be reserved for the company.

In addition, Smythe noted that the entire Millwood tract was under cultivation, "principally by negro tenants"; however, because the company was in no financial position to furnish the tenants with cash or supplies, they had been carried "for a number of years" by advances made by three neighborhood merchants, S. J. Hester, C. H. Taylor, and Ed Kieser. Each merchant had agreed to continue furnishing the tenants until the end of the season. For the first five months of 1914, $168.97, $1,777.02, and $247.76 was owed to Hester, Taylor, and Kieser, respectively. As Smythe said, these merchants had made advances to the tenants in good faith, and they were "anxious to get the money to be used in carrying out their arrangements for advances to the tenants for the present year." Smythe requested that the court allow him to pay the merchants so that the agricultural operations of the plantation could continue. Smythe's requests were granted three days later.[69]

The plan to sell Millwood Plantation was partially realized by the Calhoun Falls Company only two years later in 1916. A man named William S. Lee, from Mecklenburg County, North Carolina, who seemed to be acting alone but who was actually an agent of the Southern Power Company, a subsidiary of Duke Power Company, bought sections of the property on June 14 for $165,000. Lee had been present at the original sale but was not a successful bidder.

Lee's purchase of this land made it clear that James Edward Calhoun's original dream of developing a huge source of water power on the Savannah River was not forgotten. The plan was obviously going to be enacted by Duke Power Company. Lee receive a deed for "the bed, banks, and water powers" on the Savannah River for the entire frontage of the Calhoun estate and all the land, including the islands, up to 380 feet above mean sea level.[70] Lee was given permission to construct a dam across the river at a location of his choosing and was allowed to flood the banks up to 420 feet above mean sea level. The deed also allowed Lee to build roads, run telephone, telegraph, and transmission lines across the entire estate, and select no more than 500 acres for the construction of "power houses, canals, viaducts, flumes, commissaries, hotels, dwellings, buildings, and structures."[71] After having a careful survey made, Lee selected his 500 acres (actually 501.3 acres: 441.4 in Abbeville County and 59.9 in Elbert County) in March 1929, thirteen years later.[72]

About six months before Lee and his Duke Power Company selected their 500 acres in anticipation of the creation of their new source of water power, the Calhoun Falls Company made a conditional sale of the remainder of the estate. On September 28, 1928, Patrick Calhoun made an agreement with Philip Miner, of Cleveland, Ohio, and William Gray and Robert J. Kratky, of Saint Louis, Missouri, for the purchase of 12,500 acres for $500,000. For $100,000 in cash, the remainder to be paid at a yearly rate of $50,000, these investors would own all the land not previously sold to Lee. They also agreed to grant Lee whatever privilege he would need to fulfill his plan to develop water power.[73]

Hopes continued to run high for the industrialization of the Calhoun estate, and a map of the estate drawn by the William H. Evers Engineering Company of Cleveland, Ohio—a firm probably hired by Miner—dated December 5, 1928, shows a body of water named Savannah Lake extending to the 420-foot contour line in the old bed of the Savannah River. The map is entitled "Properties of Calhoun Falls, Inc." after the new corporation headed by Miner.[74] This "lake" and new corporation were only chimeras, and the map was obviously intended to show what was *hoped* to be not what *would* be. Only six months later, when they could not pay the $100,000 they had agreed to pay by March 1, Miner, Gray, and Kratky gave up their right to buy the property. Instead, they paid the Calhoun Falls Company $15,000 in damages.[75] Presumably, Calhoun Falls, Inc., was dissolved at this time.

The real estate maneuverings over the James Edward Calhoun estate continued into the 1930s. In February 1925, Andrew P. Calhoun sued the Calhoun Falls Company and won a judgment of $45,526.37. Being heavily in debt and unable, or unwilling, to make the payment in cash, the company was forced to sell 4,917 acres of the estate at public auction. Abbeville County sheriff F. B. McLane sold this property to I. C. Harrison, who turned it over to a new corporation called the Millwood Company. Later that same year, 1933, Harrison bought another 6,411 acres that he also turned over to the Millwood Company. This land had been held by the New York Life Insurance Company for the Calhoun Falls Company.[76] With this sale, the association of the Calhoun Falls Company with Millwood Plantation seems to have ended.

By the mid-1930s the final arrangement of private land ownership of the Calhoun estate had been made. The Duke Power Company, through its South Carolina–based Wateree Power Company, owned those lands along the Savannah River, and the Millwood Company owned the remainder of the estate.

During all the sales and resales of the Calhoun estate, when the property changed hands or almost changed hands, the tenant farmers there continued to work. They were not involved in the sales of the land and, in fact, may not have even known about them. Theirs was not a world of high finance, but one of living day to day in the effort to make a crop. Because these tenants were not involved in the larger issues of estate ownership, little written evidence of their lives exists. As a result, most current knowledge about them derives from oral information collected from the tenants themselves. Some of these tenants were descended from former Calhoun slaves. Although some of the former tenants' memories are clouded by time, they cannot be dismissed as insignificant; they provide a wealth of information available from no other source.[77]

Many tenants lived at Millwood between 1920 and 1940. The widow of the former manager during this period stated that ninety-eight tenant families lived on the estate in 1928. A former tenant said that a "swarm of people" lived on the estate in 1939, and another said that in 1940 "there were people all over the place." Another said that tenants "were everywhere" and that they lived in "just one house after another" but that they did not crowd one another "like in the city." Another added that the tenants on the estate were like "one family" and that most were blacks, or "half-whites," meaning mulattos.

Most of the former tenants remembered their tenant farms well. Almost all of them had some livestock, usually a milk cow, a few pigs, and some chickens. All the tenants raised cotton as a cash crop and corn and wheat as staples. As one said, "cotton was the main thing, because you had to pay bills with that cotton." Each family had its own garden and supplemented its diet with wild foods such as quail, geese, opossum, rabbits, squirrels, and blackberries. In addition, fish were plentiful and easy to catch in the Savannah River, even though one tenant said that he did not fish much because he had no time for it.

Foremost in many of the tenants' minds was the tenure arrangements they had made with the plantation manager. Their statements make it clear that most of them were standing renters who paid one bale of cotton as rent. One former tenant said, "We didn't have to give him [the manager] nothing but that one bale of cotton and everything else was ours." Once the tenant gave the manager a 400-pound bale of cotton, "he'd go about his business" and "you ain't got no more to do with him." One tenant remembered paying a 500-pound bale, and another said that her family paid two 500-pound bales. But all standing renters agreed that once paid, the manager "didn't have nothing to do with nothing else." Still, if they made only one bale, the manager got it for rent. One tenant said, when speaking of his years as a tenant farmer at Millwood, he had "to pay the other man the best I could."

Tenants described the various tenure arrangements practiced at Millwood. One tenant said that "if you owned your own stock, they'd rent" for a bale of cotton, but if the estate had to furnish anything to assist in making a crop, the manager received half the crop. This included fertilizer and arsenic to kill the boll weevils. Another tenant said that he started farming on the Calhoun estate "on halves." Later, when he began renting for a bale of cotton, the cotton was "understood for cash." The manager did not furnish anything except the land. Tenants had a house only if they built it themselves. Accordingly, "if you didn't build none, you didn't have none." Another former tenant said that in addition to sharecroppers, called "halvers," some "people worked for a third" because the manager had "to furnish mules and plows, plow points, gear, all, everything."

Although most of the Millwood tenants were standing renters, a couple of the former tenants stated that some were share renters. These tenants rented for one-fourth of their cotton. This kind of arrangement, however, was infrequent at Millwood.

Some of the tenants questioned mentioned the merchants with whom they dealt while they lived at Millwood. One of the former tenants said that the merchants would take a lien on the crop and would extend credit in the spring of each year. As he said, if a person bought a seventy-five-cent sack of flour, the merchants would "charge you about a dollar and a half." In September, when the cotton would be picked, ginned, and sold, the tenants would pay their bills "and usually they'd just about come out even." In addition to taking a mortgage on the crop, the merchants would mortgage "cows or horses or anything," in other words, "practically everything you had." At least one former tenant expressed his opinion that the white merchants frequently cheated the Millwood tenants because "half the time people didn't know what they was getting."

Little is known about these merchants. As noted above, the principal merchants for Millwood Plantation were Edward Kieser, the German immigrant who had begun as a Calhoun tenant, S. J. Hester, and C. H. Taylor. Of these merchants, Kieser was probably most important to the Millwood tenants.[78] Unfortunately, the exact role of the merchants on the estate cannot be assessed accurately.

While the men of the tenant families made their living raising cotton, many of their wives provided supplemental income by doing the laundry of neighboring white families. For between twenty-five cents and one dollar, tenant farm wives would walk from Millwood to Calhoun Falls, a distance as great as four and a half miles, pick up laundry, transport it back to Millwood in baskets on their heads, wash it with "nothing but an old wash board, rub board, and tub," and iron it (figure 15). These women, often accompanied by their children, would walk between Millwood and Calhoun Falls from Monday morning to Friday night. As one tenant said, these women were in a position where "wasn't nothing to do. They had to do something to make a living." One of the white tenants stated that he frequently gave these washerwomen rides in the back of his old truck. He said that when they knew he was in town "there'd be maybe half a dozen of them sitting up there under a tree at the railroad waiting for [him] to come home." He said, "I hauled many a load of them with their clothes." Once the whites in town had cars, the women stopped going there to pick up the clothes, because the whites would deliver and pick them up themselves. The black washerwoman's work, at one time an integral part of the tenant farming system at Millwood Plantation, passed away with the widespread use of washing machines during the 1940s.

The exact date that Millwood Plantation became depopulated cannot

Figure 15. Millwood Plantation washerwomen at work. (U.S. Army Corps of Engineers, Savannah District)

be determined. Although many of the reasons for the abandonment of the estate involve circumstances that extend far beyond the boundaries of the plantation, at least one reason is particular to Millwood: the use of the plantation as a campground and picnic spot for local whites.

According to the former estate manager's wife, people started camping at Millwood shortly after Calhoun died, in 1889. These people would spend the night in two deserted cabins in the landlord's part of the plantation, and camp in tents throughout the yard. The Abbeville newspaper said in 1933 that "campers and picnickers have been drawn to this estate as a favorite place for generations." Accordingly, "in years gone by people from Greenwood, Anderson, and other counties as well as Abbeville spent the summer in this beautiful spot." When the local highways were improved, people were drawn to other places, and by 1933 only nearby residents went there to fish. The article reported, "Seiners have been known to catch 300 pounds of the famous channel, sand, and blue cat in one afternoon."[79]

What the newspaper did not mention was that the influx of white campers caused considerable inconvenience and worry to the black tenant farmers. The tenants who lived at Millwood Plantation every day and called it home were put in an extremely delicate position by these campers. As one tenant said when two vacant houses were filled with campers, "The people had to put up tents all around . . . right back in our yard, and we couldn't get by [because] there was cars and different things [everywhere]." According to this tenant, whole families of whites would come to Millwood "all the way from New York and everyplace."

Not only did these white campers cause problems by their very presence, they also presented clear threats. Many of these campers often stole produce from the tenants' gardens and occasionally killed tenants' animals. One tenant remembered: "We had pear thieves, pig thieves, and things like that. They didn't ask us for nothing. . . . The only thing I know they didn't do, they didn't kill that hog, but [they did kill] your chickens." One tenant noted that the campers would pay for some of what they took, but most things were taken without any offer of remuneration.

The tension between the campers and tenants was heightened when white men came to drink on the property without their families. "They'd stay one [week] without their wives, their wives come the next week," said one tenant. Some of these men had apparently constructed a clubhouse near the river.

Although few tenants were willing to talk much about the period during which white campers came to the plantation, this time was undoubtedly a difficult one for the tenants. The problems were adequately expressed in 1942, when two men, Floyd Majors and Louis Brown, were indicted for setting fire to two camp houses at Millwood. Majors was found guilty of arson, sentenced to three years in prison, but given a suspended sentence and paroled.[80] One tenant said that the only defense against the campers was to move, "We moved, had to move." Many of the Calhoun tenants apparently moved off the estate during the 1920s and 1930s, although many still continued to frequent the property intermittently. Still, with the influx of white campers, Millwood ceased to function as a tenant plantation. By the time of the land sales to I. C. Harrison, Millwood Plantation was largely devoid of working tenants, although, as shown in the following chapter, many of their homes continued to survive.

The history of Millwood Plantation did not end when the tenants left the estate. Its end, however, was not far off.

In February 1952, John C. Williams, United States attorney, and Walter H. Sims, special attorney for the Department of Justice, filed a declaration of taking to receive by right of eminent domain those lands owned by the Millwood Company (later to merge into the South Carolina Land and Timber Corporation, which later changed its name to the Crescent Land and Timber Corporation) and by Duke Power Company.[81] This land and land much more to the north would be the site of the Trotter's Shoals Dam and Reservoir, later renamed the Richard B. Russell Dam and Lake. In 1966 a plan for the construction of the dam and lake was put forth in the United States Senate, and shortly thereafter the 89th Congress enacted Public Law 89-789 calling for the "construction of the Trotter's Shoals Reservoir on the Savannah River" at an estimated cost of $84,900,000.[82]

In January 1985, the dream of James Edward Calhoun, Patrick Calhoun, the Calhoun Falls Company, Calhoun Falls, Inc., the Millwood Company, and the Duke Power Company (but certainly not of the tenants) finally became a reality when the Richard B. Russell Dam was finished and closed, and the power pool for the generation of electrical power began to rise. Today, Millwood Plantation, with its abundant and priceless evidence about the organization and life of a postbellum Piedmont cotton plantation, lies under the waters of the Richard B. Russell Multiple Resource Area, visited only by unknowing sport fishermen and boaters. All physical and archaeological evidence not already collected is lost forever. Neither Calhoun nor anyone else who sought the development of water power at Trotter's Shoals ever foresaw the inundation of Millwood Plantation.

Chapter Six

The Material Basis
of Millwood Plantation:
Houses and Settlement

To this point, Millwood Plantation has been presented as a historical and cultural entity that gained expression through the actions of its inhabitants. The majority of its inhabitants were first slaves and then tenant farmers, and little documentation exists about them. What does exist was not written by them. As a result, the history of Millwood Plantation, as it can be compiled from the available records, is largely a history of James Edward Calhoun's activities there. This history is largely "big man" history. Other histories can be compiled through the use of other sources of information. Historical archaeology presents one way of discovering some of this information.

Historical archaeology permits Millwood Plantation to be seen as a physical entity having discrete boundaries and containing buildings, roads, fences, trees, and grass. The use of archaeological techniques for the collection of data transforms Millwood from an historical abstraction into a physical, material reality. This physical reality consists of building remains, evidence of the use of space across the plantation, and material possessions. This chapter explores the first two subjects; the next chapter, the third subject.

With the final planning of the Richard B. Russell Dam and Lake, then called the Trotter's Shoals Reservoir, a concern over the cultural resources contained within its boundaries—those sites and properties having historical or cultural significance—began to be expressed. In compliance with federal legislation, an archaeological survey of the region to be flooded or otherwise affected by construction was conducted by the

Institute of Archaeology and Anthropology at the University of South Carolina.[1] The physical remains of Millwood Plantation were located during this survey.

The archaeologists who "discovered" Millwood Plantation in January-February 1970 described it as consisting of "rather extensive remains" composed of "masonry foundations and chimney footings of the house and outbuildings, masonry foundations of millworks, and a millrace about one quarter of a mile long."[2] Although no artifacts were collected at this time, and no historical research was conducted, the archaeologists recommended further archaeological and historical research at this impressive site.

Seven years later, this simple survey was followed with a more extensive study also conducted by the Institute of Archaeology and Anthropology.[3] At this time, a small collection of artifacts was removed from the surface of the site, thirty building foundations were located, and a detailed map of the plantation was prepared. In addition, twenty-nine individual sites—mostly tenant farmsteads—were located within the boundaries of the Calhoun estate.[4] Although James Edward Calhoun's entire estate contained well over ten thousand acres, the Millwood Plantation archaeological site was restricted to about thirty-two acres.

These surveys demonstrated that the land that composed Millwood Plantation had remained largely undisturbed and that the site demanded further research attention. The information presented in this book was collected in recognition of these survey findings. This research provided extensive information about the material basis of Millwood Plantation.[5]

As shown in the preceding chapters, over the course of the plantation's history, the agricultural operations were organized into three distinct systems. From 1834 to 1865, the Millwood crops were produced through the labor of black slaves. Immediately after the war and up to 1870 or 1875, crops were produced by freed slave collectives who worked under the supervision of individual squad leaders. And finally, from 1875 to about 1925, Millwood Plantation operated as a tenant plantation worked by former slaves who were now classified as tenant farmers. Thus, Millwood Plantation was a slave plantation for thirty-one years, a transitional plantation for about 10 years (or eight years from the signing of the contract with the seven freedmen), and a tenant plantation for about fifty years. Millwood was a non-slave operated plantation twice as long as it had been a slave plantation.

Given this history, it should not be surprising that Millwood Plantation, as it lay in ruins in 1980, exhibited the general spatial organization of a postbellum plantation. Millwood's slave history had low visibility, undoubtedly because Millwood's tenants had little interest in preserving the plantation's antebellum spatial organization or buildings. For Calhoun's part, it would have been uneconomical and impractical to preserve the antebellum form of the plantation once the tenants had moved into individual tenant houses. The antebellum buildings that were no longer needed were probably either dismantled for their building materials or allowed to fall into complete disrepair and ruin if their materials were not needed. As noted in chapter 4, the change in settlement form was one important characteristic of the development of the tenant plantation.

In addition to the activities of the postbellum tenants, other factors obscured the visibility of the antebellum period. These factors were environment and the uses of the property after the tenants had left. Because the plantation was located in the Piedmont, erosion was extensive. The topography of the plantation was such that the land sloped about one hundred feet from its northernmost edge to the bank of the Savannah River. The implication of this erosion for archaeological research is that any antebellum deposits that may have existed, particularly in its yard areas, were stripped away during downpours. As a result, no information of any kind was collected from the yard areas, and all the archaeological evidence was found inside, or directly adjacent to, the extant building foundations. This evidence was overwhelmingly from the post-1865 habitation of the plantation.

Thirty-three separate building foundations were identified during the 1980–81 research at Millwood Plantation.[6] These structures were heavily overgrown, cut-granite foundations. Twenty-seven of these foundations were located by surveyors from the Institute of Archaeology and Anthropology before 1980, and six foundations were located in 1980. The foundations found during the early surveys were assigned numbers; those found later were identified by letters. Twenty-eight of these foundations were investigated as part of the 1980–81 research effort. All twenty-eight were completely exposed and mapped, but time and funds did not permit their total excavation.

Four clusters of foundations were identified (figure 16). The first cluster was an elongated collection of twenty-one foundations that extended in a northeast-southwest direction. On the southernmost limit was a

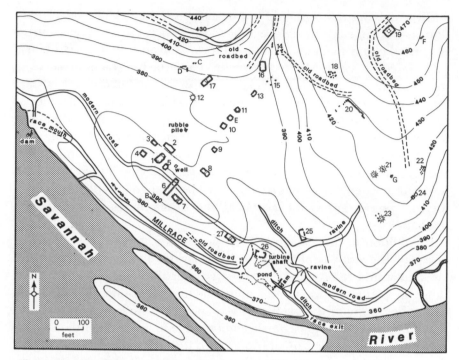

Figure 16. Foundations at Millwood Plantation, 1980–81.

long, cut-granite wall (structure B) and on the northernmost limit was a
scattering of bricks (structure 14). Included in this cluster were twelve
dwellings that were identified on the basis of the presence of fireplace
hearths (structures 1, 2, 6, 7, 8, 10, 11, 13, 14, 15, 17, and E), three
outbuildings or possible storage sheds with no chimneys (structures 3, 4,
and 5), one smokehouse (structure 9), one industrial structure (structure
16), four nonstructural features (structures 12, B, C, and D), a well, and
one large pile of cut-granite blocks. An old roadbed occurred on the
northern limit of the site running alongside structures 14 and 16. This
road probably extended to the river when the plantation was inhabited.
A modern road ran parallel to the river adjacent to structures 1, 4, and
5. This road was placed over the northern end of structure 6 and obviously postdated it.

A second cluster of three apparent dwellings (structures 25, 26, and
27) were southeast of the first cluster. These buildings were close to the
plantation millpond and were probably associated with it when oc-

cupied. The modern road extended past structures 26 and 27, and a remnant of a second old roadbed ran for a short distance parallel to the plantation millrace, which extended the length of the southern edge of the site. At the eastern edge of the dry millpond was a stone dam. The millrace extended beyond this dam and back into the Savannah River.

A third group of building foundations was located just to the northeast of those found near the millpond. These buildings were on a rise that overlooked the Savannah River. Included here were three dwellings (structures 21, 23, and 24), an outbuilding (structure 22), and a possible structure of unknown form or use (structure G). An old road extended to these buildings from the northern edge of the site.

This road also ran through the final grouping of foundations, located in the northeastern corner of the site. This cluster included one dwelling (structure 19), one wall (structure 20), and two piles of rubble that may have been the remains of buildings (structures 18 and F).

The building foundations, the old roadbeds, the millrace, the millpond and dam, the modern road, the vegetation, and the topography constituted the physical remains of Millwood Plantation in 1980–81. These physical remains provide the only information about the settlement organization and house designs.

Because Millwood's most active period of operation was after 1865, it stands to reason that the slave plantation period would have the least focus and visibility. Accordingly, the earliest history of the plantation is the most difficult to identify from the tangible remains. Although the available historical documents contain information about various construction activities on the property during the plantation's formative era, when Calhoun was still a young man trying to build his economic empire, they seldom contain references to the more mundane aspects of construction: the kinds of materials used, the designs, and the location of the buildings. Given the ambiguity or paucity of comments about Millwood's buildings from those who lived in them, the physical remains themselves must be used to provide this information. Of the buildings found, the most difficult to identify are the slave quarters.

As is mentioned in chapter 4, nineteenth-century slave quarters on cotton plantations were commonly grouped together in straight lines on short roads. Enough reference material exists, however, to suggest that other forms of slave settlements appeared on the South's antebellum cotton plantations, including settlements located along curved roads or scattered throughout the plantation.

The likelihood is strong that the Millwood Plantation slaves did not all live in one tightly packed slave quarter settlement. The geographical shape of Millwood, a linear estate along a river, precluded the typical grouping of slaves in one large settlement. If all the slaves lived in one place relatively close to Calhoun's home, some would have had to travel as much as five miles to reach the agricultural fields and the industrial complexes that were their work places. Some of them even would have had to cross the Savannah River to reach the fields in Georgia. It seems likely, therefore, that slave settlements occurred at various locations throughout the plantation. Only clues about these locations exist.

Two of the former tenant farmers who were interviewed stated that some of the slaves had been housed around the base of the hill on the northern edge of the site in the general vicinity of structures C and D. One of these informants said that a slough ran between these slave quarters and James Edward Calhoun's residence, which she and many others identified as structure 1. Evidence of this slough was found between structures 2 and 12 in the flat area on the western part of the site by botanists from Clemson University in 1981. Thus, even though no physical remains could be found, circumstantial evidence indicates that some of Calhoun's slave force may in fact have lived at the base of the hill north of his home.

The promotional map Calhoun made in 1877 (figure 13) suggests the possible location of other slave houses on the plantation. Given Calhoun's strong interest in industrialization, he probably had a couple of slaves housed near his mills. This would be the three locations along the river in South Carolina and the one across the river from his house. He also may have housed slaves on either side of the river, near his ferry just north of Cedar Island. With all these possible work stations, the Millwood slaves probably did not live in a typical quarters village. Unfortunately, physical evidence for these slave buildings could not be located in the large and densely overgrown land that was once Millwood Plantation.

Possible slave houses were discovered, however, at one place in the archaeological site. These houses were the three small, square foundations designated structures 10, 11, and E.

Located near the center of the site, these three foundations of identical cut-granite construction were placed in a straight line (figure 17). Structure 10, the southernmost foundation, was 17.4 feet by 21.3 feet (370.6 square feet), and structures E and 11 were both 16.4 feet by 19.7

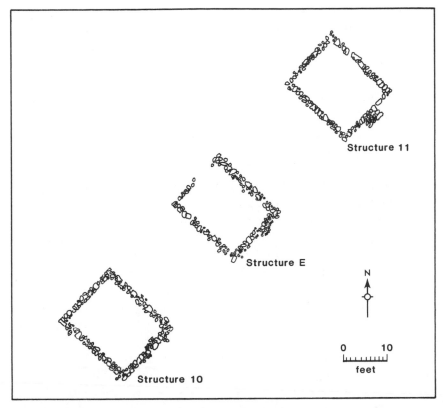

Figure 17. Three slave–wage hand cabin foundations.

feet (323.1 square feet). They were fairly evenly spaced; structure 10 was 21.3 feet southwest of structure E, and structure E was 23.0 feet southwest of structure 11. Structure 11 contained evidence of a cut-granite chimney support on its southeast wall. Stone rubble at the other structures implied that they also had chimney supports on their southeast walls.

The shape, spatial arrangement, and size of these structures imply that they were indeed intended to house slaves at Millwood Plantation. This interpretation, however, does not summarize the entire history of these buildings. Important evidence about these three buildings, and all the structures in the most densely settled part of the site, derives from two panoramic photographs of Millwood Plantation.

The first photograph, marked "about 1879," was probably taken from the road that once ran from structure 14 to structure 20 on the northern part of the site (figure 18). This view shows a cluster of buildings with the Savannah River behind. The chimneys of the three structures currently designated structures 10, 11, and E appear in the center of the photograph behind a row of small trees. The eroded hills so typical of the Piedmont appear in the foreground. The buildings are clearly visible, but little information about them can be discerned.

A second photograph of these three structures provides more detail about their construction. This photograph was probably taken from the same road, but from a slightly different angle and probably during the winter or late fall, when the leaf cover was minimal (figure 19). This photograph clearly shows structures 10, 11, and E.

These buildings were identically constructed. Each was built of logs and had a simple roof. The chimneys of each seem to stand away from the cabin gables in a manner similar to those of colonial houses in middle Virginia.[7] The construction materials of these chimneys cannot be determined. Each house exhibits an open, unglassed window in its side, and no shutters appear in the photograph. The road on the north end of the archaeological site can be seen running near these buildings, adjacent to a long, barnlike structure.

These three small, identical buildings exhibit the characteristics of typical nineteenth-century slave cabins, and it is clear from the photographs that the buildings were not in disrepair, but, rather, appeared to be livable houses. What this means, of course, is that they were occupied at the time of the photograph. Given this interpretation, the likelihood exists that these dwellings may have housed postbellum wage laborers. Located close to Calhoun's home, they were perhaps originally built as cabins for house slaves and may have been used by wage hands after the war.

Support for the notion that these structures were inhabited by postbellum laborers is increased when the dates for the artifacts found associated with them are considered. Historical archaeologists date artifacts in a number of ways, all of which are important in the study of any particular site.

Artifacts—any objects made or modified by human action—are the primary documents of the archaeologist. Archaeologists use artifacts in the same way that historians use written records; however, whereas historians may occasionally be called upon to provide a date for an undated document, archaeologists always have to date their artifacts. Historical archaeologists date artifacts using methods not available to prehistorians.

Prehistorians, because they usually explore periods spanning thousands of years, use dating techniques that offer rough dates for the ancient artifacts they find. The most well known of these measures the amount of a radioactive carbon isotope (carbon 14) within a carbon-containing object. These objects include living organisms, burned wood, and iron tools. The dates derived by this method are accurate within certain limits and include a "plus or minus factor." Thus, the date produced from an ancient object may be 1000 b.c. plus or minus 900 years. While this date may be meaningful to a prehistorian researching a past culture that existed for thousands of years, such a date is usually quite meaningless for the historical archaeologist. At Millwood Plantation, for example, a fireplace hearth dated a.d. 1850 plus or minus 85 years, or from 1765 to 1935, would have no meaning; the historical documents have already indicated that the site was occupied from 1834 to about 1925. Historical archaeologists must have means for dating their artifacts that are different from the carbon 14 method and other similar methods used by prehistorians.[8] Therefore, a number of techniques have been devised by historical archaeologists.

One tool historical archaeologists use to date artifacts generally is historical records. Records establish the dates between which a site was occupied; it can be assumed that the artifacts found there usually were used within that period, although this is not always true. Because historical records clearly establish the date that Millwood Plantation began, artifacts made and used before this period either were used by the prehistoric inhabitants of the area before the plantation was created or were brought to the plantation by someone during its existence, perhaps as souvenirs or curios. For example, the discovery of a Viking sword at Millwood Plantation would more likely suggest that a former inhabitant was interested in collecting historical artifacts than that the Vikings had settled in the area in the tenth century. The use of historical documents for dating artifacts is the weakest of all methods, however, because the records usually provide only time spans. For example, knowing that an artifact was used at Millwood sometime within the period from 1834 to 1925 provides little real information about the plantation and the people who lived there.

A second way to date historical artifacts is to know their dates of man-

*Figure 18. Panoramic photograph of Millwood Plantation, circa 1879.
(U.S. Army Corps of Engineers, Savannah District)*

Figure 19. Panoramic photograph of Millwood Plantation, undated.
(U.S. Army Corps of Engineers, Savannah District)

ufacture. Most historical artifacts made since the mid-eighteenth century were mass-produced in factories, many of which kept careful records. These records, if they still exist and can be located, often provide irrefutable proof of the date of an artifact's manufacture. These kinds of dates are particularly useful for dating ceramics. Large-scale ceramic manufacturers often kept detailed records of decorative patterns, vessel forms, and ware types that can be used to date individual specimens. Some ceramic vessels made in England during the late nineteenth century even have their date of manufacture stamped in code on their bases. Once the meaning of the code is known, the exact day of the vessel's manufacture can be determined.[9] Of course, this dating method is available only for some fine earthenware ceramic tablewares made by large factories, and not for folk ceramics.

Another method that can provide rough dates for a site is the use of the known manufacturing dates of all the ceramics found there to compute a mean date of ceramic manufacture for the entire ceramic collection. To compute this mean date of manufacture, not necessarily the date of use, the number of sherds of each kind of ceramics is multiplied by its known median manufacturing date; the product is then divided by the total number of sherds in the collection. A constant of 1798.90 is added to this quotient. Once this single date is derived, a statistical measure called the standard deviation can be calculated to increase the accuracy of the date. This standard deviation is a number that when added and subtracted from the mean ceramic date provides a date range for the collection that has more reliability than the single mean ceramic date.[10]

Used on many historical sites, the mean ceramic dating formula is a powerful dating tool that has been refined by a number of historical archaeologists. The refinement most applicable to the Millwood Plantation ceramic collection is the addition of twenty years to the generated date to account for the ceramic time lag that has been documented at rural sites associated with poor inhabitants.[11] All mean ceramic dates presented in this chapter have been increased by twenty years.

An experimental dating method similar to the mean ceramic dating method involves the dating of window glass fragments. Several historical archaeologists have realized that more-recent window glass fragments are generally thicker than older window glass fragments.[12] Using the ideas of these archaeologists and after conducting his own careful analysis, archaeologist Karl G. Roenke demonstrated that window glass was indeed made increasingly thicker during the nineteenth century.[13] Once this was realized, excavated flat-glass collections could be dated using the known thicknesses as an index. Roenke's ideas were further used to devise a formula that could establish dates for the Millwood Plantation flat-glass collections.[14] With the formula, the thickness of a particular piece of excavated flat glass could be used to produce a date. A mean date for the entire collection was computed by combining the dates. The generated dates are tentative because more experimentation with the dating method is needed, but the close agreement between the flat-glass dates and the usually reliable mean ceramic dates implies that the flat-glass dating method is generally accurate and useful.

All these dating methods were used to date the artifacts from the three small, identical foundations. The generated dates are clearly related to the postbellum period and so support the notion that these buildings were inhabited by wage hands after 1865. The mean ceramic dates for each structure are consistent: 1891.8 with a standard deviation of 1.0 year (1890.8 to 1892.8) for the southernmost foundation (structure 10), 1891.4 with no standard deviation for the northernmost foundation (structure 11), and 1892.5 with no standard deviation for the center foundation (structure E). The flat glass from structure 11 was dated to 1897.5 with a standard deviation of 1.9 years (1895.6 to 1899.4), from structure E, to 1889.1 with a standard deviation of 2.1 years (1887.0 to 1891.2). No flat glass was found in the structure 10 excavation units.

The nails found in these three buildings also substantiate their occupation during the postbellum period. Each structure contained square machine-cut nails and round wire nails. Machine-cut nails were first made in the late 1830s and reached their peak production levels between 1850 and 1888. Wire nails, those round-shanked and round-headed nails common today, were first produced in 1855 but did not gain great popularity until they replaced machine-cut nails after 1888.[15] The predominance of machine-cut nails in structures 10, 11, and E implies either that these buildings were first built with machine-cut nails and later repaired with wire nails, or that they were built at a time when both kinds of nails were commonly used. The slave cabin design of the buildings suggests the first interpretation. In any case, all the available evidence makes one conclusion possible: The three small, identical foundations were inhabited during the 1880s and 1890s.

The antebellum plantation is difficult to discern in the physical form of the plantation because of the continued use of the estate after 1865. The period after the war is equally difficult to observe in the physical remains at the site.

As is noted in the preceding chapter, Millwood Plantation was organized into a squad system in 1867. Given the structure of this system, with its small family-based groups of farmers, the physical form of the squad system should be represented by small clusters of dwellings spread across the plantation. At Millwood, seven such groups of dwellings, associated with the seven squad leaders, should have existed between 1867 and 1870 or 1875, the date of the standing rent agreement.

One such cluster of dwellings did appear in the building foundations located at Millwood Plantation. This cluster, consisting of structures 21, 22, 23, 24, and G, was located on a hill in the extreme southeastern corner of the site (figure 20). This settlement was about six hundred feet east of structures 10, 11, and E.

Each of the buildings in this apparent cluster had a different form. Structure 21, on the northwestern side of the cluster, consisted of two large double-fireplace foundations. The walls of the structure could not be located, but the building had to have been rather large to accommodate four fireplaces. The distance between the center of each fireplace was about 27 feet. Structure 23 was represented by a single fireplace hearth located in the center of the structure. Structure 24, the other residential building, consisted of two, almost identical, cut-granite foundations with chimney supports on the north end of each. The northern foundation was 20.7 feet wide and 24.6 feet long; the southern foundation was 16.7 feet wide and 20.0 feet long (including the chimney supports). The two buildings were only 7.9 feet apart. Structure 22 was a small, square cut-granite foundation measuring only 2.8 feet wide and 3.1 feet long. Structure G, a pile of cut-granite rocks, was not investigated, and its shape was not determined.

The form of these four, and possibly five, structures resembles what might be expected of a squad settlement: an isolated small group of dwellings with associated outbuildings. The three dwellings—structures 21, 23, and 24—are about equally spaced, with 125.0 feet between structures 23 and 24, 153.0 feet between structures 21 and 23, and 155.0 feet between structures 21 and 24. If the pile of rocks designated structure G was not really a structure, then an open space, or yard, existed between the three structures at some time.

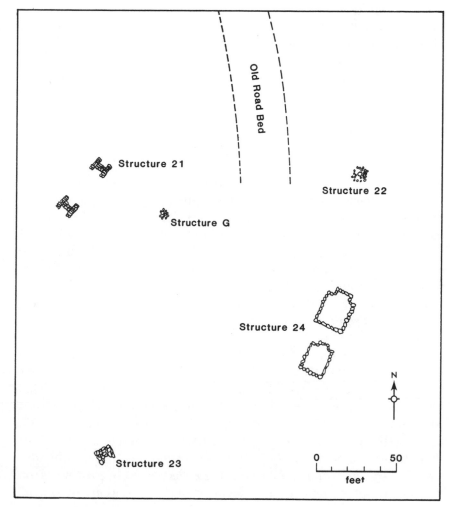

Figure 20. Foundations of possible squad settlement.

The idea that these dwellings formed a squad settlement gains further support when the dates of the artifacts from them are examined. A mean ceramic date of 1883.7 with a standard deviation of 14.2 years (1869.5 to 1897.9) was computed from the sherds found in structure 21. Of the nails, 95.4 percent were machine cut, so the collection is roughly assignable to the period from 1850 to 1888. A similar postbellum date is suggested for the structure 23 artifacts. A mean ceramic date of 1888.7

with a standard deviation of 10.2 years (1878.5 to 1898.9) was calculated for the ceramic collection. Machine-cut nails accounted for 73.2 percent of the sample, and 17.6 percent of the nails were wire. Temporally diagnostic artifacts, including a bottle fragment containing the words HEINZ CO APLD FOR dating to the post-1888 period,[16] and an 1889 penny, were also found. The dates for structure 24 are somewhat earlier than those derived from the other structures. A mean ceramic date of 1860.2 with a standard deviation of 32.9 years (1827.3 to 1893.1) was computed for the earthenware ceramics, but an embossed panel bottle fragment probably was not made until after 1867.[17] Of the nails, 97.3 percent were machine cut and probably datable to the period from 1850 to 1888.

These artifacts, when coupled with the physical clustering of the structures in this area, suggest that structures 21, 22, 23, 24, and possibly G may have served as a squad village between 1867 and 1875.[18] Although the mean ceramic dates are later than 1875 in two of the dwellings and earlier in another, the ceramic date ranges (i.e., with standard deviations) are close enough to be accepted.

The interpretation that structures 21, 22, 23, and 24 formed a postbellum squad settlement is not completely without problem, because it can be argued that structures 21 and 24 were occupied during the antebellum period. A single ceramic sherd with a blue transfer-printed design marked Ital——Flower and J.W.—— is clearly of prewar manufacture. This mark indicates that this sherd was decorated in the Italian Flower Garden pattern made at the Staffordshire, England, pottery of John and William Ridgway. The Ridgways' pottery operated from 1814 to about 1830, but the mark may have been used as late as 1855.[19] Although this one piece was the only marked sherd discovered, the other five blue transfer-printed sherds in the collection were probably from the same vessel. A similar case for an antebellum association can be made for structure 24, where five pieces of one plate contain an edge-molded decoration that can be roughly dated to the period from 1830 to 1840.[20]

Admittedly, the presence of a couple of antebellum ceramic pieces cannot be considered to be unimpeachable proof that structures 21 and 24 were inhabited during the antebellum period. Many possible explanations are possible for the presence of antebellum ceramics in a postbellum household: the dishes were keepsakes, they were acquired secondhand, the broken sherds were picked up somewhere and brought home by someone, and so on. All such alternative interpretations must be kept in mind.

When the placement and construction of structures 21 and 24 are considered, however, the case for an antebellum construction and habitation of the structures becomes even easier to accept for a number of reasons. First, the size of structure 21's double chimney bases seems to be an indication that structure 21 was an extremely large structure. If this building contained just three equal-sized rooms and if the distance between the center of the chimneys can be used to estimate room size, then each room could have been about 27.0 feet long. If the two end rooms were even half the size of the center room, then the entire building would have been about 54.0 feet long. Unfortunately, the accuracy of these speculations can never be evaluated, because the walls of structure 21 could not be located. They had presumably eroded away or were robbed for the construction of another building somewhere else on the plantation. If structure 21 was actually as large as is calculated, then James Edward Calhoun may have used the building as his first residence at Millwood Plantation. Second, the form of the structure 24 foundation must be considered. The similarities between the three slave–wage hand building foundations and the two foundations at structure 24 may not be coincidental. The southern foundation of structure 24, measuring 16.7 feet by 20.0 feet, was almost the exact size as two of the slave–wage hand foundations (16.4 feet by 19.7 feet, structures 11 and E). The northern foundation of structure 24, measuring 20.7 feet by 24.6 feet, was just 3 feet longer in both dimensions than the largest slave–wage hand foundation (17.4 feet by 21.3 feet, structure 10). These similarities in size and construction are striking. Third, the placement of structure 24 in relation to the large double fireplaces (structure 21) is provocative, and may indicate that the two small foundations are the remains of slave cabins. As noted above, the distance between these foundations was 155.0 feet. The distance between Calhoun's house (structure 1) and the southernmost slave–wage hand cabin (structure 10) was about 230.0 feet. Even though the distance between the last two structures is much greater than that between structures 21 and 24, the difference may not be meaningful, because the location of these buildings was limited by the natural slope of the land. To be located any farther away, the two small foundations would have had to be on the side of a fairly steep slope.

The probability that the building with double fireplaces (structure 21) may have been Calhoun's first home at Millwood and that the two small foundations (structure 24) may have been slave cabins is supported in the historical record. It will be recalled from chapter 2 that Calhoun occupied an overseer's house from 1834 to 1840. By at least April 1840, he is known to have begun the construction of a larger house for his new bride, Maria Simkins. Although this sequence is discussed in more detail below, it can be speculated that structure 21 was this overseer's house and that structure 24 was actually two slave cabins built for those slaves who were engaged in clearing the land that would become Millwood Plantation. If this interpretation is accepted, then the three foundations on the hill overlooking the Savannah River constituted the Millwood settlement during the plantation's earliest days.

A postbellum occupation of this hill, however, cannot be doubted. If it can be accepted that structures 21 and 24 were occupied during Millwood's earliest plantation history, another instance of building reuse, similar to that suggested for the three small structures near Calhoun's home (structures 10, 11, and E), has been identified on the plantation. Unfortunately, these plausible assertions can never be substantiated.

The physical evidence for the postbellum habitation of Millwood Plantation from 1875 to 1925 is somewhat easier to interpret. As might be imagined from the historical evidence presented in preceding chapters, the buildings at Millwood represent both the industrial and the agricultural aspects of the estate. The industrial side of the plantation is represented by a turbine shaft that protruded from the millpond floor and by a foundation referred to as structure 16.

The exposed iron turbine shaft was 34.5 feet from structure 26. In 1980 it projected approximately two feet from the surface of the dry millpond. When fully exposed about four feet below ground, the turbine was found to consist of six white oak paddles fixed to a hexagonal iron sleeve extending from the iron shaft by four large iron bolts (figure 21). Robert L. Johnson, an expert on early American industrial technology, stated that this turbine was either a spout-fed flutter wheel (the kind mentioned in the 1880 Industrial Census) or a wooden scroll-case reaction turbine.

Portions of two other turbines were also located in the millpond. One was a metal scroll-case reaction turbine, and the other was a pair of iron wheels from a rose-wheel reaction turbine. These were the machines on which Calhoun built his industrial dreams and at which his workers toiled. In addition, two thick metal blades were found in association with the scroll-case reaction turbine.[21]

The foundation nearest the millpond and the iron and wooden pad-

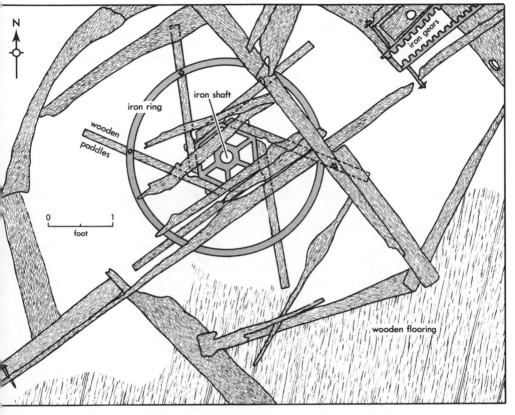

Figure 21. Turbine wheel found in millpond. Before excavation only the shaft was visible above ground.

dle-wheel turbine (structure 26) was a cut-granite foundation that was approximately 19.7 feet wide and 43.0 feet long. A thin layer of burned wood and cottonseeds was discovered on portions of its brick floor.

Although the three turbines are consistent with the kinds manufactured in the period from 1850 to 1860, the artifacts from this structure date to the late nineteenth and early twentieth centuries. The small ceramic sample, containing only nine sherds, had a computed mean date of 1895.6 with a standard deviation of 6.3 years (1889.3 to 1901.9). Of the nails, 82.4 percent were machine-cut, and 12.1 percent were wire. Both kinds of nails could have been used during the period from 1880 to

1905. In addition, a bottle fragment used by the short-lived South Carolina Dispensary dates to the 1897 to 1903 period.[22]

The thin layer of cotton found on the excavated portions of the brick floor suggests that the building may have been used for cotton processing, possibly for ginning and baling. A plantation's cotton gin and press were usually housed in a multistoried structure. The gin would have been located on the second floor so that the ginned cotton could fall directly into the presses. This kind of gin, common in postbellum South Carolina, was called the Carolina single-stand cotton gin.[23] The presence of cottonseed on the bottom floor of the gin house would be consistent with this process, and the historical records indicate that a cotton gin did exist at Millwood. The cotton press was probably a wooden screw press located outdoors and sheltered by a small roof.[24] This structure was undoubtedly located near structure 26.

The metal blades found within the millpond were probably flensing tools used to remove hair and tissue from animal hides during the tanning process. This interpretation is probable, for the Millwood Plantation workers produced seven hundred hides in 1860.[25]

The production of hides, along with the production of flour, timber, and ginned cotton, indicates that Millwood Plantation had significant industrial activity around the millpond. And, while Calhoun, his executor, or his resident manager had ultimate control over this aspect of the plantation, the millwright was the person who kept much of this industry in operation.

The exact location of this millwright's home is unknown, but a likely structure for him to have inhabited is structure 27. Located about 90 feet west of the millhouse (structure 26), structure 27 was at least a two-room dwelling measuring approximately 18 feet wide and 41.3 feet long with a central double fireplace. A mean ceramic date of 1892.2 with a standard deviation of 26.4 years (1865.8 to 1918.6) was computed from the fine earthenware collected there. Of the nails, 92.9 percent were machine cut, and 7.1 percent were wire. The flat glass from the structure yielded a tentative mean date of 1880.8 with a standard deviation of 2.1 years (1878.7 to 1882.9).

These dates correlate with the dates derived from the structure 26 artifacts well enough to suggest that the buildings were contemporary. Nothing concrete can be said about the relationship between the people who were associated with these two buildings, however. The 1880 population census does indicate that Damon Gripper, a seventy-seven-year-old black man whose parents were both born in Africa, lived in a separate house at Millwood with a seventy-one-year-old concubine named Mona Barnet. Gripper is listed as working in the Millwood gristmill.[26] Neither Gripper nor any other mill hand appears in the later censuses, and the continued operation of the Millwood mills cannot be determined. At any rate, it can be reasonably asserted that the millwrights, whoever they were, lived in the general vicinity of the millhouse, perhaps at structure 27.

In addition to this mill complex, from which the plantation received its name, a second industrial center was identified in the physical remains at Millwood Plantation. This industrial operation was on the northern portion of the site at structure 16, about 160 feet north of the northernmost slave–wage hand cabin.

Structure 16 was a cut-granite foundation 22.3 feet wide and 31.5 feet long. A carefully laid brick floor and four brick enclosures, placed in the northeastern quarter, were found inside this foundation (figure 22). The two northernmost enclosures had parallel sides and rounded ends; the southernmost enclosures were keyhold shaped. The substantial amount of charred cottonseeds and fiber, ash, charcoal, and burned brick fragments found inside the enclosures indicates that fires were once lit inside them.

The presence of only two plain white ceramic sherds makes the mean ceramic dating technique useless at this foundation, but a mean date of 1897.4 with a standard deviation of 2.1 years (1895.3 to 1899.5) was computed from the flat-glass sample. The nail sample, composed of 97.2 percent machine-cut nails and 2.8 percent wire nails, suggests that the building was constructed in the late nineteenth century. Although other interpretations are possible, enough circumstantial evidence exists to support the contention that this structure was a sorghum processing center.[27]

Sorghum was first introduced in the southern uplands in 1855, and the production of its syrup was experimented with throughout the next few years. Two years later, "thousands" were reportedly experimenting with sorghum for "syrup, green and dried forage, alcohol, and as bread corn."[28]

The production of syrup from sorghum was a relatively simple and inexpensive process that could easily have been accomplished within the

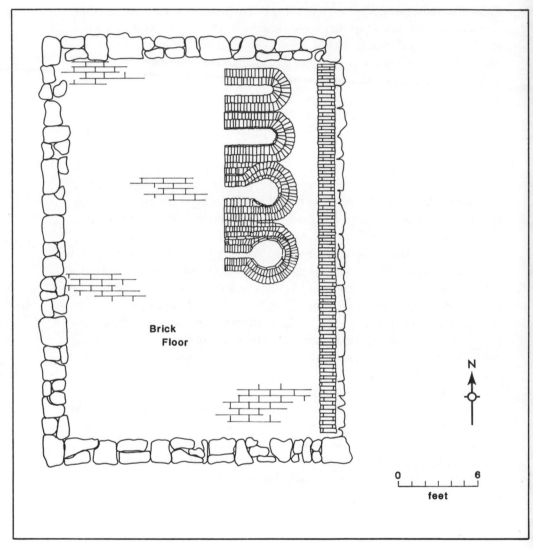

Figure 22. Foundation of sorghum-processing structure. This foundation was designated structure 16.

structure 16 enclosures. The juice of the sorghum plant, also called Chinese Sugar Cane in the nineteenth century,[29] was extracted by passing cut cane through a set of rollers turned by either a mule or an ox. This juice was then strained into iron pots or flat, metal pans called evaporators that were placed over slow-burning fires. The thin juice was boiled until it reached the desired consistency.[30]

A common method of evaporation used four large kettles of decreasing size. Cane juice, added to the largest kettle, was gradually dipped from one kettle to the next as it thickened.[31] These evaporators were frequently built of masonry or other durable materials. Brick evaporators were used as early as 1847, and by the 1870s most were constructed of brick.[32]

The production of sorghum molasses was a probable activity at Millwood Plantation before 1865 and a known activity after 1865. The agricultural census of 1860 reported that Calhoun, more accurately Calhoun's slaves, produced five hundred gallons of molasses that year.[33] This molasses was probably made from sorghum grown in the garden, because the census does not indicate that sorghum was grown as an agricultural crop at Millwood.

Some experimenters reported that between 74.4 and 274.0 gallons of molasses could be made from just one acre of the plant.[34] Thus, only 1.8 to 6.7 acres of sorghum would have been needed to produce Millwood's 500 gallons of molasses. This acreage could easily have been contained within Millwood's 1,450 improved acres in 1860 and so overlooked by census takers, who did not normally record garden crops anyway. Given Calhoun's interest in experimentation, his fascination with sorghum production is not unreasonable.

Further evidence for the production of sorghum molasses during Calhoun's later years at Millwood comes from the probate records. The inventory and appraisal of his property mentioned in the preceding chapter indicates that he owned "1 Molasses Mill & Frame" worth $25.00, "6 Molasses Boilers" worth $5.00 each, and four barrels containing seventy gallons of molasses. At the sale of Calhoun's property held on March 10 and 11, 1890, one "boiler" was sold for $2.25, and three "Molasses boilers" were sold for $1.65, $3.50, and $5.00 each, suggesting perhaps that they were of different sizes.[35] Edward Kieser bought two of the boilers, and I. H. McCalla and E. Pfeiffer, two local white farmers, bought the other two. The purchase of these boilers by area whites could be used to argue that the black tenants at Millwood were not engaged in syrup production. Photographic evidence, however, provides unique proof that Millwood Plantation tenants were indeed involved in sorghum molasses production during the postbellum period (figure 23). In this photograph, a mule-powered sorghum crusher is being fed cane. A brick continuous evaporator, with one long pan and one chimney, appears on the left. Although the exact location on the plantation of this small-scale industry is not known, at least one former tenant claimed to know the woman sitting in the front left of the photograph. All the informants stated that this picture was taken at Millwood, somewhere northeast of the archaeological site. The agricultural census of 1880 stated that at least four of Calhoun's known tenants produced a total of fifty-seven gallons of sorghum molasses.[36]

In any case, the production of sorghum molasses at Millwood Plantation did occur during the postbellum period. Exactly how much sorghum was made, and by whom, cannot be determined. That Calhoun built a large processor for experimentation is assured.

In addition to its industrial capabilities, Millwood Plantation obviously was also the home of people associated with agriculture. These people included the tenant farmers, the plantation managers, and, until 1889, Calhoun himself. The homes of each were identified at Millwood Plantation.

Little doubt exists that the foundation designated structure 1 by archaeologists was the postbellum home of James Edward Calhoun. However, Calhoun did live in other homes on the plantation before he moved into this building.

As noted earlier, a somewhat circumstantial case can be made that James Edward Calhoun first lived in the large house called structure 21 on the hill northeast of the millpond. Upon his marriage in February 1839, he began the construction of another home somewhere else on the plantation. A foundation identified as structure 6 might have been this house.

Located on the southern end of a line made by the three slave–wage hand cabins and the sorghum processing building, structure 6 was the largest foundation uncovered at Millwood Plantation. Twenty feet wide and 79 feet long (1,580.0 square feet), this foundation contained a brick floor and a brick fireplace on its northern end (figure 24). Even though the artifacts found in and near this foundation are overwhelmingly

*Figure 23. Sorghum crushing at Millwood Plantation. The location of this crusher
could not be determined. (U.S. Army Corps of Engineers, Savannah District)*

postbellum—the mean ceramic date was 1890.7 with a standard deviation of 9.5 (1881.2 to 1900.2); the mean flat-glass date was 1884.9 with a
standard deviation of 14.5 (1870.4 to 1899.4); 62.7 percent of the nails
were machine cut, and 30.9 percent were wire—enough other information exists to permit the assertion that, in this case, the dates are probably
spurious. That is, the artifacts found here are not related to the original
occupation of the dwelling. These artifacts were probably deposited
later by postbellum plantation inhabitants or by campers.

   This interpretation is not made simply for convenience. It would be
too easy, not to mention unethical, to accept those dates that conform to
one's a priori assumptions and to reject those that do not—that is, to
accept postbellum dates for foundations that are thought to be postbellum and to reject those for buildings that for some reason should be

viewed as antebellum. In the case of structure 6, however, enough con-vincing evidence exists to make an antebellum date at least feasible.

Structure 6 is remembered in the oral tradition of the nearby town of Calhoun Falls, South Carolina, as the "boat house." The origin of the boat house legend cannot be determined, but it goes back as far as Lewis Perrin, the amateur Calhoun historian who wrote at least one influential article about Millwood Plantation in a local newspaper in 1933.[37] In this article, Perrin maintains that upon the death of Maria Simkins Calhoun, James Edward had the house wherein "he and his wife had lived so hap-pily" boarded up, "declaring that no human being should ever enter it again." As an act of grief, Calhoun, the former naval officer, had a house built like a ship, "with port holes instead of windows high up" and a balcony that "ran around the wall beneath the port holes." This balcony could be reached only by a ladder that could be drawn "up to the bal-cony after ascending it."

Perrin's statements were incorporated into the area's local tradition, and today many people in the area still speak about this "boat house." This legend is so strong, in fact, that archaeologists from the University of South Carolina's Institute of Archaeology and Anthropology de-scribed the exposed rocks on the ground surface as boat-shaped, even though the foundation did not actually have this shape (figure 24).

Support for the idea that structure 6 was one of the former houses inhabited by James Edward Calhoun was offered by Francis de Sales Dundas when he wrote that in 1879 Calhoun's original home, "no doubt an impressive mansion at the outset and for many years thereafter," was abandoned and in ruins. A short distance north of these ruins, according to Dundas, was the home Calhoun occupied until his death.[38] These comments by Dundas are consistent with the physical association be-tween structures 6 and 1 (see figure 16).

Further support for the idea that structure 6 was probably the ruins of the home Calhoun built in 1839 or 1840 derives from a sketch map of the plantation made on July 6, 1955, by retired Admiral William L. Cal-houn.[39] Calhoun, who had obviously spent many summers at the planta-tion of his uncle James, identified as the "ruins of house never com-pleted" a long rectangular structure oriented in the same direction as structure 6.

Although the true locations of Calhoun's residences can never be known with certainty, the following sequence can be suggested. Calhoun

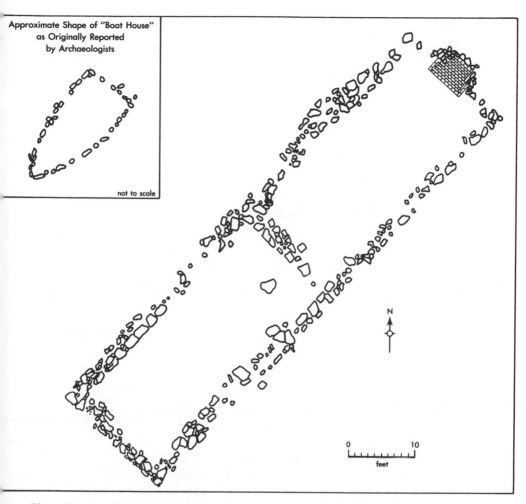

Figure 24. Possible home of James Edward Calhoun, circa 1840. This building was designated structure 6. The insert shows the supposed shape of the building. Excavation, however, revealed that the building was not boat-shaped.

first lived on the hill in the large building (structure 21), but upon his marriage, he started to have a house built closer to the river. This house, most likely structure 6, was designed as the plantation "big house." If it was completed, Calhoun closed this house when his wife died. If the house was still under construction, he did not have it finished. At any rate, he moved to a new house that, at least according to Lewis Perrin, seemed to resemble a ship. Although archaeologists from the Institute of Archaeology and Anthropology identified structure 6 as this boat house, the boat house was probably structure 1. This house may have had certain naval characteristics, but under no circumstances did it have a boat-shaped foundation.

No doubt exists that structure 1 was James Edward Calhoun's home at the time of his death. The location of his home is always consistently identified in all historical sources—written and oral—in relation to the plantation well (see figure 16). William Calhoun drew the well near a rectangular building he referred to as "Uncle James' House" when he drew a map of the plantation from memory. Similarly, both past inhabitants and frequent visitors often mentioned the well as a point of reference for locating Calhoun's home. One knowledgeable person stated that upon approaching the plantation from the road (presumably the modern road that was still there in 1980–81) "you got to the big house first, and then the well was probably at the end of the big house." This informant did not know too much about this "big house," but his father had told him that it "wasn't the first house." Another informant stated that in 1910 only two houses were standing at Millwood, hers and the "old Calhoun building." The latter was "made in front of that well."[40]

Further support for the idea that Calhoun's home was near the well and that structure 1 was that house's foundation is provided in a remarkable photograph of this part of the plantation (figure 25). This photograph, probably taken from the vicinity of structure 8, shows parts of four buildings, structures 1, 2, 3, and 5 (see figure 16). Structure 1 appears behind structure 5, a small clapboard-sided building with no chimney. The well appears to the right of this building. A carriage rests under the overhanging roof of structure 2, and a shovel hangs against the wall of the outbuilding, called structure 3. This photograph is today widely available in Calhoun Falls on postcards with a caption that reads "Home of James Edward Calhoun near Millwood—About 1875." A caption on another copy of this photograph reads "Millwood Grounds." The similarities between the spatial arrangement of the buildings in the photograph and those discovered at the site make it clear that this photograph was taken at Millwood Plantation.

This photograph shows that Calhoun lived in a one-story clapboard-sided house with a simple shingle roof. A glassed window occurs to the

Figure 25. James Edward Calhoun's home, circa 1875. (U.S. Army Corps of Engineers, Savannah District)

right of a wide doorway containing two white doors. The door on the right is missing its lower half. Simple wooden steps lead to the doorway, and an inner doorway can be seen beyond it. Two chimneys can be seen, but the two panoramic photographs (figures 18 and 19, especially figure 19) indicate that this structure contained three chimneys, one on each end and one in the center. These panoramic views also show an interesting architectural feature of the Millwood Plantation dwellings: the presence of wooden projections at the eaves of the structure at the four corners. These projections were located on other houses on the plantation (see figures 28 and 31).

The only description of the building's interior has been provided by Francis Dundas, who described this dwelling as "a long and very comfortable one story building" that contained three rooms.[41] On the west end of the building, presumably that end nearest the river, was a combination living room–office and a bedroom. Extending east was a "long hall" lined with shelves "filled with a very valuable collection of books." A dining room appeared on the east end of the hall. Unfortunately, Dundas makes no mention of the number or placement of fireplaces.

The excavation of structure 1 revealed that this building was 15.5 feet wide and 39.0 feet long (figure 26). An extended foundation running along the southeastern edge of the building added another 7.5 feet to the width of the structure, making its total width 23.0 feet. Only two brick chimneys, one on each end, were discovered. Even though the photographs clearly show the presence of three chimneys, no physical evidence could be found for the continuation of the foundation beyond the southwestern limit illustrated in figure 26.

Following Dundas's description, the bedroom, measuring about 10 feet by 15 feet, was on the extreme southwestern end of the structure and contained a fireplace. The combination living room and office, the same size as the bedroom, was located next to it. An interior wall, supported by a foundation, was placed between the living room–office and the dining room, which contained a fireplace. This last room measured about 15 feet by 20 feet. The hall, measuring 7.5 feet wide, extended along the east side of the building. The northeastern portion of this hallway contained the double doors and the window that appear in the photograph. The inner doorway led into the dining room. At least half the hall, the bedroom, and the combination office and living room had brick floors. The dining room probably contained a brick floor that had been stolen at some time after the building was abandoned.

The dates for the artifacts found in structure 1 indicate its postbellum occupation. The mean ceramic date was 1889.3 with a standard deviation of 12.2 years (1877.1 to 1901.5), the flat-glass date was 1897.4 with a standard deviation of 2.1 years (1895.3 to 1899.5), 79.0 percent of the nails were machine cut, and 3.1 percent were wire. All these artifacts provide support for the idea that this structure was occupied from the 1870s to the 1890s. An occasional antebellum artifact, however, also makes it possible to argue that the building was inhabited before 1870.

Most provocative of the antebellum materials were a number of sherds of blue transfer-printed ceramics in the Italian Flower Garden pattern. As stated earlier, similar sherds were also found on the hill in the building with the large, double fireplaces (structure 21). In structure 1, these

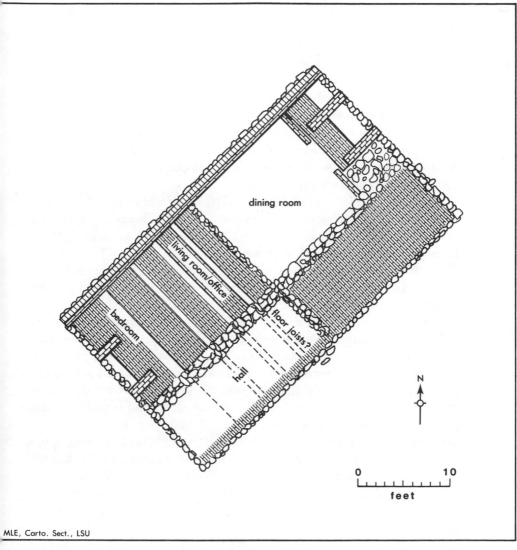

Figure 26. Foundation of James Edward Calhoun's home. This foundation was designated structure 1.

sherds were found in archaeological contexts that suggest that these sherds were used during the habitation of this building. As noted previously, this design was probably used sometime between 1814 and 1855. This finding is consistent with the assertion that Calhoun moved into this building sometime after his wife's death.

The presence of post-Calhoun-period artifacts in the structure suggests, as one informant said, that the building was still standing as late as 1910. Fragments of bottles from the South Carolina Dispensary, dating to the period from 1893 to 1907, and a bottle bearing the mark of the Adolphus Busch Glass Manufacturing Company, used from 1904 to 1907, support this contention.[42]

In summary, all the available historical and archaeological evidence supports the interpretation that structure 1 was the home in which Calhoun lived at the time of his death. Who may have lived there after Calhoun's death cannot be determined.

In addition to Calhoun's house, the home of another important plantation personage was located in this area of the plantation. This was the home of Caroline Walker "Calhoun," Calhoun's long-time servant.

The location of Caroline's house has been documented by many sources. For example, Dundas described a house "directly opposite" Calhoun's house as "a long building of two large rooms, one used as a kitchen and one as servants' quarters." William Calhoun identified a building north of Calhoun's home and oriented the same way as structure 2 as "Aunt Caroline's cottage." Similarly, a former Millwood tenant who was particularly knowledgeable about Calhoun's house stated that the house on the right of Calhoun's house (in figure 25) was Caroline's house, because one could leave Caroline's house and "go into Calhoun's house."[43] The structure 2 foundation was only 24.6 feet north of Calhoun's home.

Further evidence to substantiate that structure 2 was Caroline Walker's house derives from the archaeological research. This research supports Dundas's claim that the house directly across from Calhoun's house was long. When cleared of surface soil and leaf cover, structure 2 was found to be at least 48 feet long (figure 27). The southeastern wall of the structure could not be located, but if this section of the building was the same size as the northwestern section (and all the foundations uncovered at Millwood were symmetrical), then the entire structure would have been about 66 feet long and 15.1 feet wide. A more parsimonious explanation, however, is that structure 2 really was 48.0 feet long and was com-

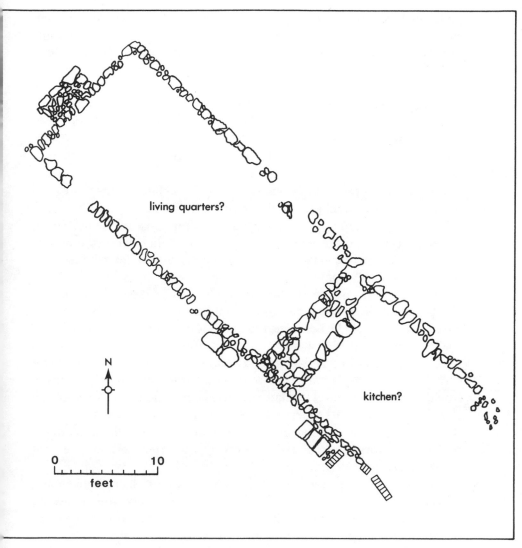

Figure 27. Foundation of Caroline Walker's home. This building was designated structure 2.

posed of two rooms: living quarters measuring 15.1 feet by 33.0 feet, with at least one fireplace on the northwest end, and a kitchen measuring 15.1 feet by about 18 feet, with a large fireplace on the northwestern wall. This explanation fits well with both the written and the physical evidence.

The distance between structures 1 and 2 and the relative size and orientation of each are indicated in the historical photographs of this part of the plantation (figures 19, 20, and 25). These photographs, along with the informants' comments, suggest the contemporaneity of structures 1 and 2.

Further evidence for the habitation of these dwellings at the same time derives from the similarity of the artifacts collected from these structures. In addition to implying a common temporal use of the buildings, the artifacts make it possible to reinforce the idea that a great amount of interaction occurred between the inhabitants of the long house and those of Calhoun's home.

The dates derived from the long house (structure 2) sample are almost identical to those for Calhoun's home (structure 1). The mean ceramic date for the structure 2 ceramic sample was computed as 1886.6 with a standard deviation of 14.1 years (1872.5 to 1900.7), or only 2.7 years less than the mean date of the structure 1 ceramics. The mean date of 1897.4 with a standard deviation of 2.1 years (1895.3 to 1899.5) for the structure 2 glass was identical to that computed for structure 1. More of the nails in structure 2 (91.2 percent) were machine cut than were those in structure 1 (where 79.0 percent were machine cut), but the percentage of wire nails was almost equal (3.6 percent for structure 2, 3.1 percent for structure 1).[44]

One unique group of artifacts found at Caroline Walker's house was a collection of nine patent medicine bottles discovered on the outside of the foundation against the chimney support on the northwestern corner of the building. The bottle collection was composed of one marked —— WITT & CO. CHICAGO, U.S.A., from Elden C. DeWitt and Company; one bottle of Simmons Liver Regulator, from J. H. Zeilin and Company in Philadelphia and Macon, Georgia; one from L. Gerstle and Company, probably somewhere in Pennsylvania, judging by the partial mark —— ENN; one bottle of Dr. King's New Discovery for Consumption, from H. E. Bucklen and Company in Chicago; one bottle of Monarch Extracts, from Austin, Nichols, and Company in New York; one bottle marked HARRISON & GAME; and one bottle of Ponds Extract Catarrh Remedy. All the bottles date from the 1860s to the 1890s. The two bottles with no identifying product name can also be dated. One, exhibiting a maker's mark A. G. CO on the bottom, was made by the Arsenal Glass Company in Pittsburgh from 1865 to 1868, and the other, with a maker's mark WT & CO A Q, signifies that it was manufactured sometime between 1857 and 1935 by Whitall-Tatum and Company of Millville, New Jersey.[45]

Interestingly, most of the blue transfer-printed ceramics found in Caroline Walker's home were decorated with the Italian Flower Garden pattern. Again, even though a number of scenarios might be devised to explain the presence of these ceramics in both structures 1 and 2, one explanation that must be considered is that structure 2 was, as Dundas has maintained, the kitchen for structure 1. On a more personal basis, it might be asserted that Caroline Walker cooked for James Edward Calhoun in her house and that the food was prepared on blue-printed ceramics and carried to Calhoun's dining room.

The presence of James Edward Calhoun's house in a cluster of structures (composed of structures 1, 2, 3, 4, and 5) identifies this part of the plantation as its administrative center. The proximity of these buildings implies their association with the landlord. Although in a very real sense the tenants operated the plantation, the administrative center housed the landlord, and he played a major role in organizing the plantation, at least formally and legally. With Calhoun's death, however, the character of the administrative center changed as agents or managers were needed to keep the plantation in operation for the Calhoun heirs. The tenants were obviously quite capable of keeping the plantation operating on their own, but the heirs needed someone on the estate to be mindful of their interests. This person was a resident plantation manager. Structure 8, located about 120 feet east of Caroline Walker's house (structure 2), was probably the home of Granville Beal, the manager of Millwood Plantation from 1894 to 1910.

Brief mention of a building that might be this building was offered by Dundas when he wrote that "near the original dwelling [of Calhoun] was a well and the home of the overseer, occupied by Mr. Keiser [*sic*] and later by Mr. McAllister." Further evidence is provided by William Calhoun, who showed a structure on his map in the exact position of structure 8, identified as "Beall's [sic] cottage."[46] This house, east of the well and south of a "red brick smokehouse," positively identified by excavation as structure 9, is in the exact location of structure 8.

Other evidence about the location of the manager's house near the well was provided by former Millwood Plantation tenants. Many of the tenants remembered Granville Beal, who most said came from Massachusetts. Beal's name was usually mentioned in conjunction with that of Dr. Joseph Hicks, Beal's brother-in-law, a dentist from Boston. One former tenant said that Hicks lived somewhere between Calhoun's house and the mill. This would mean that Hicks may have lived in structure 7, a dwelling identified by William L. Calhoun as "our cottage." No matter how ambiguous the tenants' statements about the location of Dr. Hicks's home might be, they all agreed that Beal lived near the well.[47]

The relative location of Beal's house can be placed near the well, but the construction of the house is more difficult to determine. The wife of a more recent manager who oversaw the Millwood estate from 1928 to 1972, remembered the homes occupied by Beal and Hicks as unpainted, "very plain houses" with "stone chimneys . . . at each end."[48] This description is difficult to correlate with the view of structure 8 offered in the panoramic photograph of Millwood taken sometime in or around 1879 (figure 19). Structure 8 appears on the left side of this photograph, just to the left of a tall, brick smokehouse (structure 9). Structure 7 (perhaps Hicks's house) appears behind structure 8. Structure 8 appears as a simple, clapboard-sided building supported with piers and having a central chimney. The two stone chimneys that the informant said were placed on the ends of the building do not appear in the photograph.

Further construction details of the manager's house cannot be discerned from this panoramic view; however, another photograph, perhaps of structure 8, provides clues of its possible details (figure 28). This photograph shows the eave projections and wide roof overhang apparently characteristic of Millwood Plantation dwellings before 1900. The building exhibits simple clapboard siding, a central chimney, and an unglassed window. The central chimney is consistent with the archaeological findings at structure 8, but the photograph could be of almost any building at Millwood. At any rate, the archaeological evidence clearly indicates that structure 8 was built after 1876 and used during Granville Beal's tenure at the plantation, or from 1894 to 1910.

Although its exact dimensions cannot be determined, the foundation

Figure 28. Unknown dwelling, Millwood Plantation, undated. The eave projections and overhanging roof apparently were common building features at the plantation.

of structure 8 may have been about 26 feet wide and 35.5 feet long. The most significant feature of this foundation was a central fireplace support 10.0 feet wide and 14.5 feet long (figure 29). This support, or base, was built with cut-granite stones and a series of stepped bricks. These bricks may have been added to the outside of the support for increased strength because the building was on piers.

Three separate and clearly distinct layers of stones were found within this fireplace support. The first layer was about 21.7 inches thick and consisted of small pieces of stone rubble. The second layer, about 13.8 inches thick, was a dense zone of small stones mixed with red clay. The bottom layer was about 23.2 inches thick and consisted of large, tightly packed stones. Below these stones was the dark yellowish brown sandy clay that appeared beneath the cultural deposits on some portions of the site.

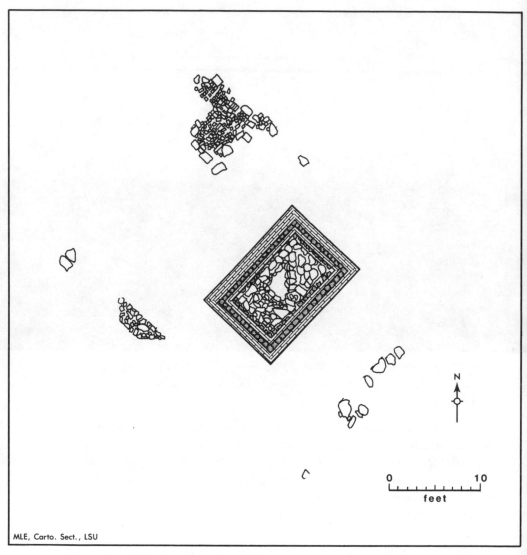

Figure 29. Chimney support of possible manager home. This support was designated structure 8.

MLE, Carto. Sect., LSU

Within the third layer of stones, about 3.4 feet below the top of the chimney base, came irrefutable proof—an 1876 Seated Liberty silver quarter—of when this support was built. Given the depth of this quarter and the density of the stones around it, this coin had to have fallen out of one of the workmen's pockets during construction; it could not have been deposited after construction. This coin serves as a *terminus post quem*—meaning "the date after which"—because it could not have been dropped before 1876. It must have been dropped sometime after 1876, but just when is open to speculation. If, however, the date on the panoramic photograph of 1879 (figure 18) is indeed accurate, then the photograph serves as a *terminus ante quem*—meaning "the date before which."[49] As such, the construction date of structure 8 can be placed between 1876 and 1879. These dates are almost twenty years before Granville Beal became the Millwood Plantation manager.

The majority of the artifacts, however, do date to the time when Beal would have occupied the house. The mean ceramic date of 1890.0 with a standard deviation of 11.5 years (1878.5 to 1901.5) and a mean flat-glass date of 1889.1 with a standard deviation of 2.1 years (1887.0 to 1891.2) are fairly consistent with Beal's tenure of from 1894 to 1910. Of the nails, 88.0 percent were machine cut, and 7.7 percent were wire. The overwhelming proportion of machine-cut nails to wire nails is consistent with what would be expected in a building built during the late nineteenth century.

The dating of the structure using only the recovered artifacts is complicated by the presence of Italian Flower Garden ceramics there. As noted above, this pre-1855 pattern may have been used by James Edward Calhoun and Caroline Walker. Its presence at structure 8 cannot be explained. Other artifacts, however, do seem to support the contention that structure 8 was occupied in the late nineteenth and early twentieth centuries. For example, a bottle base marked A.B.C. CO was made by the American Bottle Company in Chicago from 1905 to 1916, and another bottle with the mark W F & S MIL was made by William Fronzen and Son of Milwaukee, Wisconsin, from 1900 to 1929.[50]

Although the archaeological evidence sometimes conflicts with the existing historical evidence, such as that about the size of Calhoun's home, a general agreement exists between the two sources of information. All available evidence indicates that the area encompassing structures 1 through 8 housed the postbellum administrators of Millwood Plantation.

The exception, of course, was Caroline Walker, who was not an administrator.

The people who lived in the administrative area were not the only people of importance who lived at the plantation. The annual receipts for cotton sales from 1890 to 1910 mentioned in the preceding chapter (table 20) amply demonstrate that the tenants produced the economic base for Millwood Plantation. These tenants, like tenants everywhere in cotton country, were housed throughout the plantation lands after 1865.

At least two recognizable tenant homes were excavated at Millwood Plantation. These tenant houses were identified as structure 17, located near the center of the site, and structure 19, located in the extreme northeastern corner of the site.

Structure 17 was located about 275 feet north of Calhoun's home. When its foundation was completely exposed, this building measured about 14 feet wide and 39 feet long. It contained a central fireplace support and appeared to have been divided into at least two rooms (figure 30). Archaeological evidence—burned floorboards and a substantial layer of burned soil, charcoal, and artifacts—indicated that the building had burned at a time when people had lived there. Seventy-six of the 243 pieces of ceramics (31.3 percent) were burned, and 1,484 of the 2,271 fragments of glass (65.3 percent) were melted.

The artifacts from this structure, both burned and unburned, provide a clue about its date of occupation. The mean ceramic date of 1891.6 with a standard deviation of 11.9 years (1879.7 to 1903.5) and a mean flat-glass date of 1897.4 with a standard deviation of 2.1 years (1895.3 to 1899.5) suggest that the building was used in the late nineteenth century. A relatively equal proportion of machine-cut nails (52.6 percent) to wire nails (40.8 percent) (with 6.4 percent unidentifiable and 0.2 percent possibly hand-wrought) seems to suggest an early twentieth-century date.

Specific artifacts fall within the period spanning the late nineteenth and early twentieth centuries. For example, a single piece of a cup reading —FALLS 190—in gilt print is probably a section of a souvenir cup commemorating the incorporation of Calhoun Falls, South Carolina, in 1908. Two Indian-head pennies, dated 1891 and 1896, a medallion, reading SOUVENIR OF THE 1887 ICE CARNIVAL on one side and containing a picture of the Ice Palace on the other, were also found. This medal is a souvenir from the Saint Paul, Minnesota, winter carnival held each Janu-

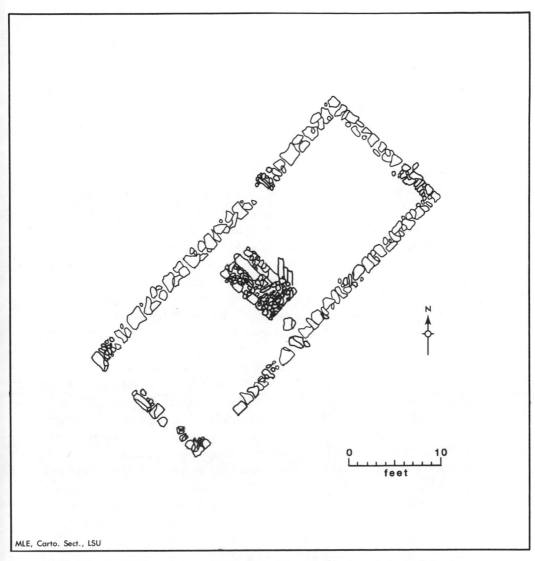

Figure 30. Foundation of tenant farmer home. These remains were designated structure 17.

ary since 1886. A central attraction of the carnival is a "palace" constructed entirely of ice. The fairs of 1886, 1887, and 1888 each attracted over 100,000 visitors.[51] The reason for the presence of this medallion in a tenant farmer's house is fascinating to contemplate, but it can never be known.

In addition to that from the archaeological evidence, further information about this structure was provided by a unique source: the woman who had lived in the house at the time of the fire. Born at Millwood in 1892 about a mile from Calhoun's residence, this woman said that she was married in 1910 to the youngest son of Calhoun's antebellum brickmason. Upon her marriage, she and her husband moved into an existing house, perhaps one that had been inhabited by her husband's father, who had recently passed away. This house was described as being located on "a little piece of ground near the Savannah where there's a barn." This suggests that this barn might be the one that appears on the extreme right of the 1879 panoramic photograph (figure 18). If so, then the small building with the overhanging roof to the right of the barn may be that building that can be seen on the left side of another photograph of a Millwood Plantation tenant farmer's house that is probably structure 17 (figure 31).

This photograph shows a long clapboard-sided building with a central chimney and a brick or stone foundation. The windows are not screened or glassed, and the eaves exhibit the characteristic projection. A simple porch and steps lead to the front door, and tools and pieces of old wood are stacked against its walls. Three log outbuildings are near the building.

The building details shown in this photograph correlate well with the recollection of the former inhabitant of structure 17. Describing her home, she said that it contained "brick up inside and weather boarding on the outside" and that "it wasn't up on no pillars." Her house was not "fine inside as the white people's house, but it was built like the white people's house." This means that the house was probably designed like the other houses at Millwood, but of a lesser quality.

Further support that structure 17 may be the building shown in the photograph comes from her comments about the foundation. She said that her family had "hogs and chickens and things like that" that would often go under the house. Accordingly, "every year" she allowed her children to go "under there with a hoe and rake, [to] clean [it] out." This comment seemingly contradicts her earlier statement that the house was

Figure 31. Tenant farmer home, Millwood Plantation, undated. (U.S. Army Corps of Engineers, Savannah District)

not up on pillars. This contradiction can be eliminated, however, by examining the tenant house shown in the photograph. A square hole on the side of the house could easily have allowed hogs, chickens, and children to go underneath the house, even though the foundation does not consist of piers.

The former tenant also provided information about the inside of her home. She said that it had a central chimney with two fireplaces and three rooms, "two bedrooms and a kitchen." The bedrooms were apparently half the size of the kitchen because they were formed by placing a "panel" in one of the two large rooms. Even though she said that the life of a Millwood Plantation tenant farmer was hard, her house was both warm and appreciably better than the houses of those who "started off with logs."

Further evidence makes the case even stronger that the tenant interviewed actually lived in structure 17. When explaining her reasons for leaving her home, she said that "we got burned out down there in the flat."[52] This statement provides excellent corroboration that structure 17 was indeed the house in which this former tenant lived, because the evidence for its burning is irrefutable. None of the other buildings excavated showed any evidence of having been burned. The historical evidence for the destruction of two buildings in 1942 mentioned in the preceding chapter, however, provides proof that other structures at Millwood were burned. The dates for the artifacts found in structure 17, however, were clearly not representative of the 1940s. The artifacts found show that structure 17 burned well before 1942.

All the available evidence can be used to make a strong case that structure 17 was a tenant farmer's house that was inhabited at least during the late nineteenth and early twentieth centuries. The date of its destruction by fire was between 1910, when the tenant who lived there said she was married, and 1925, the date she moved off the plantation. Because her family moved within the plantation "up near the spring" after the first house burned, the fire had to have occurred sometime before 1925. Unfortunately, the tenant could not recall the date of the fire.[53]

Another tenant farmer's home at Millwood Plantation is structure 19. Located in the extreme northeastern corner of the site, structure 19 was located near the top of a hill, about 660 feet away from structure 17. The old roadbed that extended as far as the possible squad settlement ran alongside structure 19.

The cut-granite foundation of structure 19 was indistinct (figure 32). Although a square, cut-granite chimney base occurred in the center of the dwelling, the outside walls were difficult to delimit. Stones that could be found indicated that structure 19 had been about 42 feet long. A single row of stones in a rough line appeared on the southeastern edge of the building. If this row of stones represented the building's wall, and if the wall on the opposite side was the same distance from this possible wall, then the structure would have been 25.5 feet wide. With these dimensions, the building would have encompassed about 1,071 square

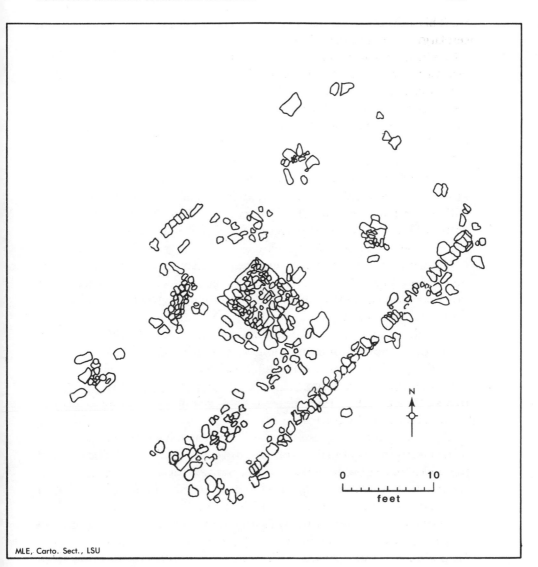

Figure 32. Foundation of probable tenant farmer home. This foundation was designated structure 19.

feet. This would have been a large tenant house; in fact, it would have been larger than Calhoun's house.

If an inner row of stones, more intermittent than the outer row, was indeed the remains of the wall (with the outer row being wall debris), then the structure would have been 15.0 feet wide. If this was the case, then structure 19 would have contained about 630 square feet. This size is more compatible with that of the known tenant farmer house, structure 17.

The artifacts found in and around structure 19 help provide a date for its habitation. A mean ceramic date of 1888.9 with a standard deviation of 7.5 years (1881.4 to 1896.4) and a mean flat-glass date of 1880.8 with a standard deviation of 2.1 years (1878.7 to 1882.9) correlate well with the finding that 97.9 percent of nails collected were machine cut, whereas only 2.1 percent were wire.

Unfortunately, no artifacts were found at structure 19 that could be dated more precisely. However, its probable size, construction, and location make it possible to argue that the building was used as a dwelling by postbellum tenant farmers.

That the archaeological site of Millwood Plantation should contain evidence of the agricultural and industrial aspects of the plantation is not surprising. After all, the former tenant's house burned down just a little over seventy-five years ago. Thus, it can be reasonably expected, given this small amount of time, that physical remnants of these industries would remain at the plantation.

Physical evidence suggests that Calhoun may have first settled on a hill overlooking the Savannah River (structure 21). Early in 1839 he decided to build a more grandiose home closer to the river (structure 6); this was the house closed or unfinished on the death of his wife in 1844. Calhoun then moved into an overseer's cabin (structure 1).

Calhoun's slaves, who actually cleared and worked the plantation, also may have lived on the hill (structure 24) and then later in cabins closer to Calhoun's new home (structures 10, 11, and E). Postbellum laborers probably lived in the same quarters, and squad members may have moved into the old buildings on the hill (structures 21 and 24) and built some new ones (structures 22, 23, and possibly G). After the breakup of the squad system before 1875, tenant farmers lived in at least two locations within the boundaries of the archaeological site (structures 17 and 19).

This sequence explains the physical settlement of Millwood Plantation. An incomplete picture of tenant settlement is presented, however, by viewing just the archaeological site. After the dissolution of the squad system, tenants were no longer required to live within the confines of what later would be considered the Millwood Plantation archaeological site. They merely had to remain somewhere within the limits of Calhoun's estate in order to be Millwood tenants.

Precise information about where these tenants actually settled has not been found. Only twenty-nine historic-period archaeological sites were located on Calhoun's lands during the original archaeological survey.[54] Because written and oral sources indicate that Millwood Plantation contained ninety-five tenants in 1890 and ninety-eight in 1928,[55] it can be expected that at least ninety-five different tenant homesites would once have existed within the boundaries of the Calhoun estate. With tenant shifting, many more buildings could have been inhabited. No source, however, contains information about the location of these homesites.

One source, a 1932 map of the soils in Abbeville County, does show the location of sixty-six individual buildings on the Calhoun estate (figure 33). This map provides clues about the settlement of tenants on the estate if it can be assumed that the structures shown are all tenant homes and that they are all accurately located.

A quick examination of the house locations shown on the map reveals that most of them occurred between the Atlantic Coast Line Railroad and the Savannah River, southeast and east of the Millwood Plantation archaeological site. This diffuse distribution is consistent with postbellum tenant settlement patterns and with comments made by two informants who said that many people lived at Millwood in the late 1930s.[56] These dates, however, are after Millwood had become a campground, and may indicate that these people were simply remembering incorrectly or that they were actually thinking about the settlement of campers.

Although this map is not a perfect source, the location of the buildings on it were analyzed as if they were tenant homesites according to a number of variables meant to indicate something about the houses' placement. (For this analysis, it does not matter whether these houses were occupied or already abandoned.) These variables were elevation, direction of ground slope, and the distances to the nearest stream, to the nearest neighbor, to the Savannah River, to the nearest road, to the nearest railroad, and to Calhoun Falls.

These variables indicate that the "typical" tenant farm on Millwood

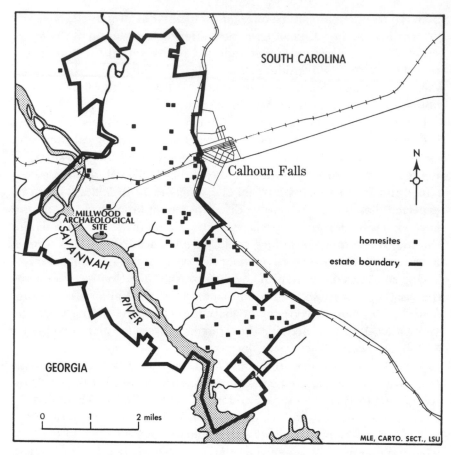

Figure 33. Location of buildings on Calhoun estate according to the 1932 soil map of Abbeville County.

Plantation (if the structures on the map were indeed farmhouses) was located about 475 feet above sea level (78.8 percent) and placed on a slope that faced southwest (16.7 percent), west (16.7 percent), or southeast (15.2 percent). This ideal farm was three-tenths of a mile from the closest stream (98.5 percent) and less than one and one-half miles from the Savannah River (63.6 percent). This farm was also less than one-half mile from its nearest neighbor (75.8 percent), less than one and one-half miles from the nearest road (84.8 percent) and the nearest railroad (86.4 percent), and more than one and one-half miles from Calhoun Falls (86.4 percent).[57]

It may never be known whether certain criteria were used to establish the location of individual tenant farms on Millwood Plantation. The descriptive statistics collected from the 1932 soil map do make it possible to argue tentatively that certain locations consciously were selected for home location. It cannot be determined whether the tenants selected their own locations or whether they were selected for them, but given the restrictions of tenancy, the last possibility seems more likely.

A better picture of the tenant houses themselves can be gleaned from the former tenants who lived in them. These comments indicate that a number of different kinds of housing were used at Millwood Plantation during the postbellum period. For example, a couple of the tenants remembered dog-trot houses with stick-and-mud chimneys: "They put mud over the sticks [in the chimney]. What they'd do is put these four rooms together. They's build them in a little separate thing, but they'd be right together [and] they'd have a chimney come out of each room. Sometimes they used to have a hallway between them." Another tenant recalled that the tenant houses of her experience were log with stick-and-mud chimneys. Wide planks were placed over the logs to keep the house warm. This house form, containing a central, double chimney with two fireplaces, seems to have been the most widely used house design on the plantation. These houses are reported to have had four rooms—a bedroom, a living room, a kitchen, and a shed or storage room—with the fireplaces facing the bedroom and the living room. One tenant stated that the fireplace in the living room was whitewashed "with white mud."

Interesting comments about the construction of the Millwood Plantation tenant homes were provided by a grandson of one of Calhoun's slaves. When asked about these homes, he replied that one or two carpenters would come, perhaps from town, and "cut a piece of board, any way it fit." These carpenters did not care whether the house was well made, because once a board was cut, "maybe it would fit, [maybe] it didn't fit." They would nail it together and then go "back to their business." They generally used rocks "with a little cement put together with mud" for the pillars on which the house sat. This description is amazingly similar to that of Nate Shaw in Alabama, who said that the typical plantation house built for the black farmer was usually "just a old common-built house" with "no special care took of how it was built."[58]

Regarding the chimneys in these houses, this informant remembered that "you had a great big fireplace there, two of them" in the center of the house. He said, "You built the chimneys with sticks and mud, a square chimney with mud between layers of sticks." This construction was the same in all parts of the chimney, except that rocks were placed at the bottom "to keep the sticks from burning." These stick chimneys, going "all the way to the tip top of the house," were daubed with mud "on the outside and on the inside." When the mud was dry and hard, a fire could be safely built in the fireplace because "it ain't going to burn because the main foundation of the fireplace is rock at the bottom."[59] The presence of central fireplaces with stone foundations is clearly supported by the archaeological findings at the tenant dwellings (structures 17 and 19) and at other structures.

A comparison of the sizes of the different foundations uncovered at Millwood Plantation generally illustrates the correlation between plantation labor status and house size. Unfortunately, the house sizes of those people who had administrative responsibility over the plantation, namely Calhoun and his resident manager, cannot be determined with total certainty. For example, as excavated, Calhoun's home (structure 1) contained 897.0 square feet within its foundation. The photographic evidence (figures 18, 19, and 25), however, indicates that his home was much larger and contained three chimneys, not just the two found by excavation. As stated above, this discrepancy remains a mystery. Calhoun's probable second house (structure 6) was the largest structure at Millwood, with about 1,580.0 square feet of living space. Similarly, the available space in the manager's home (structure 8) cannot be accurately determined because its walls could not be found.

The available living spaces for the plantation tenant homes are much easier to calculate. The smallest foundations were of homes occupied by wage hands. Structures 11 and E were 323.1 square feet, and structure 10 contained 370.6 square feet. The probable living quarters of Calhoun's longtime servant Caroline Walker (in structure 2) measured 498.3 square feet. The known tenant home (structure 17) contained 546.0 square feet, and if the walls of the other tenant home (structure 19) are located accurately, it contained 630.0 square feet. The possible home of the plantation millwright (structure 17) was 743.4 square feet. Thus, the wage-hand cabins were built somewhere in the range of 16.4 feet by 21.3 feet, and the tenant houses were somewhere around 14 feet by 42 feet.

The size and arrangement of the foundations at Millwood Plantation seem to offer good material evidence for the differences between the different plantation tenure groups. The landlord, James Edward Calhoun, had the largest house; the wage hands had the smallest homes. Although Millwood is only one plantation (and one directed by a man often referred to as eccentric), the temptation is to argue that a clear correlation existed between one's place on the agricultural ladder and the size of one's house. Additional research is required, but this interpretation based on the physical evidence seems plausible.

Unlike the analysis of physical evidence, the analysis of artifacts collected by excavation is never straightforward. So many factors intrude on archaeological deposits—past cultural practices, the natural history of a site, and the abilities and strategies of the archaeologists—that all interpretation based on artifacts must be cautious and tentative. The postbellum plantation, although remarkably recent, presents an imposing problem for archaeologists intent on studying artifact collections recovered from them.

Chapter Seven

The Material Basis
of Millwood Plantation:
Personal Possessions

IN ADDITION TO STUDYING THE CONSTRUCTION, size, patterns, and layout of buildings, it is possible for archaeologists to learn about the life at a past plantation by examining the artifacts found there. These artifacts constitute a primary source of information for archaeologists.

The reason for studying artifacts at a postbellum plantation is understandable. Because plantation inhabitants occupied various positions on the agricultural ladder from wage hand to landlord or independent owner-operator—that is, maintained a different relationship to the mode of production—it follows logically that each kind of plantation inhabitant would have a different set of material possessions. In other words, on the basis of the inequalities of postbellum plantation life (or perhaps just plantation life, in general), it can be reasonably postulated that landlords would purchase and own a different class of items than would sharecroppers. Importantly, however, this distinction is not caused by any sort of "broad culture process," as some historical archaeologists might propose,[1] but rather by the historical process of plantation life and the unequal distribution of power and wealth.

The material manifestations of this historical process are decidedly difficult to discern, because when an archaeologist recovers a particular artifact through excavation, the temporal association of this artifact must be determined. This determination process is slightly different from that discussed in the preceding chapter. In that process the archaeologist tries to provide manufacturing dates for specific items. In the analysis discussed in this chapter, the archaeologist must decide when the item was used. The subtle distinction between the dates can be illustrated by considering an object with a known manufacturing date of from 1850 to 1870. Whether that item was used by a slave or by a freed tenant farmer can make a significant difference to the plantation archaeologist. Unfortunately, traditional sources of information cannot always shed light on the answer. Most historical documents, even bills of sale, are seldom explicit enough to facilitate identification of specific artifacts, and the archaeologist's measure of time—soil stratigraphy—is often not helpful at plantation sites. While prehistorians may excavate a site with soil layers extending to a depth of three feet or more, historical archaeologists often excavate sites with soil layers only inches thick. This difference is due partly to the short time during which historic sites, compared with prehistoric sites, were inhabited. In the United States, for example, plantations for the most part were inhabited for only a short time. In addition, several nonhabitation factors must be taken into consideration when conducting analysis on excavated artifact collections. These factors include the specific circumstances of site history, excavation, and preservation.

Millwood Plantation was inhabited as a plantation for only about one hundred years. Although this one hundred years was a period of great change in the South, marked particularly by changes in plantation labor organization, it cannot be considered a long time in an archaeological sense. The archaeologist interested in postbellum plantation reorganization encounters significant difficulty in distinguishing short periods of time in the archaeological deposits. So, even though plantation life was vastly different in 1870 when compared with 1850, archaeologists cannot easily distinguish between these two dates.

None of the buildings investigated at Millwood were completely excavated. All the foundations studied were cleared of soil and underbrush, but in most cases, time constraints dictated that only two or three excavation units be placed within or around the foundations. One of the goals of the project was to recover as much physical information as possible about the plantation before its inundation. This strategy required excavation at locales with a high probability of containing archaeological information. The severe erosion of the Piedmont made the excavation of yard areas pointless; culturally sterile red clay occurred directly beneath the leaf cover. With the time limits imposed on the excavation, and with the knowledge that this would be the last archaeological research possible at Millwood, the continued examination of the yards seemed counterproductive, even though in an ideal setting such excavations would be mandatory. In addition, no dumps or trash pits could be located during the fieldwork. Thus, the archaeological information that was collected at Millwood is biased. This bias, which is present at more sites than archaeologists generally like to admit, makes it impossible to compare the deposits using inferential statistics. Nonetheless, enlightening examinations of these materials can be made.[2]

A total of 62,119 artifacts were collected at Millwood Plantation. Of this number, 1,741 (2.8 percent) were prehistoric and, perhaps, either were evidence of an indigenous, preplantation occupation of the site or were brought to the plantation as curios by plantation inhabitants. The remaining 60,378 artifacts were directly associated with the plantation, either during its operation or immediately thereafter.

Archaeologists have many options when analyzing excavated artifact collections. A major determining factor in how the collection will be examined and what interpretations will result derives from the way artifacts are classified, or formed into meaningful groups. In many ways, the classification scheme will structure the way the archaeologist "sees" the collection. Because this study of postbellum Millwood Plantation places a major emphasis on labor position, and because it was assumed that different laboring groups used artifacts that had different functions, the artifacts have been grouped into categories that reflect suspected artifact function (table 21).

This functional typology and others like it[3] are based, in part, on the idea that the items in use today are enough like those used in America's past to ensure that a commonality of function can be assumed. For example, a small, round, flat object with four holes in it can be assumed to have been used as a button in the past because it looks like the buttons used today; however, functional associations such as this can only be made with varying degrees of probability, because no guarantees can be made that the round, flat item was actually used as a button. It may have been used for something else, something that no modern archaeologist could ever imagine. Because this unusual function can never be known, the assumption must be made that a high probability exists that the object was indeed used in the usual manner. This usage usually can be determined from today's practices or from reliable historical records. In rare instances, idiosyncratic uses of artifacts are mentioned in historical

Table 21.

Functional Typology, with Examples of Artifacts in Each Subcategory

1. FOODWAYS
   a. Procurement—ammunition, fishhooks, fishing weights
   b. Preparation—baking pans, cooking vessels, large knives
   c. Service—fine earthenware, flatware, tableware
   d. Storage—coarse earthenware, stoneware, glass bottles, canning jars, bottle stoppers
   e. Remains—floral, faunal

2. CLOTHING
   a. Fasteners—buttons, eyelets, snaps, hook and eyes
   b. Manufacture—needles, pins, scissors, thimbles
   c. Other—shoe leather, metal shoe shanks, clothes hangers

3. HOUSEHOLD/STRUCTURAL
   a. Architectural/Construction—nails, flat glass, spikes, mortar, bricks, slate
   b. Hardware—hinges, tacks, nuts, bolts, staples, hooks, brackets
   c. Furnishings/Accessories—stove parts, furniture pieces, lamp parts, decorative fasteners

4. PERSONAL
   a. Medicinal—medicine bottles, droppers
   b. Cosmetic—hairbrushes, hair combs, jars
   c. Recreational—smoking pipes, toys, musical instruments, souvenirs
   d. Monetary—coins
   e. Decorative—jewelry, hairpins, hatpins, spectacles
   f. Other—pocketknives, fountain pens, pencils, inkwells

5. LABOR
   a. Agricultural—barbed wire, horse and mule shoes, harness buckles, hoes, plow blades, scythe blades
   b. Industrial—tools

documents. Obviously, the functional interpretations made by archaeologists have less probability as the time between the present and the past being studied increases.[4] Prehistorians studying the distant past can have great difficulty determining an artifact's past function.

Another problem faced by archaeologists arises in the use of artifact frequencies. For instance, one excavation unit might contain forty pieces of broken dishes, and another might contain only five. The presence of ceramics in the first location seems to outweigh significantly that in the second unit, but, further analysis may indicate that the forty pieces represent only one plate, whereas the five sherds in the second unit actually represent five different plates. The interpretation that might result from using the whole dishes would be very different from that derived from using the sherd frequencies. This problem can be partially overcome, however, by examining the frequency of ceramic vessels at the site (as reconstructed from the sherds) and the occurrence of different kinds of ceramics (on the basis of their surface decoration and shape).

For the following analysis, the recovered artifacts from six dwellings were grouped into the functional categories listed in table 21. The dwellings used were Calhoun's home (structure 1), Caroline Walker's home (structure 2), the resident manager's home (structure 8), the northernmost slave–wage hand cabin (structure 11), one of the two tenant homes (structure 17), and the millwright's home (structure 27). These dwellings were chosen because they can be fairly well identified with the major tenure groups at the plantation.

The fact that more of the foundations were completely excavated make it difficult to place too strong an emphasis on the representativeness of the collections as a means to infer the exact material differences between plantation labor groups. Most of the artifacts are commonplace—shoe parts, ceramic sherds, sewing needles, smoking pipes—and collectively suggest only that someone lived at the plantation in the past. Other artifacts—brooches, spectacles, medallions, and harmonica reeds—indicate that these lives were real and individualistic. The construction of past life from archaeological deposits is always tricky; the presence of small artifact samples makes it even more difficult. Thus, rather than speculation about the different kinds of material possessions used by the inhabitants of each dwelling, a different and more telling approach is adopted here. This analysis seeks to explore only the differences between the samples from each dwelling. The focus is on the characteristics that might have been shared by labor groups, as exemplified at one building, rather than on idiosyncracies, even though these individual differences cannot be discounted.

The artifacts collected from the dwellings can be grouped into the functional categories and examined for similarities (table 22).[5] By far, the largest category represented is that related to the procurement, preparation, and consumption of food. This category accounts for from 65.8 to 93.9 percent of the artifacts collected at the dwellings. This, perhaps, is not startling because ceramics and glass objects, included within the "foodways" category, are easily broken, preserve well in most soils, and were generally used in larger quantities than other objects. For example, a family of four might have four plates but only one plow. Still, the variation within the samples is interesting. Calhoun's postbellum home and

Table 22

Six Artifact Samples Grouped in Adjusted Functional Categories*

	Functional Category					
Sample	Foodways	Clothing	Household	Personal	Labor	Total
Calhoun	4,597 (93.9)†	88 (1.8)	104 (2.1)	103 (2.1)	4 (0.1)	4,896
Walker	458 (65.8)	27 (3.9)	17 (2.4)	194 (27.9)	0	696
Manager	1,545 (92.3)	29 (1.7)	18 (1.1)	76 (4.5)	6 (0.4)	1,674
Wage hand	59 (70.2)	9 (10.7)	5 (6.0)	6 (7.1)	5 (6.0)	84
Tenant	2,798 (88.6)	116 (3.7)	88 (2.8)	115 (3.6)	42 (1.3)	3,159
Millwright	557 (89.1)	4 (0.6)	14 (2.2)	49 (7.8)	1 (0.2)	625
Total	10,014 (89.9)	273 (2.5)	246 (2.2)	543 (4.9)	58 (0.5)	11,134

*Excluding architectural items and cottonseeds from structure 1.
†Numbers in parentheses are percentages.

the resident manager's home show high percentages of foodways items. Two structures, Caroline Walker's home and the wage hand dwelling, show lower percentages of foodways items. Walker's home has a high percentage of personal items because of the presence of medicine bottles and medicine bottle fragments (188 pieces).

When the data are presented as a graph (figure 34), the differences between the samples are easier to see. The sample from Calhoun's home is similar to those from the tenant home, and the manager and the millwright samples are somewhat similar. The wage hand sample and the Walker sample are each more or less unique.

Given the importance of labor at a postbellum plantation, the distribution of "labor" artifacts, tools and items related to agriculture, is significant. The highest percentage occurs at the foundation associated with the wage hand, but no such items were found in the Walker sample. The tenant sample contained the second-largest proportion followed by that related to the manager, the millwright, and Calhoun. Many of the artifacts placed within the labor category—horseshoes, chain links, and wagon parts—may not have been used for agriculture. Artifacts that, with some measure of probability, were used in agriculture appeared only in the tenant sample (six plow blades and one scythe blade). While it may be tempting to argue that this unique distribution related to labor organization, the presence of these items in the tenant sample may be explained by the fact that this house was the only one excavated that

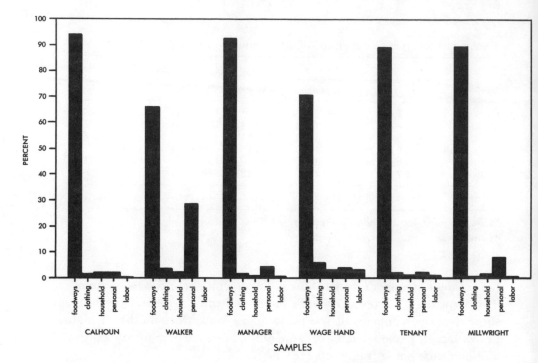

Figure 34. Distribution of artifact samples grouped in functional categories.

showed signs of having been burned. Completely charred floorboards, extensive fire marks on the foundation, and many melted artifacts indicate that this house was destroyed by fire. Thus, the number of agricultural implements found may indicate only that these items could not be saved when the house burned. Being valuable economic objects, these items would be curated and removed when plantation families moved to new locations and so would not often appear in archaeological deposits. Thus, spurious conclusions might be reached by placing too strong an emphasis strictly on the presence or absence of agricultural implements, and more profitable interpretations might result from a closer examination of the artifact samples.

More rigor can be brought to the analysis of the similarities and differences between the artifact samples by the construction of a matrix of similarity using Robinson's Index of Agreement. This measure, well used in archaeology since the early 1950s, permits the computation of a number, an *index of agreement,* that indicates the similarity between two groups of artifacts. The index was originally presented to help archaeologists order samples temporally, but it can also be used to provide an unbiased measure of the similarity between two artifact samples.

To compute the index, the largest number of artifacts in one artifact class from one site or locale is subtracted from those in the same class from a second site or locale. This procedure, producing absolute values, is completed for all artifact classes. For the Millwood Plantation artifacts, the percentage of foodways items from Calhoun's home (structure 1) was subtracted from the percentage of foodways items in Caroline Walker's home (structure 2); or vice versa, depending upon which percentage was larger. The same procedure was conducted for each of the other four categories of artifacts. The resultant differences were added, and 200 was subtracted from the sum (because 200 percent is the maximum amount of possible difference between two samples). The figure that results is the index of agreement.

The index of agreement was computed for all possible combinations of structures, and a matrix of similarity containing all the indices was produced (table 23). The index is large when the artifact samples are similar (the index is 200 when a sample is compared against itself). A low index value indicates that the samples are dissimilar.[6]

The generated matrix indicates that some pairs of samples from the dwellings are more similar than others and that some are dissimilar. The indices range from 143.6 to 194.6. The Calhoun sample is most similar to the manager sample and to the tenant sample and most dissimilar to the Walker sample and the wage hand sample; the Walker sample is not especially similar to any of the other samples; and the tenant sample is

Table 23

Similarity Matrix for Artifact Samples Grouped in Functional Categories

	Sample					
Sample	Calhoun	Walker	Manager	Wage hand	Tenant	Millwright
Calhoun	200.0					
Walker	143.6	200.0				
Manager	194.6	146.2	200.0			
Wage hand	152.6	158.4	158.4	200.0		
Tenant	189.4	151.0	151.0	163.2	200.0	
Millwright	188.1	152.9	191.1	160.7	190.5	200.0

Table 24

Artifact Samples in Functional Categories, Ranked by Index of Agreement

Samples Compared	Index of Agreement
Calhoun–manager	194.6
Manager–millwright	191.1
Tenant–millwright	190.5
Calhoun–tenant	189.4
Calhoun–millwright	188.1
Wage hand–tenant	163.2
Wage hand–millwright	160.7
Walker–wage hand	158.4
Manager–wage hand	158.4
Walker–millwright	152.9
Calhoun–wage hand	152.6
Walker–tenant	151.0
Manager–tenant	151.0
Walker–manager	146.2
Calhoun–Walker	143.6

similar to the millwright sample. These findings, then, substantiate the validity of the observation made by a visual examination of the samples.

A further understanding of these indices can be gained by ranking the samples by index of agreement (table 24). Some of the indices seem to correlate with expectations about the tenure groups at Millwood. For example, it makes sense that the Calhoun sample would be similar to the manager sample because they were both in control of the plantation; the Calhoun sample would be dissimilar from the wage hand sample because they were on opposite ends of the agricultural ladder. But the similarity between the Calhoun and the tenant samples and the great difference between the Calhoun and Walker samples is difficult to rationalize. Walker's role as Calhoun's servant agrees with this possible difference in artifact profiles, but Calhoun's will suggests that he had great fondness for her. This fondness might have been only an expression of his paternalist feelings toward her, but regrettably, this conclusion cannot be substantiated.

Although the exact nature of these differences and similarities is difficult to determine, these indices do make it possible to argue that certain regularities can be indicated in the kinds of artifacts used by the different tenure groups at Millwood Plantation, or at least by individuals who occupied those positions. That is, within certain limits imposed by the archaeological sampling design, unequal artifact preservation, site disturbance, and certain cultural practices such as shifting, it would appear that the distribution of artifacts at sites associated with different tenure groups may be distinct.

This finding can be further evaluated by focusing the analysis on that artifact class that is perhaps most responsible for the variation in the samples, the foodways group (table 25). A similar analysis, using the index of agreement and a matrix of similarity (table 26) was conducted, and the samples were ranked (table 27).

The index values range from 125.8 to 197.2, with the greatest difference being between the wage hand and the millwright samples and the greatest similarity being between the manager and the tenant samples. Interestingly, the ranks in this test are almost completely unlike those in the previous test (table 23), but again, reasonable interpretations can be offered. For example, the difference between the Calhoun sample and the tenant sample fulfills what would be expected on a postbellum plantation, as does the somewhat strong similarity between the Calhoun and the Walker samples. The strong similarity between the Calhoun sample and the wage hand sample, however, is difficult to explain.

The analysis can be taken a step further by considering the ceramics themselves and assuming that different tenure groups on a plantation would have different access to different sorts of ceramic vessels, distinctions that would be identifiable in the archaeological samples.[7] To overcome the problem of unequal breakage of ceramics, creating two pieces of one plate and sixty-five of another, the analysis of the number and kind of vessels present at particular foundations can be examined.

Table 25

Foodways Artifacts from Six Dwellings*

| | *Functional Category* | | | | |
Sample	*Procurement*	*Preparation*	*Service*	*Storage*	*Total*
Calhoun	44 (1.6)†	2 (0.1)	860 (31.6)	1,815 (66.7)	2,721
Walker	3 (1.0)	0	66 (22.1)	230 (76.9)	299
Manager	13 (1.0)	3 (0.2)	106 (7.9)	1,213 (90.9)	1,335
Wage hand	0	0	13 (37.1)	22 (62.9)	35
Tenant	13 (0.5)	10 (0.4)	173 (7.0)	2,293 (92.1)	2,489
Millwright	25 (4.5)	33 (6.0)	0	496 (89.5)	554
	98 (1.3)	48 (0.6)	1,218 (16.4)	6,069 (81.6)	7,433

*Excluding food remains.

†Numbers in parentheses are percentages.

Table 26

Similarity Matrix for Artifacts in Foodways Category

	Sample					
Sample	*Calhoun*	*Walker*	*Manager*	*Wage hand*	*Tenant*	*Millwright*
Calhoun	200.0					
Walker	179.6	200.0				
Manager	151.4	171.6	200.0			
Wage hand	189.0	170.0	169.6	200.0		
Tenant	148.6	168.8	197.2	139.8	200.0	
Millwright	136.8	155.8	181.4	125.8	180.8	200.0

Ceramic items made during the nineteenth and early twentieth centuries, were made in shapes that are recognizable and still used today (for example, plates, platters, bowls, and cups). By knowing the shapes of ceramic objects, archaeologists are able to calculate the minimum number of vessels at a structure. For example, an archaeological sample containing three ceramic sherds could represent as few as one or as many as three separate vessels. By an examination of the thickness, paste color, decoration, and shape of the sherd, archaeologists can usually determine, within reasonable limits, how many vessels are represented in a sample.

The minimum number of vessels in the six dwellings is 189 (table 28). Of these vessels, most derive from the Calhoun sample, whereas the least

Table 27

Artifact Samples in Foodways Category, Ranked by Index of Agreement

Samples Compared	*Index of Agreement*
Manager–tenant	197.2
Calhoun–wage hand	189.0
Manager–millwright	181.4
Tenant–millwright	180.8
Calhoun–Walker	179.6
Walker–manager	171.6
Walker–wage hand	170.0
Manager–wage hand	169.6
Walker–tenant	168.8
Walker–millwright	155.8
Calhoun–manager	151.4
Calhoun–tenant	148.6
Wage hand–tenant	139.8
Calhoun–millwright	136.8
Wage hand–millwright	125.8

come from the wage hand sample. The samples from the other dwellings are intermediate.

At first glance, the number of vessels at each locale makes perfect sense, because the landlord should have had more ceramic vessels than anybody else on the plantation, and the wage hand should have had the least. Unfortunately, this kind of simple interpretation, all too common in archaeological research, has certain weaknesses. For one thing, this interpretation hinges on the idea that all ceramic vessels used at the dwellings were broken and deposited in the soil, leaving sherds as evidence. Because the landlord had more dishes, greater probability existed for them to be broken and thrown away; the wage hand had fewer dishes, so fewer sherds remain as evidence. While this sort of reasoning might be justifiable, the archaeologist has no way of determining whether the landlord was just clumsier than the wage hands and simply broke more dishes. Also, the question of size of household must be considered. Theoretically, a larger household would require more dishes. But even this reasoning has weaknesses. A small family may simply have acquired more dishes than a larger one for some undeterminable reason. This last problem is not so great at Millwood, because historical records indicate that Calhoun lived alone. On the other hand, the 1900 census, noted in chapter 5, indicates that as many as six other people may have lived with Caroline Walker. Nonetheless, the Calhoun sample contained more than twice the ceramic vessels as the Walker sample.

Table 28

Ceramic Vessels in the Six Samples

	Sample						
Vessel	*Calhoun*	*Tenant*	*Walker*	*Manager*	*Millwright*	*Wage hand*	*Total*
Cup	3	7	4	2	3	–	19
Bowl	12	1	–	10	–	1	24
Cup/bowl	6	–	–	–	–	–	6
Saucer	3	1	2	7	–	1	14
Plate	23	8	4	4	–	1	40
Platter	1	–	1	–	–	–	2
Tureen	1	–	–	–	–	–	1
Jug	1	–	1	–	–	–	2
Crock	–	–	–	1	–	–	1
Crock/jug	5	6	3	5	–	1	20
Unidentified	24	12	15	1	7	1	60
Total	79 (41.8)	35 (18.5)	30 (15.9)	30 (15.9)	10 (5.3)	5 (2.6)	189

Other problems make it difficult to postulate a direct correlation between tenure affiliation and number of vessels in the archaeological sample. For example, only the tenant house was destroyed by fire. Thus, the relatively high number of ceramic vessels found in the deposits of this structure may be an indication that the people who lived there lost all of their dishes during the fire. The thirty-five vessels found may represent their entire ceramic collection, a possibility made believable by the observations of Agee and Evans. At all the other structures, the ceramic sherds were probably deposited as a result of accidental breakage. These people would have had the chance to take their dishes with them when they moved, whereas the people in the burned tenant house would not have.

To ameliorate the problems caused by the manner in which the artifacts found their way into the ground as well as the question of whether the "right" places were excavated, the ceramic vessels can be studied according to their percentage of occurrence. For this analysis, the vessels from each dwelling were divided into flat fine earthenware vessels (saucers, plates, and platters), deep fine earthenware vessels (cups, bowls, and tureens), and stoneware containers (jugs and crocks). These vessels were also classified as food-service wares or food storage wares (table 29).

A similarity matrix (table 30) was generated using the percentage of

Table 29

Ceramic Vessel Forms in the Six Samples

| | Service | | Storage | |
| | Fine Earthenware | | Stoneware | |
Sample	Flat*	Deep†	Containers‡	Total
Calhoun	27 (49.1)§	22 (40.0)	6 (10.9)	55
Manager	11 (37.9)	12 (41.4)	6 (20.7)	29
Tenant	9 (39.1)	8 (34.8)	6 (26.1)	23
Walker	7 (46.1)	4 (26.7)	4 (26.7)	15
Wage hand	2 (50.0)	1 (25.0)	1 (25.0)	4
Millwright	–	3 (100.0)	–	3
Total	56 (43.4)	50 (38.8)	23 (17.8)	129

*Saucers, plates, platters.
†Cups, bowls, tureens.
‡Jugs, crocks.
§Numbers in parentheses are percentages.

Table 30

Similarity Matrix for Vessel Forms

	Sample					
Sample	*Calhoun*	*Manager*	*Tenant*	*Walker*	*Wage hand*	*Millwright*
Calhoun	200.0					
Manager	177.6	200.0				
Tenant	169.6	186.8	200.0			
Walker	168.5	170.5	183.7	200.0		
Wage hand	170.0	167.2	178.2	193.3	200.0	
Millwright	80.0	82.8	69.6	53.3	50.0	200.0

occurrence of each vessel form, and the samples were ranked by index of agreement (table 31). The index values range from 80.0 to 193.3. The millwright sample, because of its total association with deep service vessels, has the lowest indices. In this analysis, the Walker sample is similar to the wage hand sample and to the tenant sample, and the manager and the tenant samples are similar. The Calhoun sample does not show a strong similarity to any sample, but its greatest similarity is with the manager sample, and its greatest dissimilarity is with the Walker sample (excluding the millwright sample).

To recapitulate, the three analyses conducted are intended to locate and identify differences and similarities in the artifact samples from six

Table 31

Vessel Forms in the Six Samples, Ranked by Index of Agreement

Samples Compared	*Index of Agreement*
Walker–wage hand	193.3
Manager–tenant	186.8
Tenant–Walker	183.7
Tenant–wage hand	178.2
Calhoun–manager	177.6
Manager–Walker	170.5
Calhoun–wage hand	170.0
Calhoun–tenant	169.6
Calhoun–Walker	168.5
Manager–wage hand	167.2
Manager–millwright	82.8
Calhoun–millwright	80.0
Tenant–millwright	69.6
Walker–millwright	53.3
Wage hand–millwright	50.0

Table 32

Ranks by Indices of Agreement

	Ranks		
Samples Compared	Functional Categories	Foodways	Vessel form
Calhoun–manager	1	11	5
Manager–millwright	2	3	14
Tenant–millwright	3	4	13
Calhoun–tenant	4	12	8
Calhoun–millwright	5	14	15
Wage hand–tenant	6	13	4
Wage hand–millwright	7	15	11
Walker–wage hand	8	7	1
Manager–wage hand	9	8	10
Walker–millwright	10	10	12
Calhoun–wage hand	11	2	7
Walker–tenant	12	9	3
Manager–tenant	13	1	2
Walker–manager	14	6	6
Calhoun–Walker	15	5	9

dwellings associated with individuals from different tenure classes at Millwood. The expectations are that the Calhoun (landlord) sample should bear marked differences with the tenant, wage hand, and mill-wright samples and perhaps less dissimilarity with the Walker and the manager samples. In terms of these analyses, the Calhoun–wage hand comparisons should produce consistently low indices, whereas the Cal-houn–manager or perhaps Calhoun–Walker comparisons should pro-duce higher values. When ranked according to index of agreement, the samples should produce fairly consistent values.

A comparison of the ranks (table 32) shows that the interpretation is not straightforward. The comparison of the Calhoun–wage hand sam-ples ranks low in regard to functional categories, but high in terms of foodways and fairly high in vessel form, suggesting similarity between the samples. The Calhoun–manager comparison suggests similarity in the functional categories but dissimilarity in the foodways comparison. A similarity between the Walker and the wage hand samples is reasonable to expect, because they both worked directly for Calhoun, but a strong similarity appears only in the vessel form analysis. Moderate similarities appear in the other two tests.

Clearly, one fact does emerge from these tests: the correlation of artifact samples with postbellum tenure groups at Millwood Plantation is difficult. The impulse might be to hypothesize a certain distribution or occurrence of artifacts, conduct certain tests, and then interpret the findings. In a simple way, that procedure has been followed here; however, the realities of the Millwood sample make it difficult to lean too heavily on such straightforward interpretations. It would seem that the most informative physical evidence for the material basis of the postbellum plantation, or at least the easiest to discern at this early stage of archaeological investigation, is settlement pattern and housing form and size. Both these aspects of plantation life appear to relate directly to plantation labor organization. The study of the kinds of artifacts used by each tenure class is much more difficult to understand, possibly because the wage hand found it easier to purchase a plate like the landlord's than to construct a similar house. Both the landlord and the wage hand could buy a harmonica, own a pocket watch, and eat from a blue transfer-printed plate, but only one could afford to live in a four-room house and maintain an extensive library. The artifacts collected at plantations can help archaeologists present a picture of the past, but that picture is clouded by the actions of the past inhabitants, individual choice in artifact purchase, natural elements, and the prejudices and biases of the archaeologist. Each factor makes the interpretation of artifact collections a challenging task that has only begun.

At this point, the distribution of artifacts at Millwood can be associated only with specific people. The landlord sample is the James Edward Calhoun sample, the servant sample is the Caroline Walker sample, and so forth. Whether these distributions relate to all landlords, all servants, all managers, and all tenants is far from being even preliminarily established. Further archaeological research, like the kind presented here, is required to establish the general applicability of the research findings at Millwood Plantation.

Chapter Eight

Continuing the Search for the Postbellum Tenant Plantation

With the excavation of Millwood Plantation in South Carolina, and Waverly Plantation in Mississippi, the potential of postbellum tenant plantation studies in archaeology is being revealed, but there is still a long way to go.

For this study to reach its potential, the direction of historical archaeology must change somewhat. Up to this point, many historical archaeologists have been content to study their sites as if they existed free of external influence, beyond the range of historical events. These archaeologists carefully excavate and analyze artifacts, describe soil stratigraphy in great detail, and write complex site reports as if their sites were detached from the wider historical and cultural world—as if the sites' inhabitants were unaffected by the world in which they moved. As a result, many archaeological reports remain on the shelves of libraries or state archaeologists' offices, usually used only by other archaeologists who happen to be excavating similar sites. These reports have little appeal to nonarchaeologists engaged in the study of the past.

Even some of those historical archaeologists who have considered the effects of the wider world on the past inhabitants of their sites generally have concentrated on the distance artifacts found at a site had to travel to reach that particular site. This research on the tangible evidence of marketing patterns is useful because it demonstrates the range of historical events acting on people at individual sites, but it often falls short of providing social information about the people who lived at the site. The concern of these studies is too often merely the artifacts *as* artifacts.

A better approach to the problem of artifact occurrence at a site is to determine what the artifacts *meant* to the people who lived there in the past—how the artifacts openly indicated or covertly symbolized the inhabitants' place in the world. This search for meaning, although highly desirable, is a decidedly difficult task. As modern archaeologists, we are not members of the past culture we are studying. No matter how hard we try, we will never know exactly what it meant to live in the past. All we can do is to evaluate the available evidence on the basis of our experiences, expectations, and judgments in a way that makes sense to us today. As our modern world changes, so does our perception of the past. In this respect, archaeologists are no different from anyone else; when they present pictures of the past, archaeologists are guided by who they are and what they think.

Historical archaeologists, however, do have an easier time making reasonable interpretations of the past than do prehistorians. The writings of people who participated in the past, which were in turn based on their experiences, expectations, and judgments, are usually available to historical archaeologists. Even in those situations where no directly relevant documentation exists, enough generally pertinent information, written and unwritten, exists to permit the formulation of a reasonable interpretation of that past. Herein, then, lies one strength of historical archaeology.

Nonetheless, even without directly relevant documentation, historical archaeology is a powerful means by which to study the past. This power stems in part from the examination of historical material culture. Once historical archaeologists realize that their research might be used to understand questions of power, racism, exploitation, and accommodation, in addition to the more mundane question of artifact usage, historical archaeology will be more widely used by scholars in other fields. The research of historical archaeologists will be directly relevant to others who study the past. No longer will an excavated site be of interest merely because it is a tangible representation of the past.

This transformation of historical archaeology will not be easy to effect, and many paths may be taken to bring it to fruition. This book offers a starting point: a study of the material basis of a past culture with a firm footing in historical context. Here, that culture is represented by one historical institution, the postbellum tenant plantation.

The material culture of the postbellum tenant plantation is not pre-

sented as a peculiar manifestation of the cultural milieu of the late nine-
teenth- and early twentieth-century South, but rather as a *basis* for the
eventual understanding of the relations between plantation inhabitants.
No other starting point is really possible for archaeologists. That so
many historical archaeologists have not chosen to start here is not an
indictment of the field, but rather an indication of its immaturity.

For the past few years, American historical archaeologists have shied
away from intensive historical studies of the sites they have examined,
perhaps for fear of having their research labeled "particularistic" or "humanistic."[1] In the 1980s, however, many historical archaeologists began to
realize that although the site they excavate may have once had regional,
national, and even international connections, that site is but a single expression of society and human interaction. Because of the limited data
currently available, archaeologists face great difficulties in postulating
that the artifact frequencies and building designs at one site relate to a
general pattern of life at all such sites. Perhaps in the future, archaeologists will be able to provide interpretations on postbellum labor relations, for example, based on information from a hundred different sites,
but now, the only reasonable option is to attempt to construct a historical
context for the site being studied, with the understanding that the site
may be completely idiosyncratic. This contextual historical archaeology
does not need to be called historical or anthropological, because to do so is
only to split academic hairs. As the research conducted in departments of
history and anthropology becomes more similar in terms of topic (material culture, family structure, and society) and methods of analysis, the
debate over whether historical archaeology is really history or anthropology becomes less and less relevant.

The purpose of this book is to illustrate the material basis of a postbellum tenant plantation in South Carolina. At this plantation, the landlord, James Edward Calhoun, lived in the administrative center of the
plantation in a cluster of buildings. Near him were the plantation well,
the smokehouse, and the houses of his longtime servant and of his resident manager. Also located nearby was his mill complex. The agricultural fields of his many tenants were located close enough that he
could easily visit them. The tenants lived first in seven individual squad
settlements and then in separate homesites throughout the estate. For
the entire existence of the plantation, from 1834 until 1925 or so, the
plantation agricultural producers—first field slaves and then tenant

farmers—and industrial workers—mill hands and artisans—actually kept the plantation in operation. As a distinct entity, however, the postbellum plantation was viewed in one of two ways: as providing the homes and fields of tenant farmers, or as a piece of real estate to be bought and sold.

The material basis of the plantation, or the inherent distinction between the two groups of people who perceived the plantation either as home or as real estate, appears in the historical and in the archaeological sources. For example, the appraisal of James Edward Calhoun's estate revealed that he had owned, among many other things, books, surveying instruments, and silver utensils. Archaeological excavation at the home of a tenant family revealed that they owned a commemorative cup from the nearby town of Calhoun Falls and a medallion from the Saint Paul Winter Carnival. This simple difference, exemplified by commemorative cups and silver tableware, alone emphasizes the actual social distance between one postbellum tenant plantation landlord and one tenant family. Archaeologists must do much more research to determine how widespread this distinction might have been.

The search for understanding the material basis of the postbellum tenant plantation and the social relations engendered by the basic differences between landlords and tenants must continue. Historical archaeology, offering a truly remarkable manner for investigating the postbellum tenant plantation, will become widely accepted only when its practitioners learn to view their sites in a firm historical context.

Notes

Chapter One

1. Herman Clarence Nixon, "Whither Southern Economy?" in *I'll Take My Stand: The South and the Agrarian Tradition*, ed. Twelve Southerners (New York: Harper and Brothers, 1930), p. 176.

2. Kenneth M. Stampp, *The Peculiar Institution: Slavery in the Ante-Bellum South* (New York: Vintage, 1956), pp. 29–30; Frank Lawrence Owsley, *Plain Folk of the Old South* (Baton Rouge: Louisiana State University Press, 1949).

3. Gilbert C. Fite, *Cotton Fields No More: Southern Agriculture, 1865–1980* (Lexington: University Press of Kentucky, 1984), pp. 1–29.

4. Howard W. Odum, *Southern Regions of the United States* (Chapel Hill: University of North Carolina Press, 1936); Rupert B. Vance, *Human Factors in Cotton Culture: A Study of the Social Geography of the American South* (Chapel Hill: University of North Carolina Press, 1929); Robert E. Park, "The Bases of Race Prejudice," *Annals of the American Academy of Political and Social Science* 140(1928): 11–20; Edgar T. Thompson, "The Plantation: The Physical Basis of Traditional Race Relations," in *Race Relations and the Race Problem: A Definition and an Analysis*, ed. Edgar T. Thompson (Durham, N.C.: Duke University Press, 1939), pp. 180–218; W. Lloyd Warner, "American Caste and Class," *American Journal of Sociology* 42(1936): 234–37.

5. Robert Preston Brooks, *The Agrarian Revolution in Georgia: 1885–1912* University of Wisconsin Bulletin no. 639 (Madison, 1914); Roger W. Shugg, *Origins of Class Struggle in Louisiana: A Social History of White Farmers and Laborers During*

Slavery and After, 1840–1875 (Baton Rouge: Louisiana State University Press, 1939); J. Carlyle Sitterson, "The Transition from Slave to Free Economy on the William J. Minor Plantations," *Agricultural History* 17(1943): 216–24; Willie Lee Rose, "Jubilee and Beyond: What Was Freedom?" in *What Was Freedom's Price?* ed. David G. Sansing (Jackson: University of Mississippi Press, 1978), pp. 3–20; Charles L. Flynn, Jr., *White Land, Black Labor: Caste and Class in Late Nineteenth-Century Georgia* (Baton Rouge: Louisiana State University Press, 1983); Michael Wayne, *The Reshaping of Plantation Society: The Natchez District, 1860–1880* (Baton Rouge: Louisiana State University Press, 1983).

6. Robert Redfield, *Tepoztlan, A Mexican Village: A Study in Folk Life* (Chicago: University of Chicago Press, 1930); Paul Taylor, *A Spanish-Mexican Peasant Community: Arandas in Jalisco* (Berkeley: University of California Press, 1933).

7. Allen W. Johnson, *Sharecroppers of the Sertão: Economics and Dependence on a Brazilian Plantation* (Stanford, Calif.: Stanford University Press, 1971).

8. Peggy F. Barlett, ed., *Agricultural Decision Making: Anthropological Contributions to Rural Development* (New York: Academic Press, 1980).

9. Important anthropological studies of the southern social order are Allison Davis, Burleigh B. Gardner, and Mary R. Gardner, *Deep South: A Social Anthropological Study of Caste and Class* (Chicago: University of Chicago Press, 1941); John Dollard, *Caste and Class in a Southern Town*, 3d ed. (Garden City, N.Y.: Doubleday Anchor, 1957); Hortense Powdermaker, *After Freedom: A Cultural Study in the Deep South* (New York: Atheneum, 1968).

10. Morton Rubin, *Plantation County* (Chapel Hill: University of North Carolina Press, 1951).

11. Two good reviews of North American prehistory are Jesse D. Jennings, ed., *Ancient North Americans* (New York: W. H. Freeman, 1983), and Gordon R. Willey, *An Introduction to American Archaeology*, vol. 1, *North and Middle America* (Englewood Cliffs: Prentice-Hall, 1966).

12. Robert L. Schuyler, "Historical and Historic Sites Archaeology as Anthropology: Basic Definitions and Relationships," *Historical Archaeology* 4(1970): 83–89.

13. The best general introductions to historical archaeology currently available are James Deetz, *In Small Things Forgotten: The Archaeology of Early American Life* (Garden City, N.Y.: Doubleday, 1977); Ivor Noël Hume, *Historical Archaeology* (New York: Alfred A. Knopf, 1972); idem, *Martin's Hundred: The Discovery of a Lost Colonial Virginia Settlement* (New York: Delta, 1983); Robert L. Schuyler, ed., *Historical Archaeology: A Guide to Substantive and Theoretical Contributions* (Farmingdale, N.Y.: Baywood, 1978); and Stanley South, *Method and Theory in Historical Archaeology* (New York: Academic Press, 1977).

14. Bernard L. Fontana, "On the Meaning of Historic Sites Archaeology," *American Antiquity* 31(1965): 61–65; Bruce W. Fry, "Restoration and Archae-

ology," *Historical Archaeology* 3(1969): 49–65; J. C. Harrington, "Historic Site Archaeology in the United Sates," in *Archaeology of Eastern United States,* ed. James B. Griffin (Chicago: University of Chicago Press, 1952), pp. 335–44; Frank M. Setzler, "Archaeological Explorations in the United States, 1930–1942," *Acta Americana* 1(1943): 218.

15. Ivor Noël Hume, "Archaeology: Handmaiden to History," *The North Carolina Historical Review* 41(1964):215–25; J. C. Harrington, "Archaeology as an Auxiliary Science of American History," *American Anthropologist* 57(1955): 1121–30.

16. For an excellent explanation of the anthropological practice of historical archaeology, see South, *Method and Theory.*

17. Charles Hudson, "The Historical Approach in Anthropology," in *Handbook of Social and Cultural Anthropology,* ed. John J. Honigmann (Chicago: Rand McNally, 1973), pp. 111–41; H. Stuart Hughes, "The Historian and the Social Scientist," *The American Historical Review* 66(1960): 20–46; Margaret Mead, "Anthropologist and Historian: Their Common Problems," *American Quarterly* 3(1951): 3–13. For interesting comments by a historian, see Robert Berkhofer, *A Behavioral Approach to Historical Analysis* (New York: Free Press, 1969).

18. Werner Conze, "Social History," *Journal of Social History* 1(1967): 7–16; Peter N. Stearns, "Social and Political History," *Journal of Social History* 16(1983): 3–5; Elizabeth Fox-Genovese and Eugene D. Genovese, "The Political Crisis of Social History," *Journal of Social History* 10(1976): 205–20; idem, *Fruits of Merchant Capital: Slavery and Bourgeois Property in the Rise and Expansion of Capitalism* (Oxford: Oxford University Press, 1983), pp. 179–212.

19. Stearns, "Social and Political History," p. 3.

20. James Deetz, "Material Culture and Archaeology: What's the Difference?" in *Historical Archaeology and the Importance of Material Things,* ed. Leland Ferguson (Columbia, S.C.: Society for Historical Archaeology, 1977), p. 10.

21. Ian Hodder, "Postprocessual Archaeology," in *Advances in Archaeological Method and Theory,* ed. Michael B. Schiffer (Orlando, Fla.: Academic Press, 1985), 8:5–6.

22. For important overviews, see Ian M. G. Quimby, ed., *Material Culture and the Study of American Life* (New York: W. W. Norton, 1978), and Thomas J. Schlereth, ed., *Material Culture Studies in America* (Nashville, Tenn.: The American Association for State and Local History, 1982).

23. Deetz, *In Small Things Forgotten,* p. 25.

24. Thomas J. Schlereth, "Material Culture Studies in America, 1876–1976," in Schlereth, *Material Culture Studies,* pp. 47–50; Leland Ferguson, "Historical Archaeology and the Importance of Material Things," in Ferguson, *Historical Archaeology,* p. 7.

25. Shigeyoshi Matsumae, *Materialism in Search of a Soul: A Scientific Critique of*

Historical Materialism (Tokyo: Tokai University Press, 1975); Ali Rattansi, *Marx and the Division of Labor* (London: Macmillan, 1982); August Thalheimer, *Introduction to Dialectical Materialism: The Marxist Worldview,* trans. George Simpson and George Weltner (New York: Covici-Friede, 1936).

26. Karl Marx and Frederick Engels, *The German Ideology, Part I,* ed. C. J. Arthur (London: Lawrence and Wishart, 1970); Karl Marx, *The Grundrisse,* ed. and trans. David McLellan (New York: Harper and Row, 1971).

27. Frederick Engels, Selection from "Karl Marx," in *K. Marx, F. Engels, V. Lenin on Historical Materialism: A Collection* (New York: International Publishers, 1974), p. 175.

28. P. L. Kohl, "Materialist Approaches in Prehistory," *Annual Review of Anthropology* 10(1981): 90.

29. Historical archaeologist James Deetz has a deep interest in material culture, but he is by no means a materialist. The theoretical position he has adopted is structuralism. Although Deetz's attitude toward structuralism is apparent in all his writings, one of the best explicit statements of his position appears in his "Scientific Humanism and Humanistic Science: A Plea for Paradigmatic Pluralism in Historical Archaeology," *Geoscience and Man* 23(1983): 27–34.

30. V. Gordon Childe, "Archaeology and Anthropology," *Southwestern Journal of Anthropology* 2(1946): 243–51; idem, *History* (London: Cobbett Press, 1947); idem, *Man Makes Himself* (New York: Mentor, 1951); idem, *Society and Knowledge* (New York: Harper and Brothers, 1956); idem, *What Happened in History* (Baltimore: Penguin, 1964); idem, "Prehistory and Marxism," *Antiquity* 53(1979): 93–95; Ian Hodder, ed., *Symbolic and Structural Archaeology* (Cambridge: Cambridge University Press, 1982); Matthew Spriggs, ed., *Marxist Perspectives in Archaeology* (Cambridge: Cambridge University Press, 1984).

31. Maurice Bloch, *Marxism and Anthropology* (Oxford: Oxford University Press, 1985), pp. 16–20.

32. Russell G. Handsman, "Thinking about an Historical Archaeology of Alienation and Class Struggle" (Paper delivered at the Annual Meeting of the Society for Historical Archaeology, 1985), p. 2.

33. Mark Leone, "Some Opinions about Recovering Mind," *American Antiquity* 47(1982): 757.

34. Eric R. Wolf, *Europe and the People without History* (Berkeley: University of California Press, 1982).

35. Matthew Spriggs, "Another Way of Telling: Marxist Perspectives in Archaeology," in Spriggs, *Marxist Perspectives in Archaeology,* p. 7n; Childe, *History,* pp. 71–72.

36. Philip S. Foner, ed., *Karl Marx Remembered: Comments at the Time of His Death* (San Francisco: Synthesis Press, 1983), p. 39; Thalheimer, *Introduction to Dialectical Materialism,* p. 185.

37. Bruce G. Trigger, "Alternative Archaeologies: Nationalist, Colonialist, Imperialist," *Man* 19(1984): 355–70.

38. Jacques Maquet, "Diffuse Marxian Themes in Anthropology," in *On Marxian Perspectives in Anthropology: Essays in Honor of Harry Hoijer, 1981,* ed. Jacques Maquet and Nancy Daniels (Malibu, Calif.: Undena Publications, 1984), pp. 1–2. A further exploration of this idea in archaeology appears in Charles E. Orser, Jr., "Toward a Theory of Power for Historical Archaeology: Plantations and Space," in *The Recovery of Meaning in Historical Archaeology,* ed. Mark P. Leone and Parker B. Potter (Washington: Smithsonian Institution Press, forthcoming).

39. Schuyler, "Historical and Historic Sites Archaeology," p. 84.

40. Charles H. Fairbanks, "Historical Archaeological Implications of Recent Investigations," *Geoscience and Man* 23(1983): 17–26; idem, "The Plantation Archaeology of the Southeastern Coast," *Historical Archaeology* 18(1984): 1–14; Charles E. Orser, Jr., "The Past Ten Years of Plantation Archaeology in the Southeastern United States," *Southeastern Archaeology* 3(1984): 1–12.

41. James A. Ford, "An Archaeological Report on the Elizafield Ruins," in *Georgia's Disputed Ruins,* ed. E. Coulter (Chapel Hill: University of North Carolina Press, 1937), pp. 191–225.

42. Fairbanks, "Historical Archaeological Implications," pp. 22–23.

43. Charles H. Fairbanks, "The Kingsley Slave Cabins in Duval County, Florida, 1968," *The Conference on Historic Site Archaeology Papers* 7(1974): 62–93; Robert Ascher and Charles H. Fairbanks, "Excavation of a Slave Cabin: Georgia, U.S.A.," *Historical Archaeology* 5(1971): 3–17.

44. Ascher and Fairbanks, "Excavation of a Slave Cabin."

45. See Orser, "Past Ten Years," pp. 2–3, for further comments on Fairbanks's contribution to plantation archaeology; Sue Mullins Moore, "The Antebellum Barrier Island Plantation: In Search of an Archaeological Pattern" (Ph.D. diss., University of Florida, 1981); John Solomon Otto, "Status Differences and the Archaeological Record: A Comparison of Planter, Overseer, and Slave Sites from Cannon's Point Plantation (1794–1861), St. Simons Island, Georgia" (Ph.D. diss., University of Florida, 1975); Theresa A. Singleton, "The Archaeology of Afro-American Slavery in Coastal Georgia: A Regional Perception of Slave Household and Community Patterns" (Ph.D. diss., University of Florida, 1980).

46. Vernon G. Baker, "Historical Archaeology at Black Lucy's Garden, Andover, Massachusetts: Ceramics from the Site of a Nineteenth Century Afro-American," *Papers of the Robert S. Peabody Foundation for Archaeology,* no. 8 (Andover, Mass.: Phillips Academy, 1978); idem, "Archaeological Visibility of Afro-American Culture: An Example from Black Lucy's Garden, Andover, Massachusetts," in *Archaeological Perspectives on Ethnicity in America: Afro-American and Asian American Culture History,* ed. Robert L. Schuyler (Farmingdale, N.Y.: Baywood, 1980), pp. 29–37; Sarah T. Bridges and Bert Salwen, "Weeksville: The

Archaeology of a Black Community," in Schuyler, *Archaeological Perspectives,* pp. 38–47; Joan H. Geismar, *The Archaeology of Social Disintegration in Skunk Hollow: A Nineteenth-Century Rural Black Community* (New York: Academic Press, 1982); Jerome S. Handler and Frederick W. Lange, *Plantation Slavery in Barbados: An Archaeological and Historical Investigation* (Cambridge: Harvard University Press, 1978); Robert L. Schuyler, "Sandy Ground: Archaeological Sampling in a Black Community in Metropolitan New York," *The Conference on Historic Site Archaeology Papers* 7(1974): 13–51.

47. John E. Ehrenhard and Mary R. Bullard, *Stafford Plantation, Cumberland Island National Seashore, Georgia: Archaeological Investigations of a Slave Cabin* (Tallahassee: Southeast Archaeological Center, 1981); Singleton, "The Archaeology of Afro-American Slavery"; Suzanne B. McFarlane, "The Ethnoarchaeology of a Slave Community: The Couper Plantation Site" (Master's thesis, University of Florida, 1975); Charles H. Fairbanks and Sue A. Mullins Moore, "How Did Slaves Live?" *Early Man,* Summer 1980, pp. 2–6; John Solomon Otto, "A New Look at Slave Life," *Natural History* 88(1979)1: 8, 16, 20, 22, 24, 30.

48. Henry M. Miller and Lynne G. Lewis, "Zoocultural Resource Utilization at a Low Country South Carolina Plantation," *The Conference on Historic Site Archaeology Papers* 12(1978): 250–65; Elizabeth J. Reitz, Tyson Biggs, and Ted A. Rathbun, "Archaeological Evidence for Subsistence and Diet on Coastal Plantations," in *The Archaeology of Slavery and Plantation Life,* ed. Theresa A. Singleton (Orlando, Fla.: Academic Press, 1985), pp. 163–91.

49. Michael Banton, *Race Relations* (New York: Basic, 1967), p. 70. A classic examination of acculturation and its many definitions appears in Melville J. Herskovits, *Acculturation: The Study of Culture Contact* (New York: J. J. Augustine, 1938).

50. E. Franklin Frazier, *Race and Culture Contacts in the Modern World* (New York: Alfred A. Knopf, 1957), pp. 243–46.

51. John W. Blassingame, *The Slave Community: Plantation Life in the Antebellum South,* rev. ed. (New York: Oxford University Press, 1979), pp. 21–22.

52. Singleton, "The Archaeology of Afro-American Slavery"; Thomas R. Wheaton, Amy Friedlander, and Patrick H. Garrow, *Yaughan and Curriboo Plantations: Studies in Afro-American Archaeology* (Atlanta: National Park Service, 1983).

53. Excellent contemporary comments on slave foods appear in James O. Breeden, ed., *Advice among Masters: The Ideal in Slave Management in the Old South* (Westport, Conn.: Greenwood, 1980), pp. 88–113.

54. Leland Ferguson, "Looking for the 'Afro' in Colono-Indian Pottery," *The Conference on Historic Site Archaeology Papers* 12(1978): 68–86. This paper also appears in Robert L. Schuyler, ed., *Archaeological Perspectives,* pp. 14–28; Leland Ferguson, "Struggling with Pots in Colonial South Carolina," in *The Archaeology of Inequality,* eds. Robert Paynter and Randall H. McGuire (Oxford, England: Basil Blackwell, forthcoming).

55. Ferguson, "Looking for the Afro," p. 79.

56. Handler and Lange, *Plantation Slavery,* pp. 139–44; Ferguson, "Looking for the Afro," pp. 77–78.

57. Kenneth E. Lewis, "Excavating a Colonial Rice Plantation," *Early Man,* Autumn 1979, pp. 13–17; Kenneth E. Lewis and Donald L. Hardesty, *Middleton Place: Initial Archaeological Investigations at an Ashley River Rice Plantation,* Research Manuscript Series, no. 148 (Columbia, S.C.: Institute of Archaeology and Anthropology, 1979).

58. William B. Lees and Kathryn M. Kimery-Lees, "The Function of Colono-Indian Ceramics: Insights from Limerick Plantation, South Carolina," *Historical Archaeology* 13(1979): 1–13; William B. Lees, *Limerick, Old and In the Way: Archaeological Investigations at Limerick Plantation,* Anthropological Studies, no. 5 (Columbia, S.C.: Institute of Archaeology and Anthropology, 1980).

59. Lees and Kimery-Lees, "The Function of Colono-Indian Ceramics," p. 10, table 3.

60. Wheaton, Friedlander, and Garrow, *Yaughan and Curriboo,* pp. 338–39; Thomas R. Wheaton and Patrick H. Garrow, "Acculturation and the Archaeological Record in the Carolina Lowcountry," in Singleton, *The Archaeology of Slavery,* pp. 239–59.

61. John Solomon Otto, "Artifacts and Status Differences: A Comparison of Ceramics from Planter, Overseer, and Slave Sites on an Antebellum Plantation," in *Research Strategies in Historical Archaeology,* ed. Stanley South (New York: Academic Press, 1977), pp. 91–118; idem, *Cannon's Point Plantation, 1794–1860: Living Conditions and Status Patterns in the Old South* (Orlando, Fla.: Academic Press, 1984).

62. W. E. B. DuBois, *Black Reconstruction* (New York: Russell and Russell, 1935), p. 9.

63. Otto, in *Cannon's Point Plantation,* p. 88.

64. Ronald Killion and Charles Waller, eds., *Slavery Time When I Was Chillun Down on Master's Plantation: Interviews with Georgia Slaves* (Savannah: Beehive, 1973), p. 35.

65. Robert Collins, "Management of Slaves," *DeBow's Review* 17(1854), p. 423; Breeden, ed., *Advice Among Masters,* pp. 114–39. Also see Bernard L. Herman, "Slave Quarters in Virginia: The Persona Behind Historic Artifacts," in *The Scope of Historical Archaeology: Essays in Honor of John L. Cotter,* ed. David G. Orr and Daniel G. Crozier (Philadelphia: Temple University Laboratory of Anthropology, 1984), pp. 253–83.

66. Quoted in George L. Rawick, ed., *The American Slave: A Composite Autobiography* (Westport, Conn.: Greenwood, 1977), supp. ser. 1, vol. 7, pt. 2, pp. 364–65. Although it may be true that the slave narratives provide evidence on black English (John W. Blassingame, "Using the Testimony of Ex-Slaves: Approaches and Problems," *Journal of Southern History* 41[1975]: 490), the more obvious white

interpretations of black speech patterns have been changed to Standard American English under the assumption that the interviewers were not trained linguists and may have misrepresented black speech.

67. Quoted in Rawick, *American Slave,* supp. ser. 1, vol. 6, pt. 1, p. 321.

68. Ascher and Fairbanks, "Excavation of a Slave Cabin," p. 8; Ehrenhard and Bullard, *Stafford Plantation,* p. 33; Fairbanks, "Kingsley Slave Cabins," p. 76; Otto, *Cannon's Point Plantation,* p. 38.

69. Blassingame, *Slave Community,* pp. 254–55; Robert W. Fogel and Stanley L. Engerman, *Time on the Cross: The Economics of American Negro Slavery,* 2 vols. (Boston: Little, Brown, 1974), 1:115.

70. Richard Sutch, "The Care and Feeding of Slaves," in *Reckoning With Slavery: A Critical Study in the Quantitative History of American Negro Slavery,* Paul A. David, Herbert G. Gutman, Richard Sutch, Peter Temin, and Gavin Wright (New York: Oxford University Press, 1976), pp. 297–98.

71. Ascher and Fairbanks, "Excavation of a Slave Cabin," pp. 8–9.

72. Ibid., p. 5.

73. McFarlane, "Ethnoarchaeology," pp. 86–87; Moore, "Antebellum Barrier Island Plantation," p. 206.

74. Wheaton, Friedlander, and Garrow, *Yaughan and Curriboo,* pp. 203–11, 338–39; Wheaton and Garrow, "Acculturation and the Archaeological Record."

75. For interesting comments on the affect of slaves on plantation architecture, see Carl Anthony, "The Big House and the Slave Quarters: Part II, African Contributions to the New World," *Landscape* 21(1976)1: 9–15.

76. Otto, "Status Differences"; idem, "Artifacts and Status Differences"; idem, "Race and Class on Antebellum Plantations," in Schuyler, *Archaeological Perspectives,* pp. 3–13.

77. Otto, "Status Differences," p. 360; idem, "Race and Class," p. 11. For further comments, see Charles E. Orser, Jr., "Review of *Cannon's Point Plantation, 1794–1860: Living Conditions and Status Patterns in the Old South* by John Solomon Otto," *American Ethnologist* 12(1985): 386–87.

78. Moore, "Antebellum Barrier Island Plantation."

79. James C. Bonner, "Profile of a Late Ante-Bellum Community," *The American Historical Review* 49(1944): 663–80.

80. Charles E. Orser, Jr., "The Archaeological Analysis of Plantation Society: Replacing Status and Caste with Economics and Power," *American Antiquity* (forthcoming).

81. Many reports of limited distribution explain cultural resource management in detail, but a good, if somewhat dated, widely available account appears in Thomas F. King, Patricia Parker Hickman, and Gary Berg, *Anthropology in Historic Preservation: Caring for Culture's Clutter* (New York: Academic Press, 1977).

82. William H. Adams, ed., *Waverly Plantation: Ethnoarchaeology of a Tenant Farming Community* (Atlanta: Heritage Conservation and Recreation Service, 1980).

83. John Lee Coulter, ed., "Plantations in the South," in *Thirteenth Census of the United States, Taken in the Year 1910*, vol. 5, *Agriculture, 1909 and 1910* (Washington: Government Printing Office, 1913), p. 878.

84. For further comments, see Karl Brandt, "Fallacious Census Terminology and Its Consequences in Agriculture," *Social Research* 5(1938): 19–36.

85. Jay R. Mandle, *The Roots of Black Poverty: The Southern Plantation Economy After the Civil War* (Durham, N.C.: Duke University Press, 1978).

Chapter Two

1. Francis Harper, ed., *The Travels of William Bartram*, naturalist's ed. (New Haven: Yale University Press, 1958), pp. 206–7. An excellent statement on Bartram's route through South Carolina appears in the Bartram Trail Conference, *Bartram Heritage* (Montgomery, Ala.: Bartram Trail Conference, 1979), pp. 79–81.

2. William J. Barbee, *The Cotton Question: The Production, Export, Manufacture, and Consumption of Cotton* (New York: Metropolitan Record Office, 1866), p. 13; Whitemarsh B. Seabrook, *A Memoir on the Origin, Cultivation, and Uses of Cotton* (Charleston, S.C.: Miller and Browne, 1844), p. 6; J. A. Turner, *The Cotton Planter's Manual: Being a Compilation of Facts from the Best Authorities on the Culture of Cotton* (New York: C. M. Saxon, 1857), p. 95.

3. Good geographic and geologic descriptions of the Piedmont can be found in Wallace W. Atwood, *The Physiographic Provinces of North America* (Boston: Ginn and Company, 1940), pp. 109–45; Nevin M. Fenneman, *Physiography of Eastern United States* (New York: McGraw-Hill, 1938), pp. 121–62; and Charles B. Hunt, *Natural Regions of the United States and Canada* (San Francisco: W. H. Freeman, 1974), pp. 252–303.

4. Harper, *The Travels of William Bartram.*

5. Henry S. Johnson, *Geology in South Carolina* (Columbia, S.C.: Division of Geology, 1964), p. 4.

6. E. Thomas Hemmings, *Archaeological Survey of Trotters Shoals Reservoir Area in South Carolina*, Research Manuscript Series, no. 3 (Columbia, S.C.: Institute of Archaeology and Anthropology, 1970), pp. 7–9.

7. Richard L. Taylor and Marion F. Smith, comps., *The Report of the Intensive Survey of the Richard B. Russell Dam and Lake, Savannah River, Georgia and South Carolina*, Research Manuscript Series, no. 142 (Columbia, S.C.: Institute of Archaeology and Anthropology, 1978), pp. 207, 368–87.

8. The history of Indian-white relations on the southern frontier is much too complex to be presented here. A standard work on this topic is Verner W. Crane, *The Southern Frontier, 1670–1732* (Durham, N.C.: Duke University Press, 1928). Also see W. Stitt Robinson, *The Southern Colonial Frontier, 1607–1763* (Albuquerque: University of New Mexico Press, 1979). Many excellent studies of the Cherokee and other Native Americans who lived in the South Carolina Piedmont have been written. Some of these are Roy S. Dickens, Jr., *Cherokee Prehistory: The Pisgah Phase in the Appalachian Summit Region* (Knoxville: University of Tennessee Press, 1976); Charles Hudson, *The Southeastern Indians* (Knoxville: University of Tennessee Press, 1976); Bennie C. Keel, *Cherokee Archaeology: A Study of the Appalachian Summit* (Knoxville: University of Tennessee Press, 1976); and James Mooney, *Historical Sketch of the Cherokee* (Chicago: Aldine, 1975).

9. William Gilmore Simms, *The History of South Carolina* (New York: Redfield, 1860), p. 120; Robert L. Meriwhether, *The Expansion of South Carolina, 1729–1765* (Kingsport, Tenn.: Southern Publishers, 1940), p. 134.

10. D. Huger Bacot, "The South Carolina Up Country at the End of the Eighteenth Century," *The American Historical Review* 28(1923): 695.

11. Taylor and Smith, *Report of Intensive Survey,* p. 116. A detailed examination of current archaeological and historical knowledge about Fort Independence appears in Beverly E. Bastian, *Fort Independence: An Eighteenth-Century Frontier Homesite and Militia Post in South Carolina* (Atlanta: National Park Service, 1982).

12. Quoted in Bacot, "South Carolina Up Country," pp. 690–91.

13. Francis A. Walker, *The Statistics of the Population of the United States, Ninth Census* (Washington: Government Printing Office, 1872), p. 60.

14. Important archaeological studies of the white settlement of South Carolina have been completed. The best of these are Kenneth E. Lewis, *Camden: A Frontier Town in Eighteenth Century South Carolina,* Anthropological Studies, no. 2 (Columbia, S.C.: Institute of Archaeology and Anthropology, 1976), and idem, *The American Frontier: An Archaeological Study of Settlement Pattern and Process* (Orlando, Fla.: Academic Press, 1984).

15. John H. Logan, *A History of the Upper Country of South Carolina* (Charleston, S.C.: S. G. Courtenay and Company, 1859), p. 151; Frank L. Owsley, "The Pattern of Migration and Settlement on the Southern Frontier," *Journal of Southern History* 11(1945): 145; Forrest McDonald and Grady McWhiney, "The Antebellum Southern Herdsman: A Reinterpretation," *Journal of Southern History* 41(1975): 147–66; Bacot, "South Carolina Up Country," p. 693; Lewis Cecil Gray, *History of Agriculture in the Southern United States to 1860,* 2 vols. (Washington: Carnegie Institution, 1933), 1: 33.

16. Ellis Merton Coulter, *Old Petersburg and the Broad River Valley of Georgia: Their Rise and Decline* (Athens: University of Georgia Press, 1965), pp. 109–11.

17. Reuben Gold Thwaites, ed., "François André Michaux's Travels West of Alleghany Mountains, 1802," in *Early Western Travels, 1748–1846,* 32 vols. (Cleveland: Arthur H. Clark, 1904), 3:298. An interesting study of the planters in the Piedmont during this early period is Rachel Klein, "The Rise of the Planters in the South Carolina Backcountry, 1767–1808" (Ph.D. diss., Yale University, 1979).

18. Computed from data appearing in Walker, *Statistics,* p. 61.

19. Silas Emmett Lucas, comp., *Mills' Atlas: Atlas of the State of South Carolina, 1825* (Easley, S.C.: Southern Historical Press, 1980).

20. Confusion exists over the spelling of James Edward Calhoun's last name. Sometimes his name appears as Colhoun, at others, Calhoun. The editor of the John C. Calhoun papers has stated that Colhoun is the name of the family in-laws. As such, he has changed all references to in-law Calhouns to Colhoun in the published papers, stating that the confusion probably signifies that the pronunciation of the two names was similar during the nineteenth century (Clyde N. Wilson, ed., *The Papers of John C. Calhoun* [Columbia: University of South Carolina Press, 1978], 13:xxxi). Most historians have followed this example (The History Group, *Historical Investigations of the Richard B. Russell Multiple Resource Area* [Atlanta: National Park Service, 1981], p. 106; Chalmers Gaston Davidson, *The Last Foray: The South Carolina Planters of 1860: A Sociological Study* [Columbia: University of South Carolina Press, 1971], pp. 108–9; Ernest McPherson Lander, Jr., *The Calhoun Family and Thomas Green Clemson: The Decline of a Southern Patriarchy* [Columbia: University of South Carolina Press, 1983], pp. 11–12). The confusion exists largely because James Edward himself used both Calhoun and Colhoun. His correspondence reveals that he signed his name Colhoun early in life but began using Calhoun later. He signed a letter to his mother, Floride Bonneau Calhoun (Colhoun), dated May 24, 1814, "your affectionate and most obedient son, James E. Colhoun"; throughout the 1820s, he signed his name Colhoun, but by 1834 he used, and was addressed by, Calhoun (Letters in the James Edward Calhoun Papers [hereafter JECP] in the South Caroliniana Library [hereafter SCL], University of South Carolina). Clearly, both Calhoun and Colhoun were commonly used when Mills made his map in 1820, as both names appear in western Abbeville County (Lucas, *Mills' Atlas*). Whether James Edward formally changed his name, as has been asserted, is not known (Benjamin T. Carlton, *The Country Doctor* [n.p.: National Photo Listing Company, 1967], p. 33). Because this study concentrates on Millwood Plantation's postbellum period, the surname Calhoun is used throughout. By 1866 James Edward seemed to have forgotten about *Colhoun;* thirty years had passed since he had last used it. All documents pertaining to him after 1840 use the surname Calhoun.

21. Lewis Perrin, "The Hermit of Millwood: An Account of the Life of Mr.

James Edward Calhoun," *The Press and Banner and Abbeville (S.C.) Medium,* 29 June 1933; Francis de Sales Dundas, *The Calhoun Settlement, District of Abbeville, South Carolina* (Staunton, Va.: F. de Sales Dundas, 1949).

22. Theodore C. Blegen, *Minnesota: A History of the State* (Minneapolis: University of Minnesota Press, 1963), p. 111; Lucile M. Kane, June D. Holmquist, and Carolyn Gilman, eds., *The Northern Expeditions of Stephen H. Long: The Journals of 1817 and 1823 and Related Documents* (St. Paul: Minnesota Historical Society Press, 1978), p. 24.

23. Kane, Holmquist, and Gilman, eds., *Northern Expeditions,* pp. 15–16.

24. Ibid., pp. 270–327.

25. Mary E. Moragne, *The Neglected Thread: A Journal from the Calhoun Community, 1836–1842,* ed. Delle Mullen Craven (Columbia: University of South Carolina Press, 1951), p. 45.

26. I am indebted to Professor James L. Roark of Emory University for conducting extensive historical research for the original contract completed for the National Park Service and funded by the U.S. Army Corps of Engineers, Savannah District (C-54042-80). This study could not have been written without his research efforts, support, and advice. The original study of the Millwood Plantation research is Charles E. Orser, Jr., Annette M. Nekola, and James L. Roark, *Exploring the Rustic Life: Multidisciplinary Research at Millwood Plantation, A Large Piedmont Plantation in Abbeville County, South Carolina, and Elbert County, Georgia, 3 vols.* (Atlanta: National Park Service, 1987).

27. Andrew Norris to James Edward Calhoun, September 18, 1822, JECP, SCL.

28. John C. Calhoun to James Edward Calhoun, July 23, 1824, in W. Edwin Hemphill, *The Papers of John C. Calhoun,* 16 vols. (Columbia: University of South Carolina Press, 1976) 9:241.

29. Andrew Norris to James Edward Calhoun, February 27, 1823, JECP, SCL; James Edward Calhoun to John C. Calhoun, January 20, 1826, JECP, SCL; John Ewing Calhoun to James Edward Calhoun, May 4, 1827, JECP, SCL.

30. Andrew Norris to James Edward Calhoun, September 18, 1822, JECP, SCL; John Ewing Calhoun to James Edward Calhoun, May 4, 1827, JECP, SCL.

31. John C. Calhoun to James Edward Calhoun, May 4, 1828, in Clyde N. Wilson and W. Edwin Hemphill, *The Papers of John C. Calhoun* (Columbia: University of South Carolina Press, 1977), 10:382.

32. Andrew Norris to James Edward Calhoun, February 27, 1823, JECP, SCL.

33. Andrew Norris to James Edward Calhoun, February 28, 1818, JECP, SCL; Andrew Norris to James Edward Calhoun, September 18, 1822, JECP, SCL; Andrew Norris to James Edward Calhoun, May 1, 1823, JECP, SCL.

34. John Ewing Calhoun to James Edward Calhoun, December 9, 1827, JECP, SCL; John Ewing Calhoun to James Edward Calhoun, May 4, 1827, JECP, SCL.

35. John Ewing Calhoun to James Edward Calhoun, May 14, 1828, John C. Calhoun Papers, History Department, University of South Carolina (hereafter USC). I would like to thank Professor Clyde N. Wilson for permitting Dr. Roark to examine these records.

36. Speed's length of service can be discerned from letters only. The first mention of his employment appears in Andrew Norris to James Edward Calhoun, September 28, 1818, JECP, SCL.

37. William Kauffman Scarborough, *The Overseer: Plantation Management in the Old South* (Baton Rouge: Louisiana State University Press, 1966), pp. 38–39.

38. John Ewing Calhoun to William Clark, January 27, 1825, JECP, SCL.

39. John Ewing Calhoun to James Edward Calhoun, December 9, 1827, JECP, SCL.

40. John Ewing Calhoun to William Clark, January 27, 1825, JECP, SCL.

41. John C. Calhoun to James Edward Calhoun, January 23, 1828; John C. Calhoun to James Edward Calhoun, May 4, 1828, in Wilson and Hemphill, *Papers of John C. Calhoun,* 10:336, 382.

42. James Edward Calhoun to J. Guillet, January 25, 1831; James Edward Calhoun to Francis [?], March 27, 1831, JECP, SCL.

43. Dundas, *Calhoun Settlement,* p. 11; John C. Calhoun to James Edward Calhoun, February 8, 1834, in Wilson, *Papers of John C. Calhoun,* 12:232.

44. James Edward Calhoun Diary, John Ewing Colhoun Papers, Southern Historical Collections [hereafter SHC], University of North Carolina, Chapel Hill. I am indebted to Professor Roark for examining this diary.

45. Ibid., January 3, 1832.

46. Ibid., August 7, 1832.

47. Ibid., August 1, 1832. This Trotter is a mysterious figure. Three Trotters, Nathan, Joseph, and Jeremiah, are reported in the 1790 census as living with their families in Ninety-Six District, South Carolina (*Heads of Families at the First Census of the United States Taken in the Year 1790: South Carolina* [Baltimore: Genealogical Publishing, 1978], pp. 64–65). Abbeville District was formed from Ninety-Six District in 1785.

48. James Edward Calhoun Diary, November 21, 1832; January 1, 1833; November 12, 1833; November 30, 1833; December 28, 1833; March 25, 1834.

49. Thomas H. Harris to James Edward Calhoun, November 24, 1834, bk. D-1, pp. 274–75; Thomas H. Harris to James Edward Calhoun, March 9, 1835, bk. D-1, pp. 273–74; John Ewing Calhoun and John C. Calhoun to James Edward Calhoun, bk. D-1, pp. 276–77; Edwin Reese and Martin S. McCay to James Edward Calhoun, November 13, 1838, bk. D-1, pp. 275–76; Clerk of Court, Pickens County Courthouse, Pendleton, South Carolina; Daniel Dixon to James Edward Calhoun, December 9, 1848, bk. AA, p. 111; Ajax Armistead to James Edward Calhoun, December 20, 1848, bk. AA, p. 112; Jeremiah R. Perryman to

James Edward Calhoun, March 10, 1854, bk. BB, p. 132; Estate of John B. Ward to James Edward Calhoun, June 3, 1857, bk. AA, p. 255; Henry G. Fleming to James Edward Calhoun, October 17, 1860, bk. CC, p. 447; Clerk of Court, Elbert County Courthouse, Elberton, Georgia.

50. 1830 Slave Schedule, James Edward Calhoun, Abbeville District, Magnolia Township, South Carolina [hereafter 1830 Slave Schedule].

51. 1840, 1850, 1860 Slave Schedules, James Edward Calhoun, Abbeville District, Magnolia Township, South Carolina [hereafter 1840, 1850, 1860 Slave Schedules].

52. Many good archaeological studies exist. Most of these have been mentioned in chapter 1, but for a good overview see Charles E. Orser, Jr., "What Good Is Plantation Archaeology?" *Southern Studies: An Interdisciplinary Journal of the South* 24(1985): 444–55.

53. This ledger is owned by Max Cann of Fredericksburg, Virginia, and is used with his permission.

54. 1840 Population Schedule, James Edward Calhoun, Abbeville District, South Carolina [hereafter 1840 Population Schedule].

55. Peter Bynum to James Edward Calhoun, October 8, 1842, JECP, SCL; John C. Calhoun to James Edward Calhoun, April 8, 1843, John C. Calhoun Papers, USC.

56. John C. Calhoun to James Edward Calhoun, June 19, 1845, John C. Calhoun Papers, USC; N. Wideman to James Edward Calhoun, January 21, 1856, JECP, SCL.

57. The perseverance of slave families through their own adaptivity has been brilliantly documented by Herbert G. Gutman, *The Black Family in Slavery and Freedom, 1750–1925* (New York: Pantheon, 1976).

58. 1850 Slave Schedule.

59. James Edward Calhoun to Andrew Calhoun, March 18, 1835, JECP, SCL.

60. Orser, Nekola, and Roark, *Exploring the Rustic Life*, 3:220.

61. January 23, 1833; January 5, 1834; James Edward Calhoun Diary, John Ewing Colhoun Papers, SHC.

62. Eric Kerridge, *The Farmers of Old England* (London: George Allen and Unwin, 1973), pp. 40–42.

63. Heloise Hulse Cruzat, "Sidelights on Louisiana History," *Louisiana Historical Quarterly* 1(1918): 123. A good brief description of the seigneurial system is Marcel Trudel, *The Seigneurial Regime* (Ottawa: Canadian Historical Association, 1971).

64. Gray, *History of Agriculture*, 1:406; Edmund S. Morgan, *American Slavery, American Freedom: The Ordeal of Colonial Virginia* (New York: W. W. Norton, 1975).

65. William Fitzhugh to Nicholas Hayward, April 1, 1689, in "The Letters of

William Fitzhugh," Virginia Historical Society, *The Virginia Magazine of History and Biography* 2(1895): 274.

66. Thomas Cooper, *The Statutes at Large of South Carolina* (Columbia, S.C.: A. S. Johnston, 1837), pp. 96–102, 572–80; David J. McLord, *The Statutes at Large of South Carolina* (Columbia, S.C.: A. S. Johnston, 1839), pp. 67–68; J. S. G. Richardson, *Cases at Law, December 1845–May 1846* (St. Paul, Minn.: West, 1918), p. 346; idem, *Cases at Law, November 1850–May 1851* (St. Paul, Minn.: West, 1917), p. 28.

67. Tatham's book is quoted in G. Melvin Herndon, *William Tatham and the Culture of Tobacco* (Coral Gables: University of Miami Press, 1969), pp. 100–101.

68. Marjorie Stratford Mendenhall, "The Rise of Southern Tenancy," *Yale Review* 27(1937): 112–13.

69. Lucas, *Mills' Atlas.*

70. August 7, 1832; August 19, 1832; January 1, 1833; July 15, 1833; August 16, 1833; September 13, 1833; April 17, 1834, James Edward Calhoun Diary, John Ewing Colhoun Papers, SHC.

71. This plaque was located, before the flooding of the Richard B. Russell Reservoir, on South Carolina Highway 72 at the former bridge to Elberton, Georgia. A photograph of the plaque appears in Francis de Sales Dundas, "Millwood Plantation: An Almost Forgotten Era," *Calhoun Falls* (S.C.) *Times*, 10 March 1955.

72. James Edward Calhoun to Andrew Calhoun, February 24, 1834, JECP, SCL.

73. March 13, 1834; April 25, 1834; August 6, 1834, James Edward Calhoun Diary, John Ewing Colhoun Papers, SHC.

74. James Edward Calhoun to John C. Calhoun, January 31, 1835, in Wilson, *Papers of John C. Calhoun,* 12:409.

75. John C. Calhoun to James Edward Calhoun, March 22, 1837, in Wilson, *Papers of John C. Calhoun,* 13:498.

76. John C. Calhoun to James Edward Calhoun, March 27, 1838; John C. Calhoun to James Edward Calhoun, April 21, 1838, in Wilson, *Papers of John C. Calhoun,* 14:249, 274.

77. James Edward Calhoun to Maria Simkins Calhoun, April, 1840, JECP, SCL.

78. John C. Calhoun to James Edward Calhoun, April 8, 1843; John C. Calhoun to James Edward Calhoun, April 8, 1843 [incorrect date], John C. Calhoun Papers, USC.

79. M. Tuomey to James Edward Calhoun, January 10, 1845, JECP, SCL.

80. Dundas, *Calhoun Settlement,* p. 15.

81. J. E. Boisseau to James Edward Calhoun, October 24, 1843, JECP, SCL.

82. John Hastings, Jr., to James Edward Calhoun, May 5, 1845, JECP, SCL.

83. By the 1840s it seems that Calhoun had begun to view Millwood as his main plantation. This change in perception probably occurred once Millwood became the home place. At any rate, after the mid-1830s, Millwood Plantation cannot be distinguished from Calhoun's other operations in the historical records.

84. Edward Harleston to James Edward Calhoun, February 15, 1842, November 25, 1842, JECP, SCL.

85. John C. Calhoun to James Edward Calhoun, February 28, 1843, in Wilson, *Papers of John C. Calhoun,* 16:691; John C. Calhoun to James Edward Calhoun, November 19, 1843, John C. Calhoun Papers, USC.

86. John C. Calhoun to James Edward Calhoun, April 8, 1843, John C. Calhoun Papers, USC.

87. John C. Calhoun to James Edward Calhoun, April 28, 1832, in Wilson, *Papers of John C. Calhoun,* 11:568.

88. Floride Calhoun to Patrick Calhoun, February 1, 1839, in Wilson, *Papers of John C. Calhoun,* 14:542.

89. Orville Vernon Burton, *In My Father's House Are Many Mansions: Family and Community in Edgefield, South Carolina* (Chapel Hill: University of North Carolina Press, 1985), p. 21; John C. Calhoun to James Edward Calhoun, December 24, 1826, August 26, 1827, in Wilson and Hemphill, *Papers of John C. Calhoun,* 10:239, 303, 337.

90. In a number of letters, John C. Calhoun mentions Anna Maria and Maria Simkins in one phrase. Examples are John C. Calhoun to Anna Maria Calhoun, January 25, 1838, February 7, 1838, in Wilson, *Papers of John C. Calhoun,* 14:109, 119; Gregory A. Perdicaris to John C. Calhoun, September 12, 1838, in Wilson, *Papers of John C. Calhoun,* 14:424.

91. February 22, 1834, James Edward Calhoun Diary, John Ewing Colhoun Papers, SHC.

92. For an example, see J. E. Boisseau to James Edward Calhoun, February 14, 1839, JECP, SCL.

93. James Edward Calhoun to Maria Simkins Calhoun, April, 1840, JECP, SCL.

94. James Edward Calhoun to Maria Simkins Calhoun, March 16, 1844, JECP, SCL.

95. John C. Calhoun to James Edward Calhoun, June 29, 1844, John C. Calhoun Papers, USC.

96. Dundas, *The Calhoun Settlement,* p. 11.

97. Mary Hemphill Greene, "James Edward Calhoun Marker to Be Put at Savannah River," *Greenwood* (S.C.) *Index-Journal,* 25 March 1953; Dundas, "Millwood Plantation."

98. Lewis Perrin, "The Hermit of Millwood."

99. "James Edward Calhoun: His Death Occurred on Thursday Morning, Oc-

tober 31, 1889. Something of his Life and Last Sickness . . . Notes of His Peculiarities . . . Speculations as to His Will . . . The Property Which He Owned" *Abbeville* (S.C.) *Press and Banner,* 6 November 1889.

100. Agreement between James Edward Calhoun and William Heemsoth, April 28, 1848; M. H. Keppelman to James Edward Calhoun, June 20, 1848, JECP, SCL.

101. 1850 Agricultural and Industrial schedules, James Edward Calhoun, Abbeville District, Magnolia Township, South Carolina [hereafter 1850 Agricultural Schedule and 1850 Industrial Schedule].

102. Agreement between James Edward Calhoun and D. U. Sloan, June 7, 1854, JECP, SCL.

103. 1860 Agricultural and Industrial schedules, James Edward Calhoun, Abbeville District, Magnolia Township, South Carolina [hereafter 1860 Agricultural Schedule and 1860 Industrial Schedule].

104. J. Branch to James Edward Calhoun, September 24, 1861, JECP, SCL.

105. James Edward Calhoun to Andrew Calhoun, May 1, 1864, JECP, SCL.

106. Robert H. Lowie, *Indians on the Plains* (Garden City, N.Y.: Natural History Press, 1963), p. 27.

107. John W. Lewis to James Edward Calhoun, February 12, 1864, JECP, SCL.

108. For comments on slave impressment during the Civil War, see James L. Roark, *Masters Without Slaves: Southern Planters in the Civil War and Reconstruction* (New York: W. W. Norton, 1977), pp. 79–81.

109. Mary Calhoun Garvin to James Edward Calhoun, February 27, 1863, JECP, SCL.

110. John W. Lewis to James Edward Calhoun, July 12, 1863, January 29, 1864, JECP, SCL.

111. James Gregorie to James Edward Calhoun, August 17, 1863, September 2, 1863, JECP, SCL.

112. James Edward Calhoun to Andrew Calhoun, February 24, 1864, JECP, SCL.

113. Untitled note. *Abbeville* (S.C.) *Press and Banner,* 7 March 1877.

114. James Edward Calhoun to Andrew Calhoun, May 1, 1864, JECP, SCL.

115. Ibid.

Chapter Three

1. S. "The Crops of 1866, A Failure, Why?" *Southern Cultivator* 25(1867): 198; San Marcus, "Cotton On the Brain," ibid., p. 251.

2. Henry Latham, *Black and White: A Journal of a Three Months' Tour in the United States* (London: Macmillan, 1867), p. 140.

3. Rawick, ed., *American Slave,* supp. ser. 1, vol. 7, pt. 2, pp. 566, 568; ibid., vol. 8, pt. 1, p. 106; ibid., supp. ser. 1, vol. 8, pt. 3, p. 850; ibid., supp. ser. 1, vol. 7, pt. 2, p. 750.

4. C. W. Tebeau, "Some Aspects of Planter-Freedmen Relations, 1865–1880," *Journal of Negro History* 21(1936): 132.

5. Roark, *Masters Without Slaves,* pp. 131–40; "Virginia: Her New Spirit and Development," *DeBow's Review* 2(1866): 56.

6. "System Proposed by General Banks," *DeBow's Review* 1(1866): 436–39.

7. Myrta Lockett Avary, *Dixie after the War: An Exposition of Social Conditions Existing in the South during the Twelve Years Succeeding the Fall of Richmond* (New York: Doubleday, Page, and Company, 1906), p. 212.

8. John S. Reynolds, *Reconstruction in South Carolina, 1865–1877* (Columbia, S.C.: The State Company, 1904), pp. 27–34; Francis Butler Simkins and Robert Hilliard Woody, *South Carolina During Reconstruction* (Chapel Hill: University of North Carolina Press, 1932), p. 48.

9. Richard Sutch and Roger Ransom, "Sharecropping: Market Response or Mechanism of Race Control?" in Sansing, *What Was Freedom's Price?* p. 59.

10. Alrutheus Ambush Taylor, *The Negro in South Carolina During the Reconstruction* (Washington, D.C.: Association for the Study of Negro Life and History, 1924), p. 50.

11. Anthony M. Tang, *Economic Development in the Southern Piedmont, 1860–1950: Its Impact on Agriculture* (Chapel Hill: University of North Carolina Press, 1958), p. 37. A more recent and rigorous study of the political economy of the Piedmont is Lacy K. Ford, Jr., "Social Origins of a New South Carolina: The Upcountry in the Nineteenth Century" (Ph.D. diss., University of South Carolina, 1983).

12. Joel Williamson, *After Slavery: The Negro in South Carolina During Reconstruction, 1861–1877* (Chapel Hill: University of North Carolina Press, 1965), pp. 130–31.

13. Sitterson, "Transition from Slave to Free," pp. 221–22; Ronald L. F. Davis, *Good and Faithful Labor: From Slavery to Sharecropping in the Natchez District, 1860–1890* (Westport, Conn.: Greenwood, 1982), p. 104.

14. J. T. Trowbridge, *The South: A Tour of Its Battlefields and Ruined Cities* (Hartford, Conn.: L. Stebbins, 1866), p. 391.

15. Ralph Shlomowitz, "The Origins of Southern Sharecropping," *Agricultural History* 53(1979): 561–62.

16. Thomas J. Edwards, "The Tenant System and Some Changes since Emancipation," *Annals of the American Academy of Political and Social Science* 49(1913): 39.

17. W. H. Evans, "The Labor Question," *Southern Cultivator* 27(1869): 54.

18. "System Proposed by General Banks," p. 437; John Richard Dennett, *The*

South As It Is, 1865–1866, Henry M. Christman, ed. (London: Sidgwick and Jackson, 1965), p. 281; Roger L. Ransom and Richard Sutch, *One Kind of Freedom: The Economic Consequences of Emancipation* (Cambridge: Cambridge University Press, 1977), p. 60.

19. Whitelaw Reid, *After the War: A Southern Tour, May 1, 1865 to May 1, 1866* (Cincinnati: Moore, Wilstach, and Baldwin, 1866), pp. 486–90.

20. David Crenshaw Barrow, "A Georgia Plantation," *Scribner's Monthly* 21(1881): 831. Also see, J. William Harris, "Plantations and Power: Emancipation on the David Barrow Plantations," in *Toward a New South: Studies in Post-Civil War Southern Communities,* ed. Orville Vernon Burton and Robert C. McMath, Jr. (Westport, Conn.: Greenwood, 1982), pp. 246–64.

21. Oscar Zeichner, "The Transition from Slave to Free Agricultural Labor in the Southern States," *Agricultural History* 13(1939): 22–25; Charles E. Orser, Jr., "The Continued Pattern of Dominance: Landlord and Tenant on the Postbellum Cotton Plantation," in *The Archaeology of Inequality,* ed. Robert Paynter and Randall H. McGuire (Oxford, England: Basil Blackwell, forthcoming).

22. F. W. Loring and C. F. Atkinson, *Cotton Culture and the South Considered with Reference to Emancipation* (Boston: A. Williams, 1869) , p. 10.

23. Carl Schurz, *Report on the States of South Carolina, Georgia, Alabama, Mississippi, and Louisiana,"* 39th Cong., 1st sess., S. Exec. Doc. 2, p. 30.

24. G. A. N., "Laborers Wanted!" *Southern Cultivator* 25(1867): 69; William A. Cook, in "Inquiries I: Replies Received to a Questionnaire Directed to Georgia Planters in Reference to the Reorganization of the Agricultural Labor System After 1865," ed. Robert Preston Brooks, Robert Preston Brooks Papers, Special Collections, University of Georgia Library, Athens; H. J. McCormick in Brooks, "Inquiries I."

25. Pitt Dillingham, "Land Tenure among the Negroes," *Yale Review* 5(1896): 201.

26. Jane Maguire, *On Shares: Ed Brown's Story* (New York: W. W. Norton, 1975), p. 44.

27. "What's To Be Done With the Negroes?" *DeBow's Review* 1(1866): 578; "How They Are Settling the Labor Question in Mississippi," *DeBow's Review* 5(1868): 224; Loring and Atkinson, *Cotton Culture,* p. 28.

28. Martin Abbott, *The Freedmen's Bureau in South Carolina, 1865–1872* (Chapel Hill: University of North Carolina Press, 1967), p. 80; Tebeau, "Some Aspects of Planter-Freedman Relations," p. 145.

29. Sutch and Ransom, "Sharecropping," p. 55.

30. Shlomowitz, "Origins," pp. 571–72; idem, "The Squad System on Postbellum Cotton Plantations," in Burton and McMath, *Toward a New South,*pp. 268–70.

31. John William DeForest, *A Union Officer in the Reconstruction,* ed. James H.

Croushore and David Morris Potter (New Haven: Yale University Press, 1948), p. 97.

32. Robert Somers, *The Southern States since the War, 1870–1* (London: Macmillan, 1871), p. 120.

33. Shlomowitz, "Origins," p. 572.

34. Edward Magdol, *A Right to the Land: Essays on the Freedmen's Community* (Westport, Conn.: Greenwood, 1977), pp. 12–13, 139–73.

35. W. J. Spillman, "The Agricultural Ladder," in *Papers on Tenancy,* Office of the Secretary of the American Association for Agricultural Legislation Bulletin no. 2 (Madison: University of Wisconsin, 1919), p. 29. For an excellent overview of the literature about the agricultural ladder, see Carl Frederick Wehrwein, "The Agricultural Ladder in Two Unlike Wisconsin Regions" (Ph.D. diss., University of Wisconsin, 1930), pp. 4–24.

36. Asa H. Gordon, *Sketches of Negro Life and History in South Carolina,* 2d ed. (Columbia: University of South Carolina Press, 1971), p. 161.

37. Papers and books considering the growth of southern tenancy after 1865 are too numerous to mention. Good bibliographies can be found in recent works, such as Ransom and Sutch, *One Kind of Freedom,* pp. 374–93, and in earlier works, such as Vance, *Human Factors,* pp. 321–37.

38. Harold D. Woodman, "Post–Civil War Southern Agriculture and the Law," *Agricultural History* 53(1979): 325.

39. Harrison v. Ricks, 71 N. C. 5(1871), in Tazewell L. Hargrave, 1905; Appling v. Odom and Mercier, 46 Ga. 583(1872), in Henry Jackson, 1912.

40. The State v. Gay, 1 Hill 374 (1833), in W. R. Hill, reporter, 1919; Huff v. Watkins, 15 S.C. 82 (1880), in Robert W. Shand, reporter, 1916; Loveless v. Gilliam 70 S.C. 391 (1904), in C. M. Efird, reporter; Malcolm Mercantile Co. v. Britt 102 S.C. 499 (1915), in W. H. Townsend, reporter, 1916; Lipscomb v. Johnson et al., 123 S.C. 44 (1922), in W. M. Shand, reporter, 1924.

41. Dacus v. Williamston Mills, 118 S.C. 245 (1921), in W. M. Shand, reporter, 1923.

42. E. A. Boeger and E. A. Goldenweiser, *A Study of the Tenant Systems of Farming in the Yazoo-Mississippi Delta,* U.S. Department of Agriculture Bulletin no. 337 (Washington: Government Printing Office, 1916), pp. 6–10.

43. E. S. Haskell, *A Farm-Management Survey in Brooks County, Georgia,* U.S. Department of Agriculture Bulletin no. 648 (Washington: Government Printing Office, 1918), p. 15.

44. Rawick, *American Slave,* vol. 4, pt. 1, p. 258; E. L. Langsford and B. H. Thibodeaux, *Plantation Organization and Operation in the Yazoo-Mississippi Delta Area,* U.S. Department of Agriculture Technical Bulletin no. 682 (Washington: Government Printing Office, 1939), p. 15.

45. Maguire, *On Shares,* pp. 55–59.

46. E. V. White and William E. Leonard, *Studies in Farm Tenancy in Texas,* Bulletin no. 21 (Austin: University of Texas, 1915), pp. 107–8.

47. Arthur F. Raper and Ira De A. Reid, *Sharecroppers All* (Chapel Hill: University of North Carolina Press, 1941), pp. 38–39.

48. Thomas J. Woofter, Jr., Gordon Blackwell, Harold Hoffsommer, James G. Maddox, Jean M. Massell, B. O. Williams, and Waller Wynne, Jr., *Landlord and Tenant on the Cotton Plantation,* Works Progress Administration, Division of Social Research, Monograph no. 5 (Washington: Government Printing Office, 1936), pp. 86–87.

49. Raper and Reid, *Sharecroppers All,* p. 39.

50. Maguire, *On Shares,* p. 72.

51. Ibid., p. 143.

52. C. O. Brannen, *Relation of Land Tenure to Plantation Organization,* U.S. Department of Agriculture Bulletin no. 1269 (Washington: Government Printing Office, 1924), p. 34.

53. Langsford and Thibodeaux, *Plantation Organization,* p. 15.

54. Ibid., p. 30n.

55. Arthur F. Raper, *Preface to Peasantry: A Tale of Two Black Belt Counties* (Chapel Hill: University of North Carolina Press, 1936), p. 214.

56. Brannen, *Relation of Land Tenure,* p. 34.

57. Woofter, et al., *Landlord and Tenant,* p. 10.

58. These studies abound in the literature, and good examples can be found in Lewis Cecil Gray, Charles L. Steward, Howard A. Turner, J. T. Sanders, and W. J. Spillman, "Farm Ownership and Tenancy," *Yearbook of the Department of Agriculture, 1923* (Washington: Government Printing Office, 1924), pp. 507–600; Rudolf Heberle, *Mississippi Backwater Area Study: Yazoo Segment* (Baton Rouge: Troy H. Middleton Library, Louisiana State University, 1941, Mimeographed); Brannen, *Relation of Land Tenure,* pp. 34–38; and others.

59. U.S. Department of the Interior, Census Office, *Report of the Production of Agriculture as Returned at the Tenth Census* [hereafter *1880 Census of Agriculture*] (Washington: Government Printing Office, 1883); idem, *Report on the Statistics of Agriculture in the United States at the Eleventh Census: 1890* [hereafter *1890 Census of Agriculture*] (Washington: Government Printing Office, 1895); idem, *Twelfth Census of the United States, Taken in the Year 1900: Agriculture* [hereafter *1900 Census of Agriculture*] (Washington: United States Census Office, 1902); U.S. Department of Commerce and Labor, Bureau of the Census, *Thirteenth Census of the United States, Taken in the Year 1910: Agriculture* [hereafter *1910 Census of Agriculture*] (Washington: Government Printing Office, 1913); U.S. Department of Commerce, Bureau of Census, *Fourteenth Census of the United States, Taken in the Year 1920: Agriculture* [hereafter *1920 Census of Agriculture*] (Washington: Government Printing Office, 1922); idem, *United States Census of Agriculture: 1925*

[hereafter *1925 Census of Agriculture*] (Washington: Government Printing Office, 1927). The first census used is the 1880 census rather than the 1870 census, following the reasons presented by Ransom and Sutch, *One Kind of Freedom,* pp. 273–74.

60. This increase in cash renters may be partly an illusion, because cash renters were added to the "other" category for the 1925 calculations. Because only 1,030 cash renters were reported in 1925 (only 1.5 percent of all farmers), some of the "others" were undoubtedly cash renters of some sort. In 1920, 889 cash renters were reported (1.2 percent of all farmers), but 12,890 standing renters were also noted. It seems likely that some of the "others" were standing renters. When the 1920 figures were computed, cash renters were added to standing renters. The amount of error caused by this procedure cannot be estimated; preferably it is quite small.

61. Coulter, "Plantations in the South," p. 877; Fite, *Cotton Fields No More,* p. 15.

62. Arthur R. Hall, *The Story of Soil Conservation in the South Carolina Piedmont, 1800–1860,* U.S. Department of Agriculture Miscellaneous Publication no. 407 (Washington: Government Printing Office, 1940), p. 1.

63. Gray, *History of Agriculture* 1:448.

64. Rupert B. Vance, *Human Geography of the South: A Study in Regional Resource and Human Adequacy* (Chapel Hill: University of North Carolina Press, 1935), p. 103; Hugh Hammond Bennett, *The Soils and Agriculture of the Southern States* (New York: Macmillan, 1921), p. 49; William Chandler Bagley, Jr., *Soil Exhaustion and the Civil War* (Washington, D.C.: American Council on Public Affairs, 1942), pp. 3–8.

65. Vance, *Human Geography,* pp. 85, 101–2.

66. Stanley Wayne Trimble, *Man-Induced Soil Erosion in the Southern Piedmont, 1700–1970* (Ankeny, Iowa: Soil Conservation Society of America, 1974), p. 59, Fig. 12.

67. Raper, *Preface to Peasantry,* pp. 219–20; Vance, *Human Geography,* p. 106.

68. Raper and Reid, *Sharecroppers All,* p. 220.

69. Trimble, *Man-Induced Soil Erosion,* p. 71, fig. 15.

70. Hugh Hammond Bennett, "Adjustment of Agriculture to Its Environment," *Annals of the Association of American Geographers* 33(1943): 184–85; idem, "The Increased Cost of Erosion," *Annals of the American Academy of Political and Social Science* 142(1929): 171.

71. *1910 Census of Agriculture.*

72. H. A. Ireland, C. F. S. Sharpe, and D. H. Eargle, *Principles of Gully Erosion in the Piedmont of South Carolina,* U.S. Department of Agriculture Technical Bulletin no. 633 (Washington: Government Printing Office, 1939), p. 37.

73. "Concentrated Fertilizers in the Southern States," *Report of the Commissioner*

of Agriculture for the Year 1868 (Washington: Government Printing Office, 1869), pp. 396, 398–99; W. J. McGee, *Soil Erosion,* U.S. Department of Agriculture, Bureau of Soils, Bulletin no. 71 (Washington: Government Printing Office, 1911); Rubin, *Plantation County,* p. 191.

74. Woofter, et al., *Landlord and Tenant,* p. 45, fig. 14; W. J. Spillman, *Soil Conservation,* U.S. Department of Agriculture, Farmer's Bulletin no. 406 (Washington: Government Printing Office, 1910), p. 14.

75. W. D. Hunter, "The Present Status of the Mexican Cotton-Boll Weevil in the United States," *Yearbook of the United States Department of Agriculture, 1901* (Washington: Government Printing Office, 1902), pp. 369–80.

76. Theodore Rosengarten, *All God's Dangers: The Life of Nate Shaw* (New York: Vintage, 1984), pp. 223–24.

77. W. D. Hunter and B. R. Coad, *The Boll Weevil Problem,* U.S. Department of Agriculture, Farmer's Bulletin no. 1329 (Washington: Government Printing Office, 1923), p. 3, fig. 1.

78. Bennett, *Soils and Agriculture,* p. 17; Vance, *Human Factors,* p. 87; Hunter and Coad, *Boll Weevil Problem,* p. 2; A. M. Agelasto, C. B. Doyle, G. S. Meloy, and O. C. Stine, "The Cotton Situation," *United States Department of Agriculture Yearbook, 1921* (Washington: Government Printing Office, 1922), p. 351.

79. Benjamin L. Moss, *The Boll Weevil Problem: An Analysis of Its Significance to the Southern Farmer and Business Man* (Birmingham, Ala.: Progressive Farmer, 1914).

80. Raper, *Preface to Peasantry,* pp. 201–5.

81. Merle C. Prunty and Charles S. Aiken, "The Demise of the Piedmont Cotton Region," *Annals of the Association of American Geographers* 62(1979): 286–99.

82. A detailed examination appears in Stephen J. DeCanio, *Agriculture in the Postbellum South: The Economics of Production and Supply* (Cambridge: MIT Press, 1974).

83. Coulter, "Plantations in the South," figure facing p. 880; Ransom and Sutch, *One Kind of Freedom,* p. 278, 280, table G.3; Woofter, et al., *Landlord and Tenant,* p. 45, fig. 14.

84. Demitri B. Shimkin, "Black Migration and the Struggle for Equity: A Hundred-Year Survey," in *Migration and Social Welfare,* ed. Joseph W. Eaton (New York: National Association of Social Welfare, 1971), p. 81; Emmett J. Scott, *Negro Migration During the War* (New York: Oxford University Press, 1920), p. 3.

85. William Oscar Scroggs, "Interstate Migration of Negro Population," *Journal of Political Economy* 25(1917): 1040.

86. Scott, *Negro Migration,* pp. 14–15; Carter G. Woodson, *A Century of Negro Migration* (New York: Russell and Russell, 1969), pp. 167–74; Thomas J. Woofter, Jr., *Negro Migration: Changes in Rural Organization and Population of the Cotton Belt* (New York: W. D. Gray, 1920), p. 119; Mandle, *Roots of Black Poverty,* pp. 72–74.

87. Many excellent anthropological studies of this nature have been completed. Among the most informative are Davis, Gardner, and Gardner, *Deep South;* Dollard, *Caste and Class;* Gunnar Myrdal, *An American Dilemma: The Negro Problem and Modern Democracy* (New York: Harper and Brothers, 1944); and Powdermaker, *After Freedom.*

88. Maguire, *On Shares,* p. 30.

89. Rosengarten, *All God's Dangers,* p. 144.

90. Maguire, *On Shares,* p. 55.

91. Scott, *Negro Migration,* p. 71; George Brown Tindall, *South Carolina Negroes, 1877–1900* (Baton Rouge: Louisiana State University Press, 1966), p. 176.

92. U.S. Department of the Interior, Census Office, *Statistics of the Population of the United States at the Tenth Census* [hereafter *1880 Census of Population*] (Washington: Government Printing Office, 1883); idem, *Report on the Population of the United States at the Eleventh Census: 1890* [hereafter *1890 Census of Population*] (Washington: Government Printing Office, 1895); idem, *Twelfth Census of the United States, Taken in the Year 1900: Population* [hereafter *1900 Census of Population*] (Washington: United States Census Office, 1901); U.S. Department of Commerce and Labor, Bureau of the Census, *Thirteenth Census of the United States, Taken in the Year 1910: Population* [hereafter *1910 Census of Population*] (Washington: Government Printing Office, 1913); U.S. Department of Commerce, Bureau of the Census, *Fourteenth Census of the United States, Taken in the Year 1920: Population* [hereafter *1920 Census of Population*] (Washington: Government Printing Office, 1922); idem, *Fifteenth Census of the United States, Taken in the Year 1930: Population* [hereafter *1930 Census of Population*] (Washington: Government Printing Office, 1933).

Chapter Four

1. Bruce G. Trigger, "Settlement Archaeology: Its Goals and Promise," *American Antiquity* 32(1967): 151; David L. Clarke, "Spatial Information in Archaeology," in *Spatial Archaeology,* ed. David L. Clarke (London: Academic Press, 1977), p. 9.

2. Edward T. Hall, *The Hidden Dimension* (Garden City, N.Y.: Doubleday and Company, 1969), p. 1; idem, "A System for the Notation of Proxemic Behavior," *American Anthropologist* 65(1963): 1003.

3. Edward T. Hall, "Proxemics: The Study of Man's Spatial Relationships," in *Man's Image in Medicine and Anthropology,* ed. Iago Goldston (New York: International Universities Press, 1963), pp. 429–30; idem, *Hidden Dimension,* pp. 103–12.

4. Henri Lefebvre, "Space: Social Product and Use Value," in *Critical Sociology: European Perspectives,* ed. J. W. Freiberg (New York: Irvington Publishers, 1979), pp. 287–89.

5. Bruce William Wright, *A Proxemic Analysis of the Iroquoian Settlement Pattern* (Calgary: Western Publishers, 1979).

6. K. C. Chang, *Settlement Patterns in Archaeology,* Addison-Wesley Module in Anthropology 24 (Reading, Mass.: Addison-Wesley, 1972); Bruce G. Trigger, "The Determinants of Settlement Patterns," in *Settlement Archaeology,* ed. K. C. Chang (Palo Alto: National Press, 1968), pp. 55–70; Clarke, "Spatial Information," pp. 11–13.

7. Chang, *Settlement Patterns,* pp. 17–20.

8. Merle C. Prunty, "The Renaissance of the Southern Plantation," *The Geographical Review* 45(1955): 463–66.

9. Thompson, "The Plantation," p. 189.

10. Trowbridge, *The South,* pp. 483–84.

11. James Battle Avirett, *The Old Plantation: How We Lived in Great House and Cabin Before the War* (New York: F. Tennyson Neely, 1901), pp. 35–42.

12. Charles Ball, *Slavery in the United States: A Narrative of the Life and Adventures of Charles Ball, A Black Man* (New York: John S. Taylor, 1837), pp. 137–40.

13. Lewis F. Allen, "A Southern, or Plantation House," *Southern Cultivator* 10(1852): 276; idem, *Rural Architecture: Being a Complete Description of Farm Houses, Cottages, and Out Buildings* (New York: C. M. Saxon, 1856), pp. 154–63.

14. Killion and Waller, *Slavery Time,* p. 77. Also see Rawick, ed., *American Slave,* supp. ser. 1, vol. 4, pt. 2, pp. 628–29; ibid., supp. ser. 1, vol. 6, pt. 1, p. 321; ibid., supp. ser. 1, vol. 7, pt. 2, pp. 364–65; ibid., supp. ser. 1, vol. 9, pt. 4, pp. 1639–40; and many others.

15. Ball, *Slavery in the United States,* p. 139.

16. Avirett, *The Old Plantation,* pp. 46, 51.

17. Reid, *After the War,* pp. 483–84.

18. Antoine Simon Le Page du Pratz, *The History of Louisiana,* trans. and ed. Joseph G. Tregle, Jr. (Baton Rouge: Louisiana State University Press, 1975), p. 381.

19. Rawick, *American Slave,* supp. ser. 1, vol. 6, pt. 1, p. 179; Killion and Waller, *Slavery Time,* p. 119; ibid., p. 126; Ball, *Slavery in the United States,* p. 139.

20. Social Science Institute, *Unwritten History of Slavery: Autobiographical Account of Negro Ex-Slaves,* Social Science Source Document no. 1 (Nashville: Fisk University, 1945), p. 13.

21. Lees, *Limerick,* p. 6, fig. 4; Moore, "The Antebellum Barrier Island Plantation," p. 74; Ehrenhard and Bullard, *Stafford Plantation,* p. vi; Genevieve Leavitt, "Slaves and Tenant Farmers at Shirley Plantation," in *The Archaeology of Shirley Plantation,* ed. Theodore R. Reinhart, p. 157 (Charlottesville: University of Virginia Press, 1984).

22. Rawick, *American Slave,* supp. ser. 1, vol. 6, pt. 1, p. 179; ibid., supp. ser. 1, vol. 9, pt. 4, p. 1430; ibid., supp. ser. 1, vol. 10, pt. 5, p. 2170.

23. Ibid., supp. ser. 1, vol. 11, p. 129.

24. Ibid., supp. ser. 1, vol. 8, pt. 3, pp. 891–92.

25. Killion and Waller, *Slavery Time*, p. 62.

26. Rawick, *American Slave*, supp. ser. 1, vol. 9, pt. 4, p. 1857; ibid., supp. ser. 1, vol. 10, pt. 5, p. 2064.

27. Stampp, *The Peculiar Institution*, p. 35.

28. Eugene D. Genovese, *Roll, Jordan, Roll: The World the Slaves Made* (New York: Pantheon, 1974), pp. 327–441.

29. Rawick, *American Slave*, supp. ser. 1, vol. 4, pt. 2, p. 447; ibid., supp. ser. 1, vol. 9, pt. 4, pp. 1394–95; Killion and Waller, *Slavery Time*, p. 221.

30. Frederick Law Olmsted, *A Journey in the Seaboard Slave States with Remarks on Their Economy* (New York: Dix and Edwards, 1856), p. 422; Ball, *Slavery in the United States*, p. 166.

31. Rawick, *American Slave*, supp. ser. 1, vol. 8, pt. 3, pp. 1112, 1228, 1266.

32. Ball, *Slavery in the United States*, p. 139; Killion and Waller, *Slavery Time*, p. 50; Avirett, *The Old Plantation*, p. 49; John B. Cade, "Out of the Mouths of Ex-Slaves," *Journal of Negro History* 20(1935): 296.

33. Orland Kay Armstrong, *Old Massa's People: The Old Slaves Tell Their Story* (Indianapolis: Bobbs-Merrill, 1931), pp. 68–69.

34. Edward King, *The Great South: A Record of Journeys* (Hartford, Conn.: American Publishing, 1879), p. 273.

35. David Crenshaw Barrow, "A Georgia Plantation," p. 831.

36. Rawick, *American Slave*, supp. ser. 1, vol. 8, pt. 3, p. 1347.

37. Killion and Waller, *Slavery Time*, p. 55; Rawick, *American Slave*, supp. ser. 1, vol. 7, pt. 2, p. 778.

38. Rawick, *American Slave*, supp. ser. 1, vol. 7, pt. 2, p. 566.

39. Ibid., supp. ser. 1, vol. 8, pt. 3, p. 957.

40. Barrow, "A Georgia Plantation," p. 832.

41. Sherwin H. Cooper, "The Rural Settlement of the Savannah Country," *Papers of the Michigan Academy of Science, Arts, and Letters* 47(1962): 422.

42. Somers, *The Southern States*, p. 120; George Campbell, *White and Black: The Outcome of a Visit to the United States* (London: Chatto and Windus, 1879), p. 142.

43. Prunty, "Renaissance," pp. 467–82.

44. John Fraser Hart, "Land Use Change in a Piedmont County," *Annals of the Association of American Geographers* 70(1980): 519–22; John Fraser Hart and Ennis L. Chestang, "Rural Revolution in East Carolina," *Geographical Review* 68(1978): 454.

45. Rupert B. Vance, *How the Other Half Is Housed: A Pictorial Record of Sub-Minimum Farm Housing in the South*, Southern Policy Paper no. 4 (Chapel Hill: University of North Carolina Press, 1936).

46. Rawick, *American Slave*, supp. ser. 1, vol. 6, pt. 1, p. 309.

47. Ibid., supp. ser. 1, vol. 6, pt. 1, p. 321; supp. ser. 1, vol. 11, p. 129; supp. ser.

1, vol. 8, pt. 3, p. 1228; supp. ser. 1, vol. 10, pt. 5, p. 1957; supp. ser. 1, vol. 10, pt. 5, p. 1995.

48. James J. Butler, "Management of Negroes," *DeBow's Review* 10(1851): 327.

49. Olmsted, *A Journey,* p. 111; Rawick, *American Slave,* supp. ser. 1, vol. 11, p. 129.

50. Rawick, *American Slave,* ser. 2, vol. 9, pt. 3, p. 359.

51. George Brown Tindall, *The Emergence of the New South, 1913–1945,* vol. 10 of *A History of the South,* ed. Wendell Holmes Stephenson and E. Merton Coulter (Baton Rouge: Louisiana State University Press, 1967), p. 411; Vance, *How The Other Half Is Housed.*

52. W. O. Atwater and Charles D. Woods, *Dietary Studies with References to the Food of the Negro in Alabama in 1895 and 1896,* U.S. Department of Agriculture, Office of Experimental Stations, Bulletin no. 38 (Washington: Government Printing Office, 1897), pp. 16–17. See figs. 1 and 3, facing p. 30.

53. Maguire, *On Shares,* pp. 37–38.

54. Margaret Jarman Hagood, *Mothers of the South: Portraiture of the White Tenant Farm Woman* (Chapel Hill: University of North Carolina Press, 1939), pp. 92–93.

55. A more recent study of the housing of black tenant farmers in one specific region is George W. McDaniel's brilliant *Hearth and Home: Preserving a People's Culture* (Philadelphia: Temple University Press, 1982). McDaniel's study provided a major impetus for this examination.

56. Maud Wilson, *Housing Requirements of Farm Families in the United States,* U.S. Department of Agriculture Miscellaneous Publication no. 322 (Washington: Government Printing Office, 1939); U.S. Department of Agriculture, Bureau of Home Economics, *The Farm-Housing Survey,* Miscellaneous publication no. 323 (Washington: Government Printing Office, 1939).

57. Wilson, *Housing Requirements,* p. 14, fig. 1; p. 36.

58. United States Bureau of Home Economics, *Farm Housing Survey,* pp. 3, 4, 7, 8, 9, 20–23.

59. United States Department of Commerce, *United States Census of Agriculture: 1935* [hereafter *1935 Census of Agriculture*] (Washington: Government Printing Office, 1936).

60. Warner, "American Caste"; Davis, Gardner, and Gardner, *Deep South;* Dollard, *Caste and Class.*

61. Warner, "American Caste," p. 235. Warner's ideas are expressed again in W. Lloyd Warner, "Deep South: A Social Anthropological Study of Caste and Class," in *Deep South* by Davis, Gardner, and Gardner, p. 10.

62. Thompson, "The Plantation," pp. 180–83.

63. Wilbert E. Moore and Robin M. Williams, "Stratification in the Ante-Bellum South," *American Sociological Review* 7(1942): 343–51.

64. The clearest refutations of the presence of castes in America are those by Oliver Cromwell Cox, "The Modern Caste School of Race Relations," *Social*

Forces 21(1942): 218–26; idem, "Race and Caste: A Distinction," *American Journal of Sociology* 50(1945): 360–68; idem, *Caste, Class, and Race: A Study in Social Dynamics* (Garden City, N.Y.: Doubleday, 1948). The application of the caste model has been used by Flynn, *White Land, Black Labor,* pp. 1–5, and earlier by Ball, *Slavery in the United States,* p. 287. Many other citations of the use of the caste concept could be mentioned.

65. *1925 Census of Agriculture.*

66. Raper, *Preface to Peasantry,* pp. 59–65.

67. Raper and Reid, *Sharecroppers All,* p. 20.

68. E. L. Kirkpatrick, *The Farmer's Standard of Living: A Socio-Economic Study of 2,886 White Farm Families of Selected Localities in Eleven States,* U.S. Department of Agriculture Bulletin no. 1466 (Washington: Government Printing Office, 1926), pp. 30–31.

69. James Agee and Walker Evans, *Let Us Now Praise Famous Men: Three Tenant Families* (Boston: Houghton Mifflin, 1941), pp. 135–211.

70. Ibid., p. 206.

71. Boeger and Goldenweiser, *A Study of the Tenant Systems,* pp. 10–12.

72. Woofter, et al., *Landlord and Tenant,* p. 84, table 33; p. 85, table 34; p. 87, table 34A.

73. Ibid., p. 94, table 37.

74. *1900 Census of Agriculture, 1910 Census of Agriculture, 1920 Census of Agriculture.*

75. Both years appear in U.S. Department of Commerce, Bureau of the Census, *Fifteenth Census of the United States, Taken in the Year 1930: Agriculture* [hereafter *1930 Census of Agriculture*] (Washington: Government Printing Office, 1933).

76. Michael Trinkley, "'Let Us Now Praise Famous Men'—If Only We Can Find Them," *Southeastern Archaeology* 2(1983): 31. For a disagreement with this essay, see Charles E. Orser, Jr., and Claudia C. Holland, "Let Us Praise Famous Men, Accurately: Toward a More Complete Understanding of Postbellum Southern Agricultural Practices," *Southeastern Archaeology* 3(1984): 111–20.

77. Rawick, *American Slave,* ser. 2, vol. 8, pt. 2, p. 257; ibid., p. 280.

78. Richard T. Ely and Charles J. Galpin, "Tenancy in an Ideal System of Landownership," in *Papers on Tenancy,* Office of the Secretary of the American Association for Agricultural Legislation Bulletin no. 2 (Madison: University of Wisconsin, 1919), Table ix, p. 66.

79. Brannen, *Relation of Land Tenure,* pp. 46–48, 74, Appendix D.

80. Raper, *Preface to Peasantry,* pp. 59–61.

81. E. A. Schuler, *Social Status and Farm Tenure: Attitudes and Social Conditions of Corn Belt and Cotton Belt Farmers,* U.S. Department of Agriculture, Farm Security Administration, and the Bureau of Agricultural Economics, Social Research Report no. 4 (Washington: Government Printing Office, 1938), p. 183.

82. Woofter, et al., *Landlord and Tenant,* pp. 108–10.

83. Ibid., p. 112, table 42; p. 113, table 43; p. 118, table 48.

84. *1935 Census of Agriculture.*

85. Raper, *Preface to Peasantry,* facing p. 65, facing p. 61.

86. Deetz, *In Small Things Forgotten,* pp. 94–95.

87. For an interesting debate on the archaeological visibility of tenant farms, see David G. Anderson and Jenalee Muse, *An Archaeological Reconnaissance of the Clarendon County Industrial Park,* Commonwealth Associates, Inc., Report no. 2398 (Jackson, Mich.: Commonwealth Associates, Inc., 1981); idem, "The Archaeology of Tenancy in the Southeast: A View from the South Carolina Lowcountry," *South Carolina Antiquities* 14(1982): 71–82; Michael Trinkley, " 'Let Us Now Praise Famous Men,' " pp. 30–36; David G. Anderson and Jenalee Muse, "The Archaeology of Tenancy (2): A Reply to Trinkley," *Southeastern Archaeology* 2(1983): 65–68; Michael Trinkley, "Reply," *Southeastern Archaeology* 2(1983): 68–69; Orser and Holland, "Let Us Praise Famous Men," pp. 111–20.

88. Raper, *Preface to Peasantry,* facing p. 61.

89. Quoted in Olmsted, *A Journey,* p. 698.

90. Rawick, *American Slave,* supp. ser. 1, vol. 7, pt. 2, p. 525; supp. ser. 1, vol. 7, pt. 2, p. 534; supp. ser. 1, vol. 8, pt. 3, p. 1267; supp. ser. 1, vol. 3, pt. 1, p. 64; supp. ser. 1, vol. 4, pt. 2, p. 346; supp. ser. 1, vol. 9, pt. 4, p. 1560; supp. ser. 1, vol. 9, pt. 4, pp. 1639–40; supp. ser. 1, vol. 8, pt. 3, p. 1186; supp. ser. 1, vol. 10, pt. 5, p. 1971; supp. ser. 1, vol. 10, pt. 5, p. 1995.

91. Killion and Waller, *Slavery Time,* p. 15.

92. Maguire, *On Shares,* p. 48.

93. Killion and Waller, *Slavery Time,* pp. 7, 14, 20, 49, 56.

94. Ball, *Slavery in the United States,* pp. 142–43; Killion and Waller, *Slavery Time,* p. 105; Rawick, *American Slave,* supp. ser. 1, vol. 6, pt. 1, p. 109.

95. Atwater and Woods, *Dietary Studies,* p. 17.

96. Kirkpatrick, *Farmer's Standard of Living,* pp. 22–23.

97. Raper, *Preface to Peasantry,* pp. 65–66.

98. Hagood, *Mothers of the South,* pp. 96–97.

99. Bureau of Home Economics, *Farm-Housing Survey,* pp. 11, 13, 15, 17.

100. Schuler, *Social Status and Farm Tenure,* p. 218, table 118.

101. Schuler's sample was comprised of statistics from parts of Hale County, Alabama; Jefferson County, Arkansas; Red River Parish, Louisiana; Union County, North Carolina; Beckham County, Oklahoma; Greenville County, South Carolina; Crockett County, Tennessee; Collin County, Texas; and Nacogdoches County, Texas; Schuler, *Social Status and Farm Tenure,* p. 248.

102. Schuler's sample was drawn from parts of McLean County, Illinois; Jones County, Indiana; Gentry County, Missouri; and Mercer County, Ohio.

103. Agee and Evans, *Let Us Now Praise Famous Men,* pp. 157–86.

104. Ibid., p. 175.

105. Ibid., pp. 190–92, 194–201.

106. Rawick, *American Slave,* supp. ser. 1, vol. 4, pt. 2, p. 629; ibid., supp. ser. 1, vol. 11, p. 129; ibid., supp. ser. 1, vol. 10, pt. 5, p. 1957; Rossa B. Cooley, *Homes of the Freed* (New York: New Republic, 1926), p. 121.

107. Killion and Waller, *Slavery Time,* p. 15.

108. Rawick, *American Slave,* supp. ser. 1, vol. 9, pt. 5, p. 1655; Olmsted, *A Journey,* p. 630.

109. For more information see the archaeological reports referenced in chapter 1.

110. Agee and Evans, *Let Us Now Praise Famous Men,* pp. 160–69, 172–74, 178–182.

111. John Ramsey, *American Potters and Pottery* (New York: Tutor, 1947), p. 153.

112. Anderson and Muse, *An Archaeological Reconnaissance;* idem, "The Archaeology of Tenancy."

113. This was site 38CR78. Archaeological sites in the United States are generally assigned a number that consists of three parts: the state within which the site occurs according to an alphabetized list, a county abbreviation, and a sequential number in the order in which sites are reported within that county. The state archaeologist's office in each state usually assigns these numbers and keeps files on the sites. The number 38CR78 refers to the seventy-eighth site reported in Clarendon County (CR), South Carolina (38). Sites that have not been given unique names are normally referred to by this number. Even sites given names still have numbers, but most archaeologists find it more convenient to use the names rather than the numbers.

114. Michael Trinkley, "'Let Us Now Praise Famous Men,'" p. 35; Michael Trinkley and Olga M. Caballero, *U.S. 521 Relocation, Sumter County, South Carolina: An Archaeological Survey of an Inter-Riverine Upper Coastal Plain Locality* (Columbia: South Carolina Department of Highways and Public Transportation, 1983), pp. 64–65; idem, *An Archaeological and Historical Evaluation of the I-85 Northern Alternative, Spartanburg County, South Carolina* (Columbia: South Carolina Department of Highways and Public Transportation, 1983), p. 78.

115. South, *Method and Theory,* pp. 47–164; idem, "Pattern Recognition in Historical Archaeology," *American Antiquity* 43(1978): 223–30. Archaeologists who have used, refined, and adapted South's idea are too numerous to mention.

116. South, *Method and Theory,* pp. 86–87; Daniel Little, *The Scientific Marx* (Minneapolis: University of Minnesota Press, 1986), pp. 24–29.

117. Orser and Holland, "Let Us Praise Famous Men," p. 118.

118. Adams, *Waverly Plantation,* p. 274.

119. Agee and Evans, *Let Us Now Praise Famous Men,* p. 180; Adams, *Waverly Plantation,* p. 359; Trinkley, "Let Us Now Praise Famous Men," p. 33.

120. Randall W. Moir, "Sheet Refuse: An Indicator of Past Lifeways," in *Settle-*

ment of the Prairie Margin: Archaeology of the Richland Creek Reservoir, Navarro and Freestone Counties, Texas, 1980–1981, A Research Synopsis, ed. L. Mark Raab (Dallas: Southern Methodist University, Archaeology Research Program, 1982), pp. 145–46.

121. Adams, *Waverly Plantation.*

122. Ibid., pp. 181–89.

123. Ibid., pp. 710–19 (microfiche).

Chapter 5

1. Professor James L. Roark conducted the research on the papers of the Bureau of Refugees, Freedmen, and Abandoned Lands at the National Archives, and I am deeply indebted to him.

2. C. R. Becker to John Devereau, March 20, 1866; C. R. Becker to John Devereau, April 3, 1866, Freedmen's Bureau Papers [hereafter FBP], National Archives [hereafter NA], Washington, D.C.

3. C. R. Becker to John Devereau, March 30, 1866, FBP, NA.

4. C. R. Becker to John Devereau, August 1, 1866; C. R. Becker to John Devereau, October 23, 1866, FBP, NA.

5. Contract between W. V. Clinkscales and Freedmen, January 7, 1867, FBP, NA.

6. Contract between John A. Calhoun and Freedmen, March 7, 1867, FBP, NA.

7. Contract between James Edward Calhoun and Freedmen, February 5, 1867, FBP, NA.

8. Untitled note, *Abbeville* (S.C.) *Press and Banner,* 7 March 1877.

9. M. Goldsmith to James Edward Calhoun, July 23, 1865, JECP, SCL.

10. James Edward Calhoun to Thomas Green Clemson, June 14, 1866, JECP, SCL.

11. H. G. M. Fleming [?] to James Edward Calhoun, August 8, 1867, JECP, SCL.

12. Memorandum of Agreement between James Edward Calhoun and John L. Vertrees, August 21, 1867, JECP, SCL.

13. Lander, *The Calhoun Family,* pp. 38, 237.

14. James Edward Calhoun to John L. Vertrees, November 5, 1868, JECP, SCL.

15. James Edward Calhoun to Thomas Green Clemson, June 14, 1866, JECP, SCL.

16. James Edward Calhoun to Anna Maria Clemson, June 3, 1869, JECP, SCL. For further details see Lander, *The Calhoun Family,* pp. 236–37.

17. James Edward Calhoun to Anna Maria Clemson, July 18, 1869, JECP, SCL.

18. James Edward Calhoun to W. F. Anderson, December 17, 1869, JECP, SCL.

19. James Edward Calhoun to Mr. Boyd, December 17, 1869, JECP, SCL.

20. Bill of Sale, White, Hill, and Cunningham to James Edward Calhoun, July 9, 1873; Bill of Sale, Miller and Robertson to James Edward Calhoun, July 9, 1873, JECP, SCL.

21. 1870 Agricultural Schedule, James Edward Calhoun, Abbeville County, Magnolia Township, South Carolina.

22. Contract between James Edward Calhoun and Jerry Blue, et al., February 15, 1875, Mortgage Book 5, Abbeville County Courthouse, Abbeville, South Carolina.

23. W. S. Logan to James Edward Calhoun, September 14, 1875, JECP, SCL.

24. James Edward Calhoun to Thomas C. Reynolds, June 26, 1877, JECP, SCL.

25. Thomas C. Reynolds to James Edward Calhoun, July 2, 1877, JECP, SCL.

26. Published letter of James Edward Calhoun to Cyrus M. McCormick, June 5, 1877, JECP, SCL. This letter also appears in "Wonderful Site for Huge Industry Here," *Calhoun Falls* (S.C.) *Times,* 26 May 1955, and in Dundas, *The Calhoun Settlement,* pp. 22–24.

27. George F. Swain, James L. Greenleaf, and Dwight Porter, *Reports on the Water-Power of the United States, Part I* (Washington: Government Printing Office, 1885), p. 790.

28. Q. A. Gillmore, "Examination of Savannah River above Augusta, Georgia," 45th Cong., 3d sess., 1879, *H. Exec. Doc.* 90, p. 4.

29. Memorandum of Agreement between James Edward Calhoun and Washington Hill, August 3, 1877, JECP, SCL.

30. 1880 Agricultural Schedule, James Edward Calhoun, Abbeville County, Magnolia Township, South Carolina [hereafter 1880 Agricultural Schedule].

31. 1880 Agricultural Schedule.

32. Statement of Account, George R. Sibley and Company to James Edward Calhoun, September 19, 1884, JECP, SCL.

33. 1880 Industrial Schedule, James Edward Calhoun, Abbeville County, Magnolia Township, South Carolina [hereafter 1880 Industrial Schedule].

34. William G. Le Duc to James Edward Calhoun, April 6, 1880, JECP, SCL.

35. William G. Le Duc, *Report of the Commissioner of Agriculture for the Year 1879* (Washington: Government Printing Office, 1880), p. 27.

36. Published letter by James Edward Calhoun in William G. Le Duc, "The Chinese Tea-Plant," *Report of the Commissioner of Agriculture for the Year 1877* (Washington: Government Printing Office, 1878), p. 364.

37. Living remnants of Calhoun's tea plants, *Camellia sinensis,* were found by Clemson University botanists Dr. John E. Fairey III and Caroline C. Douglass during their intensive field survey of Millwood Plantation in 1981, Orser, Nekola, and Roark, *Exploring the Rustic Life,* 3:25.

38. Bill of Sale, Forest City Foundry and Machine and Boiler Works to James Edward Calhoun, November 23, 1886; Frank Stanford to James Edward Calhoun, March 8, 1887, JECP, SCL.

39. James Edward Calhoun to G. W. Brown, April 20, 1885; James Edward Calhoun to Mrs. George Robinson and Ladies, April 18, 1887, JECP, SCL.

40. Perrin, "The Hermit of Millwood."

41. Maggie McNinch to James Edward Calhoun, February 19, 1886; Leila J. Norris to James Edward Calhoun, March 16, 1886; John A. Holland to James Edward Calhoun, July 24, 1886, JECP, SCL.

42. James Edward Calhoun to George C. Hodges, June 2, 1887; James Edward Calhoun to Henry A. Desaussure, June 2, 1887, JECP, SCL.

43. Phillips and Garbutt to James Edward Calhoun, June 17, 1887, JECP, SCL.

44. Dundas, *The Calhoun Settlement,* p. 13.

45. Edward B. Calhoun to James Edward Calhoun, December 5, 1888, JECP, SCL.

46. Deed, Reverend J. J. Monaghan, Edward Roche, and Hugh R. McElmore to James Edward Calhoun, May 5, 1883, Abbeville County Clerk of Court, Abbeville County, South Carolina; Dundas, *The Calhoun Settlement,* pp. 12–13.

47. "James Edward Calhoun," *Abbeville County* (S.C.) *Press and Banner,* 6 November 1889. The account of Calhoun's death and the reaction of his tenants was embellished by Perrin, "The Hermit of Millwood."

48. Perrin, "The Hermit of Millwood."

49. Last Will and Testament of James Edward Calhoun, October 19, 1889, probate court of Abbeville County, Abbeville, South Carolina.

50. 1870 Population Schedule, 1880 Population Schedule, 1900 Population Schedule, James Edward Calhoun, Abbeville County, Magnolia Township, South Carolina [hereafter 1870, 1880, 1900 Population Schedule].

51. Orser, Nekola, and Roark, *Exploring the Rustic Life,* 1:174, 3:220.

52. 1880 Population Schedule, 1880 Agricultural Schedule, 1900 Population Schedule.

53. The Calhoun genealogy appears in Lander, *The Calhoun Family,* frontispiece.

54. Inventory and Appraisement of the Personal Estate of James Edward Calhoun, Deceased, filed January 17, 1891. Returns no. 16, pp. 101–4, probate court of Abbeville County, Abbeville, South Carolina.

55. Sale Bill of the Personal Estate of James Edward Calhoun, Deceased, filed April 8, 1890, probate court of Abbeville County, Abbeville, South Carolina.

56. "Our Largest Tax Payers," *Abbeville* (S.C.) *Press and Banner,* 25 November 1885.

57. "Will There Be a Sensation?" *Abbeville* (S.C.) *Press and Banner,* 14 January 1891.

58. First Return on Account of the Estate of James Edward Calhoun, Deceased, 1889–1890, filed April 8, 1890; Returns on Account of the Estate of James Edward Calhoun, Deceased: 1890, filed January 27, 1891; 1891, filed February 12, 1892; 1892, filed February 17, 1893; 1893, filed November 8, 1893; 1894, filed November 13, 1894; 1895, filed November 13, 1895; 1896, filed March 13, 1897; 1897, filed December 21, 1897; 1898, filed April 22, 1899; 1899, filed December 4, 1899; 1900, filed December 31, 1900; 1901, filed November 2, 1902; 1902, filed December 29, 1902; 1903, filed December 9, 1903; 1904, filed November 19, 1904; 1905, filed November 5, 1905; 1906, filed December 5, 1906; 1907, filed April 10, 1908; 1908, filed December 14, 1908; 1909, filed November 22, 1909; 1910, filed December 1, 1910; Supplemental Return on Account of the Estate of James Edward Calhoun, Deceased, 1893, 1895, 1899, 1901, filed January 29, 1901; Supplemental Return on Account of the Estate of James Edward Calhoun, Deceased, 1901, filed January 10, 1902; probate court of Abbeville County, Abbeville, South Carolina.

59. Bill of Complaint, Patrick Calhoun v. Andrew P. Calhoun, et al., January 29, 1903; Deed, Patrick Calhoun to Andrew P. Calhoun, November 9, 1906, Book of Deeds 27, Abbeville County Clerk of Court, Abbeville, South Carolina.

60. "Big Land Sale!" *Abbeville* (S.C.) *Press and Banner,* 5 September 1906.

61. "Extensive Land Sale," *Abbeville* (S.C.) *Press and Banner,* 3 October 1906; Deed, Patrick Calhoun to Andrew P. Calhoun, November 9, 1906.

62. Augustine T. Smythe to Mrs. Andrew P. Calhoun [Isabella F. Calhoun], July 9, 1907, court of common pleas of Abbeville County, Abbeville, South Carolina.

63. Augustine T. Smythe to Mathew C. Butler, February 1, 1902; Granville Beal to Mathew C. Butler, February 18, 1902, JECP, SCL.

64. Declaration of Incorporation, Calhoun Falls Company, December 26, 1906, South Carolina Department of Archives and History, Columbia.

65. Deed, Andrew P. Calhoun to Calhoun Falls Company, January 28, 1907, Book of Deeds 27, Abbeville County Clerk of Court, Abbeville, South Carolina.

66. Ibid.

67. Testimony of John G. Carlisle, May 16, 1916, court of common pleas of Abbeville County, Abbeville, South Carolina.

68. Petition of Henry J. Bowdoin and Augustine T. Smythe v. Calhoun Falls Company, April 18, 1914, court of common pleas of Abbeville County, Abbeville, South Carolina.

69. Petition of Henry J. Bowdoin and Augustine T. Smythe v. Calhoun Falls Company, May 25, 1914; Court Order in the Case of Henry J. Bowdoin and

Augustine T. Smythe v. Calhoun Falls Company, May 28, 1914, court of common pleas of Abbeville County, Abbeville, South Carolina.

70. The Savannah River at Millwood Plantation was 330 feet above mean sea level before flooding.

71. Deed, Calhoun Falls Company to William S. Lee, June 14, 1916, Book of Deeds 35, Abbeville County Clerk of Court, Abbeville, South Carolina.

72. Untitled, undated survey map supplied by Doug Moore of the Duke Power Company, Charlotte, North Carolina; Deed, Calhoun Falls Company to William S. Lee, March 16, 1929, Book of Deeds 51, Abbeville County Clerk of Court, Abbeville, South Carolina.

73. Contract of Sale, Calhoun Falls Company to Philip Miner, et al., September 28, 1928, Book of Deeds 51, Abbeville County Clerk of Court, Abbeville, South Carolina.

74. Map entitled "Properties of Calhoun Falls, Inc.," December 5, 1928, supplied by Duke Power Company.

75. Agreement of Cancellation, Calhoun Falls Company and Calhoun Falls, Inc., March 18, 1929, Book of Deeds 51, Abbeville County Clerk of Court, Abbeville, South Carolina.

76. Deed, F. B. McLane to I. C. Harrison, July 6, 1933; Deed, I. C. Harrison to Millwood Company, September 11, 1933, Book of Deeds 58, Abbeville County Clerk of Court, Abbeville, South Carolina; "Famous Calhoun Estate on Savannah River Sold Last Week," *Press and Banner and Abbeville* (S.C.) *Medium,* 10 July 1933.

77. The oral information in this section appears in Orser, Nekola, and Roark, *Exploring the Rustic Life,* 3:223–51.

78. Miscellaneous records at the Clerk of Court, Abbeville, South Carolina, attest to Kieser's business dealings with the Millwood tenants. Kieser declared bankruptcy in 1909 and was murdered in 1927.

79. "Famous Calhoun Estate on Savannah River Sold Last Week," *Press and Banner and Abbeville* (S.C.) *Medium,* 10 July 1933.

80. Indictment against Floyd Majors and Louis Brown, September 5, 1942; Warrant of Arrest against Floyd Majors and Louis Brown, September 7, 1942; Sentence of Floyd Majors, September 29, 1942, court of common pleas of Abbeville County, Abbeville, South Carolina.

81. Declaration of Taking No. 1, Civil Action No. 1133, February 8, 1952, Book of Deeds 87, Abbeville County Clerk of Court, Abbeville, South Carolina; Records of the Office of the South Carolina Secretary of State, Columbia.

82. *Savannah River, Georgia and South Carolina, Trotter's Shoals Reservoir,* 89th Cong., 1st sess. S. Doc. 52; United States Public Law 89-789, November 7, 1966, *U. S. Statutes at Large* 80 (1967): 1420.

Chapter Six

1. Hemmings, *Archaeological Survey.*
2. Ibid., p. 58. Millwood Plantation was designated site 38AB9.
3. Taylor and Smith, *Intensive Survey.*
4. Ibid., pp. 365–88.
5. Charles E. Orser, Jr., James L. Roark, and Annette M. Nekola, *Summary Report of Phase I Testing and Evaluation at Millwood Plantation (38AB9), Abbeville County, South Carolina* (Atlanta: Interagency Archaeological Services, 1981); Orser, Nekola, and Roark, *Exploring the Rustic Life.* This research was sponsored by the Division of Archaeological Services of the Heritage Conservation and Recreation Service (now the Archaeological Services Branch of the National Park Service) and funded by the United States Army Corps of Engineers, Savannah District. The research, completed under contract C-54042(80), was conducted in 1980 and 1981.
6. The raw data contained in this chapter, unless otherwise noted, can be found in Orser, Nekola, and Roark, *Exploring the Rustic Life.*
7. Henry Glassie, *Folk Housing in Middle Virginia: A Structural Analysis of Historic Artifacts* (Knoxville: University of Tennessee Press, 1975), pp. 85, 86, 147.
8. Although carbon 14 and other radiometric dating techniques are not generally relevant to historical archaeology, the interested reader may want more information about these techniques. A good place to start is Joseph W. Michels, *Dating Methods in Archaeology* (New York: Seminar Press, 1973). The section on C-14 dating appears on pp. 148–67.
9. An explanation of this code appears in Geoffrey A. Godden, *Encyclopedia of British Pottery and Porcelain Marks* (New York: Bonanza, 1964), pp. 526–28.
10. This method was devised by Stanley South and is explained in "Evolution and Horizon as Revealed in Ceramic Analysis in Historical Archaeology," *The Conference on Historic Site Archaeology Papers* 6(1972): 71–116; idem, "Archaeological Pattern Recognition: An Example from the British Colonial System," in *Conservation Archaeology,* ed. Michael B. Schiffer and George J. Gumerman (New York: Academic Press, 1977), p. 433; idem, *Method and Theory,* pp. 207–74; idem, "Pattern Recognition," p. 225. For a discussion of the use of the standard deviation statistic for computing the mean ceramic date, see James E. Fitting, "Evolution, Statistics, and Historic Ceramics," *The Conference on Historic Site Archaeology Papers* 6(1972): 158–62.
11. Adams, *Waverly Plantation,* p. 534; William H. Adams and Linda P. Gaw, "A Model for Determining Time Lag of Ceramic Artifacts," *Northwest Anthropological Research Notes* 11(1977): 218–31.
12. Gordon L. Grosscup and George L. Miller, *Excavations at Walker Tavern, Cambridge State Historical Park: 1968* (Lansing: Michigan Department of Conser-

vation, 1969), pp. 36–38; John W. Walker, *Excavation of the Arkansas Post Branch of the Bank of the State of Arkansas* (Washington: National Park Service, 1971), p. 78; David H. Chance and Jennifer V. Chance, Kanaka Village/Vancouver Barracks, 1974, Reports in Highway Archaeology no. 3 (Seattle: Office of Public Archaeology, University of Washington, 1976), pp. 248–55.

13. Karl G. Roenke, "Flat Glass: Its Use as a Dating Tool for Nineteenth Century Archaeological Sites in the Pacific Northwest and Elsewhere," *Northwest Anthropological Research Notes*, Memoir no. 4 (Moscow: University of Idaho, 1978).

14. Orser, Nekola, and Roark, *Exploring the Rustic Life*, 2:542–46. Important comparative data needed to formulate the dating method appears in Adams, *Waverly Plantation*, pp. 491–95.

15. Excellent studies of nails appear in Bernard L. Fontana and J. Cameron Greenleaf, "Johnny Ward's Ranch: A Study in Historic Archaeology," *The Kiva* 28(1962): 44–66; Lee H. Nelson, *Nail Chronology as an Aid to Dating Old Buildings*, Technical Leaflet no. 48 (Nashville: American Association for State and Local History, 1968). An in-depth consideration appears in Orser, Nekola, and Roark, *Exploring the Rustic Life*, 2:549–65.

16. Julian Harrison Toulouse, *Bottle Makers and Their Marks* (New York: Thomas Nelson, 1971), p. 236.

17. Dessamae Lorrain, "An Archaeologist's Guide to Nineteenth Century American Glass," *Historical Archaeology* 2(1968): 40; N. Hudson Moore, *Old Glass, European and American* (New York: Frederick A. Stoles, 1924), pp. 255–56.

18. Another examination of the squad system at Millwood Plantation appears in Charles E. Orser, Jr., "The Archaeological Recognition of the Squad System on Postbellum Cotton Plantations," *Southeastern Archaeology* 5(1986): 11–20.

19. Godden, *Encyclopedia*, p. 534; E. Paul and A. Petersen, eds., *Collector's Handbook of Marks on Porcelain and Pottery* (Green Farms, Conn.: Modern Books and Crafts, 1974), p. 110; Ernest Reynolds, *Collecting Victorian Porcelain* (New York: Frederick A. Praeger, 1966), p. 64.

20. Ivor Noël Hume, *A Guide to Artifacts of Colonial America* (New York: Alfred A. Knopf, 1972), pp. 129–31.

21. Johnson, of Whistles in the Woods Museum, Rossville, Georgia, analyzed and conserved the Millwood Plantation turbines.

22. Phillip K. Huggins, *The South Carolina Dispensary: A Bottle Collector's Atlas and History of the System* (Columbia, S.C.: Sandlapper Press, 1971), p. v.

23. Charles A. Bennett, *Saw and Toothed Cotton Ginning Developments* (Dallas: Texas Cotton Ginners' Association, 1957), p. 3, fig. 4.

24. Drawings of this kind of press appear in Charles A. Bennett, *Cotton Ginning Systems in the United States and Auxiliary Developments* (Dallas: Texas Cotton Ginners' Association, 1962), p. 2, figs. 2, 3, 4.

25. 1860 Industrial Schedule.

26. 1880 Population Schedule.

27. Alternative interpretations appear in Charles E. Orser, Jr., "The Sorghum Industry of a Nineteenth-Century Cotton Plantation in South Carolina," *Historical Archaeology* 19(1985): 51–64.

28. James C. Bonner, *A History of Georgia Agriculture, 1732–1860* (Athens: University of Georgia Press, 1964), pp. 83–86; "Sorgho Sugar," *Southern Cultivator* 15(1857): 153.

29. "Sugar from Chinese Cane," *Southern Cultivator* 15(1857): 313.

30. Elliot Wigginton, ed., *Foxfire 3* (Garden City, N.Y.: Anchor/Doubleday, 1975), pp. 424–36.

31. Peter Collier, *Sorghum: Its Culture and Manufacture* (Cincinnati: Robert Clarke, 1884), pp. 327–28.

32. "Sugar—Its Cultivation, Manufacture, and Commerce," *DeBow's Review* 4(1847): 296–310; U.S. Hollister, *Handbook of Sorgo Culture* (St. Paul, Minn.: John J. Lemon, 1878), p. 1.

33. 1860 Agricultural Schedule.

34. Joseph S. Lovering, "Sugar Made from the Chinese Sugar," *Southern Cultivator* 16(1858): 111.

35. Inventory and Appraisement of the Personal Estate of James Edward Calhoun; Sale Bill of the Personal Estate of James Edward Calhoun.

36. 1880 Agricultural Schedule.

37. Perrin, "The Hermit of Millwood."

38. Dundas, *Calhoun Settlement*, p. 15.

39. William L. Calhoun to Mr. Meriwether, July 6, 1955, JECP, SCL.

40. Orser, Nekola, and Roark, *Exploring the Rustic Life*, 1:156; 3:229, and 236–37.

41. Dundas, *Calhoun Settlement*, p. 15.

42. Huggins, *South Carolina Dispensary*, p. v; Toulouse, *Bottle Makers*, p. 26.

43. Dundas, *Calhoun Settlement*, p. 15; William L. Calhoun to Mr. Meriwether, July 6, 1955, JECP, SCL; Orser, Nekola, and Roark, *Exploring the Rustic Life*, 1:160; 3:237.

44. The disparity between the machine-cut nail percentages may relate to the higher percentage of unidentifiable nails in structure 1—17.9 percent in structure 1, 5.0 percent in structure 2—rather than to an actual difference between the samples.

45. Toulouse, *Bottle Makers*, pp. 39, 544; Richard E. Fike, *The Bottle Book: A Comprehensive Guide to Historic, Embossed Medicine Bottles* (Salt Lake City: Peregrine Smith Books, 1987), pp. 83, 97, 109.

46. Dundas, *Calhoun Settlement*, p. 15; William L. Calhoun to Mr. Meriwether, July 6, 1955, JECP, SCL.

47. Orser, Nekola, and Roark, *Exploring the Rustic Life*, 3:224, 229, 234, 237.

48. Ibid., p. 234.

49. A fuller explanation of the terms *terminus post quem* and *terminus ante quem* can be found in Noël Hume, *Historical Archaeology,* p. 69.

50. Toulouse, *Bottle Makers,* pp. 30, 536.

51. The History Group, *Historical Investigations,* p. 134; Saint Paul Winter Carnival Association, *Seventy-fifth Anniversary of the Sun-Filled Saint Paul Winter Carnival, 1886–1961* (Saint Paul, Minn.: Saint Paul Winter Carnival Association, 1961).

52. Orser, Nekola, and Roark, *Exploring the Rustic Life,* 1:301; 3:246.

53. Further studies of structure 17 appear in Charles E. Orser, Jr., "Artifacts, Documents, and Memories of the Black Tenant Farmer," *Archaeology* 38, no. 4 (1985): 48–53; Claudia Croy Holland, " 'Everything on that Land was Yours Except that Bale of Cotton': The Archaeological Manifestations of a Share Renter's House on a Cotton Plantation in the South Carolina Piedmont." Unpublished manuscript.

54. Taylor and Smith, *Intensive Survey,* pp. 365–88.

55. First Return on Account, 1890; Orser, Nekola, and Roark, *Exploring the Rustic Life,* 3:243.

56. Orser, Nekola, and Roark, *Exploring the Rustic Life,* 3:241, 244.

57. A further examination of these locales along with the raw data for the analysis appears in Charles E. Orser, Jr. and Annette M. Nekola, "Plantation Settlement from Slavery to Tenancy: An Example from a Piedmont Plantation in South Carolina," in *The Archaeology of Slavery and Plantation Life,* Theresa A. Singleton, ed. (Orlando, Fla.: Academic Press, 1985), pp. 67–94.

58. Rosengarten, *All God's Dangers,* p. 102.

59. Orser, Nekola, and Roark, *Exploring the Rustic Life,* 3:240, 242, 249.

Chapter Seven

1. South, *Method and Theory,* p. 86.

2. The purpose of this explanation is not to duplicate the site report. Anyone wishing detailed analysis should see Orser, Nekola, and Roark, *Exploring the Rustic Life,* 1:34–414; 2:583–766. More traditional artifact descriptions can be found on 2:450–522.

3. See, for example, the classification scheme of Roderick Sprague, "A Functional Classification for Artifacts from Nineteenth and Twentieth Century Historical Sites," *North American Archaeologist* 2(1981): 251–61.

4. Robert L. Schuyler, "The Use of Historic Analogs in Archaeology," *American Antiquity* 33(1968): 390–92; Charles E. Orser, Jr., "Ethnohistory, Analogy, and Historical Archaeology," *The Conference on Historic Site Archaeology Papers* 13(1979): 1–24.

5. Architectural items—nails, window glass, mortar, slate, brick, and so forth—

have been excluded from this analysis because, while they are undoubtedly imperfectly related to plantation labor position, they can unfairly bias the analysis. For example, a tenant house repaired many times would have many more nails in its surrounding soil than would a landlord's house that was seldom repaired.

6. For complete explanations of the Index of Agreement, see George W. Brainerd, "The Place of Chronological Ordering in Archaeological Analysis," *American Antiquity* 16(1951): 301–13; J. E. Doran and R. F. Hodson, *Mathematics and Computers in Archaeology* (Cambridge: Harvard University Press, 1975), p. 139; William H. Marquardt, "Advances in Archaeological Seriation," in *Advances in Archaeological Method and Theory,* ed. Michael B. Schiffer (New York: Academic Press, 1978), vol. 1, pp. 263–65; W. S. Robinson, "A Method for Chronologically Ordering Archaeological Deposits," *American Antiquity* 16(1951): 293–301.

7. Pioneering research into the correlation of ceramics with plantation groups was conducted by Otto, "Artifacts and Status Differences." Although Otto used antebellum artifacts and made many serious mistakes, his basic idea seems to have a certain measure of validity; see Orser, "The Archaeological Analysis of Plantation Society."

Chapter Eight

1. South, *Method and Theory,* pp. 5–12.

Bibliography

Unpublished Material

Abbeville County Courthouse, Abbeville County, South Carolina. Clerk of Court records; court of common pleas records; mortgage books; probate court records.

Brooks, Robert Preston, ed. "Inquiries I: Replies Received to a Questionnaire Directed to Georgia Planters in Reference to the Reorganization of the Agricultural Labor System after 1865." Robert Preston Brooks Papers. Special Collections, University of Georgia Library, Athens.

Bureau of Refugees, Freedmen, and Abandoned Lands [Freedmen's Bureau] Papers. National Archives, Washington, D.C.

Calhoun, James Edward. Papers. South Caroliniana Library, University of South Carolina, Columbia.

Calhoun, John C. Papers. History Department, University of South Carolina, Columbia.

Colhoun, John Ewing. Papers. Southern Historical Collections, University of North Carolina, Chapel Hill.

Declaration of Incorporation, Calhoun Falls Company, December 26, 1906. South Carolina Department of Archives and History, Columbia.

Duke Power Company records. Charlotte, North Carolina.

Elbert County Courthouse, Elberton, Georgia. Clerk of court records.

Pickens County Courthouse, Pendleton, South Carolina. Clerk of court records.

South Carolina Secretary of State records. Columbia, South Carolina.

United States Census. James Edward Calhoun. Slave Schedules, 1830, 1840, 1850, 1860. Abbeville District, Magnolia Township, South Carolina.

———. James Edward Calhoun. Population Schedules, 1840, 1870, 1880, 1900. Abbeville District (County), Magnolia Township, South Carolina.

———. James Edward Calhoun. Agricultural Schedules, 1850, 1860, 1870, 1880. Abbeville District (County), Magnolia Township, South Carolina.

———. James Edward Calhoun. Industrial Schedules, 1850, 1860, 1880. Abbeville District (County), Magnolia Township, South Carolina.

Published Material

Abbott, Martin. *The Freedmen's Bureau in South Carolina, 1865–1872.* Chapel Hill: University of North Carolina Press, 1967.

Adams, William H., ed. *Waverly Plantation: Ethnoarchaeology of a Tenant Farming Community.* Atlanta: Heritage Conservation and Recreation Service, 1980.

Adams, William H., and Linda P. Gaw. "A Model for Determining Time Lag of Ceramic Artifacts." *Northwest Anthropological Research Notes* 11 (1977): 218–31.

Agee, James, and Walker Evans. *Let Us Now Praise Famous Men: Three Tenant Families.* Boston: Houghton Mifflin, 1941.

Agelasto, A. M., C. B. Doyle, G. S. Meloy, and O. C. Stine. "The Cotton Situation." *United States Department of Agriculture Yearbook, 1921,* 323–406. Washington: Government Printing Office, 1922.

Allen, Lewis F. "A Southern, or Plantation House." *Southern Cultivator* 10 (1852): 276–79.

———. *Rural Architecture: Being a Complete Description of Farm Houses, Cottages, and Out Buildings.* New York: C. M. Saxon, 1856.

Anderson, David G., and Jenalee Muse. *An Archaeological Reconnaissance of the Clarendon County Industrial Park.* Commonwealth Associates, Inc., Report, no. 2398. Jackson, Mich.: Commonwealth Associates, Inc., 1981.

———. "The Archaeology of Tenancy in the Southeast: A View from the South Carolina Lowcountry." *South Carolina Antiquities* 14 (1982): 71–82.

———. "The Archaeology of Tenancy (2): A Reply to Trinkley." *Southeastern Archaeology* 2 (1983): 65–68.

Anthony, Carl. "The Big House and the Slave Quarters: Part II, African Contributions to the New World." *Landscape* 21 (1976)1: 9–15.

Armstrong, Orland Kay. *Old Massa's People: The Old Slaves Tell Their Story.* Indianapolis: Bobbs-Merrill, 1931.

Ascher, Robert, and Charles H. Fairbanks. "Excavation of a Slave Cabin: Georgia, U.S.A." *Historical Archaeology* 5 (1971): 3–17.

Atwater, W. O., and Charles D. Woods. *Dietary Studies with Reference to the Food of the Negro in Alabama in 1895 and 1896.* U.S. Department of Agriculture, Office of Experimental Stations, Bulletin no. 38. Washington: Government Printing Office, 1897.

Atwood, Wallace W. *The Physiographic Provinces of North America.* Boston: Ginn and Company, 1940.

Avary, Myrta Lockett. *Dixie after the War: An Exposition of Social Conditions Existing in the South during the Twelve Years Succeeding the Fall of Richmond.* New York: Doubleday, Page, and Company, 1906.

Avirett, James Battle. *The Old Plantation: How We Lived in Great House and Cabin Before the War.* New York: F. Tennyson Neely, 1901.

Bacot, D. Huger. "The South Carolina Up Country at the End of the Eighteenth Century." *The American Historical Review* 28 (1923): 682–98.

Bagley, William Chandler, Jr. *Soil Exhaustion and the Civil War.* Washington, D.C.: American Council on Public Affairs, 1942.

Baker, Vernon G. "Historical Archaeology at Black Lucy's Garden, Andover, Massachusetts: Ceramics from the Site of a Nineteenth Century Afro-American." *Papers of the Robert S. Peabody Foundation for Archaeology,* no. 8. Andover, Mass.: Phillips Academy, 1978.

———. "Archaeological Visibility of Afro-American Culture: An Example from Black Lucy's Garden, Andover, Massachusetts." In *Archaeological Perspectives on Ethnicity in America: Afro-American and Asian American Culture History,* edited by Robert L. Schuyler, 29–37. Farmingdale, N.Y.: Baywood, 1980.

Ball, Charles. *Slavery in the United States: A Narrative of the Life and Adventures of Charles Ball, A Black Man.* New York: John S. Taylor, 1837.

Banton, Michael. *Race Relations.* New York: Basic, 1967.

Barbee, William J. *The Cotton Question: The Production, Export, Manufacture, and Consumption of Cotton.* New York: Metropolitan Record Office, 1866.

Barlett, Peggy F., ed. *Agricultural Decision Making: Anthropological Contributions to Rural Development.* New York: Academic Press, 1980.

Barrow, David Crenshaw. "A Georgia Plantation." *Scribner's Monthly* 21 (1881): 830–36.

Bartram Trail Conference. *Bartram Heritage.* Montgomery, Ala.: The Bartram Trail Conference, 1979.

Bastian, Beverly E. *Fort Independence: An Eighteenth-Century Frontier Homesite and Militia Post in South Carolina.* Atlanta: National Park Service, 1982.

Bennett, Charles A. *Saw and Toothed Cotton Ginning Developments.* Dallas: Texas Cotton Ginners' Association, 1957.

———. *Cotton Ginning Systems in the United States and Auxiliary Developments.* Dallas: Texas Cotton Ginners' Association, 1962.

Bennett, Hugh Hammond. *The Soils and Agriculture of the Southern States.* New York: Macmillan, 1921.

———. "The Increased Cost of Erosion." *Annals of the American Academy of Political and Social Science* 142 (1929): 170–76.

———. "Adjustment of Agriculture to Its Environment." *Annals of the Association of American Geographers* 33 (1943): 163–98.

Berkhofer, Robert. *A Behavioral Approach to Historical Analysis.* New York: Free Press, 1969.

"Big Land Sale!" *Abbeville* (S.C.) *Press and Banner,* 5 September 1906.

Blassingame, John W. "Using the Testimony of Ex-Slaves: Approaches and Problems." *Journal of Southern History* 41 (1975): 473–92.

———. *The Slave Community: Plantation Life in the Antebellum South.* Rev. ed. New York: Oxford University Press, 1979.

Blegen, Theodore C. *Minnesota: A History of the State.* Minneapolis: University of Minnesota Press, 1963.

Bloch, Maurice. *Marxism and Anthropology.* Oxford: Oxford University Press, 1985.

Boeger, E. A., and E. A. Goldenweiser. *A Study of the Tenant System of Farming in the Yazoo-Mississippi Delta.* U.S. Department of Agriculture Bulletin, no. 337. Washington: Government Printing Office, 1916.

Bonner, James C. "Profile of a Late Ante-Bellum Community." *The American Historical Review* 49 (1944): 663–80.

———. *A History of Georgia Agriculture, 1732–1860.* Athens: University of Georgia Press, 1964.

Brainerd, George W. "The Place of Chronological Ordering in Archaeological Analysis." *American Antiquity* 16 (1951): 301–13.

Brandt, Karl. "Fallacious Census Terminology and Its Consequences in Agriculture." *Social Research* 5 (1938): 19–36.

Brannen, C. O. *Relation of Land Tenure to Plantation Organization.* U.S. Department of Agriculture Bulletin no. 1269. Washington: Government Printing Office, 1924.

Breeden, James O., ed. *Advice among Masters: The Ideal in Slave Management in the Old South.* Westport, Conn.: Greenwood, 1980.

Bridges, Sarah T., and Bert Salwen. "Weeksville: The Archaeology of a Black Community." In *Archaeological Perspectives on Ethnicity in America: Afro-American and Asian American Culture History,* edited by Robert L. Schuyler, 38–47. Farmingdale, N.Y.: Baywood, 1980.

Brooks, Robert Preston. *The Agrarian Revolution in Georgia: 1885–1912.* Bulletin no. 639. Madison: University of Wisconsin, 1914.

Burton, Orville Vernon. *In My Father's House Are Many Mansions: Family and Community in Edgefield, South Carolina.* Chapel Hill: University of North Carolina Press, 1985.

Butler, James J. "Management of Negroes." *DeBow's Review* 10 (1851): 325–37.

Cade, John B. "Out of the Mouths of Ex-Slaves." *Journal of Negro History* 20 (1935): 294–337.

Campbell, George. *White and Black: The Outcome of a Visit to the United States.* London: Chatto and Windus, 1879.

Carlton, Benjamin T. *The Country Doctor.* n.p.: National Photo Listing Company, 1967.

Chance, David H., and Jennifer V. Chance. *Kanaka Village/ Vancouver Barracks, 1974.* Reports in Highway Archaeology no. 3. Seattle: Office of Public Archaeology, University of Washington, 1976.

Chang, K. C. *Settlement Patterns in Archaeology.* Addison-Wesley Module in Anthropology 24. Reading, Mass.: Addison-Wesley, 1972.

Childe, V. Gordon. "Archaeology and Anthropology." *Southwestern Journal of Anthropology* 21 (1946): 243–51.

———. *History.* London: Cobbett Press, 1947.

———. *Man Makes Himself.* New York: Mentor, 1951.

———. *Society and Knowledge.* New York: Harper and Brothers, 1956.

———. *What Happened in History.* Baltimore: Penguin, 1964.

———. "Prehistory and Marxism." *Antiquity* 53 (1979): 93–95.

Clarke, David L. "Spatial Information in Archaeology." In *Spatial Archaeology,* edited by David L. Clarke, 1–32. London: Academic Press, 1977.

Collier, Peter. *Sorghum: Its Culture and Manufacture.* Cincinnati: Robert Clarke, 1884.

Collins, Robert. "Management of Slaves." *DeBow's Review* 17 (1854): 421–26.

"Concentrated Fertilizers in the Southern States." *Report of the Commissioner of Agriculture for the Year 1868,* 396–404. Washington: Government Printing Office, 1869.

Conze, Werner. "Social History." *Journal of Social History* 1 (1967): 7–16.

Cooley, Rossa B. *Homes of the Freed.* New York: New Republic, 1926.

Cooper, Sherwin H. "The Rural Settlement of the Savannah Country." *Papers of the Michigan Academy of Science, Arts, and Letters* 47 (1962): 413–27.

Cooper, Thomas. *The Statutes at Large of South Carolina.* Columbia: A. S. Johnston, 1837.

Coulter, Ellis Merton. *Old Petersburg and the Broad River Valley of Georgia: Their Rise and Decline.* Athens: University of Georgia Press, 1965.

Coulter, John Lee, ed. "Plantations in the South." In *Thirteenth Census of the United States, Taken in the Year 1910.* Vol. 5, *Agriculture, 1909 and 1910,* 877–89. Washington: Government Printing Office, 1913.

Cox, Oliver Cromwell. "The Modern Caste School of Race Relations." *Social Forces* 21 (1942): 218–26.

———. "Race and Caste: A Distinction." *American Journal of Sociology* 50 (1945): 360–68.

————. *Caste, Class, and Race: A Study in Social Dynamics*. Garden City, N.Y.: Doubleday, 1948.

Crane, Verner W. *The Southern Frontier, 1670–1732*. Durham, N.C.: Duke University Press, 1928.

Cruzat, Heloise Hulse. "Sidelights on Louisiana History." *Louisiana Historical Quarterly* 1 (1918): 87–153.

Davidson, Chalmers Gaston. *The Last Foray: The South Carolina Planters of 1860: A Sociological Study*. Columbia: University of South Carolina Press, 1971.

Davis, Allison, Burleigh B. Gardner, and Mary R. Gardner. *Deep South: A Social Anthropological Study of Caste and Class*. Chicago: University of Chicago Press, 1941.

Davis, Ronald L. F. *Good and Faithful Labor: From Slavery to Sharecropping in the Natchez District, 1860–1890*. Westport, Conn.: Greenwood, 1982.

DeCanio, Stephen J. *Agriculture in the Postbellum South: The Economics of Production and Supply*. Cambridge: MIT Press, 1974.

Deetz, James. *In Small Things Forgotten: The Archaeology of Early American Life*. Garden City, N.Y.: Doubleday, 1977.

————. "Material Culture and Archaeology: What's the Difference?" In *Historical Archaeology and the Importance of Material Things*, edited by Leland Ferguson, 9–12. Columbia, S.C.: Society for Historical Archaeology, 1977.

————. "Scientific Humanism and Humanistic Science: A Plea for Paradigmatic Pluralism in Historical Archaeology." *Geoscience and Man* 23 (1983): 27–34.

DeForest, John William. *A Union Officer in the Reconstruction*. Edited by James H. Croushore and David Morris Potter. New Haven: Yale University Press, 1948.

Dennett, Richard. *The South As It Is, 1865–1866*. Edited by Henry M. Christman. London: Sidgwick and Jackson, 1965.

Dickens, Roy S., Jr. *Cherokee Prehistory: The Pisgah Phase in the Appalachian Summit Region*. Knoxville: University of Tennessee Press, 1976.

Dillingham, Pitt. "Land Tenure among the Negroes." *Yale Review* 5 (1896): 190–206.

Dollard, John. *Caste and Class in a Southern Town*, 3d ed. Garden City, N.Y.: Doubleday Anchor, 1957.

Doran, J. E., and R. F. Hodson. *Mathematics and Computers in Archaeology*. Cambridge: Harvard University Press, 1975.

DuBois, W. E. B. *Black Reconstruction*. New York: Russell and Russell, 1935.

Dundas, Francis de Sales. *The Calhoun Settlement: District of Abbeville, South Carolina*. Staunton, Va.: F. de Sales Dundas, 1949.

————. "Millwood Plantation: An Almost Forgotten Era." *Calhoun Falls* (S.C.) *Times*, 10 March 1955.

Edwards, Thomas J. "The Tenant System and Some Changes since Emancipation." *Annals of the American Academy of Political and Social Science* 49 (1913): 38–46.

Efind, C. M., reporter. *South Carolina Reports* 70, 1905.

Ehrenhard, John E., and Mary R. Bullard. *Stafford Plantation, Cumberland Island National Seashore, Georgia: Archaeological Investigations of a Slave Cabin.* Tallahassee: Southeast Archaeological Center, 1981.

Ely, Richard T., and Charles J. Galpin. "Tenancy in an Ideal System of Land-ownership." In *Papers on Tenancy.* Office of the Secretary of the American Association for Agricultural Legislation Bulletin no. 2. Madison: University of Wisconsin, 1919.

Engels, Frederick. Selection from "Karl Marx." In *K. Marx, F. Engels, V. Lenin on Historical Materialism: A Collection,* 174–78. New York: International Publishers, 1974.

Evans, W. H. "The Labor Question." *Southern Cultivator* 27 (1869): 54–55.

"Extensive Land Sale." *Abbeville* (S.C.) *Press and Banner,* 3 October 1906.

Fairbanks, Charles H. "The Kingsley Slave Cabins in Duval County, Florida, 1968." *The Conference on Historic Site Archaeology Papers* 7 (1974): 62–93.

————. "Historical Archaeological Implications of Recent Investigations." *Geoscience and Man* 23 (1983): 17–26.

————. "The Plantation Archaeology of the Southeastern Coast." *Historical Archaeology* 18 (1984): 1–14.

Fairbanks, Charles H., and Sue A. Mullins Moore. "How Did Slaves Live?" *Early Man,* Summer 1980, 2–6.

"Famous Calhoun Estate on Savannah River Sold Last Week." *Press and Banner and Abbeville* (S.C.) *Medium,* 10 July 1933.

Fenneman, Nevin M. *Physiography of Eastern United States.* New York: McGraw-Hill, 1938.

Ferguson, Leland. "Historical Archaeology and the Importance of Material Things." In *Historical Archaeology and the Importance of Material Things,* edited by Leland Ferguson, 5–8. Columbia, S.C.: Society for Historical Archaeology, 1977.

————. "Looking for the 'Afro' in Colono-Indian Pottery." *The Conference on Historic Site Archaeology Papers* 12 (1978): 68–86. Reprinted in *Archaeological Perspectives on Ethnicity in America: Afro-American and Asian American Culture History,* edited by Robert L. Schuyler, 14–28. Farmingdale, N.Y.: Baywood, 1980.

————. "Struggling with Pots in Colonial South Carolina." In *The Archaeology of Inequality,* edited by Robert Paynter and Randall H. McGuire. Oxford, England: Basil Blackwell, forthcoming.

Fike, Richard E. *The Bottle Book: A Comprehensive Guide to Historic, Embossed Medicine Bottles.* Salt Lake City: Peregrine Smith Books, 1987.

Fite, Gilbert C. *Cotton Fields No More: Southern Agriculture, 1865–1980.* Lexington: University Press of Kentucky, 1984.

Fitting, James E. "Evolution, Statistics, and Historic Ceramics." *The Conference on Historic Site Archaeology Papers* 6 (1972): 158–62.

Flynn, Charles L., Jr. *White Land, Black Labor: Caste and Class in Late Nineteenth-Century Georgia.* Baton Rouge: Louisiana State University Press, 1983.

Fogel, Robert W., and Stanley L. Engerman. *Time on the Cross: The Economics of American Negro Slavery.* 2 vols. Boston: Little, Brown, 1974.

Foner, Philip S., ed. *Karl Marx Remembered: Comments at the Time of His Death.* San Francisco: Synthesis Press, 1983.

Fontana, Bernard L. "On the Meaning of Historic Sites Archaeology." *American Antiquity* 31 (1965): 61–65.

Fontana, Bernard L., and J. Cameron Greenleaf. "Johnny Ward's Ranch: A Study in Historic Archaeology." *The Kiva* 28 (1962): 1–115.

Ford, James A. "An Archaeological Report on the Elizafield Ruins." In *Georgia's Disputed Ruins,* edited by E. Coulter, 191–225. Chapel Hill: University of North Carolina Press, 1937.

Ford, Lacy K., Jr. "Social Origins of a New South Carolina: The Upcountry in the Nineteenth Century." Ph.D. diss., University of South Carolina, 1983.

Fox-Genovese, Elizabeth, and Eugene D. Genovese. "The Political Crisis of Social History." *Journal of Social History* 10 (1976): 205–20.

———. *Fruits of Merchant Capital: Slavery and Bourgeois Property in the Rise and Expansion of Capitalism.* Oxford: Oxford University Press, 1983.

Frazier, E. Franklin. *Race and Culture Contacts in the Modern World.* New York: Alfred A. Knopf, 1957.

Fry, Bruce W. "Restoration and Archaeology." *Historical Archaeology* 3 (1969): 49–65.

G. A. N. "Laborers Wanted!" *Southern Cultivator* 25 (1867): 69.

Geismar, Joan H. *The Archaeology of Social Disintegration in Skunk Hollow: A Nineteenth-Century Rural Black Community.* New York: Academic Press, 1982.

Genovese, Eugene D. *Roll, Jordan, Roll: The World the Slaves Made.* New York: Pantheon, 1974.

Gillmore, Q. A. "Examination of Savannah River above Augusta, Georgia." 45th Cong., 3d sess., 1879. H. Exec. Doc. 90.

Glassie, Henry. *Folk Housing in Middle Virginia: A Structural Analysis of Historic Artifacts.* Knoxville: University of Tennessee Press, 1975.

Godden, Geoffrey A. *Encyclopedia of British Pottery and Porcelain Marks.* New York: Bonanza, 1964.

Gordon, Asa H. *Sketches of Negro Life and History in South Carolina.* 2d ed. Columbia: University of South Carolina Press, 1971.

Gray, Lewis Cecil. *History of Agriculture in the Southern United States to 1860.* 2 vols. Washington, D.C.: Carnegie Institution, 1933.

Gray, Lewis Cecil, Charles L. Steward, Howard A. Turner, J. T. Sanders, and W. J. Spillman. "Farm Ownership and Tenancy." *Yearbook of the Department of Agriculture, 1923,* 507–600. Washington: Government Printing Office, 1924.

Green, Mary Hemphill. "James Edward Calhoun Marker to Be Put at Savannah River." *Greenwood* (S.C.) *Index-Journal,* 25 March 1953.

Grosscup, Gordon L., and George L. Miller. *Excavations at Walker Tavern, Cambridge State Historical Park, 1968.* Lansing: Michigan Department of Conservation, 1969.

Gutman, Herbert G. *The Black Family in Slavery and Freedom, 1750–1925.* New York: Pantheon, 1976.

Hagood, Margaret Jarman. *Mothers of the South: Portraiture of the White Tenant Farm Woman.* Chapel Hill: University of North Carolina Press, 1939.

Hall, Arthur R. *The Story of Soil Conservation in the South Carolina Piedmont, 1800–1860.* U.S. Department of Agriculture, Miscellaneous Publication no. 407. Washington: Government Printing Office, 1940.

Hall, Edward T. "A System for the Notation of Proxemic Behavior." *American Anthropologist* 65 (1963): 1003–26.

———. "Proxemics: The Study of Man's Spatial Relationships." In *Man's Image in Medicine and Anthropology,* edited by Iago Goldston, 422–45. New York: International Universities Press, 1963.

———. *The Hidden Dimension.* Garden City, N.Y.: Doubleday, 1969.

Handler, Jerome S., and Frederick W. Lange. *Plantation Slavery in Barbados: An Archaeological and Historical Investigation.* Cambridge: Harvard University Press, 1978.

Handsman, Russell G. "Thinking about an Historical Archaeology of Alienation and Class Struggle." Paper delivered at the Annual Meeting of the Society for Historical Archaeology, 1985.

Hargrave, Tazewell L., reporter. *North Carolina Reports* 71 (1905).

Harper, Francis, ed. *The Travels of William Bartram.* Naturalist's ed. New Haven: Yale University Press, 1958.

Harrington, J. C. "Historic Site Archaeology in the United States." In *Archaeology of Eastern United States,* edited by James B. Griffin, 335–44. Chicago: University of Chicago Press, 1952.

———. "Archaeology as an Auxiliary Science of American History." *American Anthropologist* 57 (1955): 1121–30.

Harris, J. William. "Plantations and Power: Emancipation on the David Barrow Plantations." In *Toward a New South: Studies in Post–Civil War Southern Communities,* edited by Orville Vernon Burton and Robert C. McMath, 246–64. Westport, Conn.: Greenwood, 1982.

Haskell, E. S. *A Farm-Management Survey in Brooks County, Georgia.* U.S. Department of Agriculture Bulletin no. 648. Washington: Government Printing Office, 1918.

Hart, John Fraser. "Land Use Change in a Piedmont County." *Annals of the Association of American Geographers* 70 (1980): 492–527.

Hart, John Fraser, and Ennis L. Chestang. "Rural Revolution in East Carolina." *Geographical Review* 68 (1978): 435–58.

Heads of Families at the First Census of the United States Taken in the Year 1790: South Carolina. Baltimore: Genealogical Publishing, 1978.

Heberle, Rudolf. *Mississippi Backwater Area Study: Yazoo Segment.* Baton Rouge: Troy H. Middleton Library, Louisiana State University, 1941. Mimeo.

Hemmings, E. Thomas. *Archaeological Survey of Trotters Shoals Reservoir Area in South Carolina.* Research Manuscript Series, no. 3. Columbia, S.C.: Institute of Archaeology and Anthropology, 1970.

Hemphill, W. Edwin. *The Papers of John C. Calhoun.* Vols. 2–9. Columbia: University of South Carolina Press, 1963–76.

Herman, Bernard L. "Slave Quarters in Virginia: The Persona behind Historic Artifacts." In *The Scope of Historical Archaeology: Essays in Honor of John L. Cotter,* edited by David G. Orr and Daniel G. Crozier, 253–83. Philadelphia: Temple University Laboratory of Anthropology, 1984.

Herndon, G. Melvin. *William Tatham and the Culture of Tobacco.* Coral Gables: University of Miami Press, 1969.

Herskovits, Melville J. *Acculturation: The Study of Culture Contact.* New York: J. J. Augustine, 1938.

Hill, W. R., reporter. *South Carolina Reports* 1 (1919).

History Group, The. *Historical Investigations of the Richard B. Russell Multiple Resource Area.* Atlanta: National Park Service, 1981.

Hodder, Ian. "Postprocessual Archaeology." In *Advances in Archaeological Method and Theory,* vol. 8, edited by Michael B. Schiffer, 1–26. Orlando, Fla.: Academic Press, 1985.

Hodder, Ian, ed. *Symbolic and Structural Archaeology.* Cambridge: Cambridge University Press, 1982.

Holland, Claudia Croy. " 'Everything on the Land was Yours Except that Bale of Cotton': The Archaeological Manifestations of a Share Renter's House on a Cotton Plantation in the South Carolina Piedmont." Manuscript.

Hollister, U. S. *Handbook of Sorgo Culture.* St. Paul, Minn.: John J. Lemon, 1878.

"How They Are Settling the Labor Question in Mississippi." *DeBow's Review* 5 (1868): 224.

Hudson, Charles. "The Historical Approach in Anthropology." In *Handbook of Social and Cultural Anthropology,* edited by John J. Honigmann, 111–41. Chicago: Rand McNally, 1973.

———. *The Southeastern Indians.* Knoxville: University of Tennessee Press, 1976.

Huggins, Phillip K. *The South Carolina Dispensary: A Bottle Collector's Atlas and History of the System.* Columbia, S.C.: Sandlapper Press, 1971.

Hughes, H. Stuart. "The Historian and the Social Scientist." *The American Historical Review* 66 (1960): 20–46.

Hunt, Charles B. *Natural Regions of the United States and Canada.* San Francisco: W. H. Freeman, 1974.

Hunter, W. D. "The Present Status of the Mexican Cotton-Boll Weevil in the United States." *Yearbook of the United States Department of Agriculture, 1901,* 369–80. Washington: Government Printing Office, 1902.

Hunter, W. D., and B. R. Coad. *The Boll Weevil Problem.* U.S. Department of Agriculture, Farmer's Bulletin no. 1329. Washington: Government Printing Office, 1923.

Ireland, H. A., C. F. S. Sharpe, and D. H. Eargle. *Principles of Gully Erosion in the Piedmont of South Carolina.* U.S. Department of Agriculture, Technical Bulletin no. 633. Washington: Government Printing Office, 1939.

Jackson, Henry, reporter. *Georgia Reports* 46 (1912).

"James Edward Calhoun: His Death Occurred on Thursday Morning, October 31, 1889. Something of his Life and Last Sickness . . . Notes of His Peculiarities . . . Speculations as to His Will . . . The Property Which He Owned." *Abbeville* (S.C.) *Press and Banner,* 6 November 1889.

Jennings, Jesse D., ed. *Ancient North Americans.* New York: W. H. Freeman, 1983.

Johnson, Allen W. *Sharecroppers of the Sertão: Economics and Dependence on a Brazilian Plantation.* Stanford, Calif.: Stanford University Press, 1971.

Johnson, Henry S. *Geology in South Carolina.* Columbia, S.C.: Division of Geology, 1964.

Kane, Lucile M., June D. Holmquist, and Carolyn Gilman, eds. *The Northern Expeditions of Stephen H. Long: The Journals of 1817 and 1823 and Related Documents.* St. Paul: Minnesota Historical Society Press, 1978.

Keel, Bennie C. *Cherokee Archaeology: A Study of the Appalachian Summit.* Knoxville: University of Tennessee Press, 1976.

Kerridge, Eric. *The Farmers of Old England.* London: George Allen and Unwin, 1973.

Killion, Ronald, and Charles Waller, eds. *Slavery Time When I Was Chillun Down on Master's Plantation: Interviews with Georgia Slaves.* Savannah: Beehive, 1973.

King, Edward. *The Great South: A Record of Journeys.* Hartford, Conn.: American Publishing, 1879.

King, Thomas F., Patricia Parker Hickman, and Gary Berg. *Anthropology in Historic Preservation: Caring for Culture's Clutter.* New York: Academic Press, 1977.

Kirkpatrick, E. L. *The Farmer's Standard of Living: A Socio-Economic Study of 2,886 White Farm Families of Selected Localities in Eleven States.* U.S. Department of Agriculture Bulletin no. 1466. Washington: Government Printing Office, 1926.

Klein, Rachel. "The Rise of the Planters in the South Carolina Backcountry, 1767–1808." Ph.D. diss., Yale University, 1979.

Kohl, P. L. "Materialist Approaches in Prehistory." *Annual Review of Anthropology* 10 (1981): 89–118.

Lander, Ernest McPherson, Jr. *The Calhoun Family and Thomas Green Clemson: The Decline of a Southern Patriarchy.* Columbia: University of South Carolina Press, 1983.

Langsford, E. L., and B. H. Thibodeaux. *Plantation Organization and Operation in the Yazoo-Mississippi Delta Area.* U.S. Department of Agriculture, Technical Bulletin no. 682. Washington: Government Printing Office, 1939.

Latham, Henry. *Black and White: A Journal of a Three Months' Tour in the United States.* London: Macmillan, 1867.

Leavitt, Genevieve. "Slaves and Tenant Farmers at Shirley Plantation." In *The Archaeology of Shirley Plantation,* edited by Theodore R. Reinhart, 156–88. Charlottesville: University of Virginia Press, 1984.

Le Duc, William G. "The Chinese Tea-Plant." *Report of the Commissioner of Agriculture for the Year 1877,* 349–67. Washington: Government Printing Office, 1878.

———. *Report of the Commissioner of Agriculture for the Year 1879.* Washington: Government Printing Office, 1880.

Lees, William B. *Limerick, Old and In the Way: Archaeological Investigations at Limerick Plantation.* Anthropological Studies, no. 5. Columbia, S.C.: Institute of Archaeology and Anthropology, 1980.

Lees, William B., and Kathryn M. Kimery-Lees. "The Function of Colono-Indian Ceramics: Insights from Limerick Plantation, South Carolina." *Historical Archaeology* 13 (1979): 1–13.

Lefebvre, Henri. "Space: Social Product and Use Value." In *Critical Sociology: European Perspectives,* edited by J. W. Freiberg, 285–95. New York: Irvington Publishers, 1979.

Leone, Mark. "Some Opinions about Recovering Mind." *American Antiquity* 47 (1982): 742–60.

Le Page du Pratz, Antoine Simon. *The History of Louisiana.* Translated and edited by Joseph G. Tregle, Jr. Baton Rouge: Louisiana State University Press, 1975.

Lewis, Kenneth E. *Camden: A Frontier Town in Eighteenth Century South Carolina.* Anthropological Studies, no. 2. Columbia, S.C.: Institute of Archaeology and Anthropology, 1976.

———. "Excavating a Colonial Rice Plantation." *Early Man,* Autumn (1979): 13–17.

———. *The American Frontier: An Archaeological Study of Settlement Pattern and Process.* Orlando, Fla.: Academic Press, 1984.

Lewis, Kenneth E., and Donald L. Hardesty. *Middleton Place: Initial Archaeological Investigations at an Ashley River Rice Plantation.* Reserach Manuscript Series, no. 148. Columbia, S.C.: Institute of Archaeology and Anthropology, 1979.

Little, Daniel. *The Scientific Marx.* Minneapolis: University of Minnesota Press, 1986.

Logan, John H. *A History of the Upper Country of South Carolina*. Charleston, S.C.: S. G. Courtenay and Company, 1859.

Loring, F. W., and C. F. Atkinson. *Cotton Culture and the South Considered with Reference to Emancipation*. Boston: A. Williams, 1869.

Lorrain, Dessamae. "An Archaeologist's Guide to Nineteenth Century American Glass." *Historical Archaeology* 2 (1968): 35–44.

Lovering, Joseph S. "Sugar Made from the Chinese Sugar." *Southern Cultivator* 16 (1858): 107–11.

Lowie, Robert H. *Indians on the Plains*. Garden City, N.Y.: Natural History Press, 1963.

Lucas, Silas Emmett, comp. *Mills' Atlas: Atlas of the State of South Carolina, 1825*. Easley, S.C.: Southern Historical Press, 1980.

McDaniel, George W. *Hearth and Home: Preserving a People's Culture*. Philadelphia: Temple University Press, 1982.

McDonald, Forrest, and Grady McWhiney. "The Antebellum Southern Herdsman: A Reinterpretation." *Journal of Southern History* 41 (1975): 147–66.

McFarlane, Suzanne B. "The Ethnoarchaeology of a Slave Community: The Couper Plantation Site." Master's thesis, University of Florida, 1975.

McGee, W. J. *Soil Erosion*. U.S. Department of Agriculture, Bureau of Soils, Bulletin no. 71. Washington: Government Printing Office, 1911.

McLord, David J. *The Statutes at Large of South Carolina*. Columbia, S.C.: A. S. Johnston, 1839.

Magdol, Edward. *A Right to the Land: Essays on the Freedmen's Community*. Westport, Conn.: Greenwood, 1977.

Maguire, Jane. *On Shares: Ed Brown's Story*. New York: W. W. Norton, 1975.

Mandle, Jay R. *The Roots of Black Poverty: The Southern Plantation Economy after the Civil War*. Durham, N.C.: Duke University Press, 1978.

Maquet, Jacques. "Diffuse Marxian Themes in Anthropology." In *On Marxian Perspectives in Anthropology: Essays in Honor of Harry Hoijer, 1981*, edited by Jacques Maquet and Nancy Daniels, 1–10. Malibu, Calif.: Undena Publications, 1984.

Marquardt, William H. "Advances in Archaeological Seriation." In *Advances in Archaeological Method and Theory*, vol. 1, edited by Michael B. Schiffer, 257–314. New York: Academic Press, 1978.

Marx, Karl. *The Grundrisse*. Edited and translated by David McLellan. New York: Harper and Row, 1971.

Marx, Karl, and Frederick Engels. *The German Ideology, Part I*, edited by C. J. Arthur. London: Lawrence and Wishart, 1970.

Matsumae, Shigeyoshi. *Materialism in Search of a Soul: A Scientific Critique of Historical Materialism*. Tokyo: Tokai University Press, 1975.

Mead, Margaret. "Anthropologist and Historian: Their Common Problems." *American Quarterly* 3 (1951): 3–13.

Mendenhall, Marjorie Stratford. "The Rise of Southern Tenancy." *Yale Review* 27 (1937): 110–29.

Meriwhether, Robert L. *The Expansion of South Carolina, 1729–1765.* Kingsport, Tenn.: Southern Publishers, 1940.

Michels, Joseph W. *Dating Methods in Archaeology.* New York: Seminar Press, 1973.

Miller, Henry M., and Lynne G. Lewis. "Zoocultural Resource Utilization at a Low Country South Carolina Plantation." *The Conference on Historic Site Archaeology Papers* 12 (1978): 250–65.

Moir, Randall W. "Sheet Refuse: An Indicator of Past Lifeways." In *Settlement of the Prairie Margin: Archaeology of the Richland Creek Reservoir, Navarro and Freestone Counties, Texas, 1980–1981, A Research Synopsis,* edited by L. Mark Raab, 139–52. Dallas: Southern Methodist University, Archaeology Research Program, 1982.

Mooney, James. *Historical Sketch of the Cherokee.* Chicago: Aldine, 1975.

Moore, N. Hudson. *Old Glass, European and American.* New York: Frederick A. Stoles, 1924.

Moore, Sue Mullins. "The Antebellum Barrier Island Plantation: In Search of an Archaeological Pattern." Ph.D. diss., University of Florida, 1981.

Moore, Wilbert E., and Robin M. Williams. "Stratification in the Ante-Bellum South." *American Sociological Review* 7 (1942): 343–51.

Moragne, Mary E. *The Neglected Thread: A Journal from the Calhoun Community, 1836–1842.* Edited by Delle Mullen Craven. Columbia: University of South Carolina Press, 1951.

Morgan, Edmund S. *American Slavery, American Freedom: The Ordeal of Colonial Virginia.* New York: W. W. Norton, 1975.

Moss, Benjamin L. *The Boll Weevil Problem: An Analysis of Its Significance to the Southern Farmer and Business Man.* Birmingham, Ala.: Progressive Farmer, 1914.

Myrdal, Gunnar. *An American Dilemma: The Negro Problem and Modern Democracy.* New York: Harper and Brothers, 1944.

Nelson, Lee H. *Nail Chronology as an Aid to Dating Old Buildings.* Technical Leaflet no. 48. Nashville: American Association for State and Local History, 1968.

Nixon, Herman Clarence. "Whither Southern Economy?" In *I'll Take My Stand: The South and the Agrarian Tradition,* edited by Twelve Southerners. New York: Harper and Brothers, 1930.

Noël Hume, Ivor. "Archaeology: Handmaiden to History." *The North Carolina Historical Review* 41 (1964): 215–25.

———. *Historical Archaeology.* New York: Alfred A. Knopf, 1972.

———. *A Guide to Artifacts of Colonial America*. New York: Alfred A. Knopf, 1972.

———. *Martin's Hundred: The Discovery of a Lost Colonial Virginia Settlement*. New York: Delta, 1983.

Odum, Howard W. *Southern Regions of the United States*. Chapel Hill: University of North Carolina Press, 1936.

Olmsted, Frederick Law. *A Journey in the Seaboard Slave States with Remarks on Their Economy*. New York: Dix and Edwards, 1856.

Orser, Charles E., Jr. "Ethnohistory, Analogy, and Historical Archaeology." *The Conference on Historic Site Archaeology Papers* 13 (1979): 1–24.

———. "The Past Ten Years of Plantation Archaeology in the Southeastern United States." *Southeastern Archaeology* 3 (1984): 1–12.

———. "Artifacts, Documents, and Memories of the Black Tenant Farmer." *Archaeology* 38, no. 4 (1985): 48–53.

———. "Review of *Cannon's Point Plantation, 1794–1860: Living Conditions and Status Patterns in the Old South* by John Solomon Otto." *American Ethnologist* 12 (1985): 386–87.

———. "The Sorghum Industry of a Nineteenth-Century Cotton Plantation in South Carolina." *Historical Archaeology* 19 (1985): 51–64.

———. "What Good Is Plantation Archaeology?" *Southern Studies: An Interdisciplinary Journal of the South* 24 (1985): 444–55.

———. "The Archaeological Recognition of the Squad System on Postbellum Cotton Plantations." *Southeastern Archaeology* 5 (1986): 11–20.

———. "The Continued Pattern of Dominance: Landlord and Tenant on the Postbellum Cotton Plantation." In *The Archaeology of Inequality*, edited by Robert Paynter and Randall H. McGuire. Oxford, England: Basil Blackwell, forthcoming.

———. "Toward a Theory of Power for Historical Archaeology: Plantations and Space." In *The Recovery of Meaning in Historical Archaeology*, edited by Mark P. Leone and Parker B. Potter. Washington, D.C.: Smithsonian Institution Press, forthcoming.

———. "The Archaeological Analysis of Plantation Society: Replacing Status and Caste with Economics and Power." *American Antiquity* (forthcoming).

Orser, Charles E., Jr., and Claudia C. Holland. "Let Us Praise Famous Men, Accurately: Toward a More Complete Understanding of Postbellum Southern Agricultural Practices." *Southeastern Archaeology* 3 (1984): 111–20.

Orser, Charles E., Jr., and Annette M. Nekola. "Plantation Settlement from Slavery to Tenancy: An Example from a Piedmont Plantation in South Carolina." In *The Archaeology of Slavery and Plantation Life*, edited by Theresa A. Singleton, 67–94. Orlando, Fla.: Academic Press, 1985.

Orser, Charles E., Jr., Annette M. Nekola, and James L. Roark. *Exploring the*

Rustic Life: Multidisciplinary Research at Millwood Plantation, A Large Piedmont Plantation in Abbeville County, South Carolina, and Elbert County, Georgia. Atlanta: National Park Service, 1987.

Orser, Charles E., Jr., James L. Roark, and Annette M. Nekola. *Summary Report of Phase I Testing and Evaluation at Millwood Plantation (38AB9), Abbeville County, South Carolina.* Atlanta: Interagency Archaeological Services, 1981.

Otto, John Solomon. "Status Differences and the Archaeological Record: A Comparison of Planter, Overseer, and Slave Sites from Cannon's Point Plantation (1794–1861), St. Simons Island, Georgia." Ph.D. diss., University of Florida, 1975.

———. "Artifacts and Status Differences: A Comparison of Ceramics from Planter, Overseer, and Slave Sites on an Antebellum Plantation." In *Research Strategies in Historical Archaeology*, edited by Stanley South, 91–118. New York: Academic Press, 1977.

———. "A New Look at Slave Life." *Natural History* 88 (1979):1:8, 16, 20, 22, 24, 30.

———. "Race and Class on Antebellum Plantations." In *Archaeological Perspectives on Ethnicity in America: Afro-American and Asian American Culture History*, edited by Robert L. Schuyler, 3–13. Farmingdale, N.Y.: Baywood, 1980.

———. *Cannon's Point Plantation, 1794–1860: Living Conditions and Status Patterns in the Old South.* Orlando, Fla.: Academic Press, 1984.

"Our Largest Tax Payers." *Abbeville* (S.C.) *Press and Banner*, 25 November 1885.

Owsley, Frank Lawrence. "The Pattern of Migration and Settlement on the Southern Frontier." *Journal of Southern History* 11 (1945): 147–76.

———. *Plain Folk of the Old South.* Baton Rouge: Louisiana State University Press, 1949.

Park, Robert E. "The Bases of Race Prejudice." *Annals of the American Academy of Political and Social Science* 140 (1928): 11–20.

Paul, E., and A. Petersen, eds. *Collector's Handbook of Marks on Porcelain and Pottery.* Green Farms, Conn.: Modern Books and Crafts, 1974.

Perrin, Lewis. "The Hermit of Millwood: An Account of the Life of Mr. James Edward Calhoun." *Press and Banner and Abbeville* (S.C.) *Medium*, 29 June 1933.

Powdermaker, Hortense. *After Freedom: A Cultural Study in the Deep South.* New York: Atheneum, 1968.

Prunty, Merle C. "The Renaissance of the Southern Plantation." *The Geographical Review* 45 (1955): 459–91.

Prunty, Merle C., and Charles S. Aiken. "The Demise of the Piedmont Cotton Region." *Annals of the Association of American Geographers* 62 (1979): 283–306.

Quimby, Ian M. G., ed. *Material Culture and the Study of American Life.* New York: W. W. Norton, 1978.

Ramsey, John. *American Potters and Pottery.* New York: Tutor, 1947.

Ransom, Roger L., and Richard Sutch. *One Kind of Freedom: The Economic Consequences of Emancipation.* Cambridge: Cambridge University Press, 1977.

Raper, Arthur F. *Preface to Peasantry: A Tale of Two Black Belt Counties.* Chapel Hill: University of North Carolina Press, 1936.

Raper, Arthur F., and Ira De A. Reid. *Sharecroppers All.* Chapel Hill: University of North Carolina Press, 1941.

Rattansi, Ali. *Marx and the Division of Labor.* London: Macmillan, 1982.

Rawick, George L., ed. *The American Slave: A Composite Autobiography.* Westport, Conn.: Greenwood, 1977–79.

Redfield, Robert. *Tepoztlan, A Mexican Village: A Study in Folk Life.* Chicago: University of Chicago Press, 1930.

Reid, Whitelaw. *After the War: A Southern Tour, May 1, 1865 to May 1, 1866.* Cincinnati: Moore, Wilstach, and Baldwin, 1866.

Reitz, Elizabeth J., Tyson Biggs, and Ted A. Rathbun. "Archaeological Evidence for Subsistence and Diet on Coastal Plantations." In *The Archaeology of Slavery and Plantation Life,* edited by Theresa A. Singleton, 163–91. New York: Academic Press, 1985.

Reynolds, Ernest. *Collecting Victorian Porcelain.* New York: Frederick A. Praeger, 1966.

Reynolds, John S. *Reconstruction in South Carolina, 1865–1877.* Columbia, S.C.: The State Company, 1904.

Richardson, J. S. G. *Cases at Law, November 1850–May 1851.* St. Paul, Minn.: West, 1917.

———. *Cases at Law, December 1845–May 1846.* St. Paul: West, 1918.

Roark, James L. *Masters Without Slaves: Southern Planters in the Civil War and Reconstruction.* New York: W. W. Norton, 1977.

Robinson, W. S. "A Method for Chronologically Ordering Archaeological Deposits." *American Antiquity* 16 (1951): 293–301.

Robinson, W. Stitt. *The Southern Colonial Frontier, 1607–1763.* Albuquerque: University of New Mexico Press, 1979.

Roenke, Karl G. "Flat Glass: Its Use as a Dating Tool for Nineteenth Century Archaeological Sites in the Pacific Northwest and Elsewhere." *Northwest Anthropological Research Notes, Memoir no. 4.* Moscow: University of Idaho, 1978.

Rose, Willie Lee. "Jubilee and Beyond: What Was Freedom?" In *What Was Freedom's Price?* edited by David G. Sansing, 3–20. Jackson: University of Mississippi Press, 1978.

Rosengarten, Theodore. *All God's Dangers: The Life of Nate Shaw.* New York: Vintage, 1984.

Rubin, Morton. *Plantation County.* Chapel Hill: University of North Carolina Press, 1951.

S. "The Crops of 1866, A Failure, Why?" *Southern Cultivator* 25 (1867): 198.

Saint Paul Winter Carnival Association. *Seventy-fifth Anniversary of the Sun-Filled Saint Paul Winter Carnival, 1886–1961.* Saint Paul, Minn.: Saint Paul Winter Carnival Association, 1961.

San Marcus. "Cotton On the Brain." *Southern Cultivator* 25 (1867): 251.

Savannah River, Georgia and South Carolina, Trotter's Shoals Reservoir. 89th Cong., 1st sess. 1965. S. Doc. 52.

Scarborough, William Kauffman. *The Overseer: Plantation Management in the Old South.* Baton Rouge: Louisiana State University Press, 1966.

Schlereth, Thomas J., ed. *Material Culture Studies in America.* Nashville, Tenn.: The American Association for State and Local History, 1982.

———. "Material Culture Studies in America, 1876–1976." In *Material Culture Studies in America,* edited by Thomas J. Schlereth, 1–75. Nashville, Tenn.: The American Association for State and Local History, 1982.

Schüler, E. A. *Social Status and Farm Tenure: Attitudes and Social Conditions of Corn Belt and Cotton Belt Farmers.* U.S. Department of Agriculture, Farm Security Administration, and the Bureau of Agricultural Economics, Social Research Report no. 4. Washington: Government Printing Office, 1938.

Schurz, Carl. *Report on the States of South Carolina, Georgia, Alabama, Mississippi, and Louisiana.* 39th Cong., 1st sess. 1865. S. Exec. Doc. 2.

Schuyler, Robert L. "The Use of Historic Analogs in Archaeology." *American Antiquity* 33 (1968): 390–92.

———. "Historical and Historic Sites Archaeology as Anthropology: Basic Definitions and Relationships." *Historical Archaeology* 4 (1970): 83–89.

———. "Sandy Ground: Archaeological Sampling in a Black Community in Metropolitan New York." *The Conference on Historic Site Archaeology Papers* 7 (1974): 13–51.

———, ed. *Historical Archaeology: A Guide to Substantive and Theoretical Contributions.* Farmingdale, N.Y.: Baywood, 1978.

Scott, Emmett J. *Negro Migration during the War.* New York: Oxford University Press, 1920.

Scroggs, William Oscar. "Interstate Migration of Negro Population." *Journal of Political Economy* 25 (1917): 1034–43.

Seabrook, Whitemarsh B. *A Memoir on the Origin, Cultivation and Uses of Cotton.* Charleston, S.C.: Miller and Browne, 1844.

Setzler, Frank M. "Archaeological Explorations in the United States, 1930–1942." *Acta Americana* 1 (1943): 206–20.

Shand, Robert W., reporter. *South Carolina Reports* 16 (1916).

Shand, W. M., reporter. *South Carolina Reports* 118 (1923).

———. *South Carolina Reports* 123 (1924).

Shimkin, Demitri B. "Black Migration and the Struggle for Equity: A Hundred-Year Survey." In *Migration and Social Welfare,* edited by Joseph W. Eaton, 77–116. New York: National Association of Social Welfare, 1971.

Shlomowitz, Ralph. "The Origins of Southern Sharecropping." *Agricultural History* 53 (1979): 557–75.

———. "The Squad System on Postbellum Cotton Plantations." In *Toward a New South: Studies in Post–Civil War Southern Communities,* edited by Orville Vernon Burton and Robert C. McMath, Jr., 265–80. Westport, Conn.: Greenwood, 1982.

Shugg, Roger W. *Origins of Class Struggle in Louisiana: A Social History of White Farmers and Laborers During Slavery and After, 1840–1875.* Baton Rouge: Louisiana State University Press, 1939.

Simkins, Francis Butler, and Robert Hilliard Woody. *South Carolina during Reconstruction.* Chapel Hill: University of North Carolina Press, 1932.

Simms, William Gilmore. *The History of South Carolina.* New York: Redfield, 1860.

Singleton, Theresa A. "The Archaeology of Afro-American Slavery in Coastal Georgia: A Regional Perception of Slave Household and Community Patterns." Ph.D. diss., University of Florida, 1980.

Sitterson, J. Carlyle. "The Transition from Slave to Free Economy on the William J. Minor Plantations." *Agricultural History* 17 (1943): 216–24.

Social Science Institute. Unwritten History of Slavery: Autobiographical Account of Negro Ex-Slaves. Social Science Source Document no. 1. Nashville, Tenn.: Fisk University, 1945.

Somers, Robert. *The Southern States since the War, 1870–1.* London: Macmillan, 1871.

"Sorgho Sugar." *Southern Cultivator* 15 (1857): 153.

South, Stanley. "Evolution and Horizon as Revealed in Ceramic Analysis in Historical Archaeology." *The Conference on Historic Site Archaeology Papers* 6 (1972): 71–116.

———. "Archaeological Pattern Recognition: An Example from the British Colonial System." In *Conservation Archaeology,* edited by Michael B. Schiffer and George J. Gumerman, 427–43. New York: Academic Press, 1977.

———. *Method and Theory in Historical Archaeology.* New York: Academic Press, 1977.

———. "Pattern Recognition in Historical Archaeology." *American Antiquity* 43 (1978): 223–30.

Spillman, W. J. *Soil Conservation.* U.S. Department of Agriculture, Farmer's Bulletin no. 406. Washington: Government Printing Office, 1910.

———. "The Agricultural Ladder." In *Papers on Tenancy.* Office of the Secretary of the American Association for Agricultural Legislation Bulletin no. 2, 29–38. Madison: University of Wisconsin, 1919.

Sprague, Roderick. "A Functional Classification for Artifacts from Nineteenth and Twentieth Century Historical Sites." *North American Archaeologist* 2 (1981): 251–61.

Spriggs, Matthew. "Another Way of Telling: Marxist Perspectives in Archaeology." In *Marxist Perspectives in Archaeology,* edited by Matthew Spriggs, 1–9. Cambridge: Cambridge University Press, 1984.

————, ed. *Marxist Perspectives in Archaeology.* Cambridge: Cambridge University Press, 1984.

Stampp, Kenneth M. *The Peculiar Institution: Slavery in the Ante-Bellum South.* New York: Vintage, 1956.

Stearns, Peter N. "Social and Political History." *Journal of Social History* 16 (1983): 3–5.

"Sugar—Its Cultivation, Manufacture, and Commerce." *DeBow's Review* 4 (1847): 296–310.

"Sugar Made From Chinese Cane." *Southern Cultivator* 15 (1857): 313.

Sutch, Richard. "The Care and Feeding of Slaves." In *Reckoning with Slavery: A Critical Study in the Quantitative History of American Negro Slavery,* by Paul A. David, Herbert G. Gutman, Richard Sutch, Peter Temin, and Gavin Wright, 231–301. New York: Oxford University Press, 1976.

Sutch, Richard, and Roger Ransom. "Sharecropping: Market Response or Mechanism of Race Control?" In *What Was Freedom's Price?* edited by David G. Sansing, 51–69. Jackson: University Press of Mississippi, 1978.

Swain, George F., James L. Greenleaf, and Dwight Porter. *Reports on the Water-Power of the United States, Part I.* Washington: Government Printing Office, 1885.

"System Proposed by General Banks." *DeBow's Review* 1 (1866): 436–39.

Tang, Anthony M. *Economic Development in the Southern Piedmont, 1860–1950: Its Impact on Agriculture.* Chapel Hill: University of North Carolina Press, 1958.

Taylor, Alrutheus Ambush. *The Negro in South Carolina During the Reconstruction.* Washington, D.C.: Association for the Study of Negro Life and History, 1924.

Taylor, Paul. *A Spanish-Mexican Peasant Community: Arandas in Jalisco.* Berkeley: University of California Press, 1933.

Taylor, Richard L., and Marion F. Smith, comps. *The Report of the Intensive Survey of the Richard B. Russell Dam and Lake, Savannah River, Georgia and South Carolina.* Research Manuscript Series, no. 142. Columbia, S.C.: Institute of Archaeology and Anthropology, 1978.

Tebeau, C. W. "Some Aspects of Planter-Freedmen Relations, 1865–1880." *Journal of Negro History* 21 (1936): 130–50.

Thalheimer, August. *Introduction to Dialectical Materialism: The Marxist Worldview.* Translated by George Simpson and George Weltner. New York: Covici-Friede, 1936.

Thompson, Edgar T. "The Plantation: The Physical Basis of Traditional Race Relations." In *Race Relations and the Race Problem: A Definition and an Analysis,* edited by Edgar T. Thompson, 180–218. Durham, N.C.: Duke University Press, 1939.

Thwaites, Reuben Gold, ed. "François André Michaux's Travels West of Alle-ghany Mountains, 1802." In *Early Western Travels, 1748–1846.* 32 vols. Cleve-land: Arthur H. Clark, 1904.

Tindall, George Brown. *South Carolina Negroes, 1877–1900.* Baton Rouge: Loui-siana State University Press, 1966.

———. *The Emergence of the New South, 1913–1945.* A History of the South, vol. 10, edited by Wendell Holmes Stephenson and E. Merton Coulter. Baton Rouge: Louisiana State University Press, 1967.

Toulouse, Julian Harrison. *Bottle Makers and Their Marks.* New York: Thomas Nelson, 1971.

Townsend, W. H., reporter. *South Carolina Reports* 102 (1916).

Trigger, Bruce G. "Settlement Archaeology: Its Goals and Promise." *American Antiquity* 32 (1967): 149–60.

———. "The Determinants of Settlement Patterns." In *Settlement Archaeology,* ed-ited by K. C. Chang, 55–70. Palo Alto: National Press, 1968.

———. "Alternative Archaeologies: Nationalist, Colonialist, Imperialist." *Man* 19 (1984): 355–70.

Trimble, Stanley Wayne. *Man-Induced Soil Erosion in the Southern Piedmont, 1700–1970.* Ankeny, Iowa: Soil Conservation Society of America, 1974.

Trinkley, Michael. "'Let Us Now Praise Famous Men'—If Only We Can Find Them." *Southeastern Archaeology* 2 (1983): 30–36.

———. "Reply." *Southeastern Archaeology* 2 (1983): 68–69.

Trinkley, Michael, and Olga M. Caballero. *An Archaeological and Historical Evalua-tion of the I-85 Northern Alternative, Spartanburg County, South Carolina.* Colum-bia: South Carolina Department of Highways and Public Transportation, 1983.

———. *U. S. 521 Relocation, Sumter County, South Carolina: An Archaeological Survey of an Inter-Riverine Upper Coastal Plain Locality.* Columbia: South Carolina De-partment of Highways and Public Transportation, 1983.

Trowbridge, J. T. *The South: A Tour of Its Battlefields and Ruined Cities.* Hartford, Conn.: L. Stebbins, 1866.

Trudel, Marcel. *The Seigneurial Regime.* Ottawa: Canadian Historical Association, 1971.

Turner, J. A. *The Cotton Planter's Manual: Being a Compilation of Facts from the Best Authorities on the Culture of Cotton.* New York: C. M. Saxon, 1857.

U.S. Department of Agriculture. Bureau of Home Economics. *The Farm-Housing Survey.* Miscellaneous Publication no. 323. Washington: Government Printing Office, 1939.

U.S. Department of Commerce. *United States Census of Agriculture: 1935.* Wash-ington: Government Printing Office, 1936.

U.S. Department of Commerce. Bureau of the Census. *Fourteenth Census of the*

United States, Taken in the Year 1920: Agriculture. Washington: Government Printing Office, 1922.

———. *Fourteenth Census of the United States, Taken in the Year 1920: Population.* Washington: Government Printing Office, 1922.

———. *United States Census of Agriculture: 1925.* Washington: Government Printing Office, 1927.

———. *Fifteenth Census of the United States, Taken in the Year 1930: Agriculture.* Washington: Government Printing Office, 1933.

———. *Fifteenth Census of the United States, Taken in the Year 1930: Population.* Washington: Government Printing Office, 1933.

U.S. Department of Commerce and Labor. Bureau of the Census. *Thirteenth Census of the United States, Taken in the Year 1910: Agriculture.* Washington: Government Printing Office, 1913.

———. *Thirteenth Census of the United States, Taken in the Year 1910: Population.* Washington: Government Printing Office, 1913.

U.S. Department of the Interior. Census Office. *Report of the Production of Agriculture as Returned at the Tenth Census.* Washington: Government Printing Office, 1883.

———. *Statistics of the Population of the United States at the Tenth Census.* Washington: Government Printing Office, 1883.

———. *Report on the Statistics of Agriculture in the United States at the Eleventh Census: 1890.* Washington: Government Printing Office, 1895.

———. *Twelfth Census of the United States, Taken in the Year 1900: Population.* Washington: Government Printing Office, 1901.

———. *Twelfth Census of the United States, Taken in the Year 1900: Agriculture.* Washington: United States Census Office, 1902.

United States Public Law 89-789. *United States Statutes at Large* 80 (1967): 1420.

Untitled note. *Abbeville* (S.C.) *Press and Banner,* 7 March 1877.

Vance, Rupert B. *Human Factors in Cotton Culture: A Study of the Social Geography of the American South.* Chapel Hill: University of North Carolina Press, 1929.

———. *Human Geography of the South: A Study in Regional Resource and Human Adequacy.* Chapel Hill: University of North Carolina Press, 1935.

———. *How the Other Half Is Housed: A Pictorial Record of Sub-Minimum Farm Housing in the South.* Southern Policy Paper no. 4. Chapel Hill: University of North Carolina Press, 1936.

"Virginia: Her New Spirit and Development." *DeBow's Review* 2 (1866): 56.

Virginia Historical Society. "The Letters of William Fitzhugh." *Virginia Magazine of History and Biography* 2 (1895): 272–75.

Walker, Francis A. *The Statistics of the Population of the United States, Ninth Census.* Washington: Government Printing Office, 1872.

Walker, John W. *Excavation of the Arkansas Post Branch of the Bank of the State of Arkansas.* Washington, D.C.: National Park Service, 1971.

Warner, W. Lloyd. "American Caste and Class." *American Journal of Sociology* 42 (1936): 234–37.

————. "Deep South: A Social Anthropological Study of Caste and Class." In *Deep South: A Social Anthropological Study of Caste and Class,* by Allison Davis, Burleigh B. Gardner, and Mary R. Gardner, 3–14. Chicago: University of Chicago Press, 1941.

Wayne, Michael. *The Reshaping of Plantation Society: The Natchez District, 1860–1880.* Baton Rouge: Louisiana State University Press, 1983.

Wehrwein, Carl Frederick. "The Agricultural Ladder in Two Unlike Wisconsin Regions." Ph.D. diss., University of Wisconsin, 1930.

"What's to Be Done with the Negroes?" *DeBow's Review* 1 (1866): 578.

Wheaton, Thomas R., Amy Friedlander, and Patrick H. Garrow. *Yaughan and Curriboo Plantations: Studies in Afro-American Archaeology.* Atlanta: National Park Service, 1983.

Wheaton, Thomas R., and Patrick H. Garrow. "Acculturation and the Archaeological Record in the Carolina Lowcountry." In *The Archaeology of Slavery and Plantation Life,* edited by Theresa A. Singleton, 239–59. Orlando, Fla.: Academic Press, 1985.

White, E. V., and William E. Leonard. *Studies in Farm Tenancy in Texas.* Bulletin no. 21. Austin: University of Texas, 1915.

Wigginton, Elliot, ed. *Foxfire 3.* Garden City, N.Y.: Anchor/Doubleday, 1975.

"Will There Be a Sensation?" *Abbeville* (S.C.) *Press and Banner,* 14 January 1891.

Willey, Gordon R. *An Introduction to American Archaeology.* Vol. 1, *North and Middle America.* Englewood Cliffs, N.J.: Prentice-Hall, 1966.

Williamson, Joel. *After Slavery: The Negro in South Carolina during Reconstruction, 1861–1877.* Chapel Hill: University of North Carolina Press, 1965.

Wilson, Clyde N., ed. *The Papers of John C. Calhoun.* Vols. 11–16. Columbia: University of South Carolina Press, 1978–84.

Wilson, Clyde N., and W. Edwin Hemphill. *The Papers of John C. Calhoun,* vol. 10. Columbia: University of South Carolina Press, 1977.

Wilson, Maud. *Housing Requirements of Farm Families in the United States.* U.S. Department of Agriculture, Miscellaneous Publication no. 322. Washington: Government Printing Office, 1939.

Wolf, Eric R. *Europe and the People without History.* Berkeley: University of California Press, 1982.

"Wonderful Site for Huge Industry Here." *Calhoun Falls* (S.C.) *Times,* 26 May 1955.

Woodman, Harold D. "Post-Civil War Southern Agriculture and the Law." *Agricultural History* 53 (1979): 319–37.

Woodson, Carter G. *A Century of Negro Migration.* New York: Russell and Russell, 1969.

Woofter, Thomas J., Jr. *Negro Migration: Changes in Rural Organization and Popula-tion of the Cotton Belt.* New York: W. D. Gray, 1920.

Woofter, Thomas, J., Jr., Gordon Blackwell, Harold Hoffsommer, James G. Mad-dox, Jean M. Massell, B. O. Williams, and Waller Wynne, Jr. *Landlord and Ten-ant on the Cotton Plantation.* Works Progress Administration, Division of Social Research, Monograph no. 5. Washington: Government Printing Office, 1936.

Wright, Bruce William. *A Proxemic Analysis of the Iroquoian Settlement Pattern.* Cal-gary: Western Publishers, 1979.

Zeichner, Oscar. "The Transition from Slave to Free Agricultural Labor in the Southern States." *Agricultural History* 13 (1939): 22–32.

Index

Abbeville County: early white agriculture in, 24–25; population growth in, 24–25, 79; courthouse, 144, 165, 166

Abbeville (S.C.), 23, 25, 141, 157; named New Bordeaux, 23

Adams, William H., 134

Agee, James, 103, 127, 128, 130–32, 134, 242

Agrarian systems, anthropological study of, 3–4

Agricultural ladder, 59, 103, 110, 114, 154, 230; definition of, 55

Aiken, Charles S., 74

Anthropology: historical, xv; American, 4

Archaeology: United States, 4; prehistorical, scope of, 4–5; historic-site, definition of, 9–10; settlement, definition of, 82; spatial, definition of, 82; personal possessions and, 132; numbering of sites studied by, 280 (n. 113)

—Historical: scope of, xv–xvi, 4–5; distinct from prehistorical, 4–5,

185, 231, 247; plantations and, 6; strengths of, 247; documents and, 248; social relations and, 248–49

—Plantation: definition of, 10; history of, 10–11; scope of, 14–15

Artifacts: patterned regularity in, 133–34; dating of, 184–85, 190–91; archaeological study of, 230–34; classification of, 232–33

Atlantic Coast Line Railroad, 225

Atwater, W. O., 94, 123

Avirett, James Battle, 85–86

Bacot Plantation (S.C.), 51

Barbados, 12

Barrow, David Crenshaw, 90, 91

Bartram, William, 21, 22, 23

Beal, Granville, 162, 166, 168, 213, 214

Becker, C. R., 138–39, 140

Bienville, Jean Baptiste Le Moyne, Sieur de, 37

Black Code, provisions of, 50

Blacks, migration of, 78–79

Blassingame, John W., 12, 16